Future of Business and Finance

The Future of Business and Finance book series features professional works aimed at defining, describing and charting the future trends in these fields. The focus is mainly on strategic directions, technological advances, challenges and solutions which may affect the way we do business tomorrow, including the future of sustainability and governance practices. Mainly written by practitioners, consultants and academic thinkers, the books are intended to spark and inform further discussions and developments.

More information about this series at http://www.springer.com/series/16360

Thorsten Feix

Valuing Digital Business Designs and Platforms

An Integrated Strategic and Financial Valuation Framework

Springer

Thorsten Feix
Augsburg University of Applied Sciences
Augsburg, Germany

ISSN 2662-2467 ISSN 2662-2475 (electronic)
Future of Business and Finance
ISBN 978-3-030-83631-3 ISBN 978-3-030-83632-0 (eBook)
https://doi.org/10.1007/978-3-030-83632-0

This Springer imprint is published by the registered company Springer Nature Switzerland AG.
The registered company address is: Gewerbestrasse 11, 6330 Cham, Switzerland

Contents

1 Digital Business Designs and Platforms

Abstract

Despite fueling a once-in-a-century downturn of global business activity in spring 2020, the pandemic was more a tailwind than an impediment for the development of digital and platform Business Designs. This chapter introduces a scientific framework for such Business Designs by defining the four mission critical elements of platform firms, by describing five distinct platform patterns and by discussing the financial and strategic characteristics of platforms. Based on this framework, three novel scientific concepts to assess, design, and evaluate platform Business Designs are introduced:

- The *10C Business Design* enables the strategic analysis of existing and innovation of new business models by defining the ten mission-critical architectural cornerstones of a digital firm.
- The *eight platform value levers*, as second strategic tool, assess a platform's strength. The latter is defined by a *platform's scalability*, its *dominance* within a defined ecosystem, and its *value creation potential*.
- The *Reverse Discounted Cash Flow* (*DCF*) pairs strategic diagnostics with financial valuation. It builds upon the well-known Discounted Cash Flow concept of corporate valuation but applies it upside down. The valuation's origin is the steady-state description of a distinct Business Design embedded in a "picture-of-the-future" scenario.

T. Feix, *Valuing Digital Business Designs and Platforms*, Future of Business and Finance, https://doi.org/10.1007/978-3-030-83632-0_1

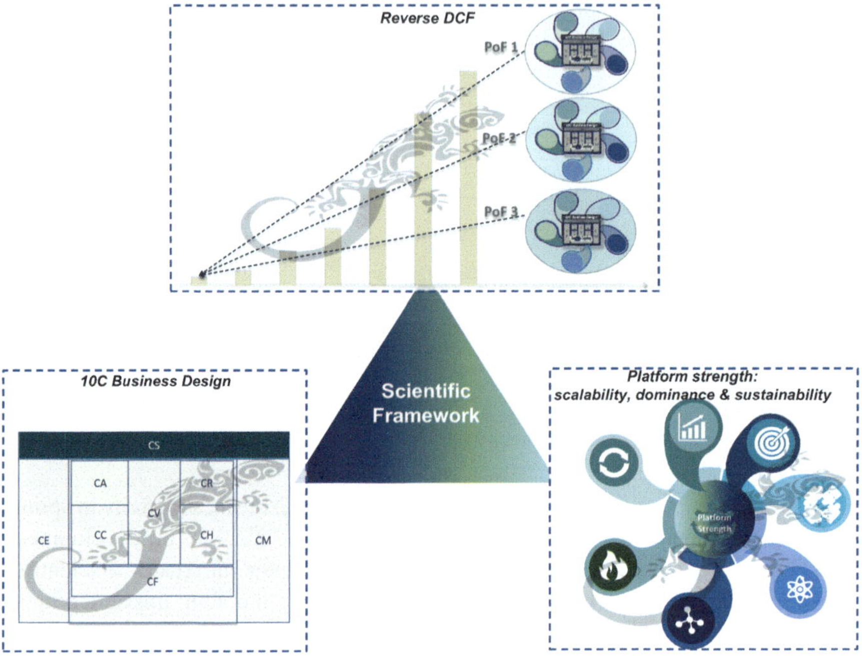

1.1 Why and How Digital Business Designs and Platforms Shape the Twenty-First Century

At the dawn of the 2020s, a once-in-a-century pandemic provoked an almighty downturn of the global economy as business activity was sheltered by social distancing and lockdown measures. A nightmarish sequence of events disrupted globally almost all social and economic activities out of a sudden and led to truncated trading days on Wall Street and other capital markets around the globe. Besides, the pandemic also highlighted the vulnerabilities of global supply chains and business models. Financial and Business Design resilience, not surprisingly, progressed from a priority to an imperative.

But, despite the uncharted downturn, this would have been still a cursory assessment. Empowered by digital technologies, a silver lining of business activity and capital markets recovery appeared below the surface. Digital tools and platforms enabled a fast scaling of home office and distance learning approaches. Online retailers, food-delivery services, and digital financial services of FinTechs and InsureTechs established, at least partially, an escape route from harsh lockdown restrictions. Streaming and gaming platforms became a convenient substitute for

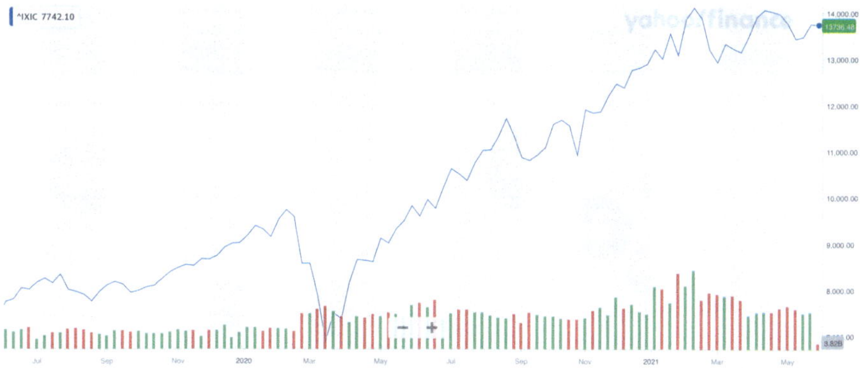

Fig. 1.1 NASDAQ composite 2020/21 YTD. *Source*: finance.yahoo.com, 2021/05/25

missing outdoor entertainment events. Overall, the pandemic was more of a tailwind than an impediment for the development of digital and platform Business Designs.

This went not unnoticed by capital markets, as described by Fig. 1.1. Propelled by aggressive expansionary monetary policies of global central banks and close to zero interest rates on “risk-free” government debt, especially technology stocks recovered surprisingly fast from their lows at the early days of the pandemic. This at first glance bizarre development was just rational as digital and platform Business Designs scaled their business activities significantly and delivered even during the downturn foremost strong cash flow improvements, significant growth, and increasing operating margins.

Besides, leading digital natives boosted their M&A activities during the pandemic with tailored pearl-of-string transaction strategies, even in more adjacent markets. Equity, including initial public offerings (IPOs), debt capital markets, M&A, as well as venture capital (VC) activity bounced back sharply. Equity prices travelled quickly to elevated levels. At the end of 2020, the market capitalization of the top ten global digital firms stood at $3.9 trillion, and their combined net profits summed up to $261 billion (Economist, 2021c), a remarkable difference to the also highly valued but loss-making business models which led to the bust of the dot.com bubble at the turn of the millennium. Nevertheless, the sky-high valuations of tech companies initiated at the time of writing this book a renewed debate about how to value such digital businesses. Also, the question, if the world lives within an equity valuation bubble, as at the turn of the millennium, which might be ready to burst, was heavily discussed (Economist, 2021b). Figure 1.2 highlights a couple of platforms which created significant shareholder value within the last decade and provides a first structure of the book.

Pausing for a breather, a fair question might be what could be learned from this empirical capital market evidence for the management of digital and platform Business Designs of the 2020s. Mission-critical strategic and financial questions might be:

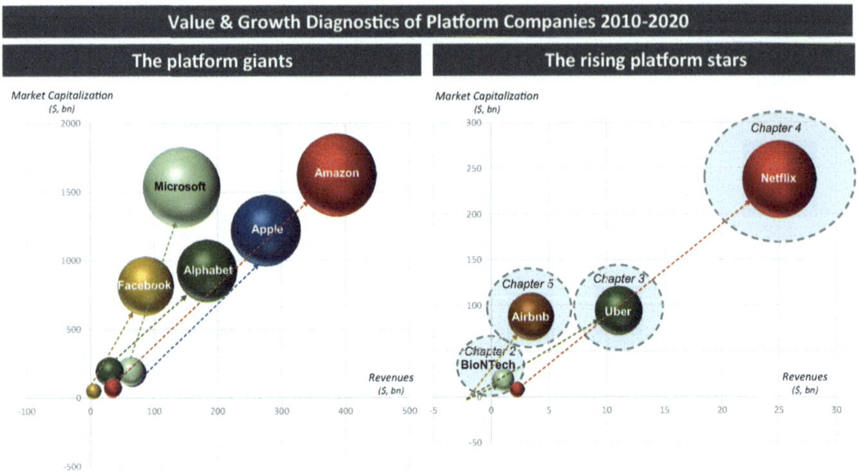

Fig. 1.2 Value and growth diagnostics of platform giants and rising platform stars: travelling north

- How will digitalization and platform economics shape new Business Designs for the 2020s like Netflix or Spotify did in entertainment streaming, Airbnb in global accommodation, Amazon in e-commerce, or Uber in urban mobility?
- If and how do such platform Business Designs pair their innovative approach with financial and strategic resilience to shape lasting competitive advantage in the 2020s?
- What are the secret success-formulas of platform Business Designs? How to evaluate if a distinct platform is scalable and will ultimately dominate global markets by deploying advanced digital technologies and exploiting economies of scale due to network effects? Beyond scalability, are such platforms and digital Business Designs sustainable, and do they capture long-term value?
- Are the elevated stock prices of asset-light platform Business Designs justified? How does their financial architecture differ from traditional business models?
- How will digital and platform Business Designs disrupt traditional industries and challenge incumbents? How should the latter respond to the risk of being side-passed and becoming irrelevant?
- And, last but not the least, what might be a fair equity value estimate or bandwidth of such new digital and platform Business Designs?

These are the bedrock of questions which will be at the center of this book. The scientific framework and applied case studies may contribute to a dynamic learning environment on how to nature the value potential of digital Business Designs and platform companies. But, the concept will also address their inherent risks.

A first glimpse on the speed and lasting impact of digital and platform Business Designs will be provided in this introductory part for the streaming revolution in global media. Netflix, Disney, and the likes reshaped the traditional global entertainment ecosystem in just a couple of years and cut the cord of traditional cable and add-based TV network businesses. Netflix passed the milestone of 200 million subscribers at the end of 2020. Disney, lagging behind originally, revitalized its traditional vertically integrated media value chain by acquiring 21st Century Fox, building a massive movie library and establishing Disney+ as viable streaming competitor, thereby challenging Netflix's first mover advantage. Disney's turnaround was honored by 100 million viewers having signed in for a monthly subscription just 18 months after the launch of Disney+.

Digital and platform Business Designs will inevitably shift the rules of competition and value creation in more or less any industry eclipsed by digital technologies. This will involve tectonic shifts on how to build and manage resilient and innovative Business Designs. Newest technologies like artificial intelligence, innovative applications of 5G technology, or virtual reality will serve in the forthcoming 2020s as enabler of such digital disruptions.

A closely linked, more macro-level—maybe even philosophical—question is thereby if the speed and impact of digitalization will be maintained by economies and societies and at what costs. Although this might be an even more important topic as the before raised questions, it might go beyond the scope of this book.

Nevertheless, to highlight what kind of meaningful impact technology breakthroughs may have on the social wider good, the first case study in Chap. 2 is dedicated to the high-speed development of mRNA-based COVID-19 vaccines which tackle the global pandemic we still try to escape. But, an even higher societal value at stake might be how we apply wisely new green technologies and digital as well as platform Business Designs for addressing environmental change and for riding the tailwinds of social responsibility and sustainability.

1.2 A First Typology of Digital Initiatives, Digital Business Designs, and Platforms

As digitalization became a buzz word since the turn of the millennium, distinct definitions are mandatory of what is understood in the following by applying terms like *digital initiatives*, *digital Business Designs*, or *platforms*, as expressed by Fig. 1.3.

Digital initiatives cover a broad range of activities, from digitalization of the manufacturing flow or processes automatization in sales to the application of predictive maintenance or the add-on of digital functionalities to supplement existing products and services. Nevertheless, these initiatives have also a common ground: Digital initiatives typically target a profound improvement of certain parts of the Business Design by applying and integrating digital tools or processes. But, such initiatives do not involve a digital-driven transformation of the whole Business Design of the underlying company. Digitalization and digital initiates are thereby understood as the application of digital technologies to improve the performance of defined business processes or practices thereby defining the digital revitalization space.

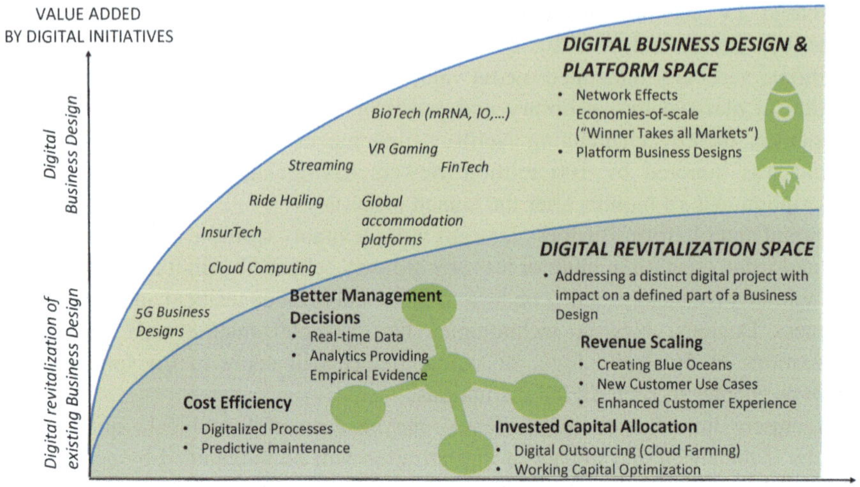

Fig. 1.3 The two playing fields of digital-driven business renewal: evolution and revolution

To classify digital initiatives, we may use the main purpose they intend to address:

- *Digital revenue scaling initiatives*: Digital initiatives might target the exploration of new market spaces or to improve existing products and services. For the latter, digitally enhanced or improved products or services may enable a company to increase prices or generate additional revenue streams. For example, some financial institutions simplified the process for opening a bank account by digital signatures paired with digital face recognition, camera systems, and online passport identification. This gave them a better access to generation X, Y, and Z customers and introducing FinTech-like products. An example for new digitally enabled markets is customer feedback analytics in B2B and B2C markets as offered by Qualtrics or Salesforce. Also, digital maintenance services for offshore wind parks might supplement wind-farm services and generate additionally service fees.
- *Digital cost-efficient initiatives*: Cost advantages initiated by digitalization projects may in principle be realized in any part of a Business Design. They have to be tailored around a specific Business Design. Examples might be the predictive maintenance initiatives reducing service and idle time in manufacturing, machine learning-enhanced digital contract assessment tools of law firms increasing speed and reducing costs-per-contract assessments, analytics application for fraud detection in insurance companies, or Google glass applications for elevator repair services.
- *Digital-driven Invested Capital allocation and efficiency improvements*: Automated warehouse and inventory management systems might substantially reduce the level of operationally required working capital. The latter may also be

achieved by digital accounts receivables management and payment processes. Besides, cloud services could reduce the necessary Invested Capital by outsourcing capital-intense assets and improve capital allocation in more productive and higher return core business investments.

- *Digitalized management decisions*: Analytics and big data assessments are applied more and more in board rooms to avoid gut feeling-based management decisions, improving thereby the quality of board discussions and decisions. An example with a wide array of application is customer data-based marketing. For consumer goods companies, market share information from external research institutes coming in with a time delay of 1 or 2 months have been for a long while the only quantified data in marketing. Nowadays, digital real-time data on volumes, the volume-price mix, price points, product preferences, or customer patterns, broken down on regional, single-line item, brand, or even marketing campaign level, become more and more standard practice.

But, digital initiatives go short of fundamental technologically driven Business Design transformations like the innovation of a new Business Design or revitalization. These digital Business Design transformations are more of the outer space of the digital change map and have the potential to reshape entire industries.

One of the most powerful digital Business Design patterns are platforms. *Platforms might be defined on highest level as digital Business Designs where the platform owner creates and orchestrates an interdependent network of different platform partners. The platform distinct role is to match the different platform partners and to facilitate their direct interaction, where the platform partners share a common interest.*[1]

A very first example of such a platform Business Design innovation might be the streaming revolution in the media ecosystem, as initiated by Netflix in the film or Spotify in the music industry, bringing together viewers or listeners with creative talents, actors, writers, or singers. Airbnb's global platform approach in the online accommodation services market bridges the interests of hosts and travelers, whereas FinTechs or InsureTechs, by substituting traditional banking and insurance services, combine new, easy-to-use, seamless, and 24/7 available financial and insurance services like digital money transfer, international money exchange, or robo-investment advisory with a wide community of financial customers and investors. Nevertheless, there exists no Carte Blanche for digital Business Design innovation or revitalization, meaning that such initiatives have high value potentials but also bear significant risks as they change every angle of the underlying Business Design or, in case of prior unmet demands, surf on untested waters.

[1] For a precise definition and a detailed discussion of platforms, see pages 22–23.

1.3 A Three-Folded Scientific Framework to Evaluate Digital Business Designs and Platforms

Digital and platform Business Designs stand at the center of this book. More precisely, the strategic and financial valuation of digital and platform Business Designs will be this book's main point of interest, not saying that digital initiatives play a less prominent role for corporate strategies or revitalizations and value generation. Also, both levels of digital change have to be evaluated in the end financially, on the same grounds, the free cash flows they will generate in the years to come. The distinct scientific framework of the book, as will be laid-out in depth in the following chapters and is described by Fig. 1.4, rests upon the following three pillars:

- The *10C Business Design* (Feix, 2020) enables the strategic analysis of existing and innovation of new business models by defining the ten mission-critical architectural cornerstones of a digital firm.
- The *platform strength diagnostics*, as second strategic tool, assesses the *platform's scalability*, its *dominance* within a defined ecosystem, and its *value creation potential* along eight distinct strategic platform evaluation criteria.

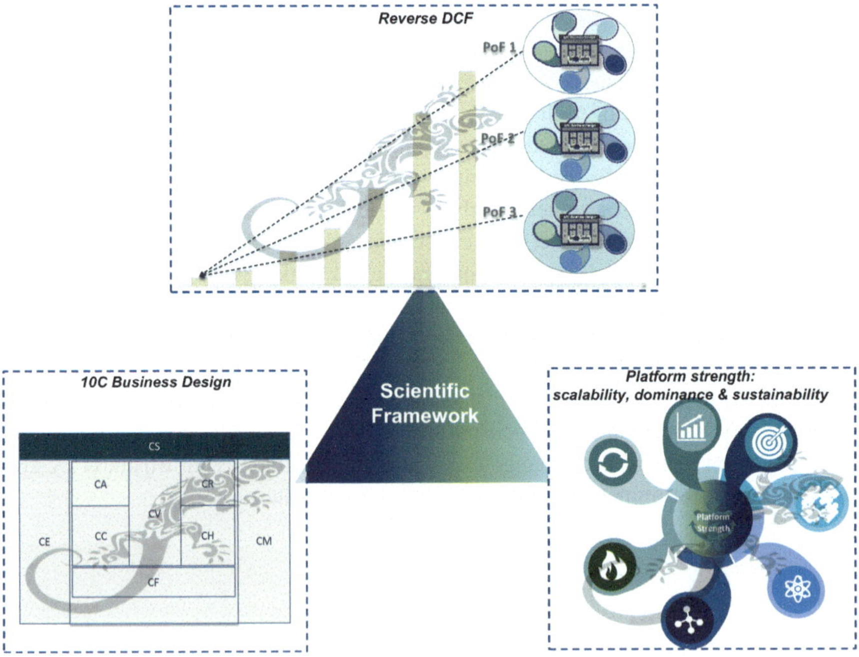

Fig. 1.4 Scientific framework for the strategic and financial valuation of digital business designs and platforms

- The *Reverse Discounted Cash Flow* (*DCF*) pairs the strategic diagnostics with the financial valuation. It references to the widely applied Discounted Cash Flow concept as traditional financial framework of corporate valuations. But, the Reverse DCF puts this concept upside down by starting with the steady-state description of a distinct Business Design and ecosystem. Based on this understanding, cash flows are consistently rolled back to the starting point of the valuation.

1.4 Strategic Patterns of Digital Business Designs and Platforms

The development and management of digital Business Designs and platform companies are enabled by an in-depth understanding of their specific strategy, business model, and ecosystem. The multitude of such digital businesses is thereby characterized by a common set of distinct patterns.

The overarching strategic rational of successful digital Business Designs and platforms is to create and exploit white spots, sometimes described as riding blue oceans. Such uncontested market spaces might create for the innovator "winners-take-all markets" where first movers exploit economies of scale advantages. Nevertheless, it may be even more important to be the first who figures out how to define and orchestrate truly beneficial interactions between the platform partners than simply being the first in the marketplace (Hagiu & Rothman, 2016). Therefore, economies of scale and network effects might be necessary, but not sufficient, to create a successful platform design.

More precisely, successful platform approaches foster a lock in on the platform by strong cross- and same-side network effects as well as economies of scale. For example, Netflix leverages streaming USPs to excel on viewers' convenience and applies a long-tail strategy with an extensive movie library, investing year by year between $12 and 16 billion, to create new entertainment content by creative talents, movie writers, and highly rewarded actors. As the entertainment streaming platform builds viewer-tailored offerings and big data-driven recommendations, based upon the analytics of viewer interests, the value of the platform increases for an individual viewer with the number of its subscribers, generating same-side network effects. But, as more viewers will also attract more creative talents to join or co-operate with the company, also cross-side network effects are generated. Netflix surpassed the milestone of 200 million subscribers in 2020 having added 37 million paying viewers on its platform during the pandemic. This enabled Netflix to reach out to the tipping point from a cash flow-negative to a cash flow-generating Business Design, a truly water shade. The streaming revolution in global entertainment will be discussed in more detail in Chap. 4.

Multi-sided platforms are especially powerful if they initiate such strong cross-side network effects between the different groups participating on the platform, meaning the platform's partners. Google, by matching users with search interests with advertisers through Google adds, or YouTube, by connecting creative talents with customer interest in creative content, might be poster boys of such platform designs.

A further common characteristic of digital Business Designs is their source of competitive advantage, which rests typically not on bricks and mortar but on intangible assets like intellectual property, patents, digital know-how, platform capabilities, brands, and technologies. Additionally, benchmarked with traditional peers, digital Business Designs are relatively asset light. This is especially the case for platform companies. The low capital investment needs allow an easy scaling of such digital Business Design based upon a convincing customer value proposition. The scalability goes financial hand in hand with high revenue growth rates, at least in the early years of such businesses.

But, there exists no free ride for a successful digital business innovation or revitalization either. The discussed significant advantages of digital Business Designs and platforms are paired with a set of downside risks. Digital and platform companies, by exploring new markets, have foremost an unproven Business Design due to their limited history. As an outcome, cash flows are hardly predictable and traditional valuation models foremost not applicable.

Additionally, early start-up losses and high cash burn rates have to be foremost accepted to establish new markets, as it was or still is the case for streaming, global accommodation, ride-hailing, or online food-delivery platforms. In case such designs do not create uncontested new markets, they compete typically with strong incumbents and their traditional Business Designs, as in the raid-hailing case, platforms like Uber or Lyft compete with a multitude of modes of transportation like public transport, car ownership, cabs, and other alternative models of urban mobility.

The point of this book is that only the combination of a thoughtful strategic assessment of the Business Design in combination with an intense financially modelling and analytics will identify the true value of such digital and platform architectures. But, also, the order is important; first comes the decoding of the strategic value. Only with this understanding at hand, a sensitive financial valuation which addresses explicitly the specific competitive advantage of a Business Design is possible, as highlighted by Fig. 1.5.

1.5 Decoding Strategic Value of Digital Businesses and Platforms: 10C Business Design

The 10C Business Design is in the following applied as the conceptual framework for the strategic evaluation of a distinct digital or platform company (Feix, 2020). The concept is derived from the latest research and literature on business model innovation approaches.

Pattern of digital Business Designs

- Most successful digital BDs and platforms target white spots (riding blue oceans) and create "winners-take-all markets" with first mover advantages
- Platform lock in by cross- and same-side network effects and economies of scale
- Competitive advantage built on intangible assets: IP, patents, knowledge, platforms and/or brands: Asset light BDs
- Platform and digital BDs foremost with unprofen performance and hardly predictable FCFs
- Digital BD value pattern:
  - High revenue growth rates (scalability!)
  - Early start up losses / cash burn rate
  - B/S light BDs, especially for platforms
  - Therefore, easily to be scaled, if successful

... and their valuation impact

- Unproven BD with high risk pattern:
  - High volatility of cash flows
  - Specific risk to be addressed by simulations of FCFs and within cost of capital
  - BD specific investments
- Due to riding Blue Oceans true peers most likely not available
  - Multiple assessment not applicable
  - VC method (pricing) w limited applicability
  - B/S light BD with dedicated CF impact
- M&A (Synergy Management): Scaling of BD and revenues (e.g. by building a platform) more important than cost synergies
- Financing structure and therefore cost of capital might change significantly through out the digital BD's life cycle

Fig. 1.5 Patterns of digital and platform Business Designs

In a broader sense, business models might be understood as [2]:

- A simplified description or holistic story of a company's strategic approach on how to conduct its business, how to fulfil the targeted customer use case, and how to compete within the competitive arena of the peer group.
- An application of newest strategy and innovation theories for the development of breakthrough and resilient Business Designs in the 2020s.
- An explanation on how to create and capture value by resilient, innovative approaches to build digital businesses and platforms or by reshaping existing ones.
- As a disruptive force that shakes up entire industries by creating fundamentally new ways of fulfilling unmet customer use cases and ride blue oceans, thereby fostering boundary-less competition.
- A fundamental transformation of capability-based core value propositions into lasting, lucrative customer and shareholder value. Lasting means that such

[2] Magretta included in his definition of business models customers and their values, the ways of delivering the promised value proposition to the customers, the revenue streams, and the cost levers. Business models are in his understanding "stories that explain how enterprises work" (Magretta, 2002; McKinsey & Company, 2021; Mody & Gomez, 2018). Osterwalder and Pigneur have a similar understanding: "A business model describes the rationale of how an organization creates, delivers and captures value" (Osterwalder & Pigneur, 2010, p. 14). The 10C Business Design (Feix, 2020) is built upon these important contributions of the newer business model research but adds a strategic linkage, a more precise financial and valuation architecture, and an organizational framework. Additionally, technical terms like "assets" or "core capabilities" are referenced explicitly to the according corporate finance and strategy literature.

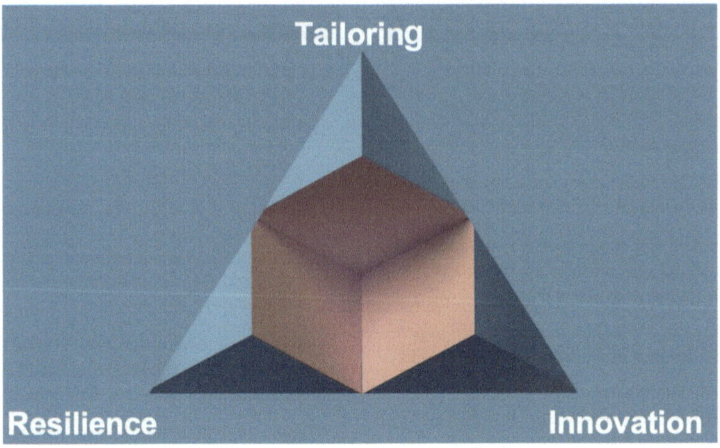

Fig. 1.6 Business Design: design principles (tfX-advisory, 2020)

Business Designs have to address the potentials but also the risks of digital approaches in the twenty-first century.

If Business Designs are interpreted as approaches for the development of breakthrough and resilient business models for the 2020s, the to be applied framework for such designs has to be specified. Any successful, value-creating, and lasting Business Design in the 2020s will rest upon three fundamental design principles as described by Fig. 1.6.

- *Tailoring*: To be successful, a Business Design has to offer a distinct customer value-added and a differentiation advantage in comparison to competing offers. A Business Design should be built upon a clearly defined, unique competitive advantage and purpose deeply engrained within the value proposition of the company. The competitive advantage in combination with the company's purpose serves as "northern star" for a tailored design of the business's skeleton.
- *Innovation (digital and platform)*: Within the 2010s, new, foremost digital technologies found an inroad into multiple industries, offering unparalleled innovation spaces for disruptive, often platform-based Business Designs which solved unmet customer needs. Such Business Designs do not only create new blue oceans (Kim & Mauborgne, 1999) but also challenged traditional industries and incumbents like in the media industry by the streaming platforms, in healthcare by personalized diagnostics and therapies, or within the automotive ecosystem by ride-hailing approaches. Whereas those technologies offer the innovators to overcome barriers of entry and to gain access to existing markets, incumbents are challenged to adjust rapidly and re-innovate their own Business Design or face the risk of being marginalized.
- *Resilience*: The pandemic of the early 2020s proved that innovation has to be paired with resilience against medical, technological, financial, or other seismic shocks in the ecosystem of a company to create a lasting and successful Business

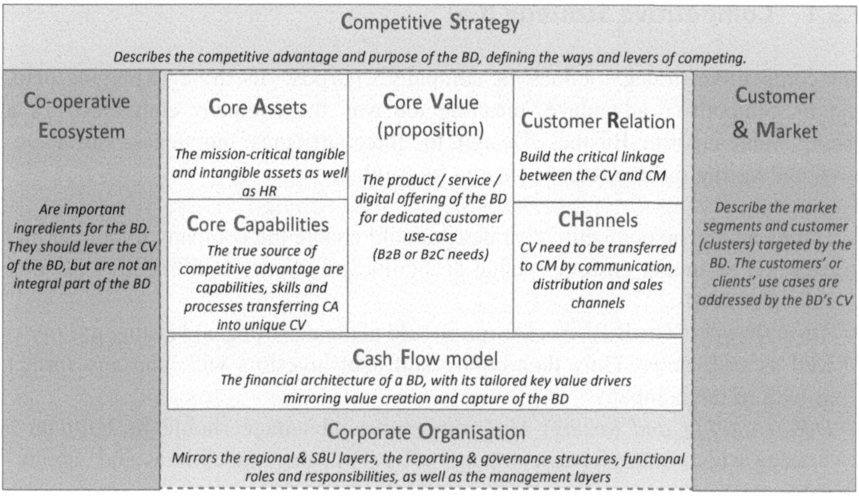

Fig. 1.7 The 10C Business Design (Feix, 2020, p. 78)

Design. Resilience requests acceptance of an ongoing change of a company's ecosystem and its competitive as well as technological playground. Transformative capabilities and a seamless recalibration of the Business Design will become mission-critical ingredients.

The 10C Business Design, as summarized by Fig. 1.7, is a tailored canvas of a business's architecture and describes its mission-critical elements as well as the relationships between those elements (Feix, 2020). The concept extends the newer research on business model innovation (Magretta, 2002; Osterwalder & Pigneur, 2010; Teece, 2010).

The corporate strategy, as the rooftop of the 10C Business Design, asks what makes the company unique, thereby defining its distinct competitive advantage as well as its purpose in comparison to its peer group. As the corporate strategy and purpose is the rooftop, the core value proposition is the heart of a Business Design and describes the company's offered services, products, or digital offering. The underlying question here is about the kind of customer needs which are addressed by the company's value proposition. The latter is framed by the company's targeted markets and customer use cases, as well as how those value propositions are realized by the combination of the company's assets, capabilities, and ecosystem partners.

Ultimately a Business Design, by defining those business elements, creates as well the financial architecture and value drivers of a company. An in-depth strategic understanding of the Business Design is a prerequisite for its financial valuation. The diagnostics of the Business Design-specific value drivers allow the modelling of the company's cash flows and, ultimately, its equity value.

The 10C Business Design's ten building blocks will be described briefly in the following.

1.5.1 Competitive Strategy (CS)

The competitive strategy defines the company's purpose, its strategic playing field, and its competitive advantage, meaning the way the company competes. For a lasting, value-creating Business Design, the three attributes, uniqueness, attractiveness, and lasting differentiation, have to be fulfilled:

- *Uniqueness*: The competitive strategy should enable the company to deliver and excel on an unmet customer value or significantly better fulfillment of existing customer needs.
- *Attractiveness*: The Business Design should generate strong and lasting returns as well as cash flows. Only then equity and debt investors will fund any further growth of the company.
- *Differentiating and lasting*: The competitive advantage should be built on a strategy which outperforms competition by its distinct capabilities and captures value creation against competitive imitation.

As shown in Fig. 1.8, the competitive strategy has to be aligned with the core value proposition (CV) and the Business Design's cash flow (CF)-generating model. Besides, it frames all other elements of the Business Design.

Implicitly, the application of newest digital technologies shifts industry boundaries and a company's competitive landscape. To understand the latter, digital Business Design peers might be more suitable benchmarks than traditional incumbents with high legacy costs.

1.5.2 Core Value Proposition (CV)

The core value proposition is at the heart of a Business Design, as described by Fig. 1.9. It defines the company's services, products, or digital offerings which address a distinct customer use case for the targeted customer segment.

The offered portfolio is also of highest importance for digital business and platform approaches as they address typically new or redefined customer use

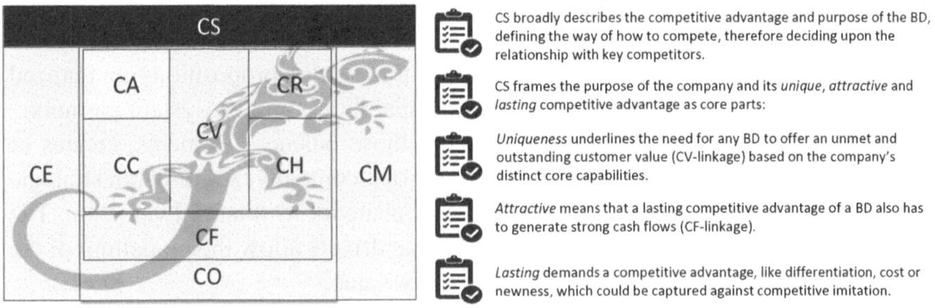

Fig. 1.8 The 10C Business Design: CS, Corporate Strategy

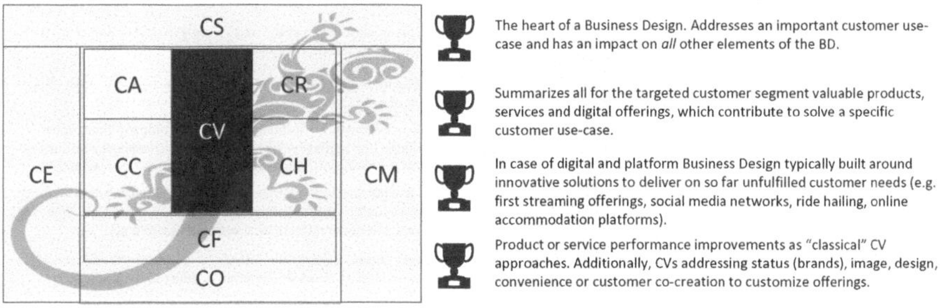

Fig. 1.9 The 10C Business Design: CV, core value proposition

cases. Such CVs offer the innovators, if successful, to ride uncontested markets and to create a valuable customer lock-in. This might especially hold true for platform approaches if they achieve a "winners-takes-all" pattern.

For example, the digital streaming platforms of Netflix, Disney+, and the likes offer unparalleled customer value in terms of convenience, variety, and seamless on-demand delivery of enticing entertainment content. These new, digitally enabled platforms revolutionize the global media industry by shifting the entertainment market from a cable and network to a streaming centric model.

Multiple digital Business Designs also integrate the customer into their service offering in the sense of a customer co-creation. The newer gaming platforms might be here a poster boy.

1.5.3 Customers and Markets (CM)

Customer and markets (CM) describe the targeted customer groups. Customer segments are thereby intertwined with the company's core value proposition and its specific product, service, or digital offerings, which fulfil a specific use case of the targeted customer segment.

The digital nature of platform Business Designs enables detailed, data-driven customer segmentation approaches. Big data assessments, artificial intelligence, and analytics support clear cut customer need definitions along a multitude of criteria beyond simple B2B versus B2C, age (generation X, Y, or Z), or purchase power-based classifications. They track the customer journey along a digital user's life cycle and identify unmet white spots for new service offerings. Additionally, they may specify psychological and behavioral patterns, which might be addressed within the core value proposition for a distinct customer segment by a tailored brand positioning and other intangible values.

The financial advantage of multi-sided platforms is thereby to combine seamless and with neglectable additional cost several customer groups and platform partners on one technology platform, whereby the participating platform parties are dependent on one another. In case of cross-sided network effects, one group's presence on the platform grows the value for the other participating groups on the platform as

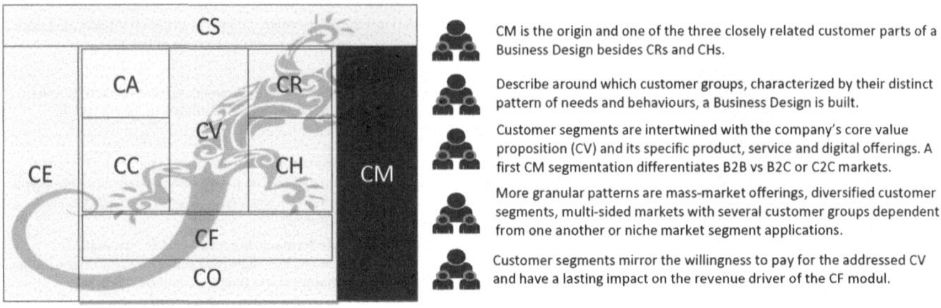

Fig. 1.10 The 10C Business Design: CM, customers and markets

well as the overall platform value. This suggests a rapid scaling of platforms to take advantage of the winners-take-all patterns, locking in more and more participants on the platform. An example of a game-changing platform is the well-known Google search engine of Alphabet, combining a powerful search engine to address the customer's search interest with Google adds as targeted marketing campaign for advertisers.

Customer segments also define the willingness to pay for a defined core value proposition and have a lasting impact on the revenue drivers of the Cash Flow Model (CF). Newer Digital Business Designs apply pay-per-use or pay-per-click models or monthly subscription fees as applied successfully by streaming on demand (SVoD) platforms. From a customer value point of view, this might lower the market entrance barriers as the pre-investment needs might be limited. This stands in stark contrast to traditional ownership approaches. At the same time, the offering company might be advantaged by a steady, monthly, or per-use-driven cash flow stream.

Figure 1.10 shows that the customer and market module is closely related to the customer relationships (CRs) and channels (CHs) as the latter serve as a bridge between the core value proposition and the customer segments.

1.5.4 Customer Relationships (CR)

Customer relationships target a deep customer understanding, including how to address the customer needs, as this understanding is mandatory for any customer acquisition and capture. Besides, customer relationships have to handle customer interaction and should initiate customer feedback loops between the company and its customers, as this enables customer retention, loyalty, and the exploitation of a share-of-wallet optimization by cross-selling opportunities. The ultimate goal of customer relationships is to create intimate customer ties, as described by Fig. 1.11.

Advanced digital Business Designs avoid the traditional simplified trade-off within customer relationship strategies between higher cost competitiveness of online solutions and the potentially deeper customer insights of personal interactions. Their deeply engrained on- and offline offerings integrate multiple newest technologies like analytics, artificial intelligence, or big data approaches.

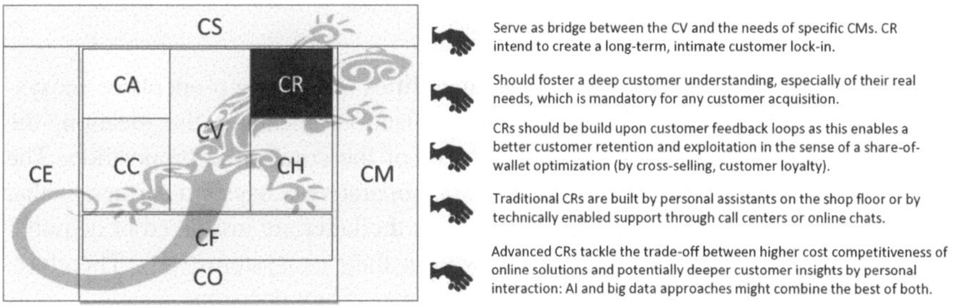

Fig. 1.11 The 10C Business Design: CR, customer relationships

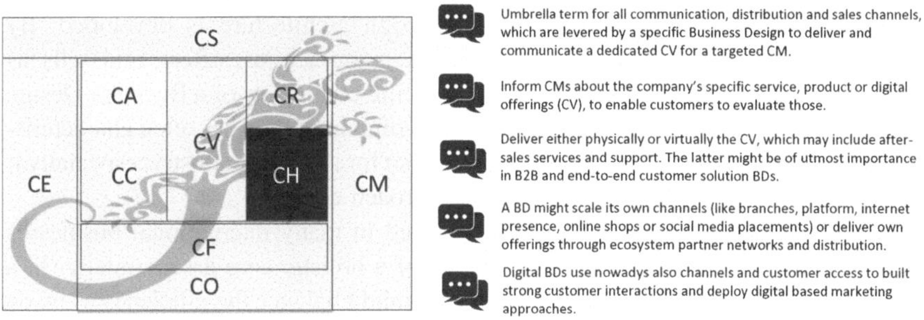

Fig. 1.12 The 10C Business Design: CH, channels

For example, analytics-driven recommendations or ratings might support to build more personalized customer relationships.

1.5.5 Channels (CH)

If the core value proposition is the malaria, the channels (CH) are the carrier to transfer the former to the customer by corporate strategy-aligned communication, distribution, and sales channel approaches. Newer Business Designs might apply for all three channels a digital-only approach, as in the case of streaming platforms, or a hybrid approach, as in ride-hailing or online food-delivery solutions.

Figure 1.12 stresses the point that channels serve a multitude of tasks like to get in contact with targeted CMs; to inform them about the company's specific service, product, or digital offerings (CVs); to enable customers to evaluate those; and, last but not the least, to physically or virtually deliver products and services, which might include as well after-sales services and support. A company might scale thereby its own channels like its proprietary branches, Internet pages, or online shops or deliver own offerings through digital or physical partner platforms and channels.

1.5.6 Core Assets (CA)

Core assets (CA) together with the core capabilities (CC) and co-operative ecosystem partners (CE) are in charge for the realization, meaning the ideation, the development, the manufacturing, and delivery of the core value proposition. The only true difference between core assets and co-operative ecosystem partners is that the former are owned by the company, whereas the latter are insourced or acquired from a company's co-operation partners within their ecosystem (CE). Therefore, investments in core assets have to tackle the make-or-buy decision.

Core assets are defined by the mission-critical tangible and intangible assets as well as human resources for the delivery of a distinct core value proposition. This is addressed by Fig. 1.13. Through targeted investments in the management and deployment of core assets, the Business Design architecture is developed. By exploiting core assets, the company develops, manufactures, offers, and sells its products, services, or digital offerings. The specific core assets of a Business Design could be described along the value stream of a company. They are often characteristic not only for a defined Business Design but also for an entire industry, especially if a dominating Business Design or platform approach exists.

The recent pandemic broke or at least rattled in many international businesses value chains and highlighted the importance of a holistic core asset strategy. In a post-COVID-19 world, financial or asset slack might balance the efficiency view on core assets of corporate boards as it was commonplace in the 2010s.

Within a digital Business Design context, intangible assets like patents, intellectual property, know-how, licenses, or brands and human resources like talents, management teams, and culture are typically more important than their tangible counterparts for shaping competitive advantage. In a digital world, intangibles assets and human resources are the crucial core assets. The management of those assets became a vital source of competitive advantage.

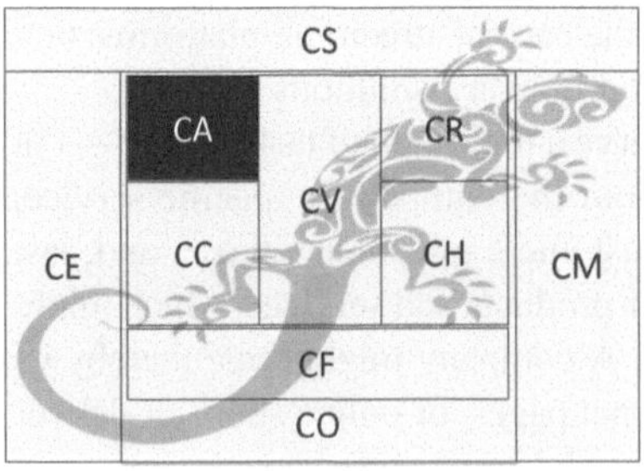

CA describe all mission-critical tangible and intangibles assets as well as human resources which enable a specific CV. In a post COVID-19 world financial or asset slack might balance the traditional efficiency view.

Through targeted investment in the management and deployment of CAs, traditional pipeline BDs develop, manufacture, offer, and sell their products or services and platform firms build their core technologies.

CA patterns are often not only characteristic for a defined BD, but as well for an overall industry (especially if a dominant BD exists).

A company might alternatively source or acquire assets from their co-operative ecosystem partners (CE). Therefore, investments in dedicated assets have to tackle as well the make-or-buy decision.

Intangible assets, like brands, patents, licenses or know-how are in digital and platform Business Designs the true source of competitive advantage (*Core* Assets).

Fig. 1.13 The 10C Business Design: CA, core assets

1.5.7 Core Capabilities (CC)

The twin of core assets are core capabilities (CC) which play also a decisive role for a lasting competitive advantage in digital and platform Business Designs. As described by Fig. 1.14, core capabilities are a unique source for the *establishment*, the *sustainability*, and the *appropriability* of competitive advantages (CS):

- *Establishment*: In case of very specific core capabilities and due to their relevance for shaping a core value proposition, they offer a perfect platform to create unique competitive advantages.
- *Sustainability*: In case core capabilities are hardly to imitate due to a limited transferability and replicability or simply scarcity, they offer a lasting competitive edge. This might be especially applicable within digital Business Designs, as proven nowadays by capabilities like AI, cloud computing, or analytics.
- *Appropriability*: IP, bargaining power, and platform embeddedness ensure that core capabilities are transferred into a strong cash flow performance and value capture.

A core capability could be best-in-class research skills in the pharmaceutical industry or analytics, network and global platform expertise in social media, e-commerce, or online search. It is a characteristic of core capabilities that they are deeply engrained within a company's tailored Business and Culture Design. On a higher level, organizational competencies might offer headroom to create dominant Business Designs.

Any successful strategy has to define the way forward to get access to mission-critical core capabilities, how to manage and how to develop them.

1.5.8 Co-operation Ecosystem (CE)

The co-operative ecosystem (CE) partners are, besides the core assets and capabilities, the third module of a Business Design for a holistic core value

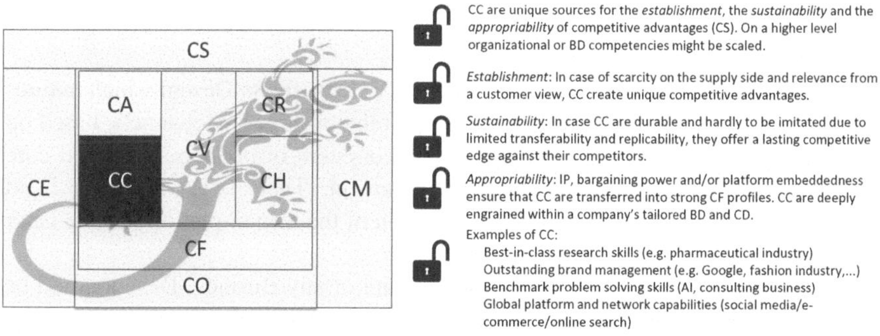

Fig. 1.14 The 10C Business Design: CC—core capabilities

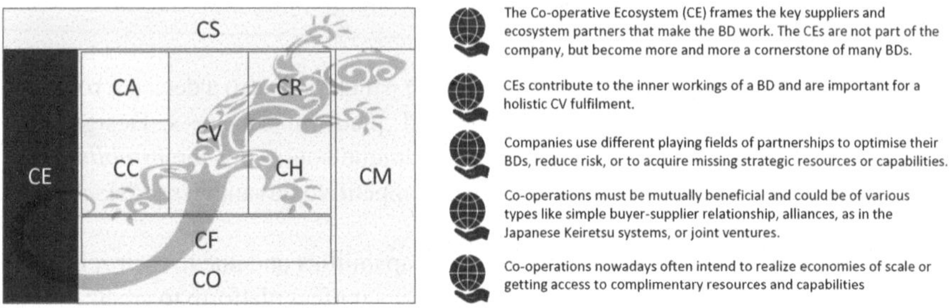

Fig. 1.15 The 10C Business Design: CE, Co-operative ecosystem

proposition fulfillment, as highlighted by Fig. 1.15. The former frame the key suppliers and ecosystem partners which contribute to the inner workings of a Business Design and supplement the company's core assets and capabilities.

Firms use different playing fields of partnerships by creating strategic alliances, forming joint ventures, building long-term contractual customer-supplier relationships, or designing deep-routed bounds between the involved companies, as in the Japanese Keiretsu systems. The ideal form of partnerships depends foremost on the intended target like optimization of the own Business Design by make-or-buy decisions, bridging missing capabilities, volume scaling due to economies of scale, risk reduction, or the acquisition of complementary resources and capabilities (Osterwalder & Pigneur, 2010).

Co-operations must be mutually beneficial for the involved partners. The sharing of the benefits depends on the criticality of the partner's assets or capabilities for the calibration of the core value proposition and the negotiation power between the two sides. In case of strong platforms like Google search or Netflix in the streaming ecosystem, the ecosystem partners might be eager to be part of powerful Business Designs, whereas in technology partnerships, as agreed, for example, between Daimler and Nvidia, the relationship might be more balanced. The ultimate target for platforms is to build a bandwagon of best-in-class ecosystem partners for the creation of an unmet core value proposition.

1.5.9 Cash Flow Model (CF)

The Cash Flow Model is the financial skeleton of a Business Design which assures value creation by delivering through customer relationships and channels, based on the company's core assets, capabilities, and ecosystem of partners, a defined core value proposition to a targeted customer segment. There exists a strong bond between the Cash Flow Model and the valuation of the firm or platform as the latter is the outcome of the first.

On the highest level, the financial architecture of any Business Design could be described by the key value drivers of corporate valuation like growth rates, the Return on Invested Capital (RoIC), and the sustainability period of competitive

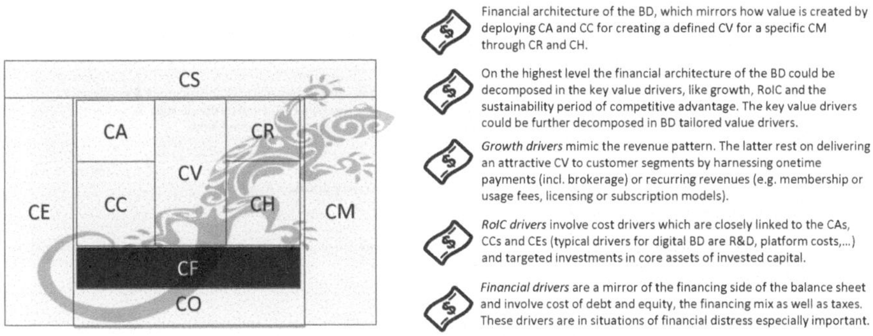

Fig. 1.16 The 10C Business Design: CF, Cash Flow Model

advantage (Feix, 2020). These value drivers of the CF model could be further decomposed in Business Design-tailored value drivers specifying dedicated growth, ROIC (including cost and Invested Capital), as well as financial drivers, as highlighted by Fig. 1.16. This extends the view of traditional business model approaches, which focus foremost on revenue and cost structures (Osterwalder & Pigneur, 2010):

- *Growth drivers* mimic the revenue pattern and are based on delivering an attractive core value proposition to targeted customer segments. Within the context of digital Business Designs, these could be harnessed by one-time payment transactions (including brokerage) or recurring revenue models, for example, pay-per-view, on-demand, or monthly-based subscription fee models. Examples for the latter are monthly subscription fees of streaming players like Netflix, Disney+, Amazon Prime, HBO, and the likes.
- *Return on Invested Capital (RoIC) drivers* involve specifically cost drivers which are closely linked to the core capabilities and investments in Business Design specific assets as part of the overall Invested Capital. The relative importance of distinct cost drivers for the value creation is significantly Business Design specific. Typical drivers are development costs, the purchase of critical ingredients from co-operation partners, the creation of digital services, and the delivery process through channel and marketing activities. On the asset side, the different case studies of the follow-on chapters will prove that digital Business Designs and platforms are often characterized by asset-light patterns. The limited amount of Invested Capital enables such Business Designs a fast scaling without burning a massive amount of cash flows.
- *Financial drivers* mirror the financing side of the balance sheet and involve the cost of debt and equity, the financing mix, as well as tax effects. These drivers are in situations of financial distress especially important.

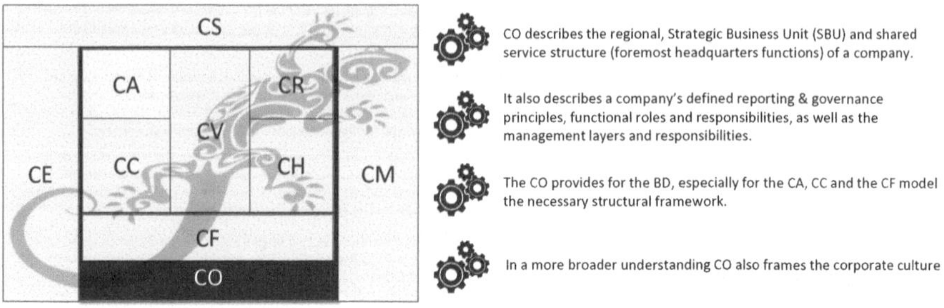

Fig. 1.17 The 10C Business Design: CO, corporate organization

1.5.10 Corporate Organization (CO)

The corporate organization is the structural and managerial framework of a Business Design. It describes the regional footprint, the strategic business units, and the shared service structure of a company. Besides, it also defines reporting and governance principles, functional roles and responsibilities, as well as management layers.

The corporate organization serves as a structural framework for the other Business Design elements, especially for the core assets and capabilities. This is pinpointed by Fig. 1.17.

These ten elements frame an entire Business Design. Platforms, as a special kind of digital Business Designs, have thereby a set of unique characteristics, which will be highlighted below.

1.6 Platform Definition, the Four Platform Elements, and Platform Patterns

Traditional Business Designs center on the production of goods or creation of services as well as on customer use cases which are typically based upon ownership models. Platform Business Designs disrupt such approaches on both angles as their core is built upon an intermediary function and not on the manufacturing of products or service delivery. They enable a dedicated, use-case tailored exchange between at least two platform partners, the user and the solution provider. Additionally, multiple platform designs substitute ownership by sharing and alternative models.

The offered solution, as in the 10C Business Design described as core value proposition (CV), might be a service, a social interaction, digital data, or knowledge transition. The solution provider and content offering are matched on the platform with the user, interested in such a content solution. As the parties participate and interact on the platform, they are creating an interdependent network in the sense of a multi- foremost double-sided, digital market place.

1.6.1 Platform Definition

Platforms might be defined as a digital Business Design where the platform owner creates and orchestrates an interdependent network of platform partners which share a common interest by matching them on the platform and facilitating their direct interaction. Thereby, one (or more) platform partner(s) create a distinct value proposition which is offered via the platform and is of interest for another (other) platform partner(s) to consume. In two-sided platforms, one platform partner offers a distinct value proposition which is of use for another platform partner, the user. Within multi-sided platforms, even three or more platform partners interact to create, distribute, and demand the underlying value proposition, whereas the platform owner acts as an orchestrator and middleman between the platform partners.[3] Networks and their interdependencies between the partners are therefore a distinct characteristic of platforms.[4] The value proposition offered and demanded on the platform might rest on a specific product or service, social interactions, digital data, or knowledge transfer. The dedicated value proposition of a platform will be used later for classifying platform patterns. The platform owner as architect of the platform facilitates and organizes the interaction and exchange between the platform partners. The platform owner sets as well the platform's rule book, meaning its guiding and governance principles, thereby defining the code of conduct for the platform participants. Another task of the former is the design of the platform's digital and standardized processes.

The value creation of platforms is embedded in their network's DNA and is typically driven by network externalities enabling economies of scale. The latter implies that the average cost of serving an additional platform participant, typically a user, declines with the number of participants already engaged on the platform. This implicitly leads to negligible costs to onboard the next (marginal) platform participant for high-volume platforms.[5] This means as well that the value of a platform is dependent on and increases significantly with the number of network participants, often measured as monthly active platform users or consumers.[6] More precisely describing the value architecture of platforms, the rational of most platforms are cross-side network effects, meaning that with an increasing number of platform participants on one side of the platform, its value increases also for the participants on the other side of the platform (Hagiu, 2014). Due to these network effects, platform Business Designs are privileged by realizing increasing returns of scale.

[3] The technical terms two-sided platforms and two-sided markets as well as multi-sided platforms and multi-sided markets will be used in the following interchangeable.

[4] The articles from Eisenmann et al. (2006) and from Hagiu (2014) underline the need for at least a two-sided pattern of a Business Design to fulfil the definition of a platform.

[5] Evans and Schmalensee define the value add of platform businesses by facilitating interactions between customers who are attracted in part by such network externalities (Evans & Schmalensee, 2010).

[6] The fundamental impact of network effects on business strategies was assessed originally in the groundbreaking article from Katz and Shapiro (1994).

They change the strategic playbook of traditional Business Designs by offering first mover advantages in "winners-take-all" markets and by creating significant barriers of entry.

In so far, platforms monetize the interaction of their platform participants. If such self-enforcing value creation loops are paired with high switching costs for platform partners (Hagiu, 2014) and barriers of entry for potential imitators, they may ultimately lead to significant competitive advantages within such winners-take-all markets, where the platform innovator may become long term the dominant player within its peer group by a fast scaling of the underlying platform.

The platform owner also defines the compensation model for the usage of the platform as well as for the participating platform parties which realize the exchange of the targeted value proposition on the platform. The former must assure by the compensation model, for example, a subscription-based revenue model, that for both platform partners, in double-sided platforms, or all partners, in multi-sided platforms, as well as for the platform owner, value is created, as otherwise any exchange on the platform would fail. In so far, the platform has to create in total a value surplus by delivering the value proposition, whereas this value surplus is shared between the participating platform parties. As the value add generated by the platform must be sizable to compensate the participating partners and the owner, it might come at no surprise that high-value-generating platforms typically rest on newly explored, uncontested markets. The customer use case might address unmatched needs or substantially redefine the solution for a distinct customer need or experience. For example, in B2C platforms, such use cases might rest on convenience through 24/7 accessibility, availability by a mouse-click, by offering through tail-end strategies an unlimited variety or creating a seamless delivery process.

1.6.2 The Four Platform Elements

Despite the diversity of platforms, such Business Designs have a set of common characteristics. Figure 1.18 summarizes the four mandatory ingredients of any platform. They define jointly a distinct platform's DNA.[7, 8, 9]

---

[7] Hagiu defines in his article *Strategic Decisions for Multisided Platforms* the number of sides to bring on board, the design, the pricing structure, and the governance principles as the fundamental drivers of a multi-sided platform. The number of sides and the governance rules are in the present concept part of the organizational structure, whereas the pricing structure is part of the platform's value creation design, and the design aspect is covered by the platform's strategic and technological architecture (Hagiu, 2014).

[8] Amit and Zott (2012) define six overarching questions for defining digital Business Design. Those questions, as platforms are a distinct form of digital Business Designs, might be interpreted as an overall framework, whereas here the specific elements of platform designs are highlighted.

[9] Staykova and Damsgaard (2015) apply for their description of multi-sided platform Business Designs the three criteria platform features, platform architecture, and platform governance.

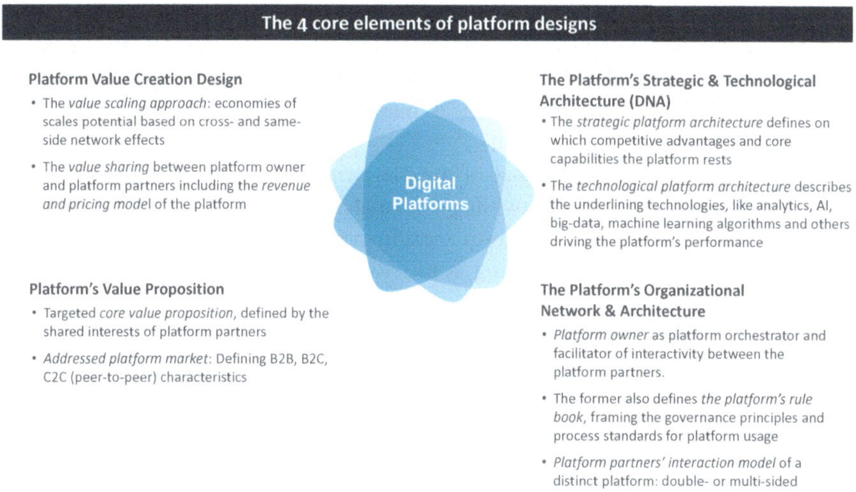

Fig. 1.18 The four core elements of platform designs

- The *platform's strategic and technological architecture*, defined by its differentiating and lasting competitive advantage paired with its underlying unique core capabilities, and its *technological architecture*, defined by the core technologies applied by the platform and their interplay.
  The platform owner shapes the competitive advantage and core capabilities of the platform and is in control of its intellectual property. Platform Business Design revolutionizes the traditional, horizontal value chain architecture and substitutes it by placing the platform owner in the center as orchestrator of the platform partners. Resource control is substituted by resource orchestration. As the platform value is defined also by the platform partner's capabilities, platform firms are partially turned inside out (Eisenmann et al., 2011). The traditional resource-based view of competitive advantage, as propelled originally by Prahalad and Hamel, with its focus on shaping a company's differentiating, lasting, and hard to imitate core capabilities has to be redefined. For platform firms, a more circular model is applicable integrating the platform partners' capabilities and resources as well as the interactivities between the platform players, besides the platform owner's own competitive advantages, capabilities, and, foremost intangible, asset architecture. The number, the depth, and the growth of interactions on the platform are the ultimate outcome of the platform parties' joint competitive advantage. The platform owner has precisely to define how his own capabilities facilitate interaction between the platform partners and create a strong and lasting platform community and bonding.

  The enabler and backbone of such interactions between the platform partners is the platform's underlying technology like demand aggregation and analytics for double-sided e-commerce platforms, advanced streaming technologies and recommendation engines for entertainment platforms, global analytics-driven engines paired with big data approaches as in the case of search platforms, or deeply engrained knowledge pools and diagnostics as well as therapeutics technologies for the development of biotechnology platforms. Especially due to the abundance of such technological innovations in recent years, platforms became more and more prevalent.

To realize the value potential of the platform, its owner controls the access point of the platform by providing the matching algorithm of the different platform partners and the platform's exclusive, proprietary content. To avoid disintermediation and side-passing is mission-critical for the platform's growth and value exploitation.

With respect to the form and mode of delivering the core value proposition to the user, convenience plays an important role for many B2C but also B2B platforms. Platforms offer a 24/7 access and availability paired with an order execution by a simple mouse click. Also, the delivery process, as digitally driven, is seamless and cost-efficient, as perceived in the case of streaming, online food-delivery, or search platforms. Typically, such platforms offer a cheer unlimited variety, as the onboarding of new content or features comes at low costs. On Airbnb's accommodation platform, potential guests might have the choice from one-room apartments up to entire castles. On Netflix, any genre and language setting might be found.

Platforms have an additional, digitally driven competitive advantage for the platform owner through the latter's direct access to the platform partners' data. These data could be exploited by big data approaches, machine learning algorithms, and analytics to better understand the platform partner's patterns and interests, to permanently improve the platform service, and to individualize customer-centric value propositions. Advanced platform architectures integrate automated feedback loops or recommendation engines to scale such advantages.

- The platform's *organizational network architecture*, defined by the platform partners connected through the platform, the platform owner, and the interactions between them.

  The platform owner has first to find the optimal interaction model before the scaling of the platform and according investments are kicked off. Fixtures of the Business Design during the critical early stage of a platform might stall growth and reduce the likelihood to achieve the infliction point which triggers exponential growth (Hagiu & Rothman, 2016). In a *double-sided network*, the platform's organizational architecture is triangular, as the two participating platform partners interact with each other through the owner's platform (Eisenmann et al., 2006). In *multi-sided platforms*, the platform partners, the nods of the network, interact through the owner's platform, the center of the platform's organizational network architecture.

  Examples for double-sided platforms might be ride-hailing, connecting drivers and riders, online accommodation platforms, connecting hosts and guests, or Apple's original iOS architecture for its smartphone, connecting app, and operating system developers with its iPhone users. The latter might be especially interesting, as it proves that within one ecosystem, even different platform architectures might exist, as evidenced by Google's triple-sided Android system, connecting users, and hard- and software developers. Other three-sided network examples might be online food delivery, connecting restaurants, couriers and diners, or professionals' networks like LinkedIn, connecting professionals with recruiters and advertisers. Sometimes platform partners even swap their role on the platform, as in the case of Airbnb, where a traveler might serve as a host on the next platform transaction (Eisenmann et al., 2011).

The trade-off in the decision on the number of platform participants must be well thought: With the number of platform partners, cross-side network effects and economies of scale might increase, revenue sources diversified, and barriers of entry due to the increasing complexity of the network even higher than in double-sided architectures. But, the latter might also become a hindrance if the complexity becomes too high or if for one or more participants the network would not offer an attractive value contribution (Hagiu, 2014).

The platform owner also has to design and implement the *platform's rule book* framing the governance principles (Staykova & Damsgaard, 2015) and setting the process standards.[10] The latter involves all processes through the platform participants' journey on the platform like the onboarding, navigating, and executing of transactions on the platform. The platform's rule book is exemplified in standardized platform online access processes, the platform's protocols, platform usage rights, and the integrated digital payment processes.

- The platform's targeted and addressed *core value proposition* which is shared by the platform partners and lurs them on the platform. The core value proposition implicitly defines the *platform's addressed markets.*
  The value proposition ultimately transferred between the platform partners represents the core of the platform. Like for the organizational design of the platform, the value proposition for all platform partners and the owner must be precisely defined before scaling the platform. A compelling value proposition for all sides of the platform will be a long-term incentive to be part of the platform community and is a prerequisite for exponential growth.

  The value proposition must also engrain a trustworthy and safe digital transaction between the platform partners. As the platform owner has no direct control over the value proposition transferred, mechanisms like ratings, feedback loops, review, and reward systems play a critical role for fostering trust between the platform partners and minimizing wrongdoings or even fraud. Likewise, Airbnb offers insurances for its hosts against property damages and Uber proposes insurance coverage for accidents. Also, escrow accounts for payments until the other side of the platform receives the promised value proposition might be an attractive safety feature (Hagiu & Rothman, 2016). Aligned with the value

[10] Eisenmann, Parker, and Van Alstyne describe such principles as platform rules (Eisenmann et al., 2006) which facilitate the platform groups' transactions.

preposition, the *platform's addressed market* is defined. This is exemplified by the platform pattern as a B2B, B2C, or C2C (peer-to-peer) matching model.

- The *platform's scaling, value creation, and sharing* approach.
  Typically, platforms are driven by economies of scales based on cross- and same-side network effects. As platform owners in principle may draw revenues from all platform partners, the definition of the *revenue and pricing model* is decisive as it defines also the *sharing of the value add created by the platform* between the platform parties. By optimizing the total ecosystem's value platforms are also in their value creation approach substantially different from traditional Business Designs with their focus on exploiting customer value (Eisenmann et al., 2011).

  The pricing strategy of platform owners has to factor in how the price setting for one platform partner might not just impact this group's demand and same-side network effects depending on price elasticity, but as well the cross-side impact on the other platform partners and their willingness to pay (Eisenmann et al., 2006). In tendency, the platform partner which is less price-sensitive and which may extract more value from the other side should be charged more (Hagiu, 2014). The pricing model based on such same- and cross-side network effects will have a lasting impact on the scalability of a platform and should be of major concern for the owner's initial platform design decisions. Nowadays, widely applied revenue and pricing models are:
  - *Subscription-based models*, where the user side of the platform, the subscriber, is charged a monthly or yearly fee for using the platform and its content like in the case of most film-streaming services.
  - *Ad-based models*, which also offer a significant cash flow pool as the global online-adds market is estimated at $350 billion. But, the perception by the network partners of advertisement placements throughout the core value proposition delivery process has to be sensitively assessed.[11]
  - *Freemium models*,[12] where one platform group, the subscribers, pays for the platform access and subsidizes another, price-sensitive group, which uses the platform for free (Carroni & Paolini, 2020). The free membership, sometimes also as basic subscription described, entails frequent commercial interruptions like in the add-based platforms. The free membership could be typically upgraded to a premium membership by paying a monthly fee. Premium members might be willing to pay such a premium for uninterrupted usage experience and access to an enlarged content offering.
- The revenue model and pricing strategy are of strategic importance for the scaling and success of a platform (Eisenmann et al., 2006): They are part of a platform's DNA as they have a lasting impact on the engagement and interaction of the platform partners, whereas each partner will define its own dedicated interest:

[11] Sánchez-Cartas and León use Evans' definition and describe platforms using add-based revenue models as audience makers (Sánches-Cartas & León, 2019).

[12] For a detailed introduction to freemium strategies, compare the landmark article from Anderson, *Free! Why $0.00 is the Future of Business* (Anderson, 2000).

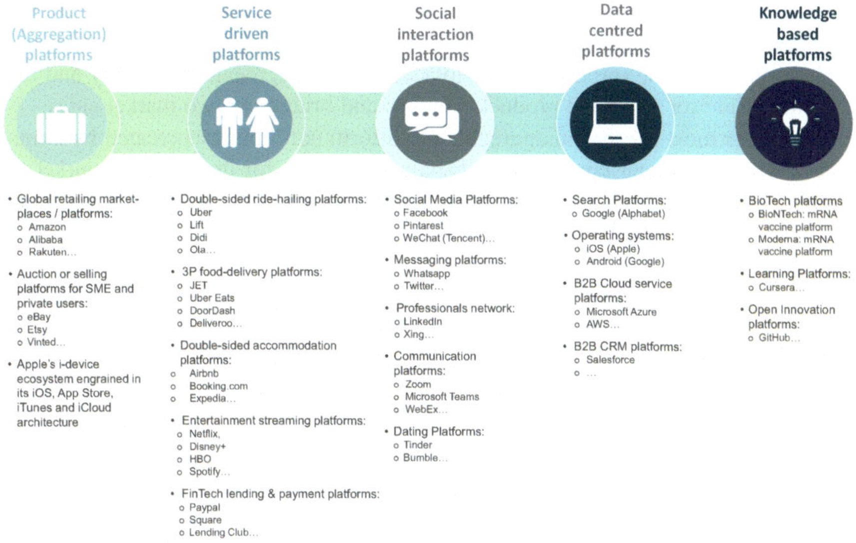

Fig. 1.19 Platform patterns defined by their core value proposition

Double-sided ride-hailing platforms coordinate the interest of drivers to earn extra money with the riders wishing to bridge the distance between point A and B at low costs, whereas global accommodation platforms lure in homeowners, also interested to earn an extra dollar, and travelers, intending to have a more individualized travel experience and affordable stay. Retail platforms bridge the distance between product suppliers and consumers through their low-cost search and matching through their app. Fintech lending platforms match investor's interest to optimize their risk-return trade-off with borrowers' needs to find a sponsor. This pattern of multi-sidedness places platforms in a prime position to create a direct link between platform partners and to orchestrate the exchange of the offered value proposition and value transfer between the parties.

1.6.3 Platform Patterns and Taxonomy

The exchange of a defined value proposition on the platform determines the use case from the platform partners' perspective. Figure 1.19 separates platform architectures in five distinct types [13].

[13] Evans and Gawer use a different classification of platform types, distinguishing between transaction, innovation, investment, and integrated platforms (Evans & Gawer, 2016). *Transaction platforms* focus on the intermediary function facilitating transactions between the platform partners, *innovation platforms* serve as a foundation for complementary technologies, *integrated platforms* combine transactional and innovation approaches, and *investment platforms* function as portfolio

- *Product (aggregation) platforms*: Platform strategies might be built around *products*. Such approaches are sometimes also described as aggregation platforms or online (product) marketplaces as they aggregate the supply and the demand side for a defined product category and bridge the two market sides.
  One of the most successful aggregation platform concepts was created by Amazon, which was later copied by Alibaba and Tencent for the Chinese market or Rakuten in Japan in the retailing space. Started as a digital book retailer platform, nowadays, a near unlimited amount of product ranges is offered on Amazon's app. In retailing platforms the platform owner serves as a facilitator of the transaction between the buyer and the seller. Nevertheless, this platform concept is still based on a traditional ownership and not a sharing model. Close to the retailing platforms are auction platforms and marketplaces for the buying and selling of used products as offered by eBay, Etsy, or Vinted.
  Within some platform concepts, the aggregator plays a twin role by also developing, producing, and delivering the offered product. Apple, for example, used the iPod success as a launchpad and extended its i-device ecosystem by introducing in sequential steps the iPhone, the iPad, and the Apple watch. This very successful but still traditional product pipeline-centered Business Design was supplemented, based on its iOS operating system, by a double-sided platform approach connecting system developers with users and was latter extended by the introduction of iTunes and its app store connecting app developers and users. This approach was lately further scaled by the iCloud service. Apple thereby engrains its hardware devices with a platform ecosystem approach. By introducing its streaming services Apple Music and Apple TV+, the tech giants even built a bridge between its double-sided iOS and app-store platform, its hardware ecosystem and such fast-growing service platforms. Apple argues to have now 660 million subscriptions across its platform services such as Apple Music, Apple TV+, news, and games (Financial Times, 2021b).
- *Service-driven platforms:* Nowadays, a multitude of service platforms are offered, from the streaming of music, film, series, and other entertainment content to double-sided ride-hailing apps or three-party food-delivery platforms.
  Streaming platforms are a dedicated subgroup of service platforms. They match different groups which share a common interest in a distinct, foremost entertainment content (Carroni & Paolini, 2020), by bringing together creative content developers with the interested community of such content like viewers, listeners, or gamers. Streaming platforms are typically based on monthly subscriptions like in the case of Netflix or Disney+, but sometimes are also paired with add-financed freemium approaches like in the case of Spotify. [14] From the 345 million Spotify

and holding approach. In contradiction to this typology, the underlying classification of this book uses the core value proposition transferred between the platform partners as reference point.

[14] Indirectly, streaming platform users pay a second "price" by contributing their data like usage, preferences, ratings, and others, allowing the platform to optimize its design for creating preference-tailored services.

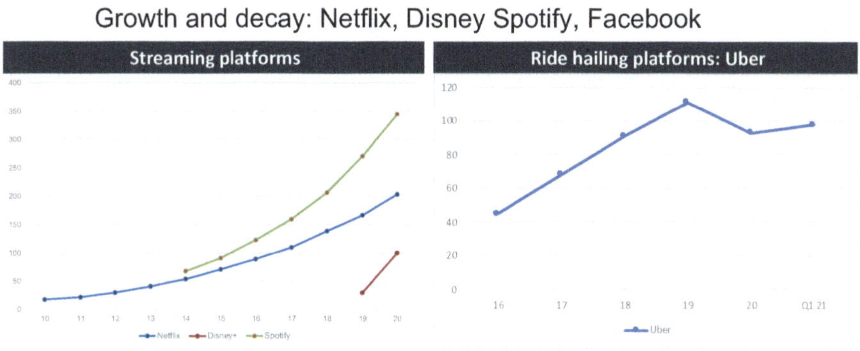

Fig. 1.20 Growth rates of service platforms: streaming and ride-hailing platforms

users in 2020 spread across 178 countries around the globe, 155 million use the subscription model, whereas the remainder the add-based model.

Not just the revenue model but also the content strategy of music and film platforms is diverse. As music-streaming platforms serve purely as an intermediate between artists and listeners, film platform owners like Netflix or Disney invest massively in own content development, branded as originals. The latter play an even more important role for the competitive advantage and differentiation strategy of film-streaming platforms. On the one side, film-streaming platforms might bear the burden of more asset-heavy balance sheets driven by multi-billion content investment needs. On the other side, they might use the creative content and aligned significant investments as a strategic and financial barrier of entry. This will be addressed explicitly within the streaming case study in Chap. 4.

The streaming platform owner controls and distributes the owned or licensed entertainment content through defined access points protecting their exclusive content. Streaming platforms are also a showcase as to how such digital Business Designs continuously enhance the technical platform capabilities by adding further advanced technologies and USPs like big data- and analytics-based recommendation engines to individualize the viewer's or listener's experience, the seamless synchronization of entertainment between different on- and offline devices, or bridging into new, adjacent networks like music-streaming platforms did with the market entrance into podcasts.

Other prominent service platform designs are ride-hailing, global online accommodation platforms, or payment and insurance services providers, labelled as FinTechs or InsureTechs. One yardstick to measure the power of platform Business Designs is the number of (monthly active) platform users or customers (MAPCs). Successful platform firms grow their MAPCs with double-digit compound annual growth rates (CAGRs) for years. This is exemplified by Fig. 1.20 for Netflix and Fig. 1.21 for Facebook. Both platforms have achieved an average CAGR of 27–28% in the last decade.

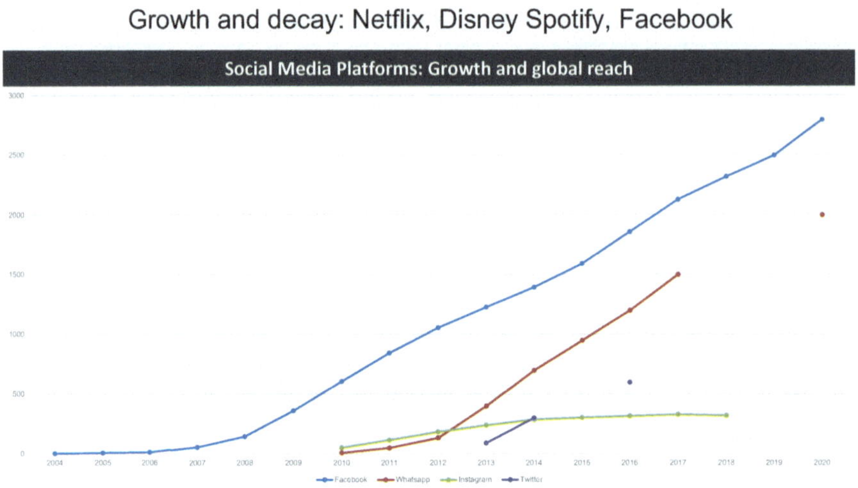

Fig. 1.21 Growth rates and global reach of social media platforms

Apple, as described in the product platform approach, is also a showcase on how to pair stand-alone product platforms with service platforms, as exemplified by the app store services or, lately, by introducing with Apple+ streaming offers and with Apple Music further entertainment options.

- *Social (media) interaction platforms:* As an alternative, and close to services platforms, digital Business Designs might focus on enabling social interactions and create a social community like in the case of Facebook, WhatsApp, WeChat, Twitter, LinkedIn, and others. They establish social networks by connecting individuals which have a common interest and lever interactivity and bonding among their platform members.
  The global reach of successful social media platforms is evidence by two decades of consistent strong growth of Facebook and its peers. The 2020 Facebook community of 2.8 billion users is astonishing, especially if compared with globally 4.9 billion Internet users or a world population of 7.8 billion.
- *Data-centered platforms*: Platforms that create data-based Business Designs, sometimes described as well as data aggregation platforms, bundle data of one platform partner, or a couple of partners on their platform or offer problem-solving services. One party might publish a need or problem or offer on the platform, and the platform owner will connect this party with a counterparty on the platform, which may fulfil the information need or solve the problem. The most powerful data-based platforms create entire new marketplaces. Data-driven platforms deploy analytics and big data approaches to design new business models, either based on business or B2C user data. For example, Alphabet's Google search engine offers such a service for search-interested users.
- *Knowledge-based platforms*: Finally, industries like finance or biotech try to copy such successful platform strategies. Already the first case study in Chap. 2 on the

BioNTech and Moderna COVID-19 vaccine development will discuss such knowledge-based platform approaches. Such biotech pioneers, using their revolutionary mRNA approach, might use their engineering and knowledge excellence to reach out beyond Sars-Cov-2 vaccines to new areas like the development of an immuno-oncology candidate pipeline or other vaccines. (Economist, 2021a). These newest platform designs might be labelled as knowledge platforms connecting the knowledge provider(s) with knowledge interests.

1.7 Decoding Platform Value: The Eight Levers of Platform Value

Platform Business Designs shift the center of gravity of competitive advantage and value creation. Where traditional Business Designs shape their competitive advantage along their value chain around the development, production, and sale of their products, platforms compete on Business Design level. The revenues and cash flows of traditional Business Designs are typically driven by the one-time sale of their products and, in a best case, supplementary aftermarket services. Platform Business Designs create value by digitally leveraging platform participants' data, thereby generating continuous revenues and cash flows through subscription or on-demand-based revenue models. In the freemium model, as described above and successfully applied by Spotify and others, one platform group may use the platform even for free, whereas another platform group has to pay a subscription or fee, therefore subsidizing the former.

Digital Business Designs are often built upon such sustainable and powerful platforms framing entire ecosystems. But, as the technical term platform is loosely defined, many companies argue to have a platform design which generates substantial value. The underlying question here is if a distinct digital Business Design rests indeed on a platform architecture and economics which keep competition at bay by low, decreasing unit costs per transaction for the market leader and, ultimately, creating a winner-takes-all market. Only if the platform's cross- and same-side network effects have increasing returns on scale, they will create outstanding RoICs by leveraging growth. And indeed, newest technologies like web- or cloud-based applications, analytics, machine learning algorithms, and big data approaches lowered the costs to reach out to global users systematically and enable for multiple Business Designs decreasing unit costs with increasing volumes.

Nevertheless, Schmalensee and Evans questioned the reliability of network effect advantages and winner-takes-all dominance for any web-based multi-sided platform (Schmalensee & Evans, 2016). Also, they highlighted the risk that network effects may work in reverse and destroy value with explosive speed, a fate suffered by multiple web-based businesses after the burst of the dot-com bubble around the millennium. For example, Myspace is still perceived as one of the early innovators of social media platforms, grew at the beginning exponentially, but became irrelevant as Facebook side-passed it.

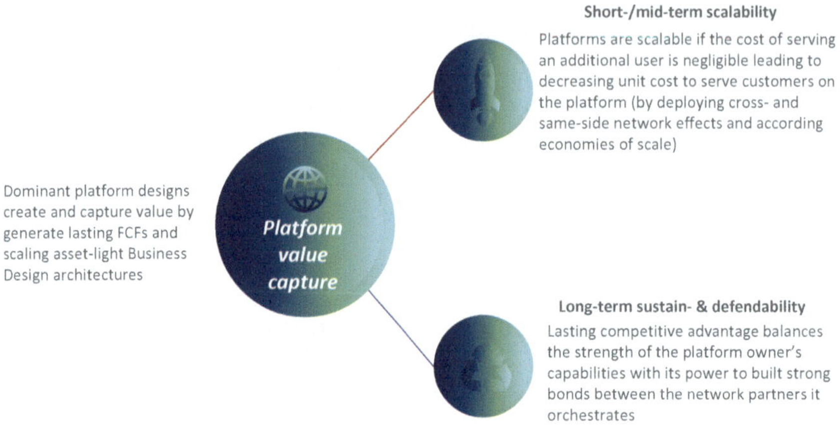

Fig. 1.22 Platform value: short-term scalability and long-term sustainability

As the existence and durability of proclaimed network effects of platforms have to be questioned, a framework is mandatory, which enables the diagnostics of long-term network and platform strengths. Platforms which create a strong and value-creating network-enticing platform participants rest on two pillars: They enable a short- and mid-term fast scalability of the Business Design and offer a long-term sustainable competitive edge which is difficult for competitors to imitate and build significant barriers of entry. Scalability and lasting competitive advantage may lead ultimately to significant cash flow generation of such platforms, as pinpointed by Fig. 1.22.

The financial tailwind of platforms is based on the principle that serving additional users or participants on the platform may be realized at negligible additional costs. Within such market spaces, the early innovator grabs a dominating market share. Besides, dominating platforms avoid value destructive price wars with competitors as the early mover could exploit those economies of scale and cost advantages in establishing the platform. The threat of the platform innovator to be in a position to counter any competitive pressure by undercutting will reduce the likelihood of imitators to enter into a price-based value-destroying competition. Dominating platforms ultimately create strong cash flows. Such Business Designs are foremost asset-light as the platform partners have to contribute typically significant inputs to fulfil on the targeted core value proposition. In contrast, the platform firm itself does focus on its technical platform capabilities like AI or analytics as well as on the design, the building, and the maintenance of the platform. Therefore, limits of successful platform Business Design in scaling the business are minor, leveraging further cash flows and value:

- *Short- and midterm scalability:* In case of substantial scalability potentials of a platform, a "winner-takes-all" pattern might be exploited. Strong growth platforms go hand in hand with intense same-side or cross-side network effects between the different platform partners participating on the platform. Examples might be Amazon in global and Alibaba in Chinese e-commerce, Facebook in social media, WhatsApp in massaging, or Airbnb in global accommodations. Short-term scalability is enforced in case of balance sheet light Business Design patterns which will be discussed in depth within Sec. 1.8.

- *Long-term platform sustainability and defendable competitive advantage*: But it might be easier to achieve platform scale than to defend and maintain it. A lasting competitive advantage of digital Business Designs balances the strength of the platform owner's capabilities with its power to build strong bonds between the network partners it orchestrates.

The sustainability of a platform Business Design depends on the health, defensibility, and dominance of the underlying platform. Zhu and Iansiti from Harvard Business School defined five platform characteristics which shape their scalability and sustainability: These five drivers of successful platforms are the existence and strength of same-side and cross-side network effects, network fragmentation or integration, the risk of disintermediation, risk of multihoming, and, last but not the least, the potential of building connected, reinforcing platform bridges (Zhu & Iansiti, 2019). These five criteria will be supplemented on the one side by the inner core of a platform's strategic approach, defined as the *platform's scalability potential* and the *platform's lasting competitive advantage*. On the other side, placed in the center of any platform approach, the platform architecture is added. The latter might be interpreted as the platform's anchor.

These *eight criteria define a framework for the strategic evaluation of platforms*, as highlighted in Fig. 1.23. This framework will be described in more detail in the following. The platform value approach will also be stress-tested, by applying the concept consistently throughout the platform case studies in Chaps. 2, 3, 4, and 5.

- *Platform architecture and core*: The platform architecture is a brief description of the four platform elements, as the framework of any platform, and their interplay. As defined prior, the platform elements encompass the platform's strategic and technological architecture, its organizational network and architecture, its value proposition, and the value creation design.
- *Platform scalability*: The platform value will be driven by the scalability of the platform, where the latter is foremost defined by the intensity of the network effects between its network partners, analyzed below in more detail, and according economies of scale (Evans & Gawer, 2016). An aligned prerequisite for catching scalability advantages and to realize robust cash flows is the design of a tailored revenue scaling model, for example, subscription-based, add-based, or as a freemium model, which is embedded in the platform's Business Design architecture. [15]

[15] Eisenmann, Parker, and Van Alstyne highlighted in their article *Strategies for Two-Sided Markets* the importance of the pricing strategy for a platform's success. For example, in freemium models, it has to be decided if and how far one platform party, which is charged for its platform

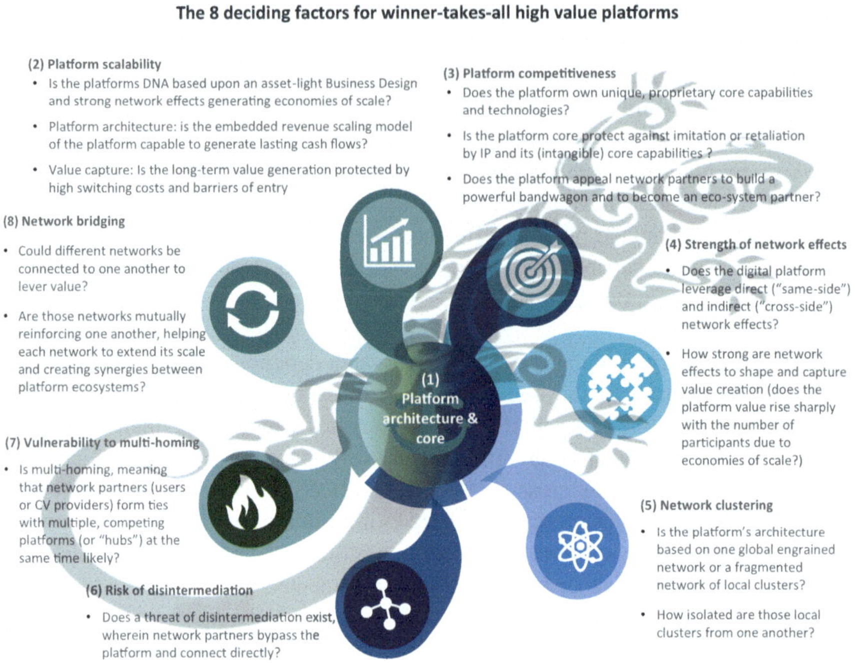

Fig. 1.23 Strategic platform patterns and the eight deciding factors of platform value

Furthermore, the diagnostics of the platform's DNA in proving its asset-light Business Design characteristics is fundamental for the forecast of the likely valuation impact in scaling the platform. Such balance sheet light patterns of Business Designs exist only, if a limited additional Invested Capital and costs are necessary to grow the business. Decreasing unit costs in combination with low Invested Capital needs foster high ROICs and cash flows.

Only under circumstances where scalability patterns of a platform are proven, a winner-takes-all strategy by aggressively scaling the installed base of the network will play out. In contrast, where such scalability advantages are not present, the scaling of a platform will burn significant cash flows.

Additionally, switching cost of platform partners to join a competing platform, an argument which is also addressed by the risk of multi-homing, and barriers of entry defend the long-term scalability potential of a platform.

- *Platform competitiveness*: A platform matches the interests of the platform partners by realizing the transfer of a distinct value proposition. But, this protects in principle not against imitation and substitution. A platform's competitiveness

participation, subsidizes another party, which may use the platform for free. A prime example is Google search, where advertisers pay and searchers use for free Google's search engine (Eisenmann et al., 2006). This is also the reason why the prior platform definition included the revenue model.

will be defined by the unique competitive advantages of the platform owner, which are hardly to be imitated by contenders. Such advantages may rest on the platform owner's core capabilities like technology skills or distinct intangible assets. Examples for the latter might be IP rights, brands, or content like for streaming platforms.
Digital technologies offer thereby novel sources of competitive advantage of platforms: Platform firms deploying big data algorithms and analytics on their ocean of users create, beside the pure matching of platform parties, more customer-tailored services, therefore increasing the platform's customer value and, ultimately, its attractiveness. Within the context of the streaming platform case in Chap. 4, this might be exemplified by the recommendation engines of Netflix or Disney+, which learn from viewer patterns and interests and suggest likely best fit next to watch movies or series. Such big data and analytics application create a segment-of-one customer profile and enable tailored streaming content experiences as a valuable strategic tool to enforce network effects. Regional and individual viewing preferences might be added by tail-end strategies offering different genres and language settings. These learning effects about the customer preferences and journeys, built upon analytics and big data approaches, ultimately increase platform value and keep competitors at bay.

Another empirical case on exploiting big data and analytics approaches might be Amazon. Its review system offers potential buyers to learn from former purchasers about the latter's purchasing experience and assessment of the product's quality or features, before their own ultimate buying decision. Additionally, the e-commerce giant's recommendation system suggests products based on prior transactions to lock in members on the platform for follow-on purchases. The linkage to same-side network effects of Amazon customers using its market place is given by the increase of its analytics-driven accuracy of its recommendations with an increasing number of platform users.

But competitive advantages of platforms are also ecosystem specific. An interesting empirical case, which also highlights the necessity to permanently renew platform defensibility and competitiveness, is the threat of Disney+ to Netflix, the early innovator of the media-streaming Business Design. As content counts in global entertainment, Disney extended its movie library significantly by multiple acquisitions besides its original content creation. This was exemplified lately by the multibillion acquisition of the 21st Century Fox franchise supplementing its own movie content and providing a launchpad to become a viable streaming competitor. This endgame in global media streaming will be analyzed in detail within Chap. 4.

Intangible assets, such as entertainment content or brands, might be applied as supplementary tools to reinforced platform strength. [16] Strong brands might build

[16] An interesting linkage to former physical networks might exist here. As Schmalensee and Evans describe, physical networks like railroads or traditional telephone networks realized barriers of entry as challengers had to invest significant amounts for tangible assets to enter such networks and still

customer trust thereby overcoming the anonymity of digital market places and distant platform partners. Amazon, eBay, Netflix, Airbnb, Uber, and others might be prime examples on how to build brands for digital platforms reinforcing their competitive advantage.

Last but not the least, the platform's appeal to network partners will define the potential to build a powerful platform bandwagon or even an entire ecosystem. This enlarged ecosystem may increase the variety and quality of the platform's value proposition.

- *Existence and strength of network effects*: Network effects describe the pattern and strength of the interdependencies between the network partners. Platforms might orchestrate two or more parties. Example for the former might be ride-hailing and streaming, an example for the latter three-party food-delivery apps. Customers represent the demand side for defined products, services, or digital offerings, whereas the supply side offers those on the platform. Network economics highlight two different sides of network effects and their strength of interconnections they build between the platform parties (Zhu & Iansiti, 2019):
- *Same-side, direct network* effects exist in case an increasing number of members of a distinct partner group participating on the platform, one side of the platform, increases the attractiveness and value of the platform also for the next marginal new member of this platform group, this side of the platform, significantly. A precondition is that the onboarding of new group members could be realized at marginal costs. The more colleagues and friends are part of a massaging or social media platform like WhatsApp, WeChat, Facebook, or LinkedIn, the more attractive the platform is for a potential new member of the network to join and to connect with mates, colleagues, or business partners.
- *Cross-side, indirect network effects* exist if an increasing number of one platform partner's members participating on the platform—one side of the platform—also increases the value for the other platform partner's members partnering on platform, the other side, as highlighted by Fig. 1.24. The origin of cross-side network effects is typically the matching of the supply and the demand of services, products, data, or knowledge on the platform. For example, the wider the scope and variety of products or services of a defined category offered on the platform, the more attractive the platform might be for potential users, luring and capturing them on the platform. Vice versa, the higher the number of active platform users, the higher the attractiveness and gravity of the platform on the supply side. [17]

---

being exposed to retaliation by the incumbent (Schmalensee & Evans, 2016). There is a fair argument that nowadays the traditional role of tangible assets is overtaken by intangibles like IPs, brands, or content. The enormous investment of streaming champions like Netflix or Disney+ highlights how platform network effects paired with multi-billion media content investments shape competitive advantage of such platforms.

[17] Same- as well as cross-side network effects might not be necessarily always positive but may also work negative. Especially for same-side effects, if competition between same-side participants

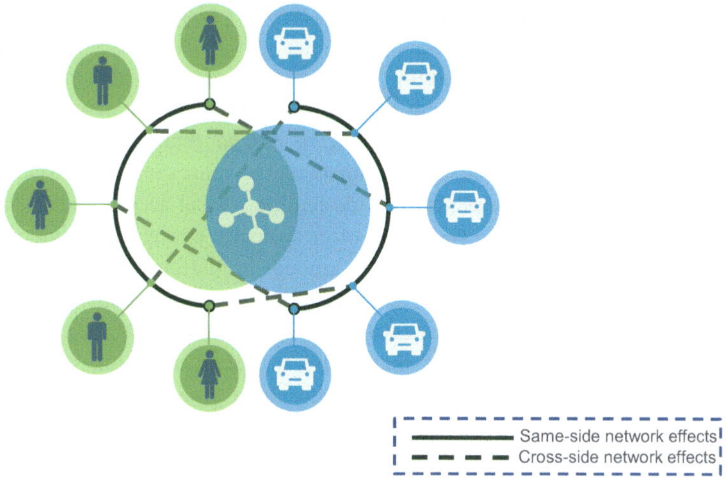

Fig. 1.24 Same-side versus cross-side network effects on platforms

An example might be Alphabet's Google search. With a higher number of individuals using the Google search engine, the value for advertisers using Google adds increases, which enables reinvestments to build an even stronger search engine and analytics tools attracting further users with search interest. Another example would be ride-hailing services as offered by Uber, Lyft, Didi, Ola, and the likes. Here, more ride-hailing drivers mean lower waiting time and fares for riders, increasing the ride-hailing platform value for riders. Vice-versa, more riders using a distinct ride-hailing app will reinforce the platform value for drivers by reducing idle time between rides and increasing their income. A vicious circle which should lock in more and more platform members, drivers, as well as riders.

The strategic and financial outcome of same- or cross-side network effects is lower unit costs or higher user satisfaction per customer or transaction with an increasing number of platform users, giving the first mover an economies-of-scale advantage. In case of strong same- and cross-side network effects, a large installed base serves as a formidable competitive advantage and will enable to shape a dominant platform design. Platform leaders lock in the first movers' market lead as they limit the attractiveness of imitation by potentially fast second

increases, they may turn out negative, e.g., the more drivers offer their services for a mobility platform, the less might be their earnings potential.

platform peers, ultimately increasing the first mover's platform's defensibility and sustainability. [18, 19]

To value a platform's strength, the *existence* of same-side or cross-side network effects plays a significant role. In a second step, the *strength* of those network effects as well as the *potential to defend* them long-term is to be analyzed. This will have a substantial impact on the value creation, sustainability, and capture potential of the platform. Ride-hailing, global accommodation, or the before-mentioned streaming platforms offer typically strong cross-side network effects. In the latter's case, an increasing amount of platform viewers will attract creative talents, actors, and movie studios to co-operate with the platform, increasing the size and content variety of the digital movie library, finally enticing more viewers on the streaming platform. For accommodation platforms, an increasing number of accommodations in global megacities and attractive destinations offered on the platform will lure in travelers. As the reach of the platform increases with the number of tenants, the platform reinforces its value for further hosts providing new accommodations on the platform.

Examples of less strong network effects might be lending-based FinTech platforms. Debtors might select simply on lowest interest rates offered by alternative lending platforms and lending capacity. Additionally, lending contracts are seldom renewed, prolonged, or supplemented, reducing the amount of interactions on the platform making true network effects marginal. The case studies in Chaps. 2, 3, 4, and 5 will highlight that network effects are mandatory for any platform to exist, but might not always be sufficient to create a winner-takes-all market and to avoid imitability.

- *Network clustering and fragmentation*: The clustering into local networks, also described as fragmentation of networks (Zhu & Iansiti, 2019), is a question of a platform's architecture and regional connectedness. Within fragmented platform patterns, and in stark contradiction to global networks, partners are matched on local level ultimately leading to a multitude of regional networks. This is highlighted in Fig. 1.25. Global networks offer substantial scaling and growth advantages if paired with strong network effects, whereas fragmentation limits the impact of scale and network advantages outside a local marketplace. Fragmentation bears the threat that parallel, isolated network universes of locally separated clusters, in different regions or for different applications, might be established and grow in parallel. Competitors may compete in another cluster by scaling their service locally, gaining critical mass and market dominance within their local

[18] By analyzing the prerequisites to build a successful platform design, Hagiu and Rothman addressed the risk of premature growth as it might put significant strains on a Business Design. Trying to adjust the latter on the run during the scaling phase might lead to a breakdown before the infliction point of exponential growth is achieved (Hagiu & Rothman, 2016).

[19] Evans and Schmalensee (2010) models of double-sided platforms assess the limitations to gain critical mass and highlight the dependency on the nature of network effects, the distribution of tastes among potential participants in both platform partner groups, and the pattern of out-of-equilibrium dynamics.

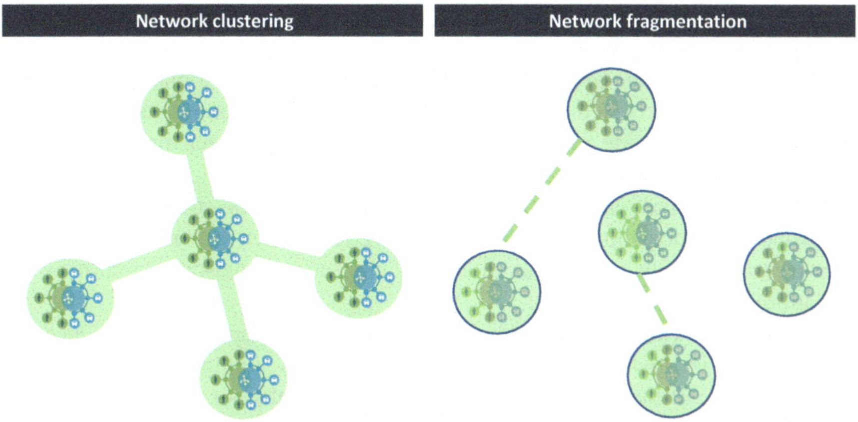

Fig. 1.25 One global platform cluster versus fragmentation into local platform clusters

hub. This ultimately may endanger the overall platform profitability, value, and sustainability of such platform ecosystems.

The ride-hailing market might bear the risk of such a network fragmentation, where the riders in one city foremost care about driver availability and pricing in their hometown or city they have travelled to, but driver availability in other cities does not offer them any advantage. Spillover advantages for ride-hailing networks in other municipalities, having established a strong position within their home turf, might be limited. This enabled Lyft as a latecomer a still successful entrance in the US ride-hailing market, starting on the West Coast, establishing a footprint against its main competitor Uber. The fierce price war between Didi and its mainland Chinese competitors is another interesting example within the regional partially fragmented ride-hailing ecosystem (Zhu et al., 2019).[20]

Some companies try to establish an overarching platform connecting regional clusters by offering additional USPs and services, therefore strengthening connectivity between the local hubs and ultimately to overcome fragmentation threats. An example might be regional FinTechs, offering lending or payment services, by introducing further financial services like international money transfer or foreign exchange services on their platform or enlarging the list of mode of payment services by introducing international credit cards and digital payments solutions. Additionally, intangible assets like brands or intellectual property may offer platform Business Designs to connect regional clusters and avoid breaking points caused by centrifugal forces of local hubs and competition. An interesting example might be here LinkedIn having bridged local and regional job markets by establishing a global network of professionals and offering them international

[20] Details of the raid hailing ecosystem and platforms will be discussed within Chap. 3 "Ride-Hailing: Is Sharing the New Owning?"

career opportunities creating ultimately a global brand and social media platform for professionals.

- *Risk of disintermediation*: Disintermediation is the risk for a platform that network partners, once having been matched on the platform for the first time, might bypass the underlying platform subsequently and to connect directly, thereby saving platform usage fees. The risk might be especially high for platform models that simply connect participating parties and which offer no additional value add beyond. If participating platform parties have found their first match, they may connect for follow-on services directly having no true reason to return to the platform.
A well-known example are platforms offering home or repair services. Once the homeowner is satisfied with such a service and trust is built up in service quality, the two sides of the platform might directly connect the next time, side-passing the platform. The risk of disintermediation might be especially high in cases of such repeated interactions once the first contact and trust is established between platform partners. Also local proximity was identified as a critical factor fostering side-passing of a platform as interaction and payments might be more easily realized off-platform than in cases where two far distant strangers interact. An example for the latter might be the first-time matching of a host and a tourist on an accommodation platform.

  Disintermediation reduces significantly a platform's sustainability and its lasting value capture potential. Not surprisingly, benchmark platforms invented a multitude of prevention mechanisms to avoid the probability of disintermediation. One possibility is simply to prohibit network participants to jump offline and connect directly by contractual service terms of the platform for their users. This strategy might be only successful as long as the network might become not too complex or attacked by simplified alternative approaches of peers.

  Another lever to protect against disintermediation is to withhold critical information for the closing of a transaction. Airbnb applies such a defense strategy by withholding the exact location of the host and by not disclosing either host or guest contact information until the transaction is finally confirmed, including payment details, on the platform.

  Ride-hailing firms offer additional, complementary services like insurances for their drivers or latest digital communication network technologies which might be important for high driver utilization rates to keep drivers on their platform. Also, rider recommendations and ratings placed on the platform might be an incentive to participate longer term on the platform. Amazon tries to lock in its suppliers by offering them, beside global customer access, a wide array of further services like lending or real-time customer data access.

  Besides, building trust by brand recognition might work as a strong barrier against platform disintermediation. Payment services like PayPal or international money transfer platforms like TransferWise offer customer financing protection and might payback transferred money if counterparty risks materialize. This may reduce the risk of digital transactions and lever trust in the platform's brand. Such additional services, closely aligned to the underlying core service, could serve a strong platform disintermediation defense tools. This might especially hold true if counterparties are not very well-known.

Another alternative is a strategic change of the payment and revenue system. Some platforms switched successfully from a direct charging of service providers and users to an advertisement funded revenue model, avoiding the direct costs for the transaction partners. The potential of a change in the payment architecture depends on the underlying value proposition offered on the network and the revolving transaction patterns. If the latter are executed only one time, alternative advertisement models might be less attractive as if a continuous flow of transactions is executed on the platform and advertisers might bond with long-term platform users.

- *Vulnerability to multi-homing*: Multi-homing means that platform partners might not just use one single platform but may join multiple platforms for the same use case. The decision to join several platforms depends on the platform partner's switching costs of multi-homing, including access costs to the platform, costs aligned with the execution of the transaction on the platform, as well as opportunity costs. If such costs are negligible or low, providers of core value propositions might place their services, products, or digital offerings on multiple platforms as users might search for them on a multitude of competing platforms. In case platform users on one side of the platform connect with multiple platforms, the number of active platform users on a single platform becomes less influential, thereby weakening network effects.
Multi-homing leads typically to a fierce competition between the different platform architectures, often accompanied by aggressive price-undercutting initiatives of competing platforms to generate short-term platform traffic. Long term, nevertheless, a degeneration of the competing platforms' value risks to destroy their core and limits the possibility to design a winning, dominant platform model or winner-takes-all characteristics.

Google's search engine escaped the risk of multi-homing by offering high-quality search hits and having reinvested fully their operating cash flows during the early days of the platform to improve performance by analytics and big data investments. Other networks like ride-hailing might be more endangered on both sides of their double-sided platform to multi-homing. Drivers might work for different, competing platforms to reduce idle time, whereas riders may switch between different ride-hailing apps based on critical USPs like cost per ride, service availability, and waiting time. Latest research (Li & Fend, 2019) provided empirical evidence that in circumstances where multi-homing on both angles of the platform exist, it will be challenging to build a winning platform, whereby reduced multi-homing on one side might push multi-homing on the other end as well. Meaning for the ride-sharing ecosystem, if fewer drivers are at the same time on Uber's as well as on Lyft's platform, riders might have an incentive to use multiple apps to reduce waiting time and compare fees. Vice versa, if less riders multi-home, drivers might do so to increase their reach and reduce idle time.

The risk of multi-homing is always then high if the costs to onboard on a single platform as well as the switching costs between platforms are low and no further

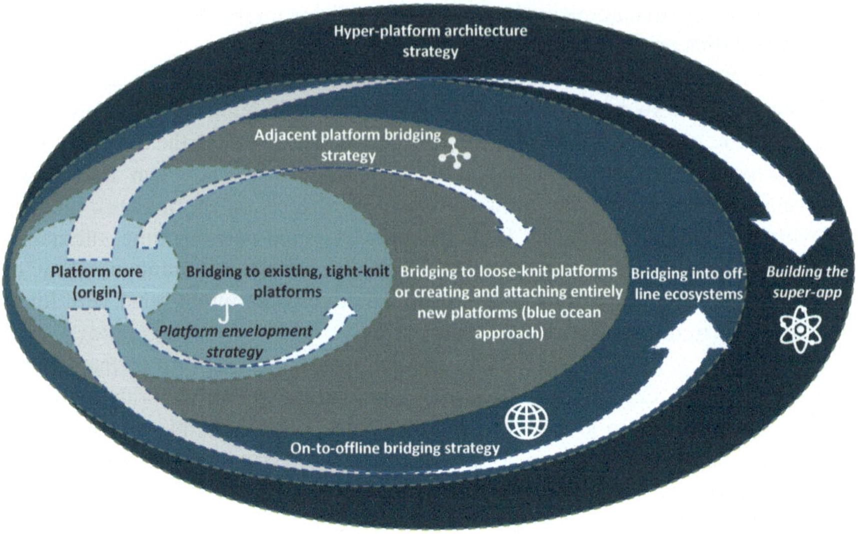

Fig. 1.26 Platform-bridging strategies: From tight-knit platform envelopment to hyper platforms. *Source*: Research project tfX-advisory on digital and platform Business Designs, 2021

platform services is able to generate a true differentiator from a platform user point of view. An interesting escape strategy to multi-homing was applied lately by streaming platforms. Leading networks lured celebrities, star actors, and movie writers on their platform by signing exclusive, highly paid contracts with them to lock in a higher number of viewers and to avoid a ruinous price competition ultimately strengthening platform value. Another interesting case is Amazon Prime's approach of avoiding multi-homing of shoppers on alternative e-commerce platforms by offering them free 2-day shipping and customer-tailored information based on their previous buys. Additionally, the e-commerce platform offers discounts for bundling purchases and use of other Amazon Prime services to lock in platform users.

- *Network bridging*: Network bridging acts as some sort of crown jewel of platform strategies by connecting distinct, initially stand-alone networks by integrating one platform's application on another platform as part of a multi-platform bundle. Network-bridging approaches blur market boundaries between such platform ecosystems. This is expressed by Fig. 1.26.

Multiple levels of platform-bridging strategies exist, but any approach has to prove that synergies could be captured by serving the targeted different platform ecosystems. *Platform envelopment*[21] *strategies* bridge a platform's core to tight-knit

[21] Eisenmann, Parker, and Van Alstyne described in their article *Platform Envelopment* platform bridging as platform envelopment (Eisenmann et al., 2011). But, as platform envelopment is understood to bridge networks between established ecosystems and thereby competing with the

ecosystems, whereas *adjacent platform-bridging approaches* reach out to more distant, loss-knit platforms with more significant differences in their platform architecture or partners. On- to offline bridging goes even beyond digital Business Designs by entering offline ecosystems. Tech giants are on the move to create super apps by building and orchestrating hyper-platforms. The attractiveness of platform-bridging approaches increases with the number of platform participants overlapping on the involved platforms. Leveraging shared partners and platform owner-to-partner relationships make bridging approaches likely.

Platform bridging starts with the definition of a platform's core, which rests often by itself on an entirely new market. Amazon originally created such a new white spot in e-commerce of books, and Netflix or Spotify did so in entertainment streaming, Airbnb in global accommodation rental, PayPal in payment services, Facebook in social networks and marketing, or Uber in ride-hailing. To grow beyond this core, two levers ultimately enable platform-bridging approaches [22]:

- On the one hand, advanced digital tools like artificial intelligence and big data-based analytics might be exploited on a multitude of platforms from diverse settings and offer platform-bridging potentials. The idea is here to leverage the data and analytics developed for one platform to reach out and scale adjacent ecosystems.
- On the other hand, in cases where one or more platform partners, for example, users, are part of multiple platform ecosystems, platform bridging might enable significant platform user synergies.

By leveraging assets and capabilities between different networks and exploiting synergies between them by serving the same platform partners or exploiting joint customer data, the platform origin might be extended beyond the original core and enforce market entrance in adjacent platform ecosystems. The original more narrow platform boundaries are extended by network-bridging strategies, whereas counterattacks of incumbents of stand-alone networks might be of limited power as the latter would miss out on the advantages of network connectivity and economies of scale between the networks. Network bridging might significantly boost the overall platform competitiveness and value creation as long as platform complexities could be handled and synergies captured.

Different platform-bridging approaches are highlighted in Fig. 1.27. Lately, the network-bridging strategies have been applied to extend to an existing platform close to the platform's core, as above defined as platform envelopment. A showcase of such a more tight-knit platform bridging is the Spotify strategy to establish beyond

---

incumbent of an adjacent network, platform bridging might be more broadly applied and goes even beyond envelopment. Platform bridging might also create entirely new platform ecosystems and uncontested blue oceans. In a further article (Eisenmann, et al., 2006), the authors explored strategies for the platform which is enveloped.

[22] Gawer and Cusumano (2008) describe the bundling of technologies, the use of the same distribution channels, and the design of unique complementarities as levers to enter other platforms.

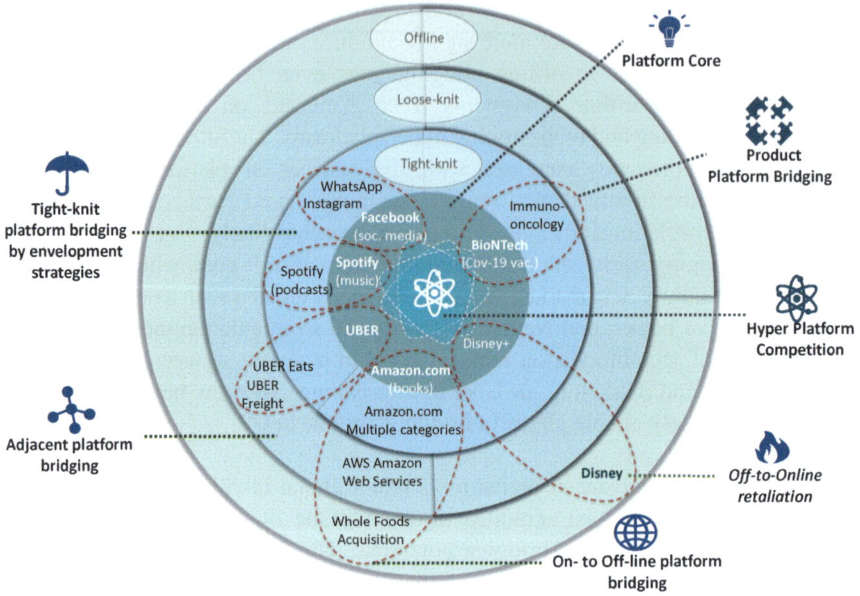

Fig. 1.27 The age of hyper-platform competition and platform-bridging strategies. Research project tfX-advisory on digital and platform Business Designs 2021

its existing core in the music-streaming business an early stronghold in the nowadays uprising and popular podcast ecosystem. Spotify invested in 2020 more than €1 billion into this new platform and acquired several start-ups to supplement its existing music-streaming core by mission-critical capabilities for this adjacent platform.

An example for an *adjacent platform-bridging strategy* might be the market entrance of Uber in the online food-delivery market by establishing Uber Eats as a stand-alone business unit within the holding company. Such food-delivery platforms are triple-sided as they connect couriers, restaurants, and consumers. Due to the architectural difference between double-sided ride-hailing platforms and three-party (3P) food-delivery architectures, the latter platforms look more distant from Uber's core than in the Spotify case reaching out from music streaming to podcasts. Nevertheless, ride-hailing and food-delivery networks have synergies as drivers and customers are for Uber on both platforms partners. Food-delivery platforms grew significantly already before the pandemic. As Uber's core ride-hailing business struggled due to the unfolding pandemic and aligned social distancing restrictions, the food-delivery platform proved to work as a hedge. Consistently, Uber extended its food-delivery footprint in 2020 by the add-on acquisition of Postmates (New York Times, 2020). The acquisition and integration of Postmates into Uber Eats gave the parent tailwinds in the hefty contested US food-delivery market against its core food-delivery competitors Grubhub and DoorDash, as will be discussed in Chap. 3 in detail.

An even *more adjacent platform-bridging approach* by Uber is given by its extension into B2B freight services and the establishment of Uber Freight as in the logistics market Uber serves two totally different user segments in comparison to its ride-hailing services: on the one side, professional logistic couriers and providers and, on the other side, firms looking for logistic services. Therefore, the platform architecture of ride-hailing as B2C platform and freight logistics platforms as B2B Business Design differ significantly and will offer less platform-bridging enabled user and data synergies as compared with the bridging from ride-hailing services to online food delivery, as the latter is as well a B2C model and shares the same platform parties.

Apple, by applying this adjacent platform-bridging approach, moved into payments by introducing Apple Pay, entertainment by offering on-demand videos through Apple TV+, and music streaming through Apple Music besides other services, balancing its hardware reliance on iPhones, iPads, and Macs. In the company's latest update to its iPhone release, the app ecosystem was further engrained into its operating system and privacy restrictions introduced, including requiring apps to get app users' explicit permission to gather advertising targeting and tracking data. Apple most likely intends to expand its own advertising business platform where the company is estimated to earn around $2 billion p.a. from search ads in the App Store, with 80% margins, by adding a "suggested" app section in its App Store search functionality. This might put the company in more direct competition to Google and Facebook, which still dominate the $350 billion digital ads market. The App Store is also assumed to be the company's biggest money-spinner and builds the core platform of its i-device hardware empire, as it connects multi-sided platform app developers with app users. Charging 30% of sales by publishers, Apple is estimated to earn $15–$18 billion from the App Store (Financial Times, 2021a). All in all, Apple's "super-cycle" continued into 2021, as the company lately communicated to have increased its Q1 2021 revenues by astonishing 54% to $90 billion, fueled by its newish 5G-capable iPhones (Financial Times, 2021b). The financial impact of Apple's multi-sided platform extension is shown in Fig. 1.28.

Amazon and Alibaba became benchmark platform powerhouses by scaling network bridging. This is exemplified by the saying "being amazoned," meaning if Amazon enters a new market or platform, it will get tough for incumbents to compete, often missing simply the digital capabilities and network bridges of the tech giant.

Amazon reached out first beyond its core book e-commerce and delivery services by offering a significant amount of further product categories on its platform. This could be interpreted as tight-knit platform extension. An adjacent platform-bridging example by Amazon might be the creation of Amazon Web Services (AWS). By deploying the established IT architecture of its original e-commerce-centered business, Amazon entered the cloud service ecosystem, and established a powerful stance and market position in this fast-growing B2B segment. In the meantime, this service line is a significant profit and cash flow pool of Amazon Inc.

In a further step, Amazon went surprisingly offline by acquiring Whole Foods, an established US high-end bricks and mortar food retailer, for more than $15 billion.

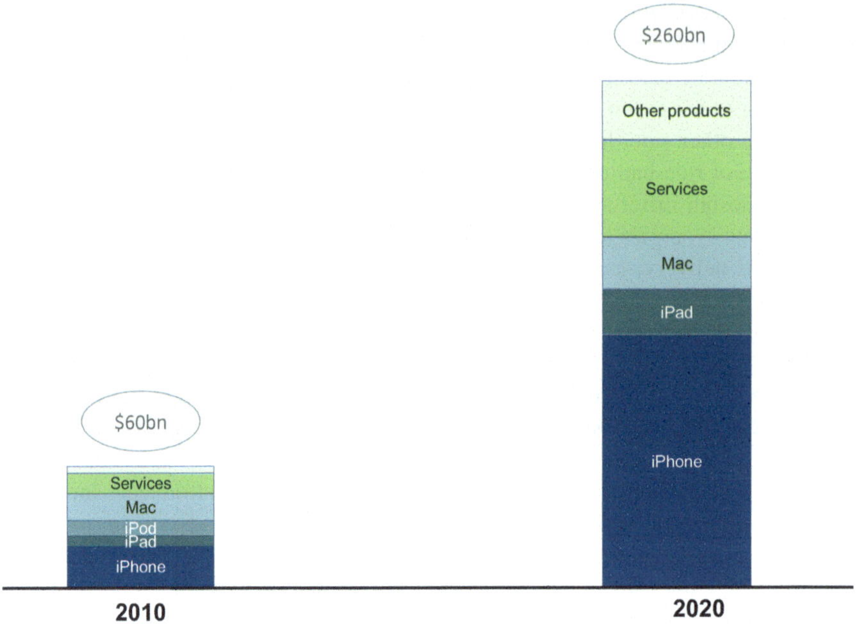

Fig. 1.28 Apple's multi-sided platform-bridging strategy. *Data Source*: Financial Times 27/01/2021

This is a more distant *on- to offline network-bridging approach*. Amazon intends to learn from and apply synergies between the off- and online food retail ecosystems. Additionally, Amazon solves with the Whole Foods transaction partially the "last-mile delivery" problem of its e-commerce franchise, as Whole Foods is present in all US states and offers with its retail outlets an ideal regional footprint for Amazon's parcel lockers.

The bridging to the offline world went not unnoticed to the bricks-and-mortar retailers and capital markets. Shortly after the announcement of the Whole Foods acquisition, the share prices of the listed food retailers plummeted by 8–10% on Wall Street. In the meantime, Amazon's competitors developed *off- to online retaliation strategies* by going flip-sided from off- to online. Walmart, the US retailer stalemate, booked $38 billion in online sales in 2020. Best Buy, Home Depot, and Target extended as well their digital stakes. Disney is another off- to online bridging example. The 98-year-old company finally cut the cord and went streaming. It achieved more than 100 million viewers in just 18 months after having introduced Disney+ and extending Hulu as well as ESPN+ as its three proprietary streaming service platforms (Economist, 2021b). The streaming revolution of Netflix and Disney's digital retaliation strategy will be discussed in depth within Chap. 4.

Alibaba went even further than Amazon by establishing a multi-network approach as some sort of super-app, supplementing its e-commerce platforms Taobao and Tmall by a multitude of financial services from payments, known as

Alipay, and lending to insurance services by its affiliate Ant Financial. It uses, for example, synergies between the platforms exploiting supplier data and rankings from their e-commerce platform by offering them tailored short-term loans, especially to fund their working capital requirements. In so far, the networks mutually reinforce one another.

A newest and maybe ultimate platform bridging might be described as *hyper-platform competition*, where digital champions like Amazon, Apple, Alphabet, Facebook, and Microsoft compete fiercely within each other's home turf. Each of those trillion-dollar giants have a clear defined core as online ads generated still 80% of Alphabet's and 98% of Facebook's revenues, 80% of Apple's revenues could be traced back to its smart i-devices, and Microsoft revenues still rely on software dominance as Amazon does on its e-commerce strengths. Nevertheless, a recent study by the Economist Intelligence Unit found that the overlaps in revenues of the top five American technology giants increased from 22% to 38% in the last 5 years (Economist, 2021b). Direct competition of platform champions is fiercest on the cloud, the profit zone of Amazon and a $63 billion business growing with a CAGR of 40%. Microsoft generates an estimated $20 billion with its Azure cloud-computing business nowadays, and Alphabet established in the last years a strong foothold in cloud services which is expected to become a $1 trillion business within the next one or two decades.

Amazon vice versa attacks Facebook and Google in their backyard by rising its stakes in digital marketing and advertising. Amazon's share in its e-commerce core business declined from 87% to 72%, as Amazon Web Services (AWS) contributes nowadays 10% and digital advertising 6% to global revenues. The latter's move snapped additionally 10% points of Alphabet's proportion from advertising (Economist, 2021c).

At the same time, PayPal intends to build a financial super-app with 750 million users competing against a multitude of FinTechs and indirectly against Apple Pay and other digital payment platforms. On this view, it has to be assessed if we are at the dawn of a new area of technology competition and if the winner-takes-all strategy might vanish at least partially long term by such hyper-competition.

1.8 Financial Valuation Patterns of Digital Business Designs and Platforms

As the strategic footprint of digital and platform Business Designs, their financial and valuation patterns bear some common characteristics which set them apart from traditional Business Designs.

A new digital but un-proven Business Design implies obviously a higher risk exposure than its traditional counterparts. Financially wise, this is mirrored by a higher volatility of the Business Design's underlying cash flows. But volatility also means that the second crucial ingredient of corporate valuations, the cost of capital, or more precisely their beta as a measure of a company's shares co-movement with a diversified peer-group, should be foremost higher than those of traditional businesses. Nevertheless, the COVID-19 case study in Chap. 2 will show that this is not necessarily always so.

Additionally, the overall funding needs and the financing mix between equity and debt and, therefore, the cost of capital might change significantly throughout the life cycle of such digital companies. A showcase here is Netflix along its journey to build a powerful streaming platform. For funding the significant investments in its originals development and content acquisition with the intent to build an unmatched, enticing catalogue of movies, the company onboarded in the peak more than $16 billion of debt. Lately, it seemed that the company's investment thesis played out. Due to the fast growth in subscribers and having propelled more than 200 million paying viewers on its streaming platform, Netflix will most likely reach the tipping point of free cash flow breakeven in 2021 finally. That will put Netflix in a position to reduce its indebtedness and probably to launch its first share buyback program.[23]

On the one side, the specific risk factors of a dedicated digital Business Design have to be addressed by tailored cash flow scenarios, by simulations or by the—in Sec. 1.9 discussed—new Reverse DCF valuation methodology applying so-called pictures-of-the-future scenarios. On the other side, the overall risks of an ecosystem and peer group as well as macro-risks have to be mirrored within the cost of capital.

Traditional multiple assessments are foremost not applicable for the evaluation of digital Business Designs. Especially in the case of digital natives riding a blue ocean true peers, most likely, will simply not exist. Also, the venture capital (VC) method might offer only limited applicability for the pricing of a digital firm. Its foremost over-simplified rule-of-thumb valuation yardstick is based on only three crucial and volatile inputs, the projected earnings, the projected but unstable price-earnings ratio of peers, and the from its investors' expected internal rate of return. Digital Business Designs have to be assessed much more in detail to get a glimpse of their "true" and long-term value.

The Invested Capital diagnostics might have not as much of an impact on the free cash flows and the valuation of digital companies as in traditional firm valuations due to the balance sheet light pattern of most digital Business Designs. Nevertheless, Business Design-specific investments in capital expenditure or intangible assets might be necessary and have to be explicitly modelled. Uber's investments in its technology platform or Netflix investments in its movie catalogue serve as prime examples. On the income statement side, the revenues might have a more prominent role in comparison to the cost drivers, as the building and scaling of a digital Business Design or platform are mission-critical for success, especially in a digital firm's early days of existence.

A more granular assessment of the financial value drivers of digital Business Designs might reference to the "tao of value": The equity value of the company is based upon the free cash flows realized by the Business Design of the company, mathematically speaking the nominator, and its distinct cost of capital,

[23] See for further details Chap. 4 on the discussion of Netflix's 10C Business Design and especially its CF module.

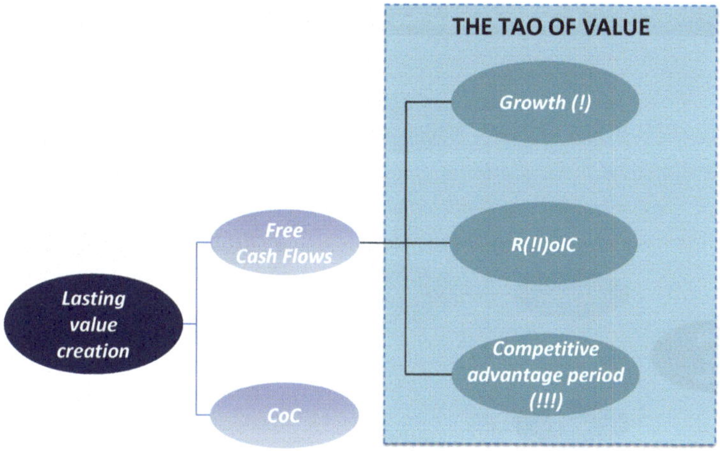

Fig. 1.29 The "tao of value": first-level value drivers of digital Business Designs and platforms

mathematically the denominator.[24] As shown by Fig. 1.29, the FCFs could be further decomposed in the three core value drivers. The latter define together the "tao of value" (Feix, 2020; Koller et al., 2020):

- The Return on Invested Capital (RoIC)
- The long-term and sustainable growth rate
- The competitive advantage period, meaning how long a Business Design could sustain returns above its cost of capital and generate lasting value

Applying those three fundamental value drivers on digital Business Designs provides first high-level insights on the financial working mechanism of digital and platform firms. Not surprisingly, the growth rates, especially in the early years of successful digital and platform companies, are often exceptional. Empirical evidence shows that companies like Facebook, Netflix, Airbnb, or Uber have been in a position to grow with double-digit rates for a long-lasting period before growth finally decays, as pinpointed in Figs. 1.20 and 1.21.

Not only the growth momentum but also the RoIC performance of successful digital and platform Business Designs is remarkable: The ROIC formula, as the second driver of the tao of value, is typically based on a combination of high EBITDA and NOPLAT performance, the nominator, paired with ultralow Invested Capital needs, the denominator, due to the foremost balance sheet light business architectures, especially of platform firms.

But two words of caution should be raised here. First, not all digital natives share the luxury of stellar returns on capital. The platform value and especially the strength

[24] Enterprise Value calculation applies foremost a weighted average cost of capital (WACC) approach and for the cost of equity assessment the Capital Asset Pricing Model (CAPM).

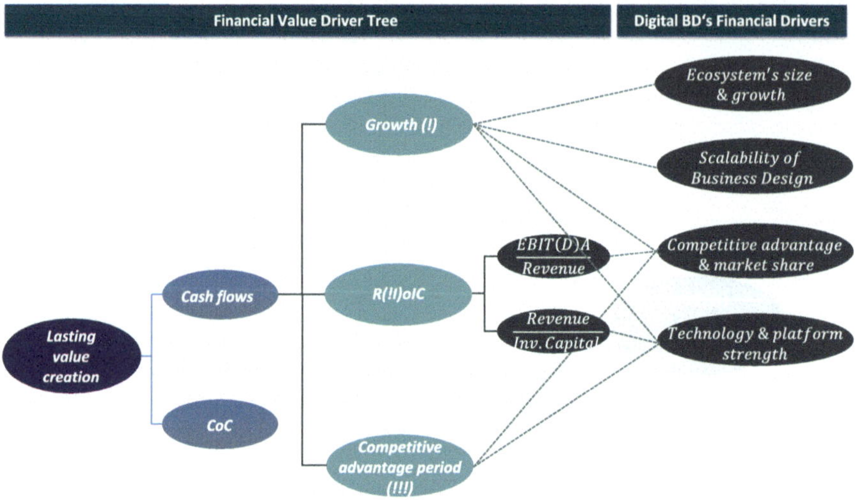

Fig. 1.30 Second-level value drivers of digital Business Designs and platforms

of network effects will determine the long-term ROIC performance and its sustainability. Second, ROICs might be artificially high in circumstances where competitive advantages rest especially on intangible investments like platform strength, brand building, or intellectual property. Intangible assets paired with asset-light Business Designs might drive ROICs to elevated levels.

The third and last value driver, the competitive advantage period, is an especially interesting one. It is defined as the time period in which companies generate returns above their or the peer group's average cost of capital. Traditional economic theory suggests that extraordinary returns should be competed away by Schumpeterian destruction and regeneration, meaning new entrants should be enticed by the early days' juicy returns. Technology companies proved this assumption wrong, e.g., Apple consistently achieved an EBITDA margin between 25 and 32%, and also platform champions like Google or Facebook proved a consistently high-profit performance level.

These top-level value drivers may be supplemented and detailed by even more tailored levers of value for a dedicated digital or platform Business Design. For example, the RoIC might be further decomposed, along the DuPont approach, in a margin (EBITDA-to-revenue) and capital turnover (revenue-to-Invested Capital) component. The first might be further detailed by sub-value levers like, as pinpointed by Fig. 1.30:

- The market size and growth of the ecosystem targeted by the core value proposition
- The scalability of the Business Design
- Its distinct competitive advantage and market share
- The Business Design's technology and platform strength

- *Market size and growth*: The size of the targeted market frames a Business Design's growth potential as well as the boundaries of its ecosystem. A close linkage exists here to the discussion on platform value: If networks and markets are fragmented, growth prospects might be limited to one or a limited number of nearby local clusters. But in case of global networks with connected clusters, growth might be nearly unlimited in the first years for the early innovator and might lead ultimately to "winner-takes-all" markets. The granularity of the market segmentation based on the addressed core value proposition of a distinct digital Business Design plays a critical role to define the potential growth momentum thereby.
- *Scalability of the Business Design*: The scalability of a Business Design rests on a number of parameters. Scalability might be propelled if the Business Design is based upon a balance sheet light approach. Also here exists a close link between the financial and strategic drivers of platform value.
  Additionally, digital and platform companies might not be limited by organizational or human barriers of growth. Building a global social media platform like Facebook, WhatsApp, or WeChat or a professional's network like LinkedIn will rest on the platform development and management capabilities, big data as well as analytics know-how, and digital marketing excellence. But, neither the number of employees nor the need to build a physical presence in every country is mandatory for the scalability of such platforms. Also ride-hailing platforms neither hold the cars of their drivers on their balance sheet nor the drivers themselves huck typically on their income statement; they just facilitate the journey between point A and B.
- *Competitive advantage and market share*: A strong and lasting competitive advantage will pivot market share from competitors onto the own platform and will be a tailwind for free cash flows. Besides, competitive advantage and uniqueness will not just define the market position but have as well a significant impact on the RoIC performance of a digital company.
- *Technology and platform strength*: The technological capabilities play a central role to create and defend competitive advantage and free cash flows. But, the granularity of the technological capability definition for a distinct Business Design is mission-critical. Besides technological core competences, the capability to build a bandwagon of partners and supplementary offers on the platform is a decisive ingredient of a platform's financial strength.

Pairing value drivers with the valuation of a digital firm, the most crucial financial terms mandatory for the valuation flow will be defined in the following briefly.

The *free cash flows*[25] *(FCFs)* of a company are the most crucial valuation ingredient. The free cash flows of the company are defined here, by applying an entity approach, as the after-tax cash flows of the company available to all investors, equity, as well as debt holders. The free cash flows might be a suitable gauge of the

[25] The technical terms *free cash flow* and *cash flow* will be used interchangeably in the following.

$$FCF =$$

$$NOPLAT - Netinvestment\ in\ Invested\ Capital =$$

$$NOPLAT + depreciation\ \&\ other\ noncash\ operating\ expenses - investment\ in\ Invested\ Capital$$

- *FCFs* are based on the two operating performance indicators of any Business Design, the *NOPLAT* performance and the investment need of the distinct Business Design.
- NOPLAT does not deduct interest payments. Therefore, free cash flows are the cash flows which are available for equity as well as for debt investors.
- As a consequence, FCF are completely *independent of the financing structure* of a company. If a company is more or less levered has no influence on the FCFs. Besides, FCFs are independent of any non-operating items.
- FCFs are therefore - in contrast to the technical term "cash flow from operations" as applied within the financial statements - a pure operational measure and therefore ideal for corporate valuation purpose

Fig. 1.31 Definition of free cash flow (FCF)

value creation of a company as they solely rest upon its operating performance, measured by its NOPLAT[26] and investment in Invested Capital (Koller et al., 2020, p. 49). Free cash flows are independent from the financing structure, meaning if a company is more or less levered, as NOPLAT is calculated prior to the deduction of interest rates:

$$\text{FCF} = \text{NOPLAT} - \text{netinvestment in Invested Capital}$$

Free cash flows rely only on the two crucial operational-driven financials, NOPLAT and Invested Capital. Thus, the free cash flows of digital Business Designs and platforms are as well derived by their NOPLAT performance and their investment need to build the Business Design. As an alternative way, the definition of free cash flows might explicitly address the add-back of non-cash items like depreciation and be defined as:

$$\text{FCF} = \text{NOPLAT} + \text{depreciation} - \text{grossinvestment in Invested Capital}$$

The gross and net perspective to calculate the free cash flows is summarized by Fig. 1.31.

Not only free cash flows but also the Return on Invested Capital (RoIC) is build upon NOPLAT and Invested Capital as ingredients. Whereas the former is an absolute, RoIC is a relative performance measure. As also a pure operational performance indicator, RoICs are suitable for benchmarks within peer groups or for corporate performance measurement purpose. RoICs are a perfect supplement of

[26] NOPLAT is used in the following as abbreviation for the technical term Net Operating Profit Less Adjusted Taxes. Adjusted taxes are to be interpreted as the normalized tax level for the operating business of a firm.

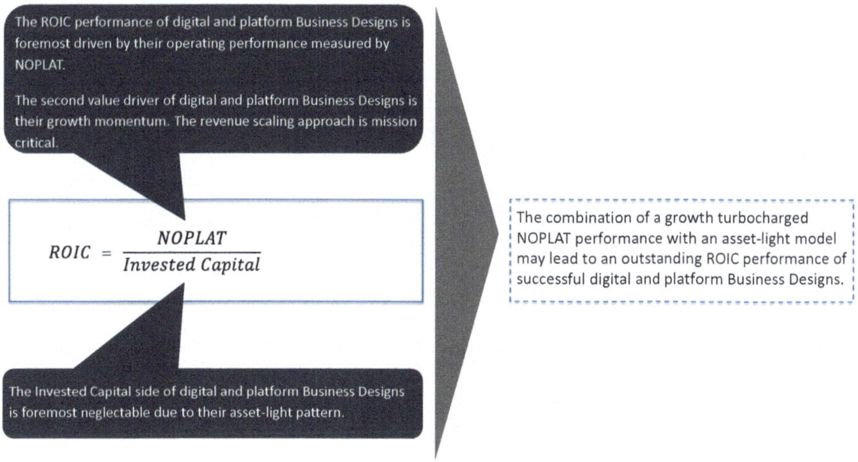

Fig. 1.32 Working principles of Return on Invested Capital (RoIC) of platform Business Designs

free cash flows. They are defined as NOPLAT divided by Invested Capital (Koller et al., 2020, p. 49):

$$\text{RoIC} = \frac{\text{NOPLAT}}{\text{Invested Capital}}$$

The ROIC of platform Business Designs is, due to their foremost asset-light pattern, driven by their operating performance, measured by NOPLAT. The second value driver of such businesses is their growth momentum. Their revenue scaling approach is mission-critical for the long-term operating performance, as measured by ROIC. In contrast, the Invested Capital of platform firms is foremost negligible, leading to an outstanding ROIC in case of a robust NOPLAT performance and successful growth scaling approach, as highlighted by Fig. 1.32.

For the ultimate valuation of a platform firm, the free cash flows have to be discounted by their distinct cost of capital (CoC). Typically, the weighted average cost of capital (WACC) approach, referencing to the market-weighted mix of the cost of equity and the after-tax cost of debt, is applied in enterprise valuation approaches, whereas here the broader-term cost of capital is used. This has the advantage that also cost of unlevered equity, e.g., in case of Adjusted Present Value (APV) valuations, could be subsumed under this definition. The latter approach provides more flexibility for modelling the changes of the debt-to-equity funding structure during the life cycle of a digital firm. In each valuation, the cost of capital approach has to be specified.

The cost of capital incorporates the time value of money as well as the non-diversifiable risk, meaning the market risk of an investment in a company. The non-diversifiable risk should be more or less identical for the companies of a defined peer-group, so should be their beta as well as the unlevered cost of equity. The latter may be re-levered to calculate with the company's specific financial

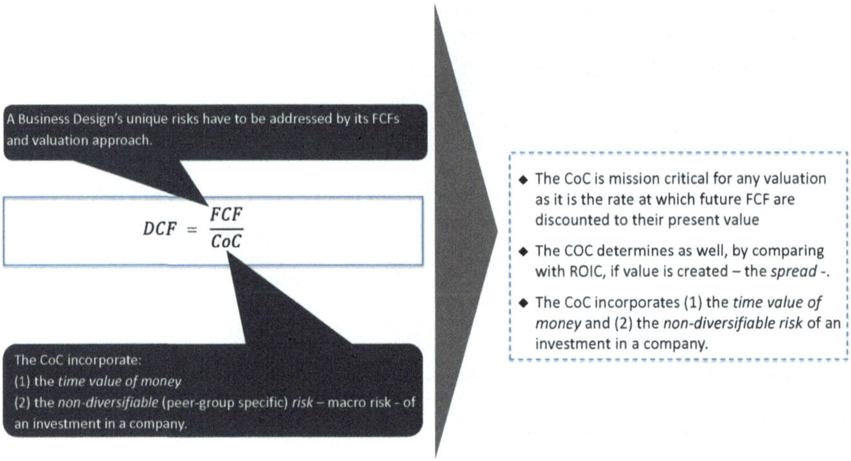

Fig. 1.33 FCFs, DCFs, CoC, and to be addressed risks

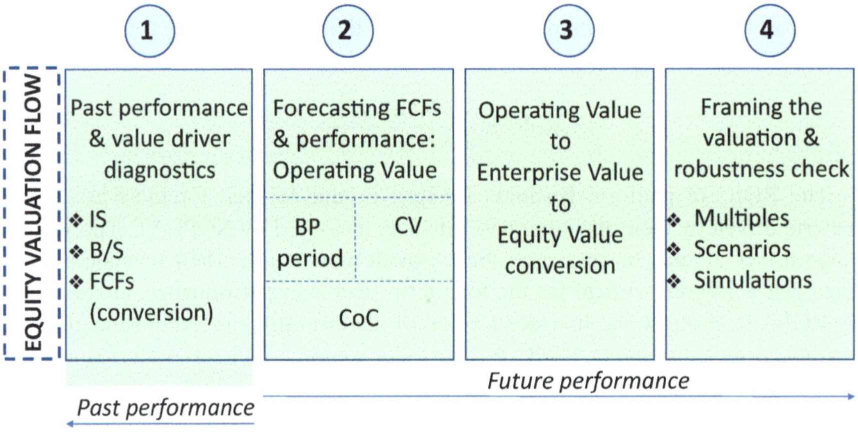

Fig. 1.34 Equity valuation flow

leverage its distinct levered cost of equity. Risk enters into corporate valuations as macro-, non-diversifiable risk through the company's cost of capital, whereas the uncertainty surrounding the specific future performance of a distinct firm is embedded in its free cash flows. That is in so far important for digital Business Designs as the unique risk of the company has to be modelled in its free cash flows and not in its cost of capital, as described by Fig. 1.33:

The cost of capital determines as well, by comparing them with the ROIC, if value is created or not within a specific time period. The spread is calculated by deducting the cost of capital from RoIC. A negative spread indicates value destruction and a positive one value creation.

Having defined the mission-critical financial terms, Fig. 1.34 shows a comprehensive equity valuation flow and forecasting process (Feix, 2020, pp. 129–135).

This distinct equity valuation process flow uses four sequential steps.

For a sound valuation based on the forecasted free cash flows of a company, the past performance has to be assessed to get a crisp understanding of the value performance and its drivers. Nevertheless, in the case of digital or platform companies, the financial diagnostics of past performance might be of limited use if no corporate history exists. Within such circumstances, other ecosystems which may rest on comparable technologies and market patterns might provide a partial substitute.

Applying an Enterprise-DCF concept, in a second step, the value of operations (OP) is calculated as the sum of the discounted cash flows (DCFs) within a to be determined planning period T in addition to the present value of the Continuing Value (DCV).[27] The latter represents the present value of the Business Design's expected DCFs beyond the explicit forecast period discounted to the date of valuation:

$$\text{Operating Value} = \sum\nolimits_{t=1}^{T} (\text{DCF}_t) + \text{DCV} = \sum\nolimits_{t=1}^{T} \frac{\text{FCF}_t}{(1 + \text{WACC})^t} + \text{DCV}$$

One caveat of the continuing value concept is that it rests on a perpetuity model and could only be applied once the steady-state free cash flow and NOPLAT performance as well as Invested Capital growth is achieved, meaning when the growth momentum of the business peters out. As digital and platform Business Designs are characterized by high growth rates, especially in the early days of the business, the planning period has to be substantially longer than for the valuation of traditional, mature companies. Additionally, a valuation bandwidth seems to be more plausible than a one-shot value estimate. How such valuation bandwidths may be addressed is discussed below within the different suitable valuation approaches for digital and platform Business Designs.

The third step in the valuation process is the walk from the value of operations (OP) to enterprise value (EV) and, ultimately, to equity value (EqV), which involves two substeps:

- Moving from operating to enterprise value, non-operating assets, often described as excess cash and other non-operating assets, have to be added:

$$\text{EV} = \text{Value of Operations OP} + (\text{ excess cash and other nonoperating assets })$$

[27] The book follows therefore the definition of Koller et al. (2020, p. 187), where the free cash flows of the firm define the operating value, whereas enterprise value includes as well excess cash and non-operating assets. For the flow to equity value, debt and debt-like items have to be deducted, and not net-debt like in alternative approaches, which are widely used. The two valuation approaches, if correctly applied, will lead ultimately to the same equity value.

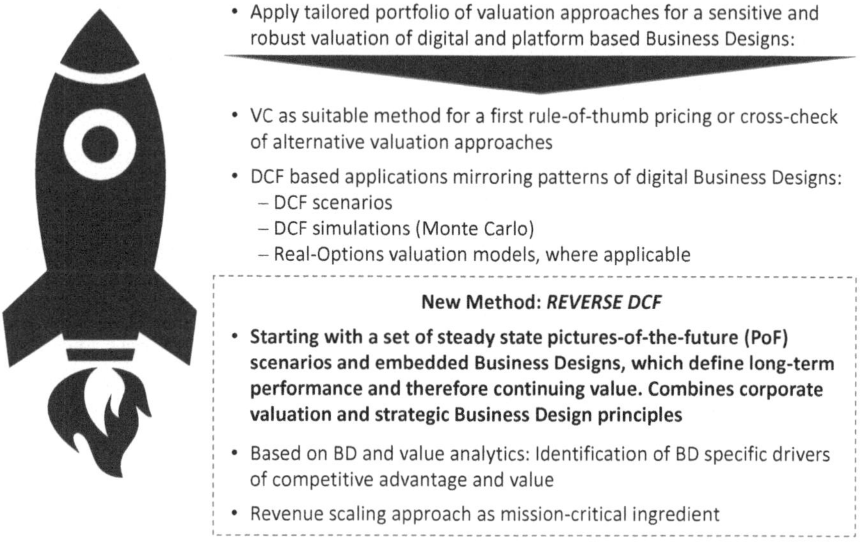

Fig. 1.35 Applicable valuation methodologies for digital and platform Business Designs

- For the final transition from enterprise to equity value, all debt and debt-like items have to be subtracted:

$$\text{Equity Value EqV} = \text{Enterprise Value} - (\text{Debt} + \text{debt like items})$$

Due to the discussed limited historical performance of digital Business Designs, as a forth step, the framing of the equity value with different scenarios and valuation methods, as well as by applying benchmarks and multiple assessments, is proposed.

Taking into consideration the pattern and value architecture of digital and platform-based Business Designs, distinct valuation approaches, which rest on the discussed Enterprise-DCF concept, could be defined. Thereby, valuation approaches which model free cash flows under uncertainty might be particularly valuable. This is addressed by Fig. 1.35.

- *Value driver sensitivities and value analytics*: The sensitivity of the projected equity value to discrete changes of the core value drivers provides an in-depth understanding of the root causes of value generation of the assessed Business Design. Based on the diagnostics of the critical value drivers, the modelling of future free cash flows is more deeply grounded. Additionally, a set of different plausible assumption for the financial drivers are mandatory ingredients for building scenarios or the modelling of simulations. Sensitivity analysis provides the framework for building scenarios which incorporate uncertainty within the forecasted free cash flows.
- *Scenarios*: A specific scenario describes one possible development path and steady state of an ecosystem at a future date which rests on a set of key

assumptions associated with this scenario. A selective set of alternative, robust scenarios in combination with their underlying assumptions enables the financial modelling of alternative development paths of a company and its ecosystem (Smith & Smith, 2019). The valuation of such scenarios must be more pulled from the idea how different futures might look like than be based on historical performance or simplified best, realistic-, and worst-case scenarios. For digital and platform Business Designs, the modelling of scenarios incorporating different scaling approaches and growth rates might be especially interesting.

- *Simulations*: The Achilles' heel of sensitivities and scenarios is their discrete number of possible outcomes. Simulations overcome the limitations of discrete scenarios. In a broad definition, simulations may be described as the design of the behavior of a complex system, here a digital or platform-based Business Design, by applying a simplified, statistical model. In case of game theory applications, even competitors' retaliation strategies may be taken into account in simulation designs.
  Simulations address the uncertainty of outcomes by interpreting each critical value driver as a statistical distribution, in most instances as a normal distribution by defining its mean and standard deviation. An alternative, often applied statistical distribution is a uniform distribution over a defined range.
  The workstreams of simulations is straightforward: In a first step, the crucial value drivers of a Business Design have to be diagnosed. Based on those mission-critical value drivers, a spreadsheet model of the Business Design is built. In a next step, the mathematical model describing the uncertainty of outcomes is designed. This model is applied by running a significant number of iterations of possible valuation outcomes, where each outcome represents a random draw from each statistical function and, by computation of all variables, their interlinkages, and ultimately their combined effect on enterprise and equity value (Smith & Smith, 2019, p. 204). The iterations of the valuation simulations are finally aggregated.
  The dispersion of simulation outcomes provides a gauge of the aggregate impact of the uncertainties surrounding the development of the core value driver of a Business Design as built into the model. An important impediment of simulations is the complexity of designing a financial model that is a reasonable mirror of the real-world Business Design.
- *Real Options*: Applying decision trees, the Real Option approach enables the valuation of staged investments. This approach applies a free cash flow-based valuation with discrete scenarios and probabilities of occurrence. For example, the biotech ecosystem is well suited for Real Option valuations. For the latter, a decision tree mirroring the approval process for drugs along the three mandatory clinical trials combined with probabilities of success to pass each of those stages, based on empirical studies, does fit well with the approach. Nevertheless, in the plausibility of such probabilities of occurrences lies also the limitation of the Real Option approach.
- *Venture Capital approach*: The Venture Capital approach is a simplified, rule-of-thumb pricing of early-stage investments and might fit as well for the valuation of

digital and platform Business Designs. Due to its simplicity, the methodology is widely applied but comes also with a couple of caveats. In the end, the VC method is based on a multiple pricing approach, but uses exit instead of actual capital market or transaction multiples.

The valuation process of the VC methodology might be arranged around four steps (Smith & Smith, 2019, p. 379): In a first step, the terminal value year (T) has to be defined as the point of time at which the new business should have achieved some sort of steady state. For this year, the free cash flow, EBITDA, or EBIT level of the business (i) has to be estimated.

In a second step, the appropriate multiple fitting to the free cash flow or earnings forecast, foremost based on a tailored peer group (PG), has to be determined. The continuing value (CV) is calculated by multiplying this multiple with the performance forecast of the to be evaluated firm.

The CV is transferred to a present value by applying in a venture capital (VC) context the Internal Rate of Return as denominator. The latter addresses the required return of the investors and compensates them for the time value of money, the underlying risk, or, vice versa, the likelihood of success. In a multiple-funding round also anticipated dilutions have to be integrated. Within a digital Business Design valuation context, the distinct cost of capital $\mathrm{CoC_i}$ will be the substitute of the IRR.

$$\mathrm{OV}_i = \mathrm{PV}\ (\mathrm{CV}_i) = \frac{\frac{\mathrm{EV_{PG}}}{\mathrm{EBITDA_{PG}}} \times \mathrm{EBITDA}_i}{(1 + \mathrm{CoC}_i)^T}$$

- The ratio of the value of the targeted VC investment to the calculated present value of the firm will provide the requested ownership share of a VC fund. In a digital Business Design context, the present value would be synonymous with the expected operating value (OV). By adding excess cash and other non-operating assets and by subtracting debt and debt-like items, the equity value (EqV) is achieved.

The VC methodology is appealing due to its simplicity and intuitiveness. Nevertheless, a couple of hurdles limit its applicability: The IRR is often arbitrary and does not include the likelihood of failure explicitly, meaning the risk that the realized performance will not match with the assumed continuing value performance. Additionally, the VC method does not include the free cash flow development of the planning period. Whereas this might be acceptable for VC valuations where the free cash flows of the planning period might be negligible in comparison to the continuing value, this might not be the case for already established digital firms having achieved already lasting free cash flows. Additionally, the VC method bears the identical caveat as the multiple approach. It cannot be applied when earnings are negative or volatile. Also, future capital market prices and multiples might rest on very vague estimates. But the most fundamental limitation of the VC method is the missing assessment of what drives ultimately the value of a Business Design.

- *Reverse DCF*: The in the following developed Reverse DCF approach intends to overcome the limitations of the so far discussed, existing valuation approaches in the context of digital Business Designs and platform companies. It rests on the hypothesis that only the pairing of an in-depth understanding of the ecosystem as well as the Business Design with the financial modelling of aligned free cash flow scenarios, embedded in tailored pictures-of-the-future (PoF) scenarios, will enable the valuation of such companies.
The Reverse DCF concept uses, as the traditional Enterprise DCF framework, for the financial valuation the underlying discounted cash flows as core ingredient. Additionally, an intense use of scenarios, the pictures-of-the- futures, is a bedrock of the Reverse DCF approach. As scenarios rest upon clearly defined underlying assumptions and their interrelations, they provide a transparent valuation (Koller et al., 2020, p. 719). A well-defined set of scenarios allows the valuation of different future ecosystems and provides a bandwidth of probable valuation outcomes. In so far, scenarios might increase the sensibility and awareness of uncertainty surrounding the development of new Business Designs.
The idea of the approach does not follow the mainstream scenario thinking to derive a single-shot equity valuation number by weighting the valuations of a distinct set of scenarios by foremost arbitrary selected probabilities of occurrence. The thinking here is much more, that uncertainty is better addressed by explicitly highlighting the spread of possible outcomes and the underlying assumptions than mixing up the different potential developments of Business Designs and ecosystems in a single number. Capital market participants might much better decide on potential investments by designing a set of certain scenario they believe to be likely to materialize and to accept uncertainty than to rest their decision on an averaged, over-simplified single number. Adding volatility and risk measures might improve investment decision in uncertain digital and platform Business Designs situations even further.
The Reverse DCF approach will be explained in more detail within the next subchapter.

1.9 Decoding Financial Value: Reverse DCF Concept

The Reverse DCF valuation approach targets the calculation of valuation bandwidths for digital and platform Business Design which became game changers for a multitude of ecosystems in the twenty-first century. One the one side, this method is applicable for the valuation of established digital Business Designs as in the case of Netflix, Amazon, Spotify, Uber, Lyft, Facebook, LinkedIn, and the likes. On the other side, it enables the valuation of digital start-ups and new business idea.

Incumbents of traditional industries are challenged by those digital natives and have to either revitalize their Business Design or face the risk to be marginalized. Therefore, the Reversed DCF methodology might also be applied for the evaluation of the strategic portfolio initiatives to renew those traditional Business Designs and strengthen their competitiveness for the 2020s.

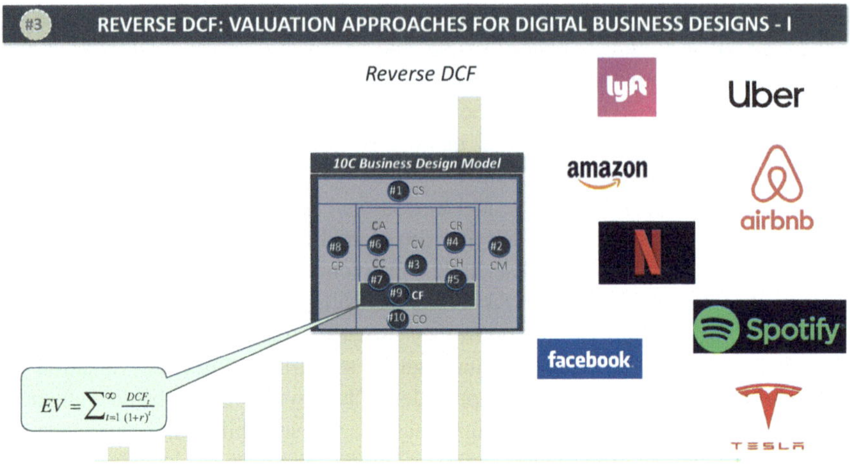

Fig. 1.36 Reverse DCF for the valuation of digital Business Designs and platform companies

The Reverse DCF develops an interwoven strategic and financial valuation framework, as pinpointed by Fig. 1.36. The approach rests on the hypothesis that only the combination of Business Design analytics—10C Business Design and platform value—with intense financial modeling, Reverse DCF, enables a true, in-depth understanding of the sources of competitive advantage and the value creation potential of such digital and platform Business Designs.

The Business Design twin of innovation is resilience to create lasting competitive advantage and capture value for the post-pandemic world of the 2020s. The Reverse DCF intends to build resilience into corporate valuation. The approach centers around the ultimate question: What is a "fair value" estimate and reasonable valuation bandwidth of digital and platform Business Designs? This might lead to second-order questions if today's elevated share prices and equity values for such companies seem to be robust.

Three elements are crucial cornerstones of the Reverse DCF concept: A detailed description of possible future scenarios of the ecosystem as "pictures-of-the-future (PoF)," the tight-knit development of aligned 10C Business Designs and platform values, and, last but not the least, the intense modelling of free cash flows, starting from the PoFs and rolling backward to the date of valuation. As this valuation concept is time-wise flip-sided to the traditional DCF valuation approach, the method is branded as Reverse DCF. Besides, taking as reference the rolling backward valuation estimate and then, in a second step, additionally rolling forward the valuation and underlying free cash flows, a robust cross-check of the revenue scaling approach is achieved.

Each of the three elements of the Reverse DCF approach plays an important, specific role within the evaluation process. But, as shown by Fig. 1.37, only their interplay will lead to a robust valuation.

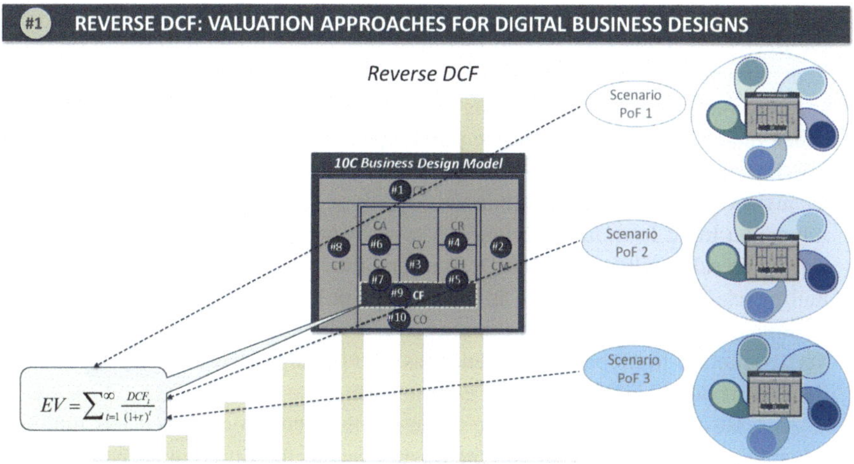

Fig. 1.37 The three cornerstones of the Reverse DCF approach

1. *PoFs—pictures-of-the-future (scenarios)*: The starting point of the Reverse DCF approach is the development of alternative views on how the future may unfold. Such pictures-of-the-future should describe holistically a full set of an ecosystem's decisive variables which will have a lasting impact on the development path of a Business Design and its free cash flows. Those ecosystem variables with Business Design impact may be clustered in five separate fields, the assessment of the underlying disruptive technology, the targeted market and use case, the competitive arena summarized by the distinct peer group including potential new entrants from other platforms or ecosystems, the Business Design's docking points, and the latter's financial diagnostics. Each of these fields will be described in more detail below.
Important is a tailored approach, whereas the number of variables plays a less prominent role. Much more has the identification of the relevant set of variables of each field of the pictures-of-the-future a profound impact on the development of a specific ecosystem and the embedded Business Design and will make a difference. The same holds true for a number of scenarios. Developing a set of powerful, consistent pictures-of-the-future is more important than the amount of scenarios. Consistent means that the variables have to match with each other for each specific scenario. The portfolio of scenarios should be as diverse and distant from one another as possible to capture a reasonable valuation bandwidth.

The diversity of distinct picture-of-the-future scenarios and the interrelatedness of their five fields will be highlighted in the case studies of Chaps. 2, 3, 4, and 5. The discussion on the future of the ride-hailing ecosystem and its impact on ride-hailing platforms like Uber, Lyft, Didi, or Ola might provide already a first idea. The potential technological part of pictures-of-the-future for the ride-hailing ecosystem might be centered around a distinct picture-of-the-future which simulates the mid- to long-term breakthrough of autonomous drive technologies as they might become a game changer to urban mobility with all involved regulatory challenges. A second picture-of-the-future might describe more limited applications and no true breakthrough of autonomous drive. The latter scenario might lead to a much tougher competitive environment of the different urban modes of transportation like public transport, local taxis, ride-hailing, and also traditional car ownership models. A third picture-of-the-future might provide a canvas of a post-pandemic urban world with more green city applications and a relocation trend from urban centers to suburbs post-pandemic. An overreaching impact on ride-hailing Business Designs and the international aspirations of ride-hailing champions like Uber might be the political development to a more regionalized world, sometimes described as "slobalization" (Economist, 2019) versus a return to globalization trends, as ride-hailing ecosystems are significant dependent on the local regulatory environment.

This Reverse DCF and picture-of-the-future-scenario approach has multiple advantages. The description and the diagnostics of the different scenarios foster the understanding of the uncertainty surrounding potential development paths into the future. Secondly, alternative Business Designs for each of those pictures-of-the-future could be developed which might have the best fit to the underlying scenario. A further lesson learned might be the comparison of the different scenarios and Business Designs. Breaking points, which might decide on which scenario of the ecosystem and Business Designs will unfold, could be identified. This will increase the sensitivity of management teams with respect to Business Design-specific early warning indicators.

Each scenario is embedded in a portfolio of alternative courses of actions and has to be evaluated against those. One caveat of traditional approaches is that typically applied base case scenarios are often of limited use, but they might be particularly misleading in a digital disruptive ecosystem framework. An example might be here the technological shifts as evidenced in the automotive ecosystem where an incumbent OEM, challenged by Tesla, has to simulate and evaluate a shift in its powertrain strategy from a combustion engine to a hybrid or electric-only approach. To evaluate such a disruptive technology impact, the point is here that a base case scenario, referencing to a business-as-usual and do-nothing combustion engine strategy world, might lead to naïve outcomes. If OEM competitors will invest in electric car concepts and technologies, the "reference" or "base" case, by evaluating a combustion engine powertrain approach, will most likely go hand in hand with significant mid-term market share losses, collapsing brand value and deteriorating financials and will not mimic simply today's financial performance till infinity. This will probably widen the value gap of a non-investment to an investment into electric powertrain scenario. The value at stake by a non-investment strategy might be in such circumstances probably significant.

Such deteriorating financial scenarios of the as-is-business are in technological disrupted ecosystems the true base case that investments into digital technologies should reference to and be compared with. Avoiding change comes at a cost.

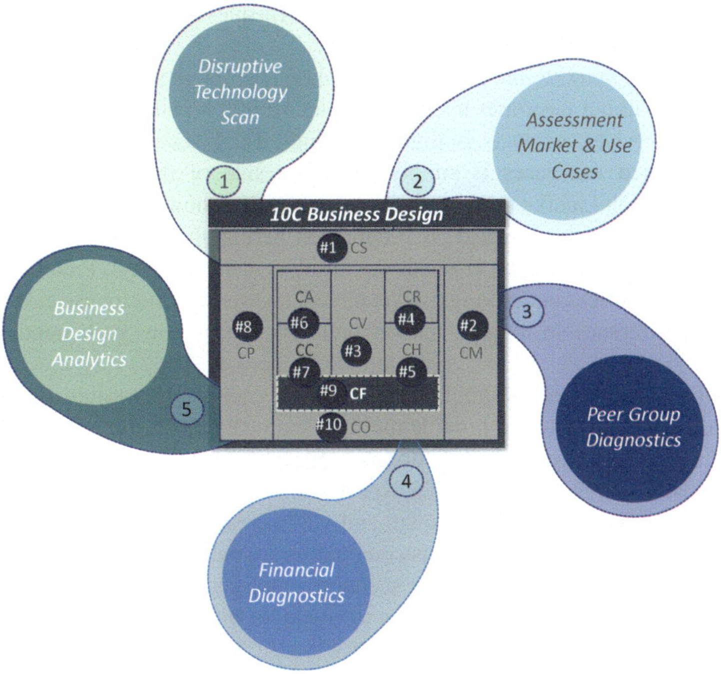

Fig. 1.38 Reverse DCF: Pictures-of-the-future elements and embedded 10C Business Design

Each of the five building blocks of the pictures-of-the-future scenario, as described in Fig. 1.38, will be elaborated below in more detail.

- *Disruptive technology scan*: A good starting point is the technological and digital framework of an ecosystem which defines as well its boundaries. The underlying technology is also tight-knit with the core value proposition of the Business Design and will define, at least partially, the customer use case as well as the requested core capabilities.
  The disruptive technology scan describes any underlying technology already used or potentially applied in the future in a defined ecosystem, or, more specifically, for a distinct customer use case. The technological framework might be dominated by one specific technology. This might be the case for specialized FinTechs like in the money transfer or cryptocurrency business. Other ecosystems might be exposed to a bundle of new technology disruptions at the same time. For the latter, an example may be the aforementioned automotive industry. The parallel evolution of the electrification of the powertrain, car-to-car communication technologies, autonomous drive approaches, and further technology shifts challenge the established automotive incumbents at the same time on multiple fronts. Such broad technology revolutions also bear the risk to entice digital

natives to bridge platforms with new digital Business Designs and to conquer technology disrupted, traditional industries.

- *Assessment of markets and potential use cases*: Disruptive technologies would be worthless without customer use cases, meaning in a broader sense, markets for such new services, products, or digital offerings. The assessment of those markets and dedicated use cases is simply the other side of the coin of disruptive technologies and marks the step from inventions to innovations.
  The challenge of the Reverse DCF approach here is that not today's but much more the long-term customer needs are at the center of interest. Pictures-of-the-future must address underlying market trends, answer how future use cases might make a difference to today's market preferences and how such trends might unfold.

  Whereas the use cases should be designed as granular as possible, the broader market perspective should provide multiple segmentations from a regional, from a business (including B2B, B2C or C2C), from a use case application, and from further Business Design-specific perspectives.
- *Peer group diagnostics*: The growth and value creation potential of a digital or platform firm will be limited by its competitors' initiatives, imitation, and retaliation moves. A picture-of-the-future scenario which should give a clear idea about the profit and cash flow potential of a steady-state Business Design has to define the competitive advantage in a relative sense by incorporating peer-group diagnostics.
  Additionally, the competitor assessment for a steady state has to be broader than the typical peer group reviews and include potential new market entrants or substitutes scaling a new or a different set of technologies. Competitive pressure might additionally be increased by network bridging whereby platform champions in adjacent ecosystems apply home turf advantages to jump into new applications and enter, often unanticipated, whole new markets. Amazon applied this strategy multiple times successfully. Its most aggressive platform extension might have been the acquisition of Whole Foods bridging on- and offline food markets. The case studies will explicitly highlight such wider peer-group settings, including new digital challengers.
- *Business Design analytics*: The dedicated digital or platform Business Design will be defined in a separate step. But, what has to be part of any picture-of-the-future is the assessment which drivers of the external or macro-environment of the Business Design have a substantial influence on its long-term performance and sustainability. This might be described by a Business Design's docking stations for specific macro-environment drivers.
  Referencing once more to the ride-hailing ecosystem, Uber's early corporate history was challenged by legal disputes with local regulators and politicians as well as taxi driver protests. If the driving allowance of Uber drivers or the business model of Uber in total is questioned or even rejected by city regulators, as shown by the back and forth discussions with the city of London authorities, this would imply an eternal financial threat to the ride-hailing company. The same may hold true for the profitability of Uber, if the ride-hailing drivers would be requested in a majority of cities to be employees of the company and, therefore,

on their payroll, as the state of California was close by to decide and London finally did lately. Additionally, the reputational value at risk and its impact on customer churn might be significant.

- *Financial impact analysis*: The severeness of the impact of external constituencies or parameters might rest on an in-depth strategic but as well quantified, financial assessment.
On the strategic side, the assessment on how many of the 10C modules and how significantly those would be impacted provides a first idea of the importance of an ecosystem driver, while on the financial side, the analysis which value drivers might be influenced and by how much adds on this understanding of mission-critical external factors. The latter have to be actively monitored to identify early potential breaking points and have to be managed for a successful development of the Business Design.
But, the financial and strategic impact assessment is not limited to the identification of the most prevalent external stakeholders and macro-trends. Even more important might be the sensitivity assessments of the inner value drivers of the Business Design. The management should focus on the selected top drivers for its most important decisions and the development of the company.

2. *10C Business Design*: Based on the understanding of the potential future ecosystem, the probable development paths, and its critical drivers, the tight-knit 10C Business Designs for each of the distinct pictures-of-the-future is developed. Each individual module of the 10C Business Design has to be embedded into a specific picture-of-the-future. From a dynamic point of view, this does request that with any change of the future development path of the ecosystem, also the Business Design has to be adjusted. But, this mirrors simply empirical management practice and should increase the applicability of the model. In so far, this approach has some parallels with the Real Options framework of staged investment decisions.
The Business Design development must also be pulled by the future ecosystem. Applied on the ride-hailing context, if the picture-of-the-future for urban mobility assumes a breakthrough of autonomous drive technologies, this has to be aligned with the design of the according 10C Business Design and cash flows. Autonomous drive would lead to value-increasing as well as value-destructive effects within a ride-hailing Business Design. On the one side, the substitution of driver costs might be a bone for the profit line of ride-hailing companies. The increased platform investments might, on the other side, lead to an additional cash flow drain. Besides, a holistic model of autonomous drive would have to answer the open question who would be the future owner of autonomous ride-hailing cars. If they would be on the balance sheet of the ride-hailing corporations, their asset-light platform advantage would be gone.
Therefore, each of the ten modules of the 10C Business Design has to fit with the underlying ecosystem. Nevertheless, the CF module of a Business Design is the internal mirror image of the Reverse DCF as it describes all mission-critical

value drivers like revenue, cost, and financial drivers. The first two will serve as crucial inputs for the income statement, and the latter will determine the structure of the balance sheet of a distinct digital firm or platform.

3. *Reverse DCF modelling*: The third pillar of the Reverse DCF is the financial modelling of the Business Design and its development by its underlying free cash flows and value drivers. The financial modelling starts, in contrast to the traditional DCF model, from the future steady state, framed by a chosen picture-of-the-future, flows backwards to the present, and then reverses from today, by revenue scaling, to the future steady state. This back-and-forth rolling of the free cash flow forecasts will work as a proof of concept of the robustness of the revenue scaling approach and as a consistency proof for the free cash flow estimates. Compared with the traditional DCF model, the ingredients are the same, free cash flows and their drivers, but the time order of their calculation is flip-sided.

STEP 1

The Reverse DCF starting point rests upon one explicit steady-state ecosystem as described in a distinct pictures-of-the-future and the corresponding Business Design. The steady-state timing should be at the tipping point where the high-growth, scaling phase enters into a more mature, sustainable long-term growth and margin path. An estimate as to how long the scaling phase through which the business could outpace the typical market growth will last is to be defined. This timespan depends on the specific industry, the market space, and how long the stand-alone competitive advantage might be probably protected. The typical scaling phase timespan of digital and platform Business Designs will be in a range of 10–15 years (Koller et al., 2020, p. 711).

The steady-state financial twin is the continuing value. The latter describes the value of a company at the point of time the steady state is achieved and rests on the then realized level of the core value drivers. For each of the pictures-of-the-future scenarios, a separate continuing value has to be estimated, as the Business Design's financials and ecosystem's economics will be fundamentally different between the different scenarios.

For a granular assessment of the steady-state performance, the key value driver formula of the continuing value will be applied (Koller et al., 2020, pp. 51, 93):

$$\mathrm{CV}_i = \frac{\mathrm{NOPLAT}_i \times \left(1 - \frac{g_i}{\mathrm{RONIC}_i}\right)}{\mathrm{CoC}_i - g_i}$$

where NOPLAT describes the Net Operating Profit Less Adjusted Tax performance in the steady-state, g the long-term growth rate, RONIC the Return on New Invested Capital, the ratio of growth-to-RONIC the reinvestment or plowback ratio, and CoC the cost of capital for a digital firm or platform *i*. The important point here is that

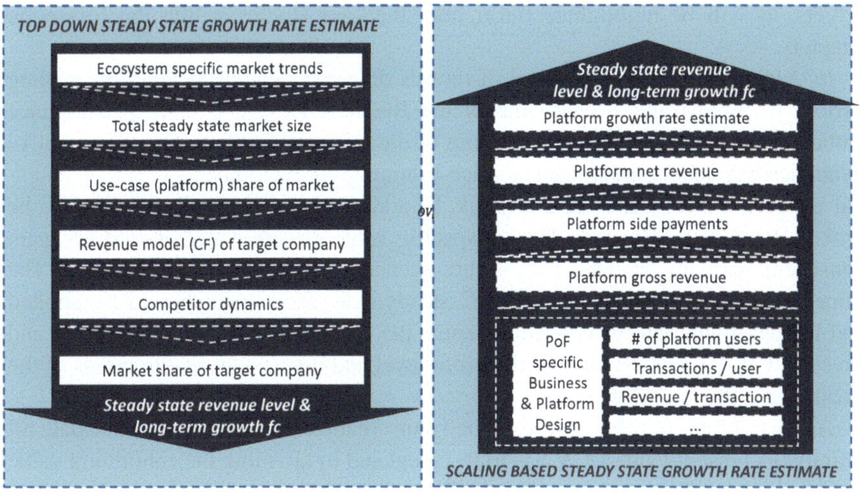

Fig. 1.39 Steady-state revenue levels and growth rates

those value drivers have to describe their steady-state level and not today's performance.

The *long-term growth* rate has to be estimated at the point of time when growth peters out from the early significant growth rates and the market begins to stabilize. The growth rate has to mirror market trends, use cases, competitor dynamics, and also the targeted revenue model (one-time sales, subscription model, add-based revenue model, etc.) of a distinct steady-state scenario. The methodology to derive the steady-state growth rate might be based on a top-down or scaling approach.

The top-down estimate of the steady-state revenue level and growth rate will start with a picture-of-the-future consistent trend assessment as a framework to derive the steady-state market volume. Based on this broad market definition, the use case or platform-specific market size will be derived. The steady-state market share estimate has to take the Business Design, specifically the targeted revenue model, into account. Additionally, the likely long-term peers and competitive environment will have an impact on a probable steady-state market share. The latter paired with the market size will give a first estimate on a scenario consistent revenue line and, from a dynamic perspective, a reasonable long-term growth estimate. The flow to derive a probable revenue development and growth rate is summarized by Fig. 1.39.

Important is the granularity of the revenue and growth model. Each revenue source must be evaluated and modelled separately as different businesses might have different competitive advantages and ecosystem economics. Therefore, also their growth, profitability, and capital needs patterns might differ significantly. Take, for example, Uber: Most probably, the growth and profitability pattern of Uber's ride-hailing and food-delivery platform might not be fully aligned, as the first is a double-sided and the latter a three-party platform. A robust revenue model should be underpinned by the Business Design's core market, customer, and value proposition drivers, as will be highlighted throughout the case studies within the follow-on chapters.

RONIC as the sustainable level of returns on new, meaning beyond the scaling period, Invested Capital has to mirror the Business Design's future performance embedded in the fundamental economics of the business and long-term competitive dynamics. Especially the impact of price-to-unit cost developments based on potential network effects has to be analyzed. To add more detail, the RONIC has to be broken down in its Business Design-specific value drivers which should be again consistent with the picture-of-the-future scenario and competitor dynamics. The same flow of thoughts of the RONIC steady-state assessment has to be applied and broken down onto its core ingredients, the steady-state level of NOPLAT, and Invested Capital, consistent with the profit level and investment requirements of the steady-state Business Design.

As the continuing value describes the value creation from the steady-state date till infinity, its present value DCV has to be calculated by dividing the continuing value CV by the according cost of capital CoC:

$$\mathrm{DCV}_i = \frac{\mathrm{CV}_i}{(1 + \mathrm{CoC}_i)^T}$$

STEP 2

After the steady-state value drivers and continuing value are set, the free cash flows of the interim period between the steady-state and the point of date of the valuation have to be modelled. This is achieved by rolling them backward from the steady state to the current financial performance. This rolling backward ensures the linkage between the steady-state revenue, profitability, and cash flow performance with the current performance by explicitly modelling the scaling phase.

The free cash flows of the interim or scaling period have to be transferred to discounted cash flows by dividing the periodic free cash flows by the period specific discount factor. The discounted cash flows of the interim scaling period will be summed up to their present value of the interim scaling period PV:

$$\mathrm{PV}_{t=1}^{T} = \sum\nolimits_{t=1}^{T} \frac{\mathrm{FCF}_t}{(1 + \mathrm{CoC})^t} = \sum\nolimits_{t=1}^{T} \mathrm{DCF}_t$$

The transition from free to discounted cash flows has an important side impact by addressing the time value of money. The pace of the scaling from the current to the steady-state performance is not just a timing issue but has as well a significant value impact. The scaling process of the free cash flows should mimic the crucial ecosystem trends. Questions like how fast underlying digital technology developments will progress and will become a standard, how fast customer adoption rates will take off, and how competition develops have to be answered for the financial modelling of the scaling phase in line with strategic assumptions. This will answer, if, when, and at which volumes platforms or digital Business Designs will become free cash flow positive, how fast their capital turnover driven by asset-light characteristics will take off, and, last but not the least, how fast the steady-state ROIC performance will be achieved.

STEP 3

The present value of the interim scaling period PV will be finally added to the discounted continuing value DCV to calculate the operating value OV of the digital or platform Business Design:

$$\mathrm{OV}_i = \mathrm{PV}_{i;\,t=1}^{T} + \mathrm{DCV}_i$$

The last step is the transfer of the operating value OV to enterprise value EV by adding excess cash and non-operating assets:

$$\mathrm{EV}_i = \mathrm{OV}_i + \text{excess cash and other nonoperating assets}$$

and ultimately equity value (EqV) by subtracting from the enterprise value EV debt, meaning interest bearing liabilities, and debt-like items:

$$\mathrm{EqV}_i = \mathrm{EV}_i - (\text{debt} + \text{debtlike items})$$

This reverse modelling of the equity value will be framed and cross-checked with a forward build-up of the free cash flows based on the scaling approach of the Business Design. The comparison of the backward and forward valuation outcomes should improve the robustness of the scaling approach of the Business Designs and the reasonability of the valuation bandwidth of the different picture-of-the-future scenarios.

The concept of this tailored strategic-financial framework, more specifically the strategic valuation with the 10C Business Design approach and platform value concept as well as the financial valuation with the Reverse DCF approach, will be applied in the following chapters on a set of high-profile case studies. These case studies will highlight the working principles of the concept:

- Chapter 2: *Developing a COVID-19 Vaccine Platform to Save the World*
- Chapter 3: *The Hottest Question on Wall Street: Ride-Hailing Platforms —Is Sharing the New Owning?*
- Chapter 4: *The Streaming Platform Revolution in Global Media: The Endgame Between Netflix and Disney+*
- Chapter 5: *Airbnb: From Double-Sided Accommodation to Multi-sided Experience Platform?*

References

Amit, R., & Zott, C. (2012). Creating value through business model innovation. *MIT Sloan Management Review, 53(3)*, 41–49.

Anderson, C. (2000, February 25). *Free! Why $0.00 is the future of business.*https://www.wired.com/2008/02/ff-free

Carroni, E., & Paolini, D. (2020, September). Business models for streaming platforms: Content acquisition, advertising. *Information Economics, 52.*

Economist. (2019, January 24). *Slowbalisation—The steam has gone out of globalisation.*https://www.economist.com/leaders/2019/01/24/the-steam-has-gone-out-of-globalisation

Economist. (2021a, March 27). *Bright side of the moonshots?* Bright side of the moonshots. https://www.economist.com/leaders/2021/03/27/bright-side-of-the-moonshots?

Economist. (2021b, February 25). *Tech competition—The rules of the tech game are changing.* https://www.economist.com/leaders/2021/02/27/the-rules-of-the-tech-game-are-changing?

Economist. (2021c, February 27). *The new rules of competition in the technology industry.*https://www.economist.com/business/2021/02/27/the-new-rules-of-competition-in-the-technology-industry

Eisenmann, T., Parker, G., & Van Alstyne, M. (2006, October). Strategies for two-sided markets. *Harvard Business Review, 84(10)*, 92–101.

Eisenmann, T., Parker, G., & Van Alstyne, M. (2011). Platform envelopment. *Strategic Management Journal, 31(12)*, 1270–1285.

Evans, D., & Schmalensee, R. (2010). Failure to launch: Critical mass in platform businesses. *Review of Network Economics, 9(4)*, 61–69.

Evans, P., & Gawer, A. (2016, January). The rise of the platform economy—A global survey. *The Emerging Platform Economy Series No. 1. The Center for Global Enterprise.*

Feix, T. (2020). *End-to-end M&A process design—Resilient business model innovation.* Springer Gabler.

Financial Times. (2021a, April 22). *Apple to boost ads business as iPhone changes hurt Facebook.* https://www.ft.com/content/5527ddd1-77a8-4cd0-82fd-4568be5da80f

Financial Times. (2021b, April 30). *Apple: Supercharged iPhone sales signpost $3tn valuation.* https://www.ft.com/content/eee8bca7-e7fb-4506-a0e2-579fa707de81

Gawer, A., & Cusumano, M. (2008). How companiesd become platform leaders. *MIT Sloan Management Review, 49(2)*, 28–35.

Hagiu, A. (2014). Strategic decisions for multisided platforms. *MIT Sloan Management Review, 55 (2)*, 71–80.

Hagiu, A., & Rothman, S. (2016, April). Network Effects aren't enough. The hidden traps in building online marketplaces. *Harvard Business Review, 94(4)*, 65–71.

Katz, M., & Shapiro, C. (1994). Systems competition and network effects. *Journal of Economic Perspectives, 8n(2)*, 93–115.

Kim, C., & Mauborgne, R. (1999). Creating new market space. *Harvard Business Review, 77(1)*, 83–93.

Koller, T., Goedhart, M., & Wessels, D. (2020). *Valuation—Measuring and managing the value of companies.* John Wiley & Sons.

Li, H., & Fend, Z. (2019). Information transparency, multi-homing, and platform competition: A natural experiment in the daily deals market. *Harvard Business School Working Paper No. 20-065.*

Magretta, J. (2002). Why Business Models Matter. *Harvard Business Review, 80(5)*, 86–92.

McKinsey & Company. (2021, January). *The risks and challenges of the global COVID-19 vaccine rollout.* https://www.mckinsey.com/business-functions/risk/our-insights/the-risks-and-challenges-of-the-global-covid-19-vaccine-rollout:https://www.mckinsey.com/business-functions/risk/our-insights/the-risks-and-challenges-of-the-global-covid-19-vaccine-rollout

Mody, M., & Gomez, M. (2018). Airbnb and the hotel industry: The past, the present, and future of sales, marketing, branding and revenue management. *Boston Hospitality Report. Boston University.*

New York Times. (2020). *Pfizer's Covid vaccine and allergies: How concerned should you be.* https://www.nytimes.com/2020/12/11/health/Covid-Pfizer-vaccine-allergies.html

Osterwalder, A., & Pigneur, Y. (2010). *Business model generation: A handbook for visionaries, game changers, and challangers.* Wiley.

Sánches-Cartas, J. M., & León, G. (2019). *Multisided platforms and markets: A literature review.* Researchgate.

Schmalensee, R., & Evans, D. (2016). *Why winner-take-all thinking doesn't apply to the platform economy.* https://hbr.org/2016/05/why-winner-takes-all-thinking-doesnt-apply-to-silicon-valley

Smith, J., & Smith, R. (2019). *Entrepreneurial finance—Venture capital, deal structure & valuation.* Stanford University Press.

Staykova, K. S., & Damsgaard, J. (2015). A typology of multi-sided platforms. The core and the periphery. *Copenhagen Business School - CBS Research Papers.*

Teece, D. (2010). Business models, business strategy and innovation. *Long Range Planning, 43 (2–3)*, 172–194.

tfX-advisory. (2020). tfX consulting approach. www.tfx-advisory.de

Zhu, F., & Iansiti, M. (2019, January–February). Why some platforms thrive ... ... and others don't. *Harvard Business Review*, 118–125.

Zhu, F., Xinxin, L., Valavi, E., & Iansiti, M. (2019). Network interconnectivity and entry into platform markets. *Harvard Business School Working Paper No 19-062.*

Developing a COVID-19 Vaccine to Save the World

2

Abstract

The containment of the human and health disaster of the COVID-19 pandemic progressed from a priority to an imperative for global politics in the early 2020s. It became fast clear that the development and global rollout of Sars-CoV-2 vaccines with high efficacy might be the most promising strategy to vanquish the coronavirus. Firms like BioNTech or Moderna developed in record time, based on their novel mRNA technology, such vaccines with outstanding efficacies. The mRNA approach is thereby a poster boy of knowledge-based platforms. The starting point of this chapter is the comparison of the different biotechnology approaches and contenders addressing COVID-19. Thereafter, BioNTech's and their co-operation partner Pfizer's 10C Business Designs will be decoded, as the two partners developed the first approved vaccine to combat COVID-19. Based on the understanding of the working mechanisms of the mRNA Business Design, the platform strength of mRNA approaches will be evaluated along the eight platform value drivers, as developed within Chap. 1. The platform strength evaluation includes also a detour on how mRNA approaches might offer platform-bridging approaches like for immuno-oncology. Finally, the financial valuation of BioNTech is derived by applying the Reverse DCF concept embedded in a "jo-jo deceleration" picture-of-the-future scenario.

"Any of various types of germs that are a cause of disease" (Cambridge-Dictionary, 2021), the definition of a virus according the Cambridge Dictionary, brought the world in early 2020 to a standstill. As the novel coronavirus SARS-CoV-2[1] spread around the world and triggered the highly infectious COVID-19[2] disease, lockdown and social distancing measures have been implemented on a global scale. "Flatten

[1] SARS stand for severe acute respiratory syndrome.

[2] COVID stands for coronavirus disease.

T. Feix, *Valuing Digital Business Designs and Platforms*, Future of Business and Finance, https://doi.org/10.1007/978-3-030-83632-0_2

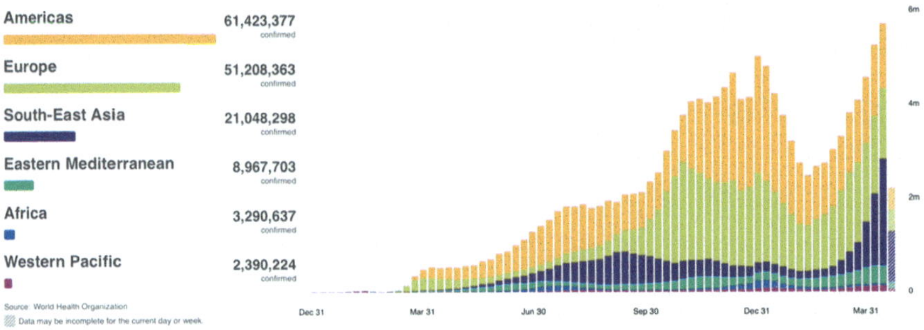

Fig. 2.1 WHO coronavirus disease dashboard. *Source*: WHO.com (2021)

the curve" to avoid the collapse of hospitals and social infrastructure became the new political mantra especially in the Western hemisphere, which was caught by the black swan effect of SARS-CoV-2 more or less unprepared. Till April 28, 2021, the world suffered from 148 million confirmed COVID-19 infections and more than 3.1 million deaths related to the disease (WHO, 2021), as described by Fig. 2.1.

The containment of the human and health disaster progressed from a priority to an imperative for global politics. Under the backdrop of this once-in-a-century pandemic economic activity phased an almighty downturn. Not surprisingly, the drop of the cliff in global GDP was accompanied by nightmarish trading days on global capital markets with unseen volatility at the early stage of the pandemic. To stabilize global economic activity, central banks flouted capital markets by aggressive, expansionary monetary policies, and governments implemented bailout measures to avoid a tsunami of insolvencies.

As even countries successful in managing to flatten the curve in spring and summer 2020 found themselves backsliding in winter 2020, it became fast clear that the only human, medical, and economic robust escape route out of the pandemic is the development of an effective vaccine on a global scale, supported by a portfolio of diagnostic tools and therapeutics like antibody drug conjugates.[3] At the writing of this book, there seems to shimmer light at the end of the tunnel foremost due to a revolutionary vaccine technology based on the novel messenger ribonucleic acid (mRNA) approach. The hope is that the coronavirus could be vanquished by a global vaccine rollout which will enable societies to hand back normality we have been taken for granted to our life.

The pandemic triggered a feverish hunt of biotechnology and pharma companies to develop an effective COVID-19 vaccine. The WHO listed as of December 2020 more than 200 vaccine candidates for COVID-19 to be developed. Of those, at least 52 candidate vaccines are in human trials. But so far, just four of them, made by

[3] Eli Lilly's antibody-based therapy bamlanivimab was granted an emergency use authorization (EUA) by the responsible US medical care regulator FDA. Besides, Regeneron Pharmaceuticals applied as well for an EUA for its antibody cocktail Regn-CoV2 which proved a significant reduction of viral load in medical test series.

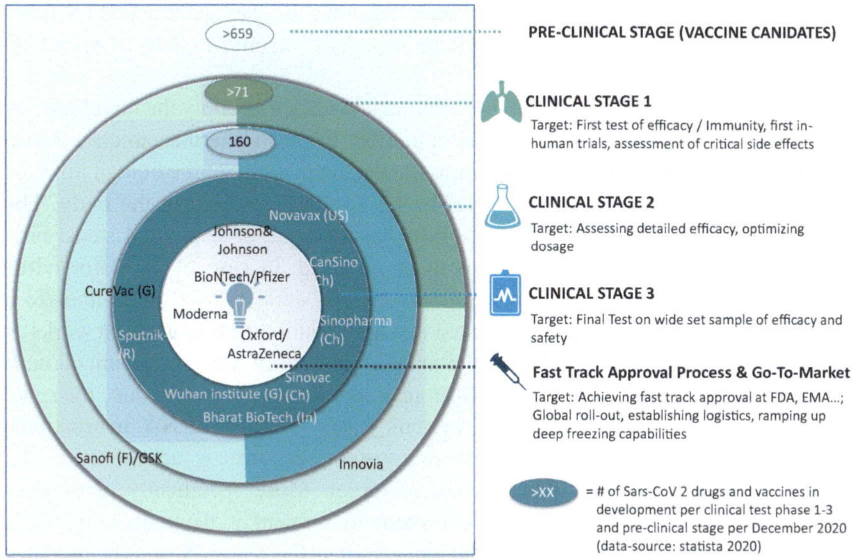

Fig. 2.2 Covid-19 vaccine developers and producers. *Source*: tfX-advisory research 2021

BioNTech/Pfizer, Moderna, AstraZeneca/Oxford University, and Johnson & Johnson, passed clinical stage 3 tests and the stringent rules of regulatory approval. Additionally, a couple of further vaccine candidates like the ones from Novavax, a US vaccine company, CureVac which is on fast-track testing in Europe, and others are on late-stage development. Besides, two vaccines from China and Russia's Sputnik V achieved authorization in some countries (Economist, 2021c). Figure 2.2 may frame some of the most promising coronavirus vaccines.

2.1 mRNA Platform as Breakthrough Sars-CoV-2 Vaccine Innovation

To target the coronavirus, different vaccine technologies have been explored. From the so far officially approved and the late-stage clinical phase 3 vaccines especially two main approaches seem to stand out in addressing the Sars-CoV-2 virus pattern:

- The vaccines of AstraZeneca/Oxford University and of Johnson & Johnson rest upon the more traditional non-replicative viral vectors technology, which was successful applied for diseases like polio or measles. Those vaccines use a weakened or inactivated virus to trigger an immune response. Coronavirus vaccines contain genes from Sars-CoV-2 triggering COVID-19 symptoms. As soon as the vaccine is injected into a human cell, an immune system response targets the spike protein of the coronavirus. The antibodies and memory cells produced during this process work as a protective shield against a true

coronavirus infection. As the viral vector vaccines are well established for other human diseases, they were thought to face less skepticism and to speed up approval processes.
- The vaccines of BioNTech/Pfizer, Moderna, and CureVac apply the novel mRNA technology, a method never applied before for licensed pharmaceuticals. Those mRNA technology-based vaccines provide via the messenger the human immune system genetic information to diagnose the virus and immunize the body. The more detailed immunization process flow has a couple of sequential steps: First the genetic sequence of a virus has to be decoded, in case of the coronavirus especially the virus's spike protein. This genetic code is used to synthesize a mRNA sequence, which is then packed in a lipid nanoparticle and which works as a protective shield. The mRNA is the main ingredient of the vaccine injection. It provides as messenger the ribosomes an instruction plan how to produce the spike protein. As soon as the immune system, based on the mRNA instructions, produced the viral protein, an immune system response is activated via the T-cells to eliminate the spike protein as target. More specifically, antibodies will bind to the Sars-CoV-2 spike protein to prevent it from docking while simultaneously calling on T-cells to phagocytize the virus. Scanning modules engrained in the first T-cell CD8 are able to detect and combat infected cells if they encounter any virus while also reducing the reproduction of the pathogen. The second T-cell CD4 ensures that antibodies target the right part of the virus and bind strongly. Additionally, they also support CD8 cells by orchestrating support from multiple other parts of the immune system. Ultimately, immunization is achieved (Financial Times, 2020).

As only the genetic code is encapsulated in the lipid nanoparticle, no real particles of SARS-CoV-2 are included in the vaccine which might endanger a patient of being infected with the virus, a significant advantage in comparison with alternative vaccines approaches. Additionally, the mRNA approach enables due to its "engineering" approach a cost-efficient development process and fast scaling for mass production. These so-called next-generation vaccines might also be relatively fast re-engineered and adjusted to new strains of the main virus.

Based on this groundbreaking biotechnological research, BioNTech/Pfizer and Moderna developed in record time vaccines to combat COVID-19. Also, clinical trials proved the mRNA-based vaccines' outstanding efficacies.

A rough comparison of the different vaccine approaches, as developed by the biotech companies, might apply the following six criteria:

- *Time-to-market*: Being in the midst of a global pandemic, *time-to-market* of a vaccine is of upmost importance. Time-to-market in a vaccine context might frame the time span along which the vaccine is developed, but should as well incorporate the regulatory required three clinical trials and the final approval by medical authorities like the FDA or EMA. BioNTech/Pfizer's BNT162b2 vaccine was approved in December 2020 as the first vaccine addressing Sars-CoV2 and was therefore a true breakthrough.

- *Efficacy*: The newly developed vaccines outperformed initial expectations of vaccination experts with respect to their efficacy. BioNTech's vaccine is with a 95% efficacy the frontrunner, but Moderna's vaccine mRNA1273 is a close second with 94% protection, and AstraZeneca/University of Oxford vaccine is within an interval of 62–82%, depending on the timing interval between the doses and the trial protocol, somewhat lagging (McKinsey, 2021). Recently, Johnson & Johnson's vaccine was tested with a 66% immunity. The two mRNA vaccines also proved along the clinical trials an encouraging immune response by eliciting high titters neutralizing antibodies and strong T-cell response. To achieve lasting immunity and maximum efficacy, all three early approved vaccines require two shots, whereas Johnson & Johnson's has the advantage of a one jab-based immunization.
- *Side effects:* One important task of the clinical trials is to prove empirically that an analyzed drug has no severe side effects. So far, no significant side effects of the replicative viral vectors or mRNA technology have been identified. Lately, some allergic reactions, most probably based on polyethylene glycol used for the wrapping of mRNA ion nanoparticles, have been identified. But, as only fragments of a virus have to be encrypted in a mRNA vaccine, its immunogenicity is limited. One caveat of the Sars-Cov-2 vaccines is their unknown ultimate time span of immunity against the coronavirus.
- *Logistical ease of delivery*: The logistical challenges of the global Sars-CoV-2 vaccine rollout are multitude. In a research paper, the management consulting firm McKinsey highlighted the risk of raw material constraints delaying the rollout, quality-assurance challenges in manufacturing, cold-chain logistics and storage demands, wastage at point-of-care, and IT challenges as major arrays of distribution challenges (McKinsey, 2021). Of all those hurdles, the cold-chain requirements of the jabs to ensure thermostability, the monitoring of the temperature, as well as the timing of arrival and storage at the point-of-use might stand out as most significant logistical caveats. Due to a storage requirement at −70 °C, BioNTech/Pfizer's vaccine is disadvantaged and has to use a cold-chain distribution approach, whereas for the cooling of AstraZeneca's and Moderna's vaccine, which require temperature levels of −20°, respectively a standard refrigerator or standard freezer is required. The former's vaccine could also be stored at 2–8° for at least 6 months (Jibilian, 2020).
- *Platform pattern*: If COVID-19 continues to circulate in non-vaccinated populations, it bears the risk to rapidly mutate and find ways of evading the currently developed vaccines. For example, the AstraZeneca/Oxford University vaccine appears to offer no protection against mild and moderate disease caused by the highly contagious 501.V2 variant first detected in South Africa (Financial Times, 2021a). A platform vaccine approach offers the potential to develop adjusted vaccines for such new strains. With respect to the development of spin-off vaccines, the mRNA approach might be perfectly suited with its engineering potential based on the genetic sequence of mutants.

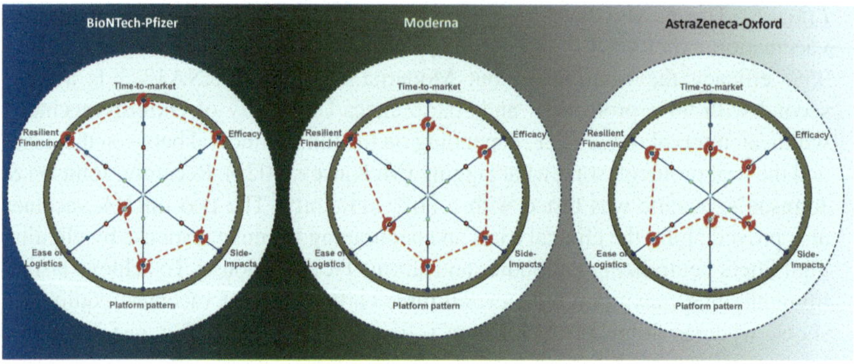

Fig. 2.3 Competitive advantage hexagon of COVID-19 vaccine innovators. *Source*: Research project tfX-advisory, 2021

- *Financial resilience*: All three already approved innovators have a similar and diversified financing structure which balances fast funds for the scaling of the rollout with financial resilience. BioNTech, Moderna, and also CureVac have, due to their listing on the NASDAQ stock exchange, access to equity markets. They also enticed broad equity investor interest in biotechnology, especially COVID-19 vaccine developers, due to the omnipresence of the pandemic. Besides equity and debt markets, an unconventional source of fund is provided by government grants. As the latter have an interest in the access to and fast scaling of COVID-19 vaccines, they directly financed the COVID-19 vaccine biotech frontrunners partially. For example, in the case of BioNTech, the EU, using its Horizon 2020 fund, and the German government invested significant amounts. So, especially the mRNA innovators are well positioned with respect to their funding needs to scale mass manufacturing.

The competitive advantage canvas of the three vaccine innovators is described by Fig. 2.3.

This first overview of the competencies and competitive advantage map of the COVID-19 vaccine contenders will be detailed within the next subchapter on the core capabilities (CC) of BioNTech's and its partner Pfizer's 10C Business Design. As these co-operation partners have developed the first approved vaccine to combat COVID-19, their cooperation will be taken as reference point for the strategic and financial valuation of mRNA platforms.

The masterminds behind BioNTech are their founders, Dr. Özlem Türeci, a molecular biologist, and her husband Dr. Ugur Sahin, an immunotherapy specialist (Financial Times, 2020). They anticipated, at the early days of the pandemic, that their intense research on the mRNA technology, as prior applied foremost in the field of immuno-oncology (IO), might also be applicable for the development of a coronavirus vaccine and might enable a breakthrough that could offer a route out of the COVID-19 pandemic.

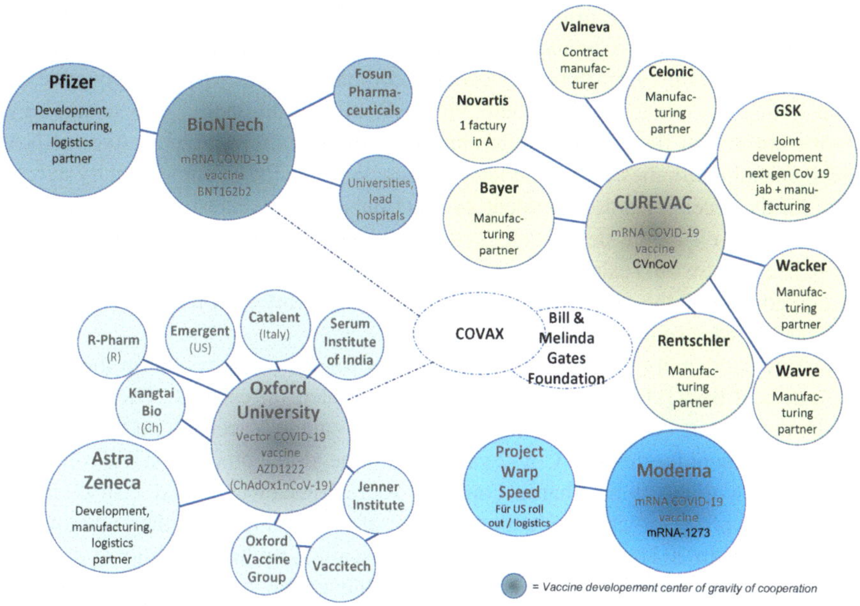

Fig. 2.4 COVID-19 vaccine alliances and partnering strategies. Exemplary overview: Research project tfX-advisory, 2021

BioNTech launched the COVID-19 vaccine development program immediately after the genetic sequence of Sars-CoV-2 emerging in China's Hubei province was made public on January 12, 2020. BioNTech announced on the 17th of March 2020 a co-operation with the global pharma company Pfizer for the development, testing, mass manufacturing, and distribution of a mRNA-based COVID-19 vaccine, intensifying a well-established partnership built for the development of influenza vaccines in 2018 (Reuters, 2020).

As biotechnology start-ups like BioNTech, Moderna, and CureVac, or university spin-offs like in the Oxford case, have their core capabilities in the development of innovative vaccines, the pairing with pharma champions for the global manufacturing, rollout, and distribution of the COVID-19 vaccines became commonplace, as pinpointed by Fig. 2.4.

As BioNTech's core capability relies more on biotechnological research and offered originally a more niche-specialist manufacturing footprint, the company paired with Pfizer for the global mass manufacturing scaling and to tackle the unprecedented logistical challenges for the vaccine distribution, especially due to the demanding cold temperature requirements of −70 °C of their coronavirus vaccine.

CureVac, following the likes of BioNTech on a proprietary mRNA approach for their Sars-CoV-2 vaccine, offers a higher temperature resilience. Nevertheless, CureVac, for facilitating large-scale vaccination, established a bandwagon of co-operations supplementary to its own research and development excellence. To develop an integrated European vaccine manufacturing footprint, the company partnered with Wacker Chemie AG, whereas for the demanding sterile filling and finishing process, the French pharmaceutical company Fareva will be responsible by contributing its plants in Pau and Val-de-Reuil. Additionally, the technology co-operation with the big pharma company GSK intends to develop five mRNA vaccines and antibodies for infectious diseases. With CEPI, a supplementary agreement for the accelerated development, production, and clinical testing of coronavirus vaccines as well as the development of a full range vaccine platform was signed lately. Besides, with Tesla's German Grohmann division, the company announced an agreement for the shipment of portable mRNA printers which may solve the logistical hassles of mRNA-based vaccines.

Oxford University centered its competencies for vaccinology within the Jenner Institute and the Oxford Vaccine Group, both located on campus. The two small academic institutes co-operate with the spin-off company Vaccitech on the research and development for the Sars-Cov-2 vaccine. For the global production and rollout, a partnership with the global pharma company AstraZeneca was agreed. AstraZeneca/Oxford University target a production volume of up to 3 billion of their adenovirus vaccine doses in 2021. To achieve this massive scaling, multiple additional partnership agreements have been signed to ensure the global supply of their vaccine AZD1222, as with the Serum Institute of India. But, this network advantage for scaling comes with the challenge to orchestrate the sub-licenses and to assure mission-critical vaccine quality. Their vaccine will be available for \$3–\$4 as the cooperation partners agreed on a nonprofit model. As the pricing and the limited cooling requirements of their vaccine are perfectly suited for higher-temperature zones in emerging markets, AstraZeneca/Oxford University co-operate through the global initiative COVAX and the Bill & Melinda Gates Foundation with 92 countries.

2.2 Decoding Strategic Value: BioNTech's 10C Business Design

For the decoding of BioNTech's Business Design and the co-operation with its partner Pfizer, the 10C Business Design framework, as defined within the first chapter, will be deployed.

2.2.1 The BioNTech/Pfizer Co-operation

Pfizer's global clinical research and development capabilities as well as the company's robust testing processes for vaccines on a global scale seemed to be a perfect complement to BioNTech's research excellence regarding the mRNA technology and its' applications. By combining their respective strengths, the two co-operation partners accomplished what was unthinkable, to develop their vaccine against the COVID-19 virus, based on BioNTech's codenamed BNT162b2 patent, in less than a year with an efficacy of 95% tested in 43,000+ patients (Sahin, 2021).

Other advantages Pfizer will contribute to the co-operation are its global manufacturing footprint and distribution infrastructure capabilities. Last but not the least, Pfizer's strong financial performance and cash conversion within its core pharma business will serve as a potential financial fund for the accelerated joint vaccine development and rollout.

The following description of BioNTech's 10C Business Design as well as its co-operation with Pfizer will have a primary lens on the Sars-CoV-2 vaccine development and rollout, but will as well expand the view on mRNA approaches beyond the coronavirus application, especially on immuno-oncology approaches.

2.2.2 Competitive Strategy and Purpose (CS)

BioNTech's origin, since its inauguration in 2008, lies in the development of biotechnological-based immuno-oncology (IO) and vaccine research, foremost centered around its novel mRNA technology. The underlying strategy of this approach is, in contradiction to the traditional mainstream cancer treatments like chemotherapies, an individualized treatment of tumor patients (BioNTech, 2020g) by improving the latter's immune response. According to this approach, each cancer patient's tumor is unique, and only an individualized treatment-based diagnostic, therapeutic, or vaccine concept seems to address the world's largest illness appropriate. The individualized therapy's starting point is the assessment of the genetic footprint and features of the tumor pattern in combination with the immune cells of a patient in order to enable a tailored development of targets and treatments, for example, by antibodies.

BioNTech's medical strategy intends to design a holistic biotech platform based on patented intellectual property. The latter is built around four distinct fields of expertise, mRNA therapy development, the engineering of cell therapies, as well as the development of antibodies and small molecule immunomodulators. The mRNA approach seems to be the most important and differentiating competitive advantage of BioNTech.

Newer biotechnology research found that the mRNA plays a predominant role for the gene regulation taking place at the RNA level. The mRNA molecule could be interpreted as the transport vehicle of genetic information to access the ribosomes as the cell's centers where proteins are formed. Within the ribosomes, the genetic information of the mRNA is then translated into a corresponding protein response.

This knowledge is applied for the development of therapies triggering an immune response: As the mRNA molecule works as a messenger, it synthesizes proteins within the patient's target cells to trigger an intended immune response.

Based on this biotechnological framework, BioNTech develops mRNA therapeutics to combat cancer and infectious and rare diseases (BioNTech, 2020h). The company works on mRNA vaccines targeting especially prostate, ovarian, pancreatic, and other cancers. The competitive advantage and success formula behind the mRNA approach is the possibility of programming. Once the researchers sequence how to program the mRNA as a messenger, the mRNA could be used to trigger an immune response, foremost by T-cells, to attack a specific tumor or other disease.

2.2.3 Core Value Proposition (CV)

The BioNTech products and services centered originally on the abovementioned four major fields of treatments developed by the company (BioNTech, 2020d):

- mRNA (messenger RNA) therapeutics
- Engineered cell therapies
- Distinct antibodies for immuno-oncology treatments and other severe illnesses
- Small molecules immunomodulators

Beyond cancer therapies, this approach was applied by BioNTech for other infectious diseases as well.

Based on the genetic sequencing of the Sars-CoV-2 virus, BioNTech kicked off in January 2020 the development of a distinct mRNA-based vaccine to program an appropriate immune response to the new coronavirus. Based on first promising data, BioNTech agreed already in March 2020 to extend its 2018 cooperation with Pfizer to develop a mRNA-based influenza vaccine. The agreement targeted the testing and ultimately manufacturing of the COVID-19 vaccines, also applying the mRNA approach (Financial Times, 2020). From the different test trials, the vaccine candidate BNT162b2 was identified as the most promising.

The working principles of BioNTech's mRNA COVID-19 vaccine are based upon the specific pattern of the virus: SARS-CoV-2 viruses are characterized by spherically shaped viral particles covered with spike proteins. The latter enable the virus to enter and infect human cells. Thus, the spike proteins is an ideal vaccine target. This was exactly the Trojan horse for BioNTech in developing a vaccine using the genetic material of the virus to build the spike protein. Accordingly, the vaccine consists of the genetic material (mRNA) that carries the blueprint for a human cell to produce an innocuous version of a target protein that activates the human body's immune response against the coronavirus. After injection, the vaccine will stimulate the immune system to generate protective antibodies. The immune system is then already prepared to identify the virus and prevent an infection that potentially could spread within the human body. To ensure vaccine protection, the vaccine must be administered twice at a 21-day interval. Each vial of the vaccine contains two doses of 0.3 mL (BioNTech, 2020a).

BNT162b2 proved effective with an efficacy rate beyond 90% in phase 3 clinical trials (Medicine, 2020). But, also the development, testing, and approval processes of the vaccine were accomplished with stunning pace: It took BioNTech/Pfizer less than 1 year from the first idea of a mRNA-based vaccine to test the latter along the mandatory three clinical trials and to launch ultimately an accelerated approval processes by national health authorities like the FDA (US) or EMA (EU). Just the three clinical test phases take for an average drug development project typically between 6 and 8 years.

BioNTech, together with its partner Pfizer, targeted at the beginning to produce 1.35 billion BNT162b2 vaccine doses in 2021. The co-operation partners upgraded multiple times their joint manufacturing capabilities and extended their manufacturing target lately to up to 3 billion shots in 2021, as will be discussed later in more detail.

2.2.4 Customer and Markets (CM)

The Sars-CoV-2 virus triggered a global COVID-19 pandemic. In principle, the global population of 7.8 billion humans should be the addressable market for a potential COVID-19 vaccine. But, vaccines were tested with respect to efficacy at the beginning of the pandemic within the prioritized adult test groups as children seemed to be less or not endangered by the virus. So, the vaccines market was thought to be restricted to the world's 5.8 billion adults. Tests of BioNTech's and Moderna's vaccine were lately extended to adolescence and proved also in this younger-aged group their efficacy.

To combat the pandemic, ultimately herd immunity has to be fulfilled. To realize this target, the WHO expected that 60–70% of the global population has to be vaccinated (WHO, 2020). And indeed, first empirical evidence among the over 60s in Israel where the number of vaccinated reached 70% sees the number of hospitalizations dropping significantly (Economist, 2020). But, in case of more aggressive coronavirus strains, this hurdle rate might shift north to 80%. The first rough volume indication of the global Sars-CoV-2 demand is in a magnitude of 5.5–6 billion to be vaccinated humans globally to keep the pandemic at bay. As governments have been reluctant to declare COVID-19 vaccination as mandatory, each person has to make his or her own decision. The ultimate demand will depend on the acceptance of the vaccines within the population.

With respect to the applicability of the BioNTech vaccine, additional limitations do exist. The cold-chain requirements of −70 °C might be a caveat for applications in countries exposed to warmer climates and only limited access to cooling and freezing infrastructure. Additionally, people with severe allergies might have to be excluded due to potential side impacts of the vaccine (New York Times, 2020a). Additionally, for the mRNA-based vaccines of BioNTech/Pfizer and Moderna, it is already known that *two jabs* are mandatory for a full immunization. The first-line estimate of up to 6 billion vaccine shots must be significantly enlarged to probably 8–9 billion vaccine doses, if mRNA-based vaccines might be the dominant approach to combat COVID-19.

Due to the rising numbers of COVID-19 infections and a limited supply, especially at the early stage of the vaccine production, multiple governments decided on the order of prioritized groups being most in need to be vaccinated first. Foremost, care home residents, the elderly, as well as frontline health- and social-care workers will have highest priority, as the first are the most severe hit by COVID-19 and the latter the most exposed to the virus. With respect to age, a couple of governments like in the USA, the UK, or Germany even developed a multi-staged process depending on the age classes. Typically, second in order will be those who have mission-critical jobs for the proper working of highest-priority societal organizations and are at the same time at risk of an infection as their jobs preclude them to work from home like it is the case in law enforcement, education, critical infrastructure, agriculture, and others (New York Times, 2020b).

For a fast rollout and to accomplish the ultralow cooling requirements of the mRNA-based vaccines, the first wave of jabs will be distributed through highly qualified hospitals or especially for the purpose of the vaccination programs ramped up vaccine centers. Later, also doctors having fulfilled the freezing infrastructure requirements and being qualified will be or have been allowed to inject the jabs.

The frontrunners in ordering a significant amount of vaccine doses have been foremost countries which have been extensively hit by the pandemic. For example, the USA signed early a contract with BioNTech/Pfizer for the supply of 100 million doses, with an order option of up to 500 million additional jabs in 2021. The European Union signed a contract for the delivery of 300 million doses of the vaccine immediately after its efficacy was proven by the EMA in December 2020. The UK ordered 40 million jabs and was the first European country that has started with injections of the vaccine. Further agreements for the delivery of the BioNTech/Pfizer vaccine have been signed with multiple governments like Brazil, Switzerland, Israel, Canada, and others (Financial Times, 2020).

Not to be neglected should be BioNTech's pre-pandemic focus on individualized tumor treatments. Oncology was before the pandemic the biggest pharma market growing consistently with a CAGR of 12–14%. An additionally pharma market addressed by BioNTech is the development of vaccines for influenza, where BioNTech formed the original co-operation with Pfizer. Both markets have in common with COVID-19 that they are broad public disease markets.

2.2.5 Customer Relationship (CR)

The go-to-market route, meaning the way to win, capture, and retain customers or clients, is a multichannel effort in the biotechnology and pharma market. In almost all countries, the distribution of prescriptive drugs to end consumers, doctors, and authorized medical professionals is regulated, due their potential significant health impact, by strict laws. Typically, pharmaceutical companies are only allowed to sell prescription medicine to "qualified counterparties" like pharmacies, hospitals, or doctors, but not directly to the patient. Additionally, the prescription of a doctor or hospital is mandatory for the purchase of prescription drugs.[4] As BioNTech/Pfizer's

[4] In contradiction to prescriptive medicine, over-the-counter (OTC) drugs may be bought without a prescription. Nevertheless, end consumers can only buy those products exclusively in a pharmacy which acts for OTCs as a third-party intermediary.

biotechnological treatments address severe human illnesses in all their fields of expertise, prescriptions are requested for the distribution of their drugs and vaccines.

The difference between prescriptive and over-the-counter drugs is also in so far important as for the first patients have to rely more or less exclusively on the qualified advice of their medical counterpart. Not surprisingly, doctors have typically to obey that they act in the best and only interest of their patients as well as prescribe drugs based on their curing potential, missing side impacts, and best-in-class performance. Therefore, trust plays a preeminent role in prescriptive medicine. This might play an even more prominent role for the COVID-19 vaccination programs, as a part of the population is skeptical due to the accelerated development and approval processes as well as the novel, on global scale untested mRNA technology. This skepticism could only be overcome by a transparent sharing of all information about the mRNA working principles and the vaccine's advantages, but also their risks. To address these complex issues around the customer interface, BioNTech and its co-operation partner Pfizer established a multi-sided CR strategy:

- On the one side, the cooperation partners offer doctors, healthcare professionals, and hospitals detailed information about the applicability, working principles, as well as benefits and risks of their vaccine, but at the same time respecting their counterparties' independence. BioNTech and Pfizer also confirmed their adherence to all applicable laws in the countries they filed for their vaccine approval. On the other side, potential patients are directly addressed by increasing the awareness of the distinct Sars-CoV-2 risks, by explaining the corona vaccine's targets, impacts, and risks. Also, discussions between patients and doctors are encouraged.
- Additionally, BioNTech and Pfizer co-operate closely with governments and health agencies as in the end, it is their ultimate responsibility to offer a safe and fair distribution of vaccines for their citizens. These authorities are also in charge for monitoring, testing and approval processes. The handling of government relationships is a delicate and privileged issue for biotechnology and pharma companies. This complexity and sensitivity with respect to political relationships is even enforced in the COVID-19 vaccine case, as the governments of the USA, the EU, the UK, and others rushed to sign multi-billion delivery contracts to ensure access to highly effective, approved vaccines.
- On top to the national level, supranational organizations like the WHO with their COVAX facility or global charity organizations like Oxfam try to assure access also for less-wealthy emerging countries to qualified vaccine programs. Only if all nations have access to effective Sar-CoV-2 vaccines, herd immunity on a global scale might be achieved and the risks of dangerous mutant strains avoided.

2.2.6 Channels (CH)

In most countries, regulatory provisions significantly limit or even prevent pharma companies to advertise prescribed drugs. A sensitive and multichannel communication strategy is prevalent to inform and educate the interested population about the working principles, advantages, and risks of a vaccine. Especially in the early stage of a vaccination program and as the BioNTech/Pfizer vaccine is based on the novel mRNA technology, the educational part might be even more important than the marketing aspect. Addressing skepticism by transparent information is in such circumstances top priority.

Pfizer seems to have the core responsibility with respect to the communication strategy of the co-operation. One pillar is intense discussions with scientists and reputable doctors, as well as educational campaigns. Besides, Pfizer built a bold social media and web presence. Besides its corporate website, innovative formats like podcast, Instagram posts, or videos on YouTube explaining the simplified working principles of the vaccine (Pfizer, 2020e) have been developed for a broad communication strategy.

Specifically for the COVID-19 vaccine, a stand-alone website was built by Pfizer, to provide more detailed information (Pfizer, 2020a). An interesting move of the co-operation partners to increase transparency and reduce skepticism was lately their public pledge on integrity and ethical standards (Cushing & Kohler, 2020).

After having promising vaccines on hand, the center of interest shifted to the global manufacturing and distribution of vaccines to combat the pandemic. This might especially hold true for the BioNTech/Pfizer vaccine due to its demanding ultra-cooling requirements.

The starting points for the vaccine supply chain are BioNTech's and Pfizer's mRNA manufacturing hubs in Europe and the USA. The vaccines are transported to their point of use in suitcase-sized thermal shippers, which use dry ice to uphold the required temperature of $-70\ ^{\circ}\mathrm{C} \pm 10\ ^{\circ}\mathrm{C}$ for up to 10 days. GPS-based sensors permanently monitor the real-time temperature (TheGuardian, 2020). BioNTech and Pfizer are also in intense discussion with global logistic companies like UPS and DHL to optimize deliveries. Finally, last-mile issues like the storage of the vaccine doses at the point of delivery, the delivery of jabs from storage centers especially to rural areas, or the logistics of the patients to the point of vaccination have to be solved for such global vaccination campaigns.

2.2.7 Core Assets (CA)

A multitude of core assets, tangible, intangible, and human, are mandatory for the development, manufacturing, and distribution of complex mRNA-based vaccines.

On the management side, the entrepreneurs and early founders of BioNTech, Dr. Özlem Türeci and her husband Prof. Dr. Ugur Sahin, play a dominant role for the development of the company as they combine biotechnology capabilities with entrepreneurial rigor. As soon as Prof. Sahin read about a new virus from China in January 2020, he worked on an action plan on how to develop a vaccine against COVID-19 with high efficacy and convinced the board to approve this endeavor under the code name "Project Lightspeed" just a couple of days later.

A second pillar of the HR strategy of BioNTech are its highly skilled, diverse, and young employees: 60 nationalities, an average age of less than 35 years, and 25% of the employees with a PhD are outstanding key statistics. Over a third of BioNTech's overall staff of 1300 employees at year-end 2019 are involved in Project Lightspeed (BioNTech, 2020d, p. 3) and are the most important ingredient for the high-speed development of the mRNA-based vaccine and its approval.

A core tangible asset is BioNTech's manufacturing footprint. Its headquarters as well as one of its manufacturing sites are located in Mainz (Germany) and a second site in Idar-Oberstein (Germany). An additional manufacturing site was acquired from Novartis in Marburg (Germany) and is expected to be fully operational in March 2021. This hub will supplement the existing footprint and will be among the largest factories for mRNA in Europe producing more than 1 billion jabs per year, based on updated forecasts (BioNTech, 2020b).

Pfizer will complement the manufacturing footprint with four factories, thereof three US sites in St. Louis, Andover, and Kalamazoo as well as in Puuh, Belgium (Pfizer, 2020d). Additionally, the partners will use Pfizer's global logistics network for the global distribution of the vaccine.

But, the most crucial assets might be intangible assets, especially IP rights, for biotechnology companies. This also holds true for BioNTech. Per September 2020, the company had invested more in intangible assets than tangible assets like property, plant, and equipment. BioNTech also developed more than 100 patent platforms and protected those by IP rights. Additionally, the company in-licenses supplementary IP.

Last but not the least, its vast cash position of close to €0.9 billion per May 2021 gives the company enough headroom for a massive further extension of its development program and scaling of its manufacturing footprint. This will be further detailed in the Cash Flow (CF) model subchapter.

2.2.8 Core Capabilities (CC)

BioNTech's origin, since its inauguration in 2008, lies in mRNA-based immuno-oncology (IO) research. The idea is, in contradiction to the mainstream cancer therapies, to enable a patient-individualized, biotechnological-driven therapy approach. The company's uniqueness and competitive advantage was shaped along the following core competencies which also frame their product lines (BioNTech, 2020d, p. 17; CNBC, 2020):

- mRNA (messenger RNA) therapeutics development and manufacturing capabilities
- Engineered cell therapies development know-how
- Distinct antibodies knowledge, development, and manufacturing capabilities
- Small molecules immuno-modulation capabilities
- Advanced T-cell understanding embedded in wider immune system knowledge

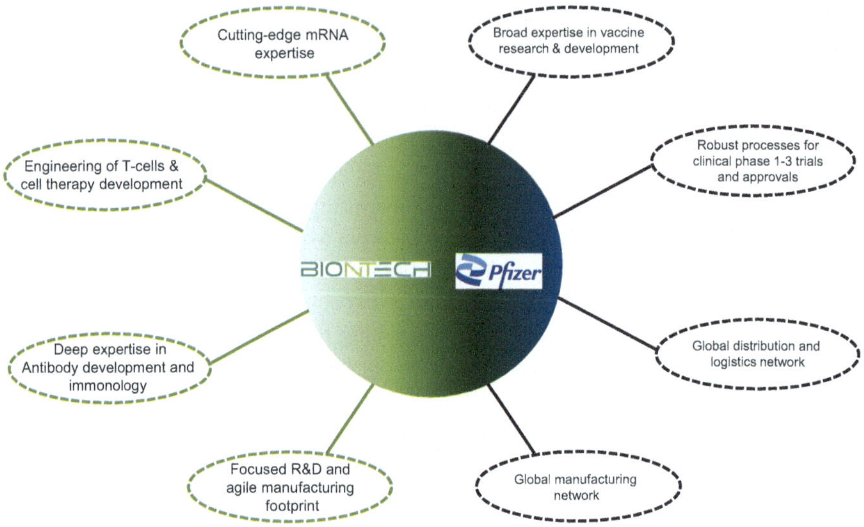

Fig. 2.5 BioNTech's core and Pfizer's supplementing capabilities

The development of a COVID-19 and, finally, the distinct BNT162b2 vaccine took advantage from the existing mRNA technology know-how BioNTech's team built up along the years. The mRNA approach was never applied before for a high-scale vaccine program. In so far, the BioNTech innovation strategy is also a showcase how knowledge-based core capabilities may shape true competitive advantage. But, even more fundamentally, the COVID-19 vaccine case serves also the social wider good, especially as it was tested in stage 3 clinical trials with an efficacy of more than 90% and might play a crucial rule in combating the Covid-19 pandemic.

Figure 2.5 describes how BioNTech's capabilities reach out beyond the development stage as the company has also expertise in highly sensitive biotechnology GMA manufacturing processes. BioNTech leveraged those in-house manufacturing capabilities by producing the critical first batches for the mandatory clinical trials and now scales its manufacturing capabilities (CNBC, 2020).

For a never-seen scaling from scratch to 3 billion jabs in just a single year, BioNTech supplemented its own manufacturing capabilities with the manufacturing processes and excellence of its co-operation partner Pfizer. Additionally, Pfizer will contribute with its broad expertise in partially blinded and placebo-controlled test designs as well as by its knowledge about fast-track global regulatory approval processes. In so far Pfizer was in charge for the late-stage phase 3 study of the COVID-19 vaccine candidate BNT162b2 (CNBC, 2020) which finally indicated that the jointly developed vaccine is meeting all primary efficacy endpoints with a 95% proven rate for every age, gender, or ethnicity demographic (Pfizer, 2020d; Sahin, 2021). Indicating the outer space of innovations in the field of biotechnology testing and development, BioNTech and Pfizer invest also in newest technologies like AI or predictive analytics (Pfizer, 2020b). Besides, Pfizer's overall vaccine research and development know how as well as its global distribution network supplement the partners' joint capabilities (BioNTech, 2020c).

In addition to its tailored core capability strategy and its intense co-operation strategy, as pinpointed in the next subchapter, BioNTech uses targeted transactions to further extend its capabilities. Examples are the acquisition of the service provider JPT Peptide Technologies GmbH in 2009, production sites like EUFETS GmbH in 2009, or the Novartis plat in 2020 as well as technology centers like Neon Therapeutics in 2020.

2.2.9 Core-Ecosystem Partners (CE)

To partner with corporations and institutions which offer supplementary capabilities or assets is part of BioNTech's DNA. Vice versa, BioNTech seems to be an attractive cooperation partner due to its' research excellence in mRNA, antibody development, and further biotechnological fields as applied successfully for the COVID-19 vaccine program or immuno-oncology.

In the scientific field, BioNTech built a bandwagon by multiple co-operations with scientific institutions, research hospitals, think tanks, and biotech peers to leverage its capabilities as well as to accelerate therapy and vaccine developments. But, also co-operations with global pharma champions are used with whom the company typically agrees on advanced payment and profit sharing-based targeted development programs as within the original co-operation with Pfizer. For the global COVID-19 vaccine rollout, the company also co-operates with global logistics companies.

In the financing part, the partial funding by the German BMBF[5] stands out. One the one side, this funding enables an even faster scaling of the vaccine development, manufacturing scaling, and rollout. On the other side, the ministry assures a timely delivery of the vaccine within the EU and globally.

The co-operation with Pfizer not only supplements BioNTech's leverage on cutting-edge technology development and testing capabilities but complements the co-operation with the pertner's global manufacturing, supply chain, and distribution scale, as well as with its holistic marketing approach, as discussed prior.

2.2.10 Corporate Organization (CO)

BioNTech was founded in 2008 and is listed as BioNTech SE since 2019 on the NASDQ stock exchange. The company has with its management and its supervisory board a dualistic board structure, which is common practice for listed companies in Germany. Stressing BioNTech's strategic emphasis on high-end biotechnological

[5] Federal Ministry of Education and Research

research, the company installed on the highest level a scientific advisory board, which is sourced exclusively from members of the supervisory board with medical or biotechnological background.

BioNTech is the holding company and consolidates 16 subsidiaries as centers of expertise at five locations in Germany, Austria, and the USA. These include JPT Technology GmbH, BioNTech Manufacturing Service GmbH, BioNTech Small Molecules GmbH, and the BioNTech Diagnostics GmbH which are run as development departments or branches and also provide services to third parties. Besides, the subsidiaries enabled BioNTech to extend its production sites for proprietary manufacturing of mRNA therapeutics and cell therapy products (BioNTech, 2020e, p. 1).

2.2.11 Cash Flow Model (CF)

The Cash Flow (CF) Model as the financial skeleton of the company references to the financial statements of BioNTech, its SEC reports, its capital market valuation, the value drivers of its biotechnological and research-centered Business Design, as well as its financing structure. Nevertheless, the audited financial statements, mirroring past performance, will provide only limited insights for BioNTech's future performance as the global COVID-19 vaccine rollout in 2021 will boost revenues, profits, and cash flows of the company. As a consequence, the financial architecture of the company will change in 2021 significantly. Therefore, the BioNTech valuation is a perfect case study for the picture-of-the-future (PoF)-based Reverse DCF methodology, as described in Chap. 1.

The most crucial *revenues drivers* of BioNTech have been in the past revenues from contracts with clients, subsuming co-operation and license payments, as well as advanced payments out of those co-operation agreements.[6] The cost and revenue sharing models of such agreements most probably served also as a blueprint for the co-operation agreement with Pfizer on the COVID-19 vaccine development and rollout.

2021 will be on the revenue side a game-changer for BioNTech. The US government signed early on an agreement with BioNTech/Pfizer. The contract detailed that upon delivery of 100 million jabs, the partners will receive a payment of $1.95 billion. The contract as well included a further delivery option for additional 500 million vaccine doses. The EU signed a contract shortly after for the delivery of 200 million doses of the vaccine for €3.1 billion with an option for the delivery of additional 100 million for a total payment obligation of €4.65 billion. After those significant breakthrough orders, many other governments like the UK, Japan, Australia, Canada, Chile, Mexico, Peru, Qatar, Kuwait, and others placed, after approval by their local drug authorities, as well orders for BioNTech's COVID-19

[6] In 2019 and 2020 especially from Genentech Inc. as partner for the neoantigen immuno-therapy vaccine "INeST" and Pfizer for the joint mRNA-based influenza vaccine program BNTN161

vaccine. The Chinese market was carved-out from the BioNTech/Pfizer agreement, as BioNTech already signed prior to the agreement with the US pharma giant with the Chinese pharma company Fosun Pharmaceuticals an exclusive agreement for the local market.[7]

The latest order book of Q1 2021 detailed the breakdown of the 1.8 billion doses contracted for 2021 so far (BioNTech, 2021a):

- EU: 600 million doses
- USA: 300 million doses
- Japan: 144 million doses
- UK: 90 million doses
- Others: 680 million doses

With respect to its profit pattern, BioNTech had so far a typical start-up company profile: Due to significant investments and expenses in R&D, the company was still loss making and operating cash flow negative till 2019. In early April 2021, BioNTech provided first insights on its 2020 financials which highlighted already the significant tailwinds of its Sars-CoV-2 vaccine. Consolidated revenues increased more than fourfold to €482 million, whereby the last quarter of 2020 alone contributed €345 million. And also 2019 losses of €179 million turned already in the financial year 2020 into a small profit of €15 million (BioNTech, 2021b).

Figure 2.6 highlights that the tipping point of BioNTech's financial performance will be ultimately 2021. According its Q1 2021 report, the company's revenues and operating profit skyrocketed, respectively, to $2.048 billion and $1.642 billion, implying a 80% operating margin (BioNTech, 2021a). As the company's effective income tax rate stands at 31%, BioNTech's net income, by deducting €514 million in income tax from operating profits and financing costs, was €1.128 billion. The Q1 2021 financials of its core mRNA Sars-CoV-2 vaccine peer Moderna showed a similar strong performance with revenues of $1.9 billion and an operating profit of $1.2 billion, implicitly a 70% margin.

Splitting consolidated revenues along the agreements between BioNTech and its cooperation partner Pfizer and Fosun Pharma with respect to distribution rights, €1.752 billion comprise BioNTech's share of gross profit from COVID-19 vaccine sales in Pfizer's territories,[8] €64 million sales are allocated to BioNTech by collaboration partners for products manufactured by BioNTech, and €200 million direct COVID-19 vaccine sales to customers within BioNTech's territory.

Based on its signed supply contracts of roughly 1.8 billion doses, BioNTech updated on May 10, 2021, its COVID-19 vaccine revenue guidance for the year

[7] In the Reverse DCF subchapter, a more detailed breakdown of delivery volumes and revenue estimates is provided.

[8] A 50:50 gross profit sharing was agreed between the two co-operation partners (Sahin, 2021).

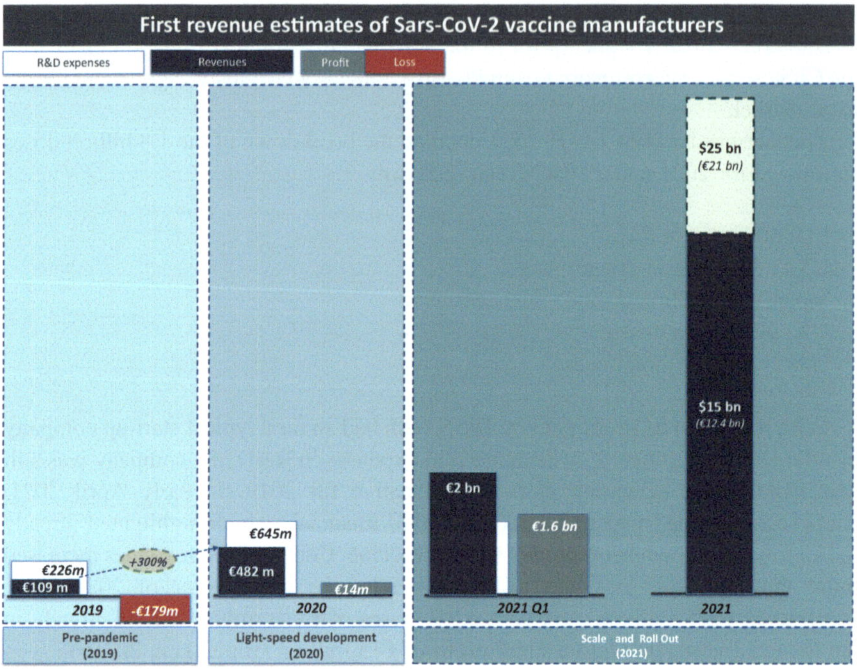

Fig. 2.6 BioNTech's profit, revenue, and R&D cost driver diagnostics

2021 to €12.4 billion or equivalent[9] $14.9 billion (BioNTech, 2021c).[10] This is pinpointed in Fig. 2.6 as baseline revenue for the company. Taking into account the updated increased vaccine manufacturing target of up to 3 billion jabs, revenues might even come in with up to €21 billion, providing an extended target line.

In line with BioNTech's core capabilities in biotechnological research, especially mRNA-based vaccines and therapies, the main *cost drivers* of BioNTech's Business Design are foremost its R&D costs, besides its cost of sales for the production and selling of its developed vaccines:

- R&D expenses: The company pushed forward the development of its' pioneering novel COVID-19 vaccine, especially its BNT162 program, by extending its R&D expenses by 185% from €227 million in 2019 to €645 million in 2020 (BioNTech, 2021b). The specific development costs for the BNT162b2 vaccine

[9] At a spot foreign exchange rate of $1.2/€

[10] This revenue forecast includes expected revenues from direct COVID-19 vaccine sales to customers in BioNTech's territory (Germany, etc.), expected revenues from vaccine doses manufactured by BioNTech for sales to collaboration partners like Pfizer and Fosun Pharma, expected sales milestone payments from collaboration partners, and expected revenues related to share of gross profit from COVID-19 vaccine sales in the collaboration partners' territories.

will be split equally by the co-operation partners, whereas Pfizer will cover 100% of the costs until after the vaccine is commercialized improving BioNTech's interim cash position and financing headroom. R&D expenses were further extended in Q1 2021 to €216 million compared year on year with €65 million (BioNTech, 2021a). This increase was again mainly driven by BioNTech's BNT162 program.[11] Further R&D expense levers were increases in the company's R&D headcount and expenses linked to a new share-based payment program.
- CoGS: First quarter cost of sales were €233 million in Q1 2021, where with €223 million the bulk of such costs was recognized with respect to BioNTech's COVID-19 vaccine sales.

BioNTech's balance sheet is also a perfect showcase of a biotechnology company and mirrors its core assets as well as its platform potential. Besides property, plant, and equipment, summarizing the company's investment in its R&D centers of excellence and its manufacturing footprint, intangible assets, and herein foremost licenses, play a dominant role on the asset side. As total non-current assets of €669 million are just 16% of its total assets, the asset side mirrors the asset-light characteristics of a typical platform firm, as described within Chap. 1. Nevertheless, working capital needs, as mirrored foremost by additional €2.2 billion in trade receivables within Q1 2021 (BioNTech, 2021a), might have to be financed along the further growth of the company.

For financing its significant growth ambitions, BioNTech strengthened its funding structure in the last years by multiple equity market transactions: Already before the pandemic, in August 2019, BioNTech concluded one of the largest European biotechnology VC financing rounds raising close to €200 million. On October 10 of the same year, BioNTech went public on the NASDAQ stock exchange under the symbol "BNTX." Through the IPO, BioNTech issued American Depository Shares for $15/share and realized IPO proceeds of €143 million (BioNTech, 2020d, pp. 66–69). At the time of the IPO, BioNTech became the second most valuable listed German biotechnology company. To scale its COVID-19 vaccine program, BioNTech issued in July 2020 further 5.5 million shares at an issue price of $93, six times higher than the IPO issue price, and raising additional €435 million. In a private funding round, two investors bought additional shares for €124 million (BioNTech, 2020f).

Since then, the share price from BioNTech more than doubled till May 2021, as described by Fig. 2.7. Especially in March 2021, BioNTech's share price rose significantly, as needs for its vaccines still increased due to a third coronavirus wave in a couple of regions like Europe. As of the writing of this book, BioNTech' market capitalization stood at an all-time high of €49 billion.

[11] R&D expenses included purchased R&D services, which were initially incurred by Pfizer and charged to BioNTech in line with the partners collaboration agreement.

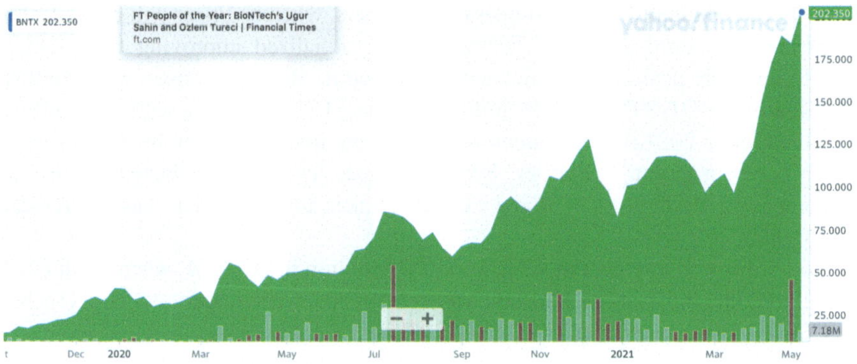

Fig. 2.7 BioNTech's share price development since its IPO. *Source*: finance.yahoo.com, 2021

To support the fast ramp up of COVID-19 vaccine development, manufacturing, and distribution, BioNTech received from the German Federal Ministry of Education and Research €375 million in September 2020 (BioNTech, 2020f, p. 3) as well as a €100 million loan from the European Investment Bank. Last but not the least, BioNTech's co-operation partner Pfizer contributed $185 million as an advanced one-time payment, including an equity investment of $113 million, and up to $563 million may be paid as additional milestone payments, summing up to maximum proceeds of $748 million (Pfizer, 2020c). Even for the intended significant scaling of BioNTech's Business Design, the financing side seemed quite robust.

As the company realized its first cash flows from its vaccine sales, BioNTech further improved its financial resilience in Q1 2021 by increasing its cash reserves, including cash equivalents, to €891 million and its total equity to close to €2.5 billion (BioNTech, 2021a). As the company's debt position stood at €657, BioNTech was even net debt positive at the end of the first quarter 2021, giving the company further financial headroom for its intended significant growth.[12]

2.2.12 10C Business Design Canvas: BioNTech

A summary of BioNTech's ten interrelated modules is provided by the 10C Business Design canvas of Fig. 2.8.

Before stress-testing today's capital market valuation of the COVID-19 vaccine pioneer and developing a long-term valuation perspective, BioNTech's strategic platform strength will be evaluated.

[12] Defined for BioNTech as non-current interest-bearing loans and borrowings, other non-current financial liabilities, current interest-bearing loans and borrowings, and other current financial liabilities

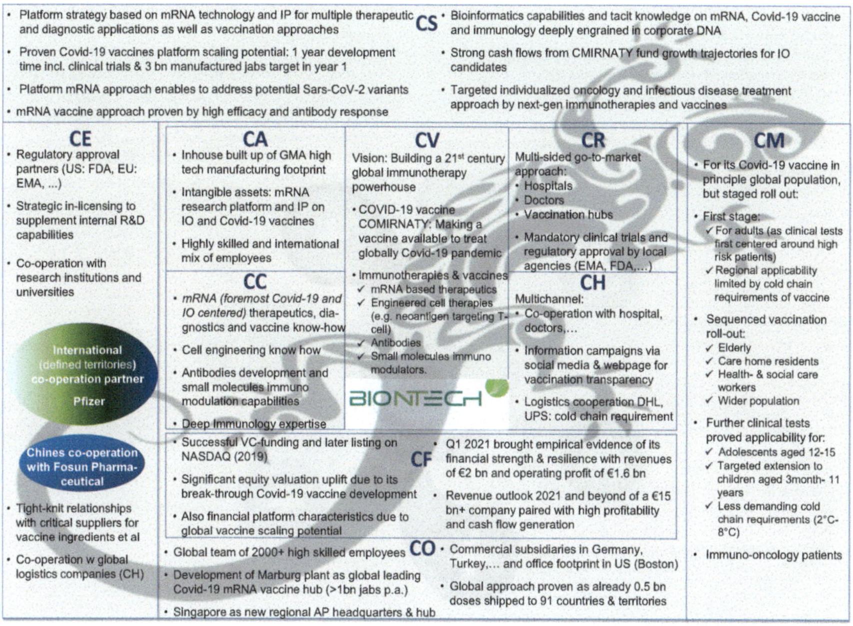

Fig. 2.8 10C Business Design canvas: BioNTech

2.3 Decoding Platform Value: The Novel mRNA Platform

BioNTech's Business Design platform value will be benchmarked along the eight criteria of platform strength, as developed in Chap. 1. These criteria, as summarized within Fig. 2.9, comprise the mRNA platform architecture, its scalability, the platform's competitiveness, its strength of network effects, the platform's cluster pattern, the risks of disintermediation as well as multi-homing, and, finally, the potential of platform bridging. The latter includes scaling potentials into immuno-oncology and further areas of medical diagnostics and therapies. Such a granular assessment of those criteria and their interlinkages will enable a detailed evaluation of the mRNA platform potentials. It will also serve as a strategic reference point for the later financial valuation.

- *Platform architecture*: BioNTech's Business Design rests on its Messenger RNA platform. The vaccines, as its COVID-19 vaccine, are built on BioNTech's novel mRNA capabilities, connecting the multitude of powerful research capabilities of BioNTech and its ecosystem partners with the vaccine-interested population. BioNTech's mRNA-backed Business Design architecture could be interpreted as a knowledge-based, double-sided platform connecting deep-routed biotechnological and bioinformatic knowledge with a multibillion population. As the

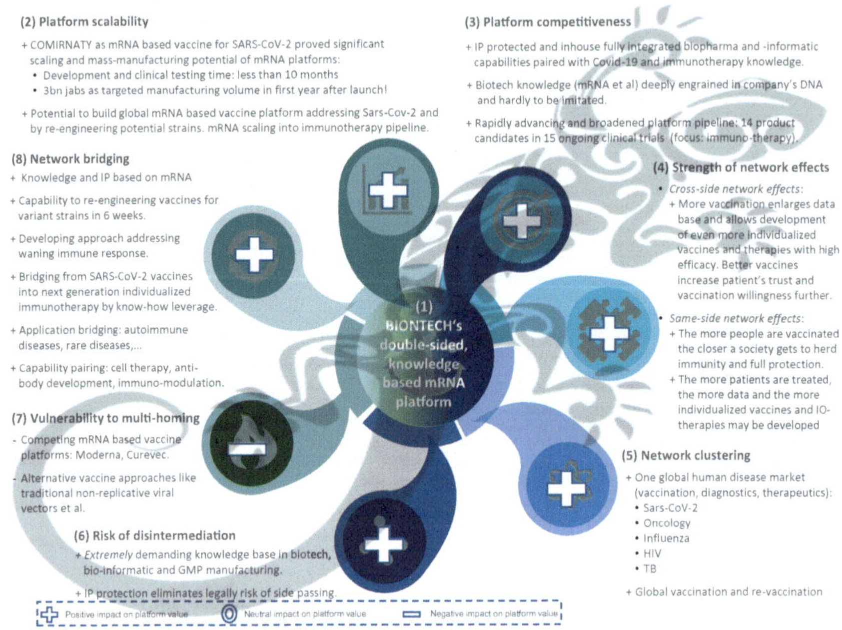

Fig. 2.9 BioNTech's platform value and its eight strategic levers of platform strength

mRNA platform in principle reaches out to the global population, it offers a powerful design.

- *Platform scalability*: BioNTech stated in one of its latest shareholder presentations its intent and potential to build a global, multi-product immunotherapy pipeline firm. The development, manufacturing, and rollout of its vaccine COMIRNATY based on its novel mRNA technology to fight the COVID-19 pandemic in record time proved this approach in the last 18 months.
  The development and demanding clinical testing of COMIRNATY along the three clinical stages including the final approval by the national health authorities, starting from the first notice of the SARS-CoV-2 virus in China in January 2020, took the company just 10 months, whereas normally such demanding developments take at least 5–7 years. In parallel, the company together with its co-operation partner Pfizer scaled the mass manufacturing of the vaccine, based on its inhouse GMP manufacturing capabilities of mRNA vaccines. The partners increased multiple times their vaccine manufacturing target, lately targeting 3 billon jabs for 2021, the first year of its coronavirus vaccine's biotech life cycle. This development will create a multi-billion mRNA biotech powerhouse on short notice.
- *Platform competitiveness*: As BioNTech's COVID-19 vaccines and further pipeline candidates are globally IP protected, as it is standard practice in the biotech industry, a one-by-one imitation is, at least within the patent runtime of the next

two decades, prohibited. Nevertheless, also other biotech start-ups like Boston-based Moderna or Germany-based CureVac have already or will most likely have promising mRNA-based COVID-19 vaccines with high efficacies in the making.

A second strategic competitive strength of BioNTech are its fully inhouse integrated biopharma and bioinformatic capabilities, from vaccine development and testing up to GMP-based manufacturing of the vaccine as well as its most crucial ingredients. Especially the deeply in the company's DNA engrained tacit mRNA knowledge, but also its immuno-oncology and Sars-Cov-2 knowledge might serve as a prime barrier to imitate.

As BioNTech reinvests its COVID-19 vaccine revenues, the company funds its broadened clinical stage pipeline to 14, foremost immuno-oncology candidates (BioNTech, 2021a), extending its COVID-19 vaccine breakthrough on immuno-oncology therapies as the globally biggest human disease market.

- *Strength of network effects:* Interesting wise, network effects have been not addressed so far in the biotech ecosystem or research. Nevertheless, they may become mission-critical for the development of lasting, effective, and efficient diagnostic and therapeutic solutions by pairing individualized medical treatment advantages with platform scaling advantages.
- *Cross-side network effects*: The Sar-CoV-2 vaccines are a showcase, how an increasing number of vaccinations provides crucial real-world data about efficacies and side impacts for global large-scale vaccination programs. Through a large bio-tech data lake based on in-human applications also further treatments for important niche applications and further bio-technological insights are gained. Especially for mRNA approaches, this plays an enormous role for the development of even more individualized vaccines and therapies with high efficacy, for example, for adolescents aged 12–15 years or children from 3 months to 11 years. Such tailored vaccines are of highest importance for patients and, in principle, for the global population.
- *Same-side network effect*: Additionally, more and transparent data will create trust by patients. The turbulences around the AstraZeneca vaccine early 2021 proved the importance of trust for global vaccination programs and new medical therapies lately. This is in so far also for pandemics critical, as the higher the number of vaccinated people and the higher the speed of the rollout, the more likely and faster societies might be protected by achieving herd immunity and by avoiding the development of variant strains, a powerful same-side network effect.
- *Pattern of platform clusters*: The pharma and biotech ecosystem is a global market as human diseases simply do not stop on boarders, as shown by the COVID-19 pandemic, where the Sars-CoV-2 virus spread from China in breathtaking speed around the world. But also other important human disease markets like diagnostic and therapeutic treatments for oncology or vaccine developments for influenza, HIV, and tuberculosis have to be addressed from a global perspective and may only be ultimately eliminated by coordinated, joint global efforts.

An additional empirical evidence of the global pattern of the biotech and pharma market is the competitive landscape as, especially on the pharma side, companies with global reach dominate the industry.

- *Disintermediation*: The development of mRNA COVID-19 vaccines rests upon demanding, in the company's talents engrained tacit knowledge and capabilities. Additionally, these capabilities must be paired with the understanding of to be treated illness like the Sars-CoV-2 virus or cancer patterns. Also, as proof of efficacy, harmless side effects and the vaccine's superiority in comparison to existing treatments must be proven by a massive amount of clear-cut data within the three clinical stages Side-passing seems therefore technically simply not possible.

Additionally, global IP rights protect legally against the risk of side-passing, as such rights could be, in case of global patent fillings, enforced around the world.

- *Multi-homing:* What is a bone for societies might be the only limitation for BioNTech's platform strength, the competition and accessibility of alternative vaccines. The tight-knight contenders are biotech firms which compete also on mRNA-based grounds.

Additionally, alternative vaccine approaches compete with BioNTech's vaccine platform to address the Sars-CoV-2 virus. The vaccines from AstraZeneca and Oxford University, Johnson & Johnson, or Gamaleya reference to the traditional non-replicative viral vectors approach, whereas the inactivated virus approach is applied for the vaccines from Bharat BioTech or Sinopharm. A partial protection of multi-homing approaches is the outstanding efficacy of mRNA vaccines of more than 90%.

- *Platform-bridging:* Novel biotechnology approaches have a common ground. They combine innovative diagnostic, vaccination, and therapeutic approaches paired with rapid efficiency gains, building on economies of scale. Latest applications on genetic decoding brought empirical evidence therefore. Test costs for reading and editing a single DNA in a human genome hoovered still in 2007 around $10 million, whereas today it takes less than $1000 and takes a fraction of the time. This builds the foundation of revolutionary, individualized medical approaches (Economist, 2021a).

The mRNA vaccination technology of BioNTech deploys such an approach as the messenger written in genetic code instructs the human body's cells to produce the viral protein designed to build up the immune response and protection against the Sars-Cov-2 virus. This development might be seen as a general proof of concept. MRNA-based therapies or vaccines might be developed on the general gained knowledge about mRNA working principles for multiple diseases like cancer or others, creating a formidable bridging approach into further disease applications.

Additionally, the mRNA capabilities might serve as a holistic knowledge platform how to instruct immune cell responses, leading ultimately to individualized therapeutical approaches, which are fundamentally tailored around the distinct patients' DNA. This might promise new diagnostics and therapies for further, even rare diseases or genetic abnormalities at affordable costs. This might be the ultimate platform promise of the revolutionary mRNA approach of BioNTech, CureVac, Moderna, and the likes.

And indeed, BioNTech intends to invest the cash flows from its COVID-19 vaccine to accelerate its portfolio diversification and to advance its broad pipeline of biotechnological product candidates. Targeted are specifically vaccines and immunotherapies in multiple therapeutic areas. One important pillar is the financing of the clinical phase 1–3 tests of its product pipeline (Sahin, 2021). This would ultimately allow the company to bridge from its SARS-CoV-2 vaccine breakthrough into next-generation individualized immunotherapies by leveraging its knowledge and IP on mRNA paired with its capabilities in cell therapy, anti-body development, and immunomodulators.

All in all, the eight platform levers prove the significant platform strength of BioNTech's mRNA drug pipeline and platform. This strategic strength will be in the following paired with the financial valuation of the mRNA innovator.

2.4 Decoding BioNTech's Financial Value: Reverse DCF

The Reverse DCF approach references to a distinct picture-of-the-future scenario of an ecosystem in which a Business Design is embedded. Such a picture-of-the-future scenario will be exemplary and briefly described as a reference point for the follow on rough first financial valuation of BioNTech's mRNA platform:

2.4.1 Picture-of-the-Future Scenario: "The Jo-Jo Deceleration"[13]

The pictures-of-the-future scenarios for a COVID-19 vaccine ecosystem have to pencil answers for the crucial unknowns which will determine the future course of the global coronavirus pandemic. Just to describe a few of those:

- How effective will be the blockbuster COVID-19 vaccines long-term? Will they have long-term side impacts?
- How fast will the manufacturing scaling and distribution of existing vaccines be realized? How long will it take to immunize the global population, and are those immunized still capable of passing on the coronavirus?

[13] Alternative pictures-of-the-future developed for BioNTech's Reverse DCF valuation have been the "awake from a nightmare" pictures-of-the-future framing a full vaccination immunization and fast Sars-CoV-2 deceleration scenario and the "long Covid doom" pictures-of-the-future describing a challenging scenario of multiple infection rounds due to variant strains and uncoordinated vaccine response policies around the globe. Those two alternative pictures-of-the-futures will be briefly discussed in this subchapter, but not separately used for the Reverse DCF.

- How fast will the various new variant strains of the original coronavirus spread? This leads to second-order questions like how well today's vaccines will work against the new mutants, or how soon new vaccines better attuned to those will become available?
- How coordinated will be the global political, social, and medical response to address the pandemic challenges? How accepted will be regional and local vaccine programs targeting herd immunity?
- How fast will the vaccine-related immune protection wane against the original virus and its different variant strains? Will second- or third-dose renewal vaccinations offer a long-term protection?
- How effective will be long term the so far available COVID-19 vaccines, and how fast could their applications broaden for the so far unaddressed, but mission-critical groups of the adolescents and children?

The severeness of those questions will be exemplary highlighted along the first question: The vaccines' protection patterns play here a prominent role. In one scenario, the same number of infections occurs after vaccination as would occur in a non-vaccination case, but the consequences of these infections are systematically downgraded, e.g., infections which would lead to severe cases lead to moderate or mild cases. The alternative is that the total number of infections is being reduced, but the ratio of severe to mild cases stays roughly the same. The third and so far evidenced global pandemic path combines both developments.

Parts of the population might still for a while be not vaccinated as the jabs' side impacts might endanger their preexisting health condition, because there might be simply too less vaccine supply, or people might strictly refuse vaccination. A COVID-19 vaccine that is highly effective in preventing transmission protects also the unvaccinated population, making them particularly useful and enables a faster way to achieve herd immunity. To put these questions into context, three different picture-of-the-future scenarios have been developed, as summarized by Fig. 2.10.

These pictures-of-the-future addressing the coronavirus case may basically be differentiated by two core variables, the vaccines' efficiency to limit transmission and the probability that multiple, more dangerous variant strains will spin off from the original Sars-CoV-2 virus as well as if the latter are neutralized by existing vaccines.

Nevertheless, all three scenarios have also a common ground, based on recent knowns. After the first wave of COVID-19 doses have been administered by "early-movers" like Israel, empirical evidence is emerging that those vaccines reduce indeed greatly the death toll rate as well as hospitalizations and might also lower, even as the degree of blocking is not fully understood jet, transmission (Economist, 2020). The vaccines' distribution worked well in the USA, by executing program Warp-Speed, and the UK. The distribution in Europe seems to have improved lately by an increased availability of vaccines. Israel, the USA, and the UK will have enough vaccine jabs to vaccinate all adults till the end of Q2 2021 most probably, and Europe will be in the same position most likely till the end of the third quarter 2021.

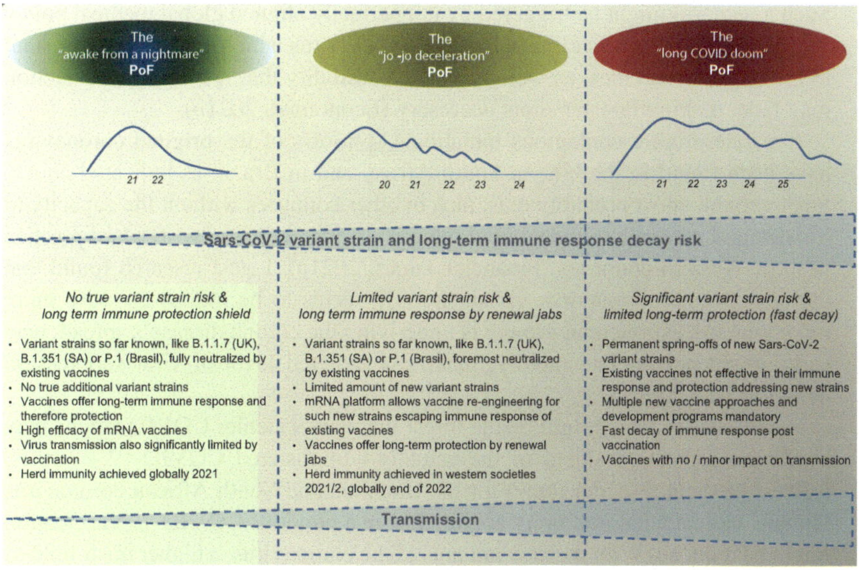

Fig. 2.10 Picture-of-the-future scenarios for the COVID-19 pandemic evaluation

1. The "awake from a nightmare" picture of the future: The "awake from a nightmare" scenario is built on the assumption that jabs come with huge benefits also for most strains of the original virus. As described, especially real-world evidence in Israel, the USA, and the UK proved that the Sars-CoV-2 vaccines of BioNTech/Pfizer, Moderna, and their peers work to address the main strain of the virus with high efficacy, by reducing hospitalizations as well as the death toll rate. This should hold true in this scenario also for the mutants, making a re-engineering of existing vaccines not necessary. Also more evidence might underline that transmission of the virus will also be mid- to long term considerably reduced by vaccination.
   This "awake from a nightmare" picture of the future builds on those assumptions as it assumes that the immune response against variant strains so far known like in the UK by the codenamed strain B.1.1.7, in South Africa where B.1.351 is now the dominant strain, and in Brazil with its mutant P.1. is fully provided by existing vaccines. It is also assumed within this scenario that no additional variant strains will emerge with the potential to escape the immune response. Further, existing one- or two-shot vaccines offer long-term immune response and protection, besides proving also long term as highly effective. As virus transmission is assumed to be significantly limited by global coordinated vaccination programs, global herd immunity may be achieved at year end 2021 in Western countries and mid-2022 globally within this scenario.
2. The "jo-jo deceleration" picture-of-the-future: The "jo-jo deceleration" picture-of-the -future is a multi-wave, but slowly decelerating COVID-19 pandemic scenario.

Such a scenario might be triggered by not perfectly aligned global medical policy responses, by multiple strains of the Sars-Cov-2 virus which are partially resistant to the original vaccines, as well as by the possibility that the vaccine protection may fade, making booster shots necessary (Economist, 2021b).

Separate, higher contagious mutational spin-offs of the original coronavirus have been found in the UK, in South Africa, and in Brazil, as indicated above. Such variants most probably exist also in other countries without the capacity to run detailed genomic sequencing of the coronavirus as it is now standard practice in most Western countries (Financial Times, 2021a). Latest research found that the new British coronavirus variant B.1.1.7 seems to be indeed 25–40% more infectious. As exponential growth is underlying the corona disease's spread, new cases might accumulate rapidly, making a targeted level of viral suppression harder to be achieved.

Additionally, there might be the threat that new, catchier COVID strains may evade the protection shield of the actually administered COVID-19 vaccines. Newest medical research found for the Brazilian and South African coronavirus mutants indicate that immunity acquired from a previous COVID-19 vaccination might be reduced. With the new mutants of the coronavirus, a higher trash-hold of vaccination level might have to be achieved so that the R-factor drops below one, meaning an infected person, on average, transfers the virus to less than one contact person. Only then, a pandemic ultimately subsides (Economist, 2021b). In so far, herd immunity within this picture-of-the-future will be achieved globally at year-end 2022, with Western countries, where vaccination programs faster progressed probably escaping slightly earlier in Q3 2021 the pandemic.

A platform vaccine approach might be a significant advantage to develop re-engineered and tailored vaccines for mutants in this scenario. Additionally, it is assumed that renewal jabs will become mandatory to achieve long-term immunity. Some vaccine manufacturers like CureVac, BioNTech, and GSK are in the development stage of "multivalent" vaccines which intend to work for multiple coronavirus mutations. Also, the latest management presentation from BioNTech provided a bit of a relief as it seems that its original BNT162b2 Sars-Cov-2 vaccine might be effective to neutralize at least the known strains B.1.1.7, B.1.351, and P.1. The "jo-jo deceleration" picture-of-the-future assumes that a deceleration of the pandemic is achieved in waves, transmission is ultimately suppressed long term by addressing also spin-off strains, and herd immunity is achieved in Western countries end of 2021 and globally end of 2022 to mid-2023.

3. The "long Covid-19 doom" picture of the future: The "long Covid-19 doom" *scenario* assumes that the coronavirus is not easily eradicated and translates much more into an endemic disease. Even as COVID-19 vaccines are making the Sars-CoV-2 virus less infectious and protect people against death, evolving new viral variants might undo in this scenario multiple times the first-order positive effect and trigger at least some level of COVID-19's persistence. Also, a potential fast decay of immune response protection might limit the efficacy of existing vaccine approaches.

Nevertheless, BioNTech's mRNA gene sequencing technologies may offer as well an efficient platform to treat potential dangerous mutants of the original Sars-Cov-2 strain. If the latter would transform the COVID-19 pandemic into an endemic, the company might re-engineer its original BNT162b2 vaccine and offer regular booster shots.

The following Reverse DCF valuation build-up is exemplary shown for the "jo-jo deceleration" picture of the future.

2.4.2 Steady State and Continuing Value

BioNTech's long-term competitive advantage as a global COVID-19 vaccination developer and producer seems to be strongly embedded in the "jo-jo deceleration" picture-of-the-future. The company was with its coronavirus vaccine first to market in December 2020, including the necessary approvals by the local medical authorities, the mRNA approach proved to be highly effective as well as with very limited side effects, and the company together with its cooperation partner Pfizer achieved a fast scaling of its demanding vaccine manufacturing process. Besides, lately achieved project milestones and order intakes underpin those strategic strengths of BioNTech:

- In May 2021, the EU, after its first order of 0.6 billion doses included in BioNTech's baseline revenue forecasts, placed an additional order of up to 1.8 billion[14] jabs for delivery in the next years.
- Lately, BioNTech with its cooperation partner Pfizer applied for emergency use authorization at the US and European medical authorities to expand its COVID-19 vaccine BNT162b2 to adolescents aged between 12 and 15 years, after medical trials provided empirical evidence that inoculations were 100% effective at preventing symptomatic disease among those adolescence. The US FDA and its European counterpart EMA are set to approve the BioNTech/Pfizer COVID-19 vaccine for this age group most probable on short notice. This might be an additional step to achieve herd immunity and might prove vital for full reopening of schools in autumn 2021 (Financial Times, 2021b). For BioNTech, the approval would open up a new, vast market segment.
- Additionally, the company is in ongoing studies and late-stage clinical trials testing its vaccine efficacy and side impact in children from 6 months to 11 years aged.

[14] The potential order volume of up to 1.8 bn Sars-Cov-2 vaccine doses includes a fixed agreed order volume of 0.9 bn jabs of BioNTech/Pfizer's vaccine for 2021–2023 and an option for the EU to buy an additional 0.9 bn jabs. Assuming an average price per dose of 14–15€, the deal would be worth up to €27–28 billion.

- BioNTech also submitted to the US and European medical authorities data to broaden temperature requirements to a 4-week storage at 2–8 °C. This would allow the rollout of BNT162b2 in more demanding hotter climate regions.
- The company is also in test mode of the immune response and virus protection by a third "renewal" shoot in case the immune response of the first two jabs would wane.

For the steady state of the "picture-of-the-future "the jo-jo-deceleration," it is assumed that a one-shot renewal vaccination per year will become standard practice. From the global world population of 7.4 billion inhabitants, China, due to its strict local policies, and India, due to its local pharma footprint, might be hardly to be captured markets. This reduces the addressable market to round about 5 billion global inhabitants. Assuming further that 70% of the population might get vaccinated per year, which might be also the political target to achieve herd immunity, 50% of the vaccinations might rest upon the mRNA approach and that the bulk of that market segment will be shared between the frontrunners BioNTech/ Pfizer and Moderna, a likely 0.8–1 billion jabs of BioNTech's BNT162b2 jabs will be sold per year long-term.

By assuming a 28–30% price decrease due to competing vaccine approaches, this would translate into a steady-state COMIRNATY revenue of $8 billion, or of $4 billion for BioNTech. Also, the extraordinary high EBIT margin of close to 80% in Q1 2021 might decrease to 70% longterm by slightly higher operating costs due to its new Marburg factory, its new AP headquarters in Singapore and its office in Boston, as well as slightly increasing SG&A. This would lead to a long-term EBIT level of close to €3 billion.[15] For the steady state of a biopharma product, the prices drop typically drastically after the expiration of the underlying patent. As BioNTech filed most likely most patents in 2020 and the scaling period is simulated along 10 years, the steady state would frame, in contradiction to most other valuation cases, a reduced time frame of additional 10 years, as drug patents have typically a patent protection of 20 years in most jurisdictions. All in all, this would lead to a continuing value CV in 2031 of €14 billion, applying weighted average cost of capital of 6.5%:

$$\mathrm{CV}_{2031}^{\mathrm{BNT}} = \sum_{t=2031}^{2040} \frac{\mathrm{FCF}_t^{\mathrm{BNT}}}{(1+\mathrm{CoC})^t} = \mathrm{EUR}14\ \mathrm{bn}$$

Or an equivalent present value of the continuing value from today's perspective of €7.4 billion:

[15] Additionally, as in the scaling period, the actual marginal tax rate of 31% and cost of capital of 6.5% are assumed.

$$\mathrm{DCV}_{2021}^{\mathrm{BNT}} = \frac{\mathrm{CV}_{2031}^{\mathrm{BNT}}}{(1+\mathrm{CoC})^{T}} = \frac{\text{EUR 14 bn}}{(1+6.5\%)^{10}} = \text{EUR7.4 bn}$$

2.4.3 Scaling Period and Free Cash Flows

Most of the 1.35 billion doses of the COVID-19 vaccine that BioNTech planned originally to manufacture with Pfizer by the end of 2021 were early earmarked for the USA, the EU, the UK, and Japan. Several other countries, including Brazil and Switzerland, scrambled to secure any remaining supply. Due to the high demand, BioNTech indicated in spring 2021 to lever its manufacturing capacity first up to 1.6 billion and later, by expanding its Marburg factory, to 2.0 billion doses for 2021 (Sahin, 2021). In its Q1 earnings call in May 2021, the management of BioNTech announced to increase once more its manufacturing target due to the massive vaccine needs around the world to up to 3 billion jabs for 2021 and beyond 3 billion jabs for 2022 (BioNTech, 2021c). BioNTech's partner Pfizer even indicated for 2022 a 4 billion jab target line.

Based on its signed supply contracts of roughly 1.8 billion doses, BioNTech estimated in May 2021 its COVID-19 vaccine revenues for the year to come in at €12.4 billion or equivalent $14.9 billion.[16] This is pinpointed in Fig. 2.11 as baseline revenue for the company and will be used as a reference point for the revenue planning within the scaling period. As the company indicated potentially additional revenues related to further supply contracts for deliveries in 2021 and beyond, a very rough stretched revenue was calculated, based on BioNTech's manufacturing target of 3 billion jabs. This stretched target would indicate a revenue line of up to €21 billion or $25 billion. Therefore, a second, stretched valuation will be provided and based upon this higher revenue line. This stretched target is also highlighted by Fig. 2.11 and compared with BioNTech's COVID-19 vaccine peers.

As the first vaccine protection needs two shots and the renewal probably a yearly one-shot vaccination, based on the 2021 baseline manufacturing target of 1.8 billion jabs and the manufacturing capacity of 3 billion jabs, a 2.3–2.5 billion dose sales target for the next 2 years seems to be a plausible estimate. With achieving herd immunity in 2022/2023 in the underlying picture-of-the future "jo-jo deceleration," this first double-shoot vaccination wave might decelerate to the one-shot renewal demand of the steady state of 0.8–1 billion jabs, consistent with continuing value assumptions.

[16] This revenue forecast includes expected revenues from direct COVID-19 vaccine sales to customers in BioNTech's territory (Germany, etc.), expected revenues from vaccine doses manufactured by BioNTech for sales to collaboration partners like Pfizer and Fosun Pharmaceuticals, expected sales milestone payments from collaboration partners, and expected revenues related to share of gross profit from COVID-19 vaccine sales in the collaboration partners' territories, whereas the latter contribute most to the company's consolidated revenues.

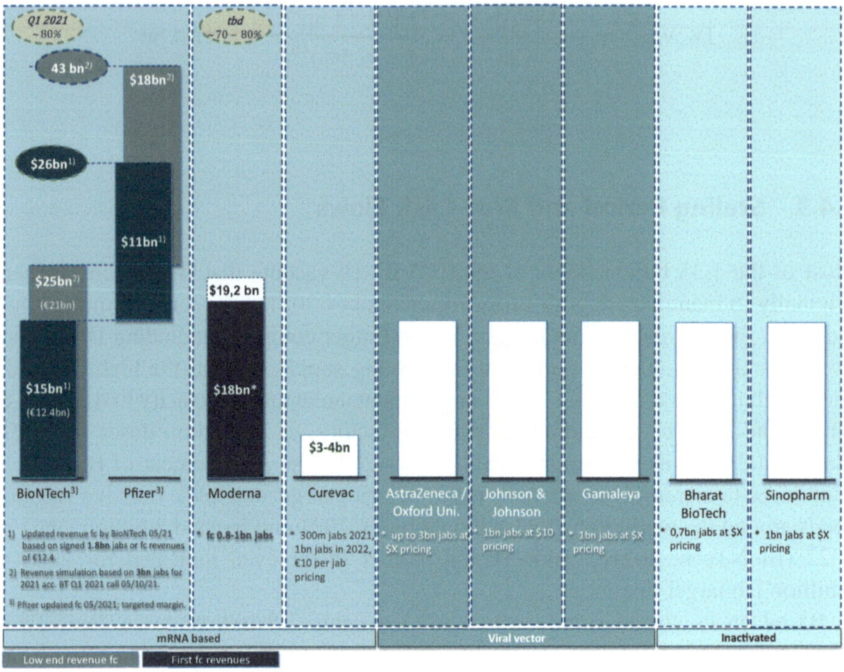

Fig. 2.11 First financial forecasts for COVID-19 jab developers and manufacturers

Prices are assumed, as pinpointed above, to decrease within the scaling period by a quarter, as competitive vaccine approaches might be less effective but also less expensive. But, as Moderna's mRNA competing vaccine is said to be higher priced than BioNTech's vaccine, the direct peer comparison might limit partially this downside price pressure.

For BioNTech's cost position in 2021, its forecast as provided in May 2021 (BioNTech, 2021c) and its Q1 2021 report (BioNTech, 2021a) have been used as references:

- R&D expenses of €750–€850 million to ramp up R&D investments in the second half of 2021 and beyond to broaden and accelerate BioNTech's candidate pipeline development within different stages of clinical trials
- SG&A expenses of up to €200 million
- Capital expenditures of €175–€225 million to rebuild its Marburg facility to a global benchmark mRNA vaccine factory, as well as to establish its presence in Singapore and Boston (USA)
- An underlying corporate tax rate of 31%

All in all, this might allow BioNTech to realize high EBIT margins, but decelerating from 80% to 70%.

	2021	2022	2023	2024	2025	2026	2027	2028	2029	2030
	1	2	3	4	5	6	7	8	9	10
Revenues	**12,4**	**17,3**	**14,7**	**12,0**	**8,3**	**5,0**	**5,0**	**5,0**	**4,0**	**4,0**
yoy growth		*39%*	*-15%*	*-18%*	*-31%*	*-39%*	*0%*	*0%*	*-20%*	*0%*
EBIT	**10**	**13**	**11**	**9**	**6**	**4**	**4**	**4**	**3**	**3**
EBIT margin (%)	*77%*	*77%*	*76%*	*75%*	*74%*	*73%*	*72%*	*72%*	*71%*	*70%*
Taxes (31%)	*3,0*	*4,1*	*3,4*	*2,8*	*1,9*	*1,1*	*1,1*	*1,1*	*0,9*	*0,9*
NOPLAT	**6,6**	**9,1**	**7,7**	**6,2**	**4,2**	**2,5**	**2,5**	**2,5**	**2,0**	**1,9**
NOPLAT margin (%)	53%	53%	52%	52%	51%	51%	50%	49%	49%	48%
Depreciation & Amortization	*0,1*	*0,1*	*0,1*	*0,1*	*0,1*	*0,1*	*0,1*	*0,1*	*0,1*	*0,1*
Operating CF	6,7	9,2	7,8	6,3	4,3	2,6	2,6	2,6	2,1	2,0
Invested Capital	5,8	6,2	4,7	4,0	3,1	2,3	2,3	2,3	2,0	2,0
Net Investment in Invested Capital	#BEZUG!	0,4	-1,5	-0,7	-0,9	-0,8	0,0	0,0	-0,3	0,0
FREE CASH FLOWS	**1,4**	**8,7**	**9,2**	**6,9**	**5,1**	**3,3**	**2,5**	**2,5**	**2,2**	**1,9**
DISCOUNTED CASH FLOWS	1,3	7,7	7,6	5,3	3,8	2,3	1,6	1,5	1,2	1,0

Fig. 2.12 BioNTech's core financials and value drivers for the PoF "the jo-jo deceleration"

On the Invested Capital side for non-current assets, comprising foremost BioNTech's PP&A, rights of used assets, and intangibles, forecasts for 2021 are in a range of €200 m. The same amount was assumed for 2022 for allowing the company to complete its global development and manufacturing footprint. For the outer years of the scaling period, it was assumed, as revenues might decline within this scenario, that further investments will compensate depreciation, allowing the company to update its factories and regional headquarters. On the working capital side, trade receivables are the dominant position. Whereas in Q1 2021 they came in at more than 100% of quarterly revenues burning significant cash flows, it is assumed for the valuation that midterm 90-day payment terms might be a probable target rate, as the co-operation agreement with Pfizer seems to have agreed on quarterly payments and also governments might have longer payments terms than global industry standards of 30 days.[17]

As BioNTech is net-debt positive and generates significant cash flows due to its COMIRNATY sales, the company bears the luxury to be in position to fund its further mRNA platform extension from COVID-19 into immuno-oncology without the need to on-board debt. This simplifies the definition of the company's cost of capital, being in the end cost of equity. For the latter's calculation, 10-year US government bond yields for the risk-free rate of 1.6% points as well as Damodaran's studies for the unlevered beta of bioinformatic peers of close to 1 and the market risk premium of 4.5% points have been taken into consideration. The cost of capital, using the capital asset pricing model assumptions, are therefore round about 6.5%.

This financial skeleton of BioNTech's Business Design would lead to a strong cash flow generation, as summarized by the excerpt of the Reverse DCF scaling period model in Fig. 2.12, enabling the company to fund its intended immune-oncology platform extension and maybe realizing its vision to "build a twenty-first century immunotherapy powerhouse" (BioNTech, 2021c, p. 6):

[17] Further distinct working capital positions included in the valuation, based on BioNTech's capital market reports and Business Design, are as current operating assets working cash and inventories and as operating liabilities accounts payables and contract liabilities.

The present value of the discounted cash flows of the scaling period mirrors the value creation of BioNTech within the picture-of-the-future "the jo-jo deceleration":

$$PV_{2021}^{BNT} = \sum_{t=2021}^{2030} \frac{FCF_t^{BNT}}{(1 + CoC)^t} = EUR33.3\ bn$$

2.4.4 Enterprise and Equity Value of BioNTech Embedded in the "Jo-Jo Deceleration" Scenario

The present value of the scaling period would generate the bulk of the total value, fully in contradiction to typical new Business Design and platform valuations, as will be shown in Chaps. 3, 4, and 5:

BioNTech's value of operations (OP) is calculated as the sum of the COVID-19 vaccine pioneer's DCFs within the scaling period and the present value of the continuing value (DCV):

$$\begin{aligned} \text{Operating Value}^{BNT} &= \sum\nolimits_{t=1}^{\infty} (DCF_t) + DCV = EUR33.3\ bn + EUR7.4\ bn \\ &= EUR40.7\ bn \end{aligned}$$

For the valuation walk from operating to enterprise value, the excess cash of close to €0.9 billion has to be added:

$$\begin{aligned} EV^{BNT} &= \text{Value of Operations OP} + \text{excess cash} = EUR40.7\ bn + EUR0.9\ bn \\ &= EUR41.6\ bn \end{aligned}$$

For the final walk from enterprise to equity value debt and debt-like items, in BioNTech's case, long- and short-term interest-bearing liabilities, other financial liabilities, and government grants of in total €0.7 billion have to be subtracted:

$$EqV^{BNT} = \text{Enterprise Value} - \text{Debt} = EUR41.6\ bn - EUR0.7\ bn = EUR40.9\ bn$$

Dividing BioNTech's equity value of €40.9 billion by the company's 241.5 million undiluted shares outstanding would provide a first indicative share price estimate of "the jo-jo deceleration" picture-of-the-future of €203 per share. The valuation flow is provided by Fig. 2.13.

To achieve a more robust valuation bandwidth than a single equity value, the valuation's sensitivity to an interest rate increase might be of particular interest as potential interest rate spikes due to increasing inflation concerns spoked capital markets in spring 2021: A 1%-point rise in the cost of capital on BioNTech's equity value would lead to an implicit share price drop to €192 per share.

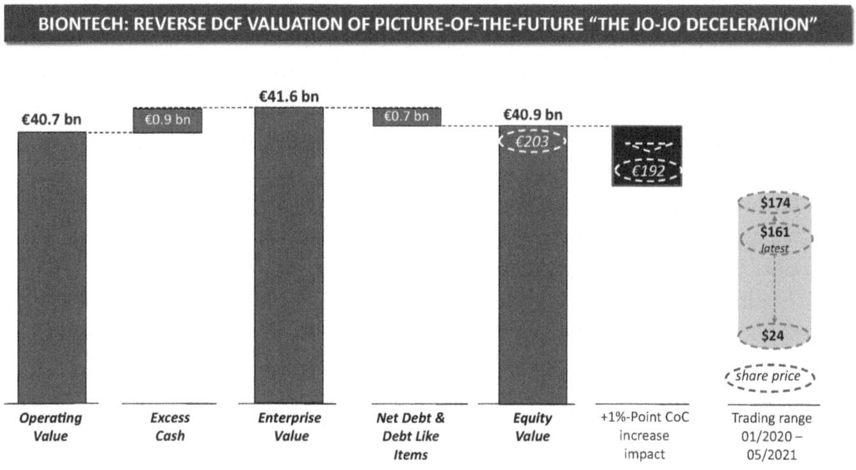

Fig. 2.13 BioNTech's valuation walk from operating to equity value

2.4.5 Platform Bridging from COVID-19 Vaccines to an Immuno-oncology mRNA Powerhouse

This indicative valuation of BioNTech embedded in a picture-of-the-future scenario "the jo-jo deceleration" addresses the company's commercialization of its Sars-CoV-2 vaccine candidate. But, as BioNTech reinvests its free cash flow to develop, based on its mRNA knowledge and patent platform, further applications, the latter might be interpreted financially as an on-top call option for BioNTech in developing drugs or vaccines for further mission-critical human diseases:

BioNTech's product platform pipeline centers around the following area:

- *Flu vaccines*: Based on the company's mRNA platform, the influenza vaccine candidate BNT161 will be designed to encode influenze antigens selected by the WHO in advance of a given flu season. BNT161 is expected to start clinical trials in Q3 2021.
- *Infectious diseases*: In a research cooperation with the University of Pennsylvania, BioNTech develops and commercializes exclusive immunotherapies for the treatment of infectious disease indications. This approach might be extended to the development of HIV as well as tuberculosis vaccines and immunotherapies in cooperation with the Bill & Melinda Gates Foundation.
- *Immuno-oncology*: The most promising extension of BioNTech is expected by its accelerated development of a broad oncology platform with 14 product candidates in 15 ongoing clinical trials. The portfolio frames five therapeutic modalities:
  - Next-generation CAR-T-cell immunotherapies targeting personalized neoantigens like in its first in-human trials for CARVac (e.g., BNT211).

- BioNTech's modified mRNA designed RiboCytokines (BNT151, BNT 152, and BNT 153) encoding secreted cytokines.
- mRNA-based cancer vaccines like BioNTech's patient-specific cancer immunotherapy iNeST (BNT122) or FixVac (BNT111 or BNT113), e.g., its FixVac candidate is built upon a distinct combination of pharmacological optimized uridine mRNA encoding known cancer-specific shared antigens.
- Its targeted cancer antibodies development (e.g., BNT321).
- Next-generation checkpoint and small immune-modulators (e.g., BNT311 and BNT312) intending to stimulate antitumor immune response by activating T-cells. Some candidates are add-on therapies of prior PD-1/PD-L1 inhibitor applications, one of the significant breakthroughs in newer cancer research.

The backbone of BioNTech's cancer candidates is its mRNA platform, which might be described as a platform-bridging approach from COVID-19 vaccines to immuno-oncology applications. All in all, this manifold potentials of mRNA applications beyond COVID-19 offer for BioNTech indeed the potential to build a twenty-first-century mRNA powerhouse and further lever its capital market valuation. For the second edition of this book, having more details on the immono-oncology pipeline of BioNTech on hands, a Real-Option valuation of this pipeline will be provided.

References

BioNTech. (2020a). *Aiming to address the global coronavirus pandemic: Project Lightspeed.* https://BioNTech.de/covid-19

BioNTech. (2020b). *BioNTech to acquire GMP manufacturing site to expand COVID-19 vaccine production capacity in first half 2021.*https://investors.biontech.de/news-releases/news-release-details/biontech-acquire-gmp-manufacturing-site-expand-covid-19-vaccine

BioNTech. (2020c). *COVID-19.*https://biontech.de/covid-19

BioNTech. (2020d). *Financial statements 2019—Form 20-F SEC report.*https:investors.biontech.de/static- files/2fe81830-7ae3-498b-b862-2e0a79221702; https://investors.biontech.de/static-files/63bc1b07-08ad-48d2-945b-bc78b0dc1172

BioNTech. (2020e). *Konzernlagebericht für das Geschäftsjahr 2019.*https://investors.biontech.de/static-files/9d250563-102c-4e7a-9346-26f27a12f3b3

BioNTech. (2020f). *United States securities and exchange commission, form 6-K.*https://investors.biontech.de/static-files/6b471789-bbd6-456c-9ae8-6e1895a0a3ab

BioNTech. (2020g, September 12). *Ushering in a new era of cancer medicine.*https://BioNTech.de/science/individualized-cancer-medicine

BioNTech (2020h, September 12). *Why mRNA represents a disruptive new drug class.*https://BioNTech.de/how-we-translate/mrna-therapeutics

BioNTech. (2021a, May 11). *BioNTech SE quarterly report for the three months ended March 31, 2021.*https://investors.biontech.de/news-releases/news-release-details/biontech-announces-first-quarter-2021-financial-results-and/

BioNTech. (2021b). *Form 20-F filing for SEC—financial year 2020.*https://investors.biontech.de/static-files/e862a8ea-5d90-4672-acfb-34de57b58806

BioNTech. (2021c, May 10). *First quarter 2021: Corporate update an financial result.*https://investors.biontech.de/news-releases/news-release-details/biontech-announces-first-quarter-2021-financial-results-and/

Cambridge-Dictionary. (2021). https://dictionary.cambridge.org/de/worterbuch/englisch-deutsch/virus

CNBC. (2020). *What you need to know about BioNTech the European company behind Pfizer's Covid-vaccine.*https://www.cnbc.com/2020/11/11/biontech-the-european-company-behind-pfizers-covid-19-vaccine.html

Cushing, J., & Kohler, J. (2020, November 24). *The credibility of pharmaceutical companies is on the line. Will they get it right.* The Globe and Mail. https://www.theglobeandmail.com/opinion/article-the-credibility-of-pharmaceutical-companies-is-on-the-line-will-they/

Economist. (2020, February 13). *When covid-19 vaccines meet the new variants of the virus.*https://www.economist.com/briefing/2021/02/13/when-covid-19-vaccines-meet-the-new-variants-of-the-virus?

Economist. (2021a, March 27). *Bright side of the moonshots?* Bright side of the moonshots. https://www.economist.com/leaders/2021/03/27/bright-side-of-the-moonshots?

Economist. (2021b, February 13). *How well will vaccines work?*https://www.economist.com/leaders/2021/02/13/how-well-will-vaccines-work

Economist. (2021c, February 13). *Jabs and jabs-nots.*https://www.economist.com/graphic-detail/2021/02/13/there-will-be-enough-vaccines-for-all-if-rich-countries-share

Financial Times. (2020, November 13). *Inside the hunt of a Covid-19 vaccine—How BioNTech made a breakthrough.*

Financial Times. (2021a, February 11). *Vaccines vs variants: The race to immunise the developing world.*https://www.ft.com/content/797e3d7b-0091-4bfd-8cae-c0b5be380772

Financial Times. (2021b, May 4). *US set to approve Pfizer Covid vaccine for 12- to 15-year-olds.* https://www.ft.com/content/68721f4c-7635-43c3-aa9d-4caf7870ea18

Jibilian, I. (2020). *Here is how the top coronavirus vaccines compare when it comes to efficacy, cost, and more.* Business Insider. https://www.businessinsider.com/how-covid-vaccines-compare-cost-astrazeneca-oxford-pfizer-biontech-moderna-2020-11?r=DE&IR=T

McKinsey. (2021). *When will the COVID-19 pandemic end*? March 2021 update.

New York Times. (2020a, December 10). *DoorDash soars in its first day of trading.* https://www.nytimes.com/2020/12/09/technology/doordash-ipo-stock.html

New York Times. (2020b, July 5). *Uber buys postmates for $2.65 billion.* https://www.nytimes.com/2020/07/05/technology/uber-postmates-deal.html

Pfizer. (2020a). *Coronavisus disease (COVID-19) resources.*https://www.pfizer.com/health/coronavirus

Pfizer. (2020b). *Leading innovation in trials.*https://www.pfizer.com/science/clinical-trials/partnering-with-pfizer/clinical-innovation

Pfizer. (2020c). *Pfizer and BioNTech announce further details on collaboration to accelerate global COVID-19 vaccine development.*https://www.pfizer.com/news/press-release/press-release-detail/pfizer-and-biontech-announce-further-details-collaboration

Pfizer. (2020d). *Pfizer and Biontech conclude phase 3 study of Covid-19 vaccine candidate, meeting all primary efficacy endpoints.*https://www.pfizer.com.newspress-release/press-release-detail/pfizer-and-biontech-conclude-phase-3-study-covid-19- vaccine

Pfizer. (2020e). *To all the participants...*https://www.youtube.com/watch?v=nY7cLRM11ss&list=UUzoP7l5bzSzi2gUUNn0I79w

Reuters. (2020, March 17). *Pfizer, BioNTech to co-develop potential coronavirus vaccine.*https://www.reuters.com/article/us-health-coronavirus-pfizer-biontech-%20idUSKBN2140LM

Sahin, U. (2021, January). *Next generation immunotherapy.*https://investors.biontech.de/static-files/82c9e451-7503-4217-a51f-ee7fb6497b17

The Guardian. (2020). *Pfizer and BioNTech's vaccine poses global logistics challenge.* The Guardian. https://www.theguardian.com/business/2020/nov/10/pfizer-and-biontechs-vaccineposes-global-logistics-challenge

WHO. (2020). *COVID-19 vaccines.*https://www.who.int/emergencies/diseases/novel-coronavirus-2019/covid-19-vaccines

WHO. (2021). *WHO coronavirus disease (COVID-19) dashboard.*https://covid19.who.int

Ride-Hailing: Is Sharing the New Owning? 3

Abstract

It is expected that the way people get around in metropolitan areas will change within the next decade more than any time since the breakthrough of the automobile. At the epicenter of this technology disruption in urban mobility stands the transition from owning a car to on-demand ride-hailing and food-delivery service platforms, which goes hand in hand with the rise of the sharing economy. Chapter 3, after having introduced the new "technological alphabet" of the automotive industry, discusses the 10C Business Design of the early ride-hailing innovator Uber. But, as Uber supplemented its double-sided ride-hailing platform Uber Mobility with its three-party food-delivery platform Uber Eats, also the latter will be analyzed. Based on the 10C Business Design understanding, the eight value levers of Uber's ride-hailing and food-delivery platform will be discussed. On the one side, Uber is a typical asset-light platform matching the riders' demand to bridge the distance between two urban locations with a driver who is registered on the platform willing to satisfy the rider's demand with his own car. On the other side, such platforms are exposed to an intense platform competition with significant side payments for the capture of platform partners, to the risk of multi-homing, and to partially fragmented networks. The financial Reverse DCF valuation of Uber, as "the hottest question on Wall Street," closes Chap. 3.

The development of newest digital and platform Business Designs goes hand in hand with the rise of the sharing economy: The traditional ownership model of goods, services, and data is more and more perceived to come along with significant investment needs, high usage costs, and increased risks of ownership, which might have to be insured (Jahromi & Zhang, 2020). Not surprisingly, consumers, especially those of the technology-affluent generations X, Y, and Z, are substituting

T. Feix, *Valuing Digital Business Designs and Platforms*, Future of Business and Finance, https://doi.org/10.1007/978-3-030-83632-0_3

owning by sharing, thereby driving collaboration and disrupting traditional Business Designs.

Additionally, by the pairing of the sharing idea with the application of newest technologies like digital network connectivity, big data approaches, as well as analytics and artificial intelligence, platform companies are collecting, analyzing, and deploying wide oceans of customer data. With this in-depth understanding of customer use cases, new digital Business Designs could be tailored around individual needs, making traditional mass-market solutions obsolete. Ownership is replaced by customer USPs like individuality and convenience, leading to a segment-of-one competition, perceived highest service quality, and real-time delivery. This is exemplified in the urban mobility ecosystem by the move from owning a car to on-demand ride-hailing services at a fingertip on a smartphone, as offered nowadays by Uber, Lyft, Didi, Ola, and the likes in metropolitan areas around the world (Feix, 2020).

One of the epicenters of technology and new Business Design-driven disruptions will be most probably urban mobility in the 2020. It is expected that the way people get around in metropolitan areas will change within the next decade more than any time since the breakthrough of the automobile. Platform-based ride-sharing or ride-hailing as well as micro-mobility concepts rapidly supplemented the portfolio of urban modalities. This new urban mobility market segment is estimated as of today by the investment bank Goldman Sachs at a size of $90–100 billion, growing at a CAGR of 15% within the next decade to a $350–400 billion market. This was echoed by significant venture capital funding of over $100 billion alone in the 5 years prior to the pandemic, whereby a substantial part of these funds was concentrated on a limited number of high-profile start-ups and new Business Designs (Goldman Sachs, 2019, p. 22).

Nevertheless, as these businesses are in start-up mode, they are characterized by a significant profit and cash flow drain. Recent capital market flotations of ride-hailing and food-delivery champions brought more financial transparency and highlighted the massive payments to attract platform partners like drivers and riders in the form of extensive capture and retention bonuses. Besides, the fierce price competition between these new mobility firms intending to scale their platform and to become a "winner-takes-all" champion led to a profit and cash flow drain, partially questioning the sustainability of such Business Designs.

But, many equity capital market investors expect, as mirrored in the high market capitalizations of such platform firms, in the years to come a transition to more profitable Business Designs, achieving ultimately cash flow breakeven. Such a transition will demand more rational competitive strategies limiting price pressure and side payments as well as operational improvements of such platform Business Designs.

The strategic and financial valuation of ride-hailing and food-delivery Business Designs applies again the three pillars, the 10C Business Design, the platform value assessment, as well as the Reverse DCF valuation. The assessment will be exemplified by its most prominent player Uber. A brief assessment of the ongoing, multiple technology disruptions within the automotive ecosystem will frame the discussion on platform strategies within urban mobility.

3.1 The New Alphabet of the Automotive Ecosystem

The global automotive industry is unsettled by multiple technological disruptions, which may be described broadly as the automotive ecosystem's "new technological alphabet" (Feix, 2020). These technologies have a lasting and massive impact on the automotive industry, thereby shifting industry boundaries:

- "A" for autonomous drive technology is the technological precondition and backbone for the development of driverless cars. It is as well an umbrella term incorporating subsystems like advanced camera, radar, and lidar technologies. Only the demanding integration and merging of the billons of data points provided by those systems enables the real-time mapping of the car vector and its environment as well as integrating latest traffic information. Autonomous drive technologies are also a showcase on how digital natives like Google enter the home turf of incumbents by building and scaling disruptive technologies. The latter dissolve traditional industry boundaries.
- "B" as Business Design innovation may exactly describe what ride-hailing is all about by overcoming and substituting the traditional car ownership model. Business Design innovation goes beyond traditional product innovation as it defines an entire new mobility ecosystem. As will be discussed, especially the architecture of platform companies enables such players to redefine the way to compete. Besides, by deploying asset-light strategies, they stand in stark contrast with respect to their financial structure if compared with the traditional asset-heavy automotive OEMs or urban railway operators.
- "C" like connectivity and car-to-car communication is realized through advanced 5G technologies, driver assist, and infotainment solutions. By providing a real-time car-to-car communication and fleet learning environment, new safety and infotainment solutions are realized.
- "D" like the digitalization of the car as well as of the complex processes of automotive OEMs from R&D and manufacturing to marketing, sales, and after-market services increases efficiency and will define new customer use cases.
- "E" as the electrification of the powertrain, either as electric pure play or as plug-in hybrid powertrain, is driven by Tesla and the likes. It is also the poster boy of how fundamentally and fast innovative technologies change traditional industries and challenge incumbents to revitalize their strategies and Business Designs.

From all those technological disruptions of the automotive, or even broader, mobility ecosystem, the Business Design innovations are of paramount interest, as they fundamentally reshape customer use cases and competition. Ride-hailing is at the forefront of such trends in urban mobility.

3.2 Decoding Strategic Value: Uber's 10C Business Designs

Uber was founded as UberCap in 2009 based on the vision to develop a smartphone application (app) that enables its user to order a ride in the most convenient and personal way. Ride-hailing, as the term was established then for this kind of service, is a double-sided platform matching a rider's demand to travel from point A to B with a driver who is registered on the platform willing to satisfy the rider's demand with his own car (Shaheen, 2018). As, at least in its origin, neither the drivers are on Uber's payroll nor the driver's cars on Uber's balance sheet, the platform is perceived as asset-light and, therefore, easily to be scaled. The company was rebranded in 2011 in Uber Technologies Inc. (Uber, 2019b).

Already a year after its inauguration, first ride-hailing services were offered in San Francisco at a price 1.5 times higher than traditional taxis. Since then, Uber revolutionized urban mobility. The company levered its business internationally by offering its services in 100 cities by 2012, 500 cities till 2016, and 900 municipalities by 2020. Uber built a stronghold in its US home market but extended its business as well to Europe and other international markets. Besides, Uber supplemented its original high-end Uber Black services by UberX for more price-sensitive riders and Uber Pool for ride-sharing. Also in 2012, Uber kicked off its first test trials in food-delivery, specifically for on-demand ice cream delivery services, followed by the bundling of those activities in 2015 in a stand-alone business unit named Uber Eats.

Further extensions of Uber's portfolio have been Uber Freight, a B2B platform for freight companies and carriers, and Uber Air which intended to offer favorable air taxi services by 2023 but was divested in 2020 or the acquisition of JUMP for e-bike rental services. The latter service was merged with Lime's e-scooter business as part of Uber's investment in Lime and streamlining of its portfolio during the pandemic.

Nowadays, Uber is established as one of the global leading mobility and food-delivery as-a-service platforms serving 98 million monthly active users (Uber, 2021a). The platform's services, being available in more than 71 countries, generated gross bookings of $19.5 billion in its most recent quarter (Uber, 2021b).

3.2.1 Competitive Strategy and Purpose (CS)

Uber's original purpose was to become a game changer in smart and seamless urban mobility creating the dominant on-demand ride-hailing and ride-sharing app-based platform and substituting thereby the traditional car ownership model. A strong belief that ride-hailing is a platform Business Design with a winner-takes-all pattern is deeply engrained in its corporate DNA. Therefore, growth scaling is a core pillar of Uber's corporate strategy.

The platform strategy is grounded on the assumption of strong cross- and same-side network effects and that those network effects build a "vicious ride-hailing circle," as described by Fig. 3.1: By entering a new city with its ride-hailing service,

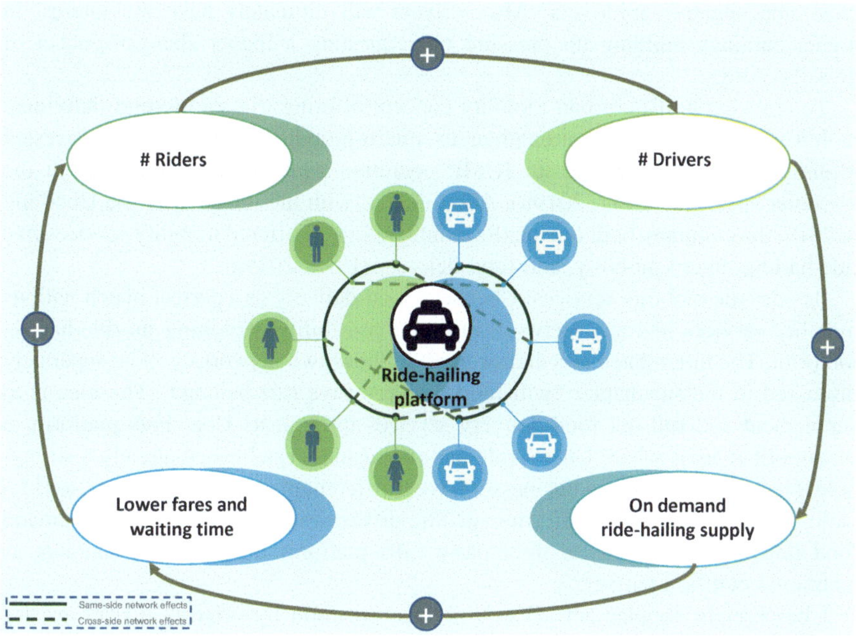

Fig. 3.1 Uber's ride-hailing platform approach built upon cross- and same-side network effects

the starting point for Uber is to assign as many as possible drivers offering rides on its platform. The number of drivers serves as the springboard for cross-side network effects. The more drivers offer their ride-hailing service on a platform, the shorter the waiting time and the price-per-mile for the ride, increasing ultimately the platform attractiveness for the riders. As more and more riders lock on to the app, a second cross-side network effect is set into motion. As higher utilization rates mean lower idle time and higher earnings for the drivers, further drivers get attracted by rising rider numbers. The latter leads back to square one of this ride-hailing circle intensifying rider and driver lock-in and strengthening the revenue and cash flow performance of the platform. As the costs to build the platform have a more one-time, fix-cost pattern, the operating unit costs per ride should drop with the increasing number of rides (Uber, 2019b), enabling the early innovator to achieve a dominant market share.

Same-side network effects on the riders' side might be realized by applying analytics and big data approaches on rider preferences, routs, demand patterns and peaks, as well as traffic information. As more and more riders join a platform and based on the according multitude of customer data, the platform might optimize routs, reduce the time for the drive, and additionally might individualize offered services along customer preferences.

However, there might as well be certain limitations within this vicious circle. As the platform attractiveness is foremost based upon lowest costs per ride for the customer this might be to the detriment of the driver's interest, leading to cross-side negative spillovers. Also, drivers will ultimately have the interest in higher earnings building up pressure on requesting a higher share-of-pocket of gross bookings.

To realize a holistic urban mobility concept offering true end-to-end individual mobility solutions and to strengthen its micro-mobility business, Uber invested recently in Lime by selling its JUMP operation against an equity stake in the e-scooter specialist (Uber, 2019b). Additionally, with the relaunch of the Uber app in 2019, the company built one platform integrating all offered mobility services like ride-hailing, micro-mobility, and food-delivery (Uber, 2019a).

Besides the mobility services, Uber sees food-delivery as a perfect match with its mobility services and as a network bridging possibility exploiting its ride-hailing footprint. The interrelatedness and strength of those two networks will be separately discussed in the subchapter "will food delivery save ride-hailing?" The idea is to supplement and roll out food-delivery services through its Uber Eats platform in metropolitan areas where Uber's ride-hailing business established already a stronghold. Nevertheless, the two businesses have a different platform architecture, as ride-hailing is a double-sided platform matching drivers and riders, whereas on-demand food delivery is typically a three-party (3P) platform integrating restaurants as additional platform partner.

Uber Freight supplements Uber's service portfolio by offering a platform for carrier and freight business services. But also here, platform architectures differ. The common ground of ride-hailing as double-sided platform and food-delivery as 3P platform is that both serve B2C markets. In contradiction, Uber Freight encounters as a B2B platform a totally different strategic architecture as well as market and competitive landscape.

In the ride-hailing core business Lyft is Uber's key competitor in its US home market, while on the international ride-hailing market prominent players are Didi for the Chinese market and Ola and Grab in the Indian and Southeast Asian markets (AD Little, 2020). Further, indirect competition exists with OEMs offering mobility services like Daimler's and BMW's ride-hailing joint venture Share Now or GM's Cruise, as well as with car rental services like Sixt, Hertz, Budget, or EuropCar. Additionally, traditional taxi companies might be the closest competitors of ride-hailing platforms on the level of local municipalities. From an overall urban mobility lens, also e-scooters and e-bike platforms compete with ride-hailing, at least for short distances. Due to missing switching costs, alternative offerings just a fingertip away, and riders focusing on cheapest rides, competitive pressure is significant within the ride-hailing market space.

As a 3P platform Uber Eats competes with an even more diverse set of competitors: Direct peers are Grubhub/Just Eat Takeaway, DoorDash, Deliveroo, or Delivery Hero. But meal kit-providing companies such as HelloFresh, Kochbox, Gobble, or Home Chef are competing as well from a customer USP point of view with Uber Eats by offering shipments of packaged food ingredients including the recipe on how to cook the food at home to customers' doorstep. From a broader industry boundary view, also restaurants and fast-food outlets have to be seen as contenders.

Uber Freight is perceived as a digitally enabled, reliable freight broker. The B2B Uber Freight platform competes directly with global logistics champions like UPS, FedEx, or DHL as well as national and local fleet operators. The latter developed in the last years, by recognizing their competitive exposure to Uber, their own proprietary digital platforms enabling digital booking of carriers. A direct challenger of Uber Freight is Flexport, which is a fully cloud-based freight forwarder, offering shipments via truck, rail, and air.

3.2.2 Core Value Proposition (CV)

Uber's vision statement "we ignite opportunity by setting the world in motion" frames the platform's purpose. From a broad core value proposition lens, Uber aims, through its offerings, to become the number one service provider of individual mobility and logistics services in the global metropolitan market by connecting through its platform supply and demand, specifically for individual mobility, on-demand food-delivery and freight services. Nevertheless, the three platforms of Uber, as pinpointed in Fig. 3.2, address different use cases and have distinct core value propositions.

Uber's mobility on-demand platform promises the rider convenience, reliability, as well as time and safety advantages on their ride combined with a competitive and transparent pricing. The relative USP in comparison with other modes of urban

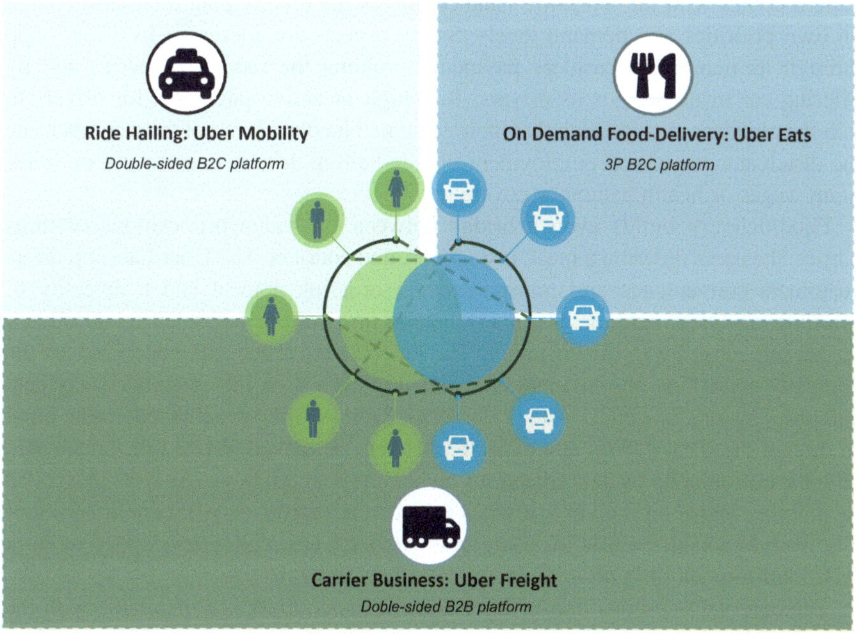

Fig. 3.2 Uber's corporate portfolio and platform Business Designs

transportation, especially cabs, is foremost the convenience aspect by comparable pricing: By ordering a ride by a fingertip on the smartphone and having a significant number of drivers assigned to the platform, waiting times should be shortened for riders, picking the latter up at their desired location. Contactless and integrated digital payment solutions like Apple Pay or credit or debit cards should contribute to the convenience perception of the ride. Additionally, the digital route tracking and optimization on Uber's app offer multiple advantages: The app calculates the best possible route from pickup to drop-off even before the rider starts the journey and is visible for both parties in advance, whereas the driver is obliged to follow the proposed route. This avoids the potential hassle with traditional taxi services in case the driver takes an extra mile or does simply not know how to navigate to the drop-off point. A reliable and transparent price setting is achieved in advance to the ride as the price for the ride and the estimated duration are calculated digitally based on the optimized route setting and current traffic diagnostics. Trust is addressed by deploying in-car camera systems, driver ratings, and Uber's reward system which provides the driver a bonus based on customer satisfaction.

The challenge for Uber's ride hailing platform is its double-sided nature, as it has to offer as well a convincing value proposition for its drivers. The latter is designed around financial rewards, capacity utilization, work-life flexibility, and safety. The first two are closely connected, as Uber's big data and analytics capabilities enable precise demand forecast and promise thereby the driver higher utilization rates compared with the concept of traditional taxi firms. The implicitly reduced idle time will increase the driver's earnings. Uber argues that the self-employment pattern comes with the work-life balance bon as the drivers plan their shifts based on own priorities and demand levels. Safety aspects are addressed by Uber's app through its mandatory cashless payments avoiding the risk of robberies and by offering car insurance for its drivers. But, high incentive payments for drivers to join the platform may indicate that their generated income does not fully compensate the disadvantages of self-employment of ride-hailing drivers missing out on minimum wages or health insurance coverage.

Food-delivery builds even a bridge between the value propositions of three parties, the users ordering a meal, restaurants, and couriers. The Uber Eats app offers customers convenience and transparency in ordering a meal and a diversity of offerings. By localizing the customer, the app first indicates all open food-delivery restaurants close by to the customer. The latter's preferences are addressed, as the company applies its big data and analytics approaches on the customer's payment and order history as well as taste preferences. Transparency is achieved, as the point of time of the meal pickup and expected delivery is tracked in real time and shared with the customer by push notifications on her or his smartphone. As Uber integrated its mobility and food-delivery services in one app, customers will benefit additionally from financial rewards for using both services. Fast deliveries depend on both B2C platforms on high driver availability (Uber, 2019b).

The core value proposition of Uber Eats for its couriers is comparable with the one offered by its ride-hailing service for its drivers. The only main difference might be that the competition between drivers is more intense as in food delivery multiple modes of transport, meaning scooters or bikes besides cars are used for the delivery of a meal. But, by orchestrating both platforms, Uber promises synergies as drivers may work for both services, thereby reducing idle time and optimizing their income.

The third party of the Uber Eats platform are the restaurants offering their meals through the app. The core value proposition for restaurants is to generate additional revenues by extending their services beyond their in-house restaurant dining offers to home-delivery customers without the need to invest in own delivery logistics. This played out as a significant advantage for restaurant owners during the COVID-19 induced lockdown and social distancing measures where restaurants have been forced to close. Ease of use in the onboarding process and latest data on menus, pricing, or opening hours optimize the interface between the restaurants, customers, and Uber's app. Additionally, and based on Uber Eats' algorithms, individualized marketing campaigns, depending on customer eating preferences, are enabled.

The advantages of B2C ride-hailing and food-delivery platforms have been translated lately to the B2B freight market, where carriers and brokers were the traditional players to coordinate and fulfill shipments. [1] Uber Freight's B2B platform promises as overall value proposition to overcome inefficiencies of the traditional trucking and carrier industry by digitalizing freight delivery processes on its platform. The platform does not only offer seamless logistic services booking but also offers price transparency and reliability, which are even more important in B2B than in B2C markets. Uber Freight supports companies in need of carrier services by a convenient process of requesting logistic offers and booking such logistic services. Uber algorithms update price settings on a daily basis guaranteeing full price transparency. The digitalization of the freight booking process through the Uber Freight app should reduce overall freight costs and increase efficiency by online, on-demand bookings. For such clients, the all-time availability of logistic services increases their flexibility and the potential to focus own activities on their core capabilities.

Uber leverages its established B2C platforms to facilitate freight logistics by taking over the role of a technology-enabled, reliant, and cost-of-ownership efficient freight broker. As Uber Freight is also a double-sided marketplace, the second platform participant, the carriers, aims to increase their efficiency by applying Uber's simplified workflow to reduce standstill times of their truck fleet and to decrease their fleet's cost of ownership. On Uber Freight's platform, carriers have access to all uploaded requests, routes, and price settings. Uber's algorithms optimize loading specifications taking into account additional shipments or follow-up loads with the intent to decrease empty rides and increase utilization rates of their platform partner's fleets. Carriers are offered a multitude of filter functions like truck type, time, route, location of client, or price per mile. The agreement between the

[1] Brokers are intermediaries facilitating freight transport services between the shippers and the carriers offering supplementary services like contract documentation, pricing, or insurance, but have no ownership of truck assets. Carriers own such truck assets and are responsible for the freight transport from pickup to drop-off.

carrier and the company looking for logistic services is fully digitalized as a confirmation of the transportation agreement is automatically triggered after acceptance and sent to the parties. Integrated digital payment solutions support transparency as well as trust and ease the overall process flow further. Like in the Uber ride-hailing app, rating systems enable Uber Freight participants to build long-term client relationships. Besides, an instant communication of warehouse and backlog data is ensured.

Other bets of Uber like Uber Air or its autonomous drive and robotics division ATG have been either divested or closed due to subcritical scale and the financial needs triggered by the pandemic's negative impact on Uber's ride-hailing core business. Nevertheless, this is of strategic importance as Uber argued for a long while that full autonomous drive technologies will provide the advantage to ultimately substitute the driver and, therefore, eliminate the most crucial cost factor in ride-hailing. With the divestment decision of Uber's own self-driving technologies to Aurora, the company is now dependent on third parties, especially automotive OEMs, to develop fully autonomous drive technologies (Financial Times, 2020c). Autonomous drive solution might come delayed to the ride-hailing market.

3.2.3 Customer and Markets (CM)

Ride-hailing platforms connect drivers with riders, whereas the latter are described by Uber as Monthly Active Platform Consumers (MAPC) (Uber, 2019b). Ride-hailing platforms serve as double-sided platforms. On the riders' side, Uber's MAPCs are typically the digital- and smartphone-affluent generations X, Y, and Z (AD Little, 2020). A latest US survey found that slightly less than half of all US citizens in the reference group aged between 18 and 29, followed by the 30–49-year-olds, are using ride-hailing platforms already. As Uber services are app based, smartphone ownership is mandatory for the efficient use of its services. The second limitation is that its services are foremost offered in urban, but not in rural areas.

Since its inauguration, Uber adjusted its focus from an exclusive black-cap service to ride-hailing offerings for price-sensitive digital natives. It might seem counterintuitive that higher-income individuals tend to have a higher ride-hailing utility rate (Reihart, 2018), but this might be explained by their technology affluence. Uber argues to have a global approach, but does focus on the Americas and Europe. The company does also focus on metropolitan centers. Uber's services are available in 900 cities, but 25% of Uber's ride-hailing revenues just stem from the five megacities Los Angeles, New York City, San Francisco, London, and Sao Paolo.

The second customer group of Uber's double-sided ride-hailing platform are its drivers, who are typically not part of Uber's original Business Design as they are working typically on a self-employment contractual level. This is also a significant difference to taxi firms and leads often to frictions with the latter. In principle, every person owning a valid driving license, a car meeting the companies' requirements, and a smartphone, as well as having passed a background check, might become an Uber driver. The company stresses work time flexibility as a USP for its drivers as the latter can decide on the frequency and time length of their ride offering. Older riders often use the ride-hailing payments as second or post-retirement income.

Food-delivery is a three-party platform as such apps connect users ordering a meal, couriers, and restaurants: An Uber Eats driver picks up the restaurant's food and delivers it to the end customer who ordered the food on the Uber Eats platform. As proximity between the parties is crucial for fast delivery, Uber Eats does, as in its ride-hailing service, focus on metropolitan areas.

The customer side of Uber Eats and Uber Mobility is slightly synergistic: for both services are smartphone connectivity and digital affluence mandatory. Besides, Uber reported that its riders use the app often also for Uber Eats orders. These double users of the company's services order more than twice as many trips for both, riding and food-delivery, on average compared with single-service users. Whereas Uber Eats customer's age is similar to its riders, with top users in their 20s and second those between 30 and 44 years, the income structure is flip-sided as customers of the lowest income group favor most food-delivery services, whereas food-delivery usage is decreasing with higher-income levels. Uber accounts food-delivery customers also as part of its reported MAPCs (Uber, 2019b). In the first quarter of 2021, close to 100 million MAPCs used Uber's services.

Uber Eats drivers are even more overlapping with Uber's ride-hailing ones, and multiple drivers offer their services for both applications to reduce their idle time and increase their income. Restaurants, as the third party on the food-delivery platform, could register without a charge on Uber Eats' platform to offer takeaway food, thereby increasing their meals availability and revenues.

The significant impact of the COVID-19 pandemic on Uber's Business Design is exemplified in Fig. 3.3 describing the shift in gross bookings of its two main platforms, ride-hailing and food-delivery.

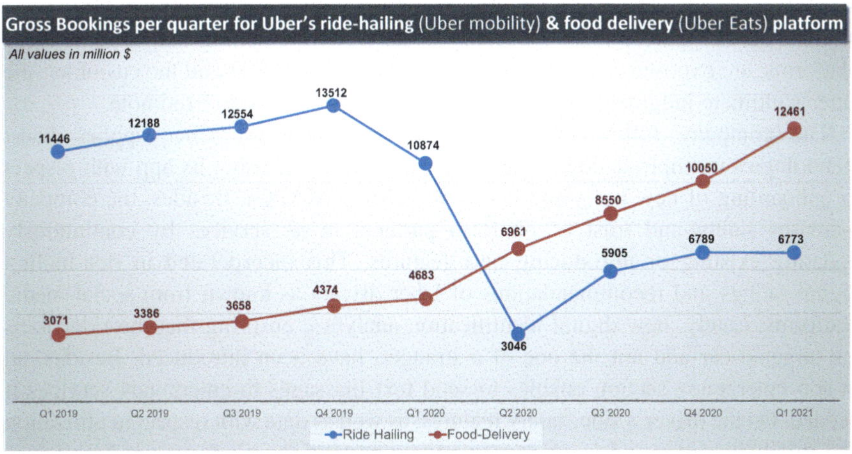

Fig. 3.3 Gross bookings development for Uber's main platforms ride-hailing and on-demand food-delivery. *Data source*: Uber Technologies, Inc. supplementary data on Q1 2021 earnings (Uber, 2021b)

The demand for ride-hailing services dropped off a cliff at the early days of the pandemic and decreased by close to 75% in spring 2020 due to the induced social distancing measures and lockdowns to combat the coronavirus, whereas on-demand food-delivery services skyrocketed. The latter increased threefold from pre-pandemic levels till early 2021. Lately, ride-hailing services recovered partially due to the progress in vaccine programs. Nevertheless, the decomposition of Uber's platform business volumes is nowadays still flip-sided, if compared with pre-pandemic levels. Whereas in Q1 2019 ride-hailing contributed 79% to Uber's consolidated gross bookings and food-delivery 21%, 2 years later in Q1 2021, food-delivery represented with 65% the bulk of gross bookings, and ride-hailing stood still at just a third of Uber's gross bookings (Uber, 2021b, p. 5). Nevertheless, total gross bookings increased in Q1 2021 by 22% year over year and by a third in comparison to the last quarter.

Uber Freight is, as described prior, in contradiction to ride-hailing and food-delivery a B2B service by connecting as double-sided platform companies who want their goods to be shipped with carriers. The service is offered foremost in the USA, but as well in selected European countries. Uber Fright expects to lever its business especially for small and midsized companies in the freight market and intends to scale their business. Shippers are enabled by Uber's freight platform to create and tender shipments, to agree on capacity on demand and pricing upfront, and to track shipments in real time. The freight platform promises efficiency improvements in comparison to traditional freight brokerage providers.

3.2.4 Customer Relationship (CR)

Uber's customer onboarding and capture is at first sight for all its service lines and platform partners a pure digital play through its app and platform. But, as the ultimate service perceptions, especially of its B2C ride-hailing and food-delivery platforms, are exposed to a direct interface between the driver and the customer, the latter's ultimate judgment on service quality has also a personalized note.

The company follows a double-edged CR strategy: Uber applies latest technologies to improve consistently the convenience in using its app with respect to onboarding of new users and usage by existing MAPCs. Besides, the company increases safety and trust of platform partners in its services by continuously updating existing or introducing new features. This incorporated in ride-hailing digital ratings and recommendations of Uber drivers as known from social media platforms. Lately, new digital identification analytics, ensuring that the rider joins the targeted car and not the one of a stranger, have been introduced. Besides, an in-app emergency section enables to send text massages to emergency services if needed. On the driver's side, safety features, as well as data with respect to utilization and ride-hailing demand levels, are ingrained parts of the platform and build close ties between the riders and Uber. For the B2B freight platform, the 24/7 possibility of booking shipments, e-mail notifications on critical milestones along the shipment execution, and real-time tracking of the freight load are examples of how customer services are tailored around the distinct use case.

Additionally, the personal and intimate note of the customer-platform interface is addressed by Uber's brand strategy, which should create an emotional bond to the platform. The consistent brand perception might have been a core reason why Uber integrated its two B2C platform services in one app.

3.2.5 Channels (CH)

Uber's three platforms are pure digital plays, requiring a smartphone, and an online access in addition to Uber's app. Therefore, Uber's communication strategy is foremost build around more or less all digital channels like social media networks, digital marketing initiatives, and advertisements or sponsored digital campaigns.

As cross- and same-side network effects are believed to scale Uber's platform, word-of-mouth initiatives and promotions in all customer segments, but as well for riders, drivers, and restaurant owners play a supplementary role to digital communication and marketing initiatives.

Additionally, referrals and other financial incentives are used to onboard and lock in riders or food-ordering consumers as well as drivers and restaurant owners on the platform: Examples are free rides for first-time platform users and referral programs incentivizing existing riders of the platform with customer credits in case of successfully gaining new MAPCs for the platform. Supplementary, drivers are incentivized to gain or enable Uber to successfully hire new drivers. All in all, those programs should bolster word-of-mouth support by the existing platform users. Only very selectively, Uber uses traditional print or TV marketing campaigns.

3.2.6 Core Assets (CA)

As Uber is a typical platform firm, the company has an asset-light Business Design, and intangible instead of tangible assets shape its true competitive advantage. Comparing a ride-hailing platform firm with a traditional taxi company exemplifies the impact of this difference. As Uber's drivers are still self-employed in most jurisdictions the company offers its services, neither the employees are on its payroll nor the cars of the drivers are part of Uber's balance sheet. The opposite holds true for traditional taxi firms. A ride-hailing platform has advantages in terms of more flexible cost structures and offers a much easier scalability of its Business Design.

Uber's platform and app technology as well as its IP are its core ingredients of intangible assets. The company continuously invests in newest technologies like artificial intelligence, the development of analytic algorithms, and big data approaches to lever such assets for ride-hailing, food-delivery, and logistic services: The company applies diagnostics on historical data and matches them with data on the current traffic observations for a fast and seamless delivery of its mobility and food-delivery services. Besides, analytics models are applied to get an in-depth understanding of its riders' and diner's preferences, to model rider and order demand, and to run its pricing models based on real-time data of driver supply and rider or diner demand.

By comparing the locations of potential riders and drivers based on geo-location mapping data, the platform analyzes a nearly unlimited amount of potential rider/driver matches with respect to a driver's distance to the point of pickup, targeted route, calculated ride time, real-time traffic, and other data points. The app ultimately indicates for the chosen driver the fastest way to reach out to the rider's pickup point and the targeted drop-off destination. At the final destination, the app sends a push notification to the rider's smartphone for final confirmation of the ride quality and safety recognition. The latter is further supported by the app's tracking functionality (Uber, 2019b). Last but not the least, Uber invests consistently in the optimizing of its cash- and contactless payment functionalities, a must-have especially during corona times.

A further mission-critical intangible asset is Uber's brand. As the ride-hailing and the food-delivery market are, despite their young age, already in a competitive endgame and network effects are thought to create winner-takes-all markets, an empowered and trustworthy international brand might serve as an important differentiator and competitive advantage. In addition, Uber's IP in autonomous drive supplemented its intangible asset portfolio, but was divested lately to Aurora.

On the human resources side, Uber represents as well a typical platform company. Employees and talents, as intangible assets, are mission-critical. Especially for talents in highly demanded technology niches like AI, platform design, or algorithm development, Uber competes with other digital natives and automotive incumbents.

3.2.7 Core Capabilities (CC)

The establishment, sustainability, and appropriability of competitive advantage set core capabilities apart from necessary, but not mission-critical capabilities. Uber's global double-sided and 3P platform and app development excellence is definitely such a core capability.

The management of its technological architecture includes not only the development but also the continuous scaling and redesign of the Uber platform architecture. This might play an even more prominent role since the integration of the company's ride-hailing and food-delivery app. The permanent update with latest technologies is mandatory not only for its supply and demand matching but also for its routing and payment functionalities. Only such technological capabilities allowed Uber to build an efficient network which serves consistently millions of drivers, consumers, restaurants, and other platform partners at the same time.

USPs like convenience, a seamless driver-rider matching, a smooth pick up navigation, or algorithms for decreased waiting times require deep-routed technology skills. Big data management, artificial intelligence, and analytics paired with mapping and visualization technologies are therefore core capabilities. Such technologies must also ensure the platform's robustness as Uber's services have to handle a massive amount of data with respect to trips, distance, locations, waiting time, or prices. Additionally, such customer data have to be matched with real-time traffic data and driver availability. Autonomous drive knowledge was seen for a long while as well as a core capability by Uber itself and analysts, but due to Uber's divestment became less relevant, at least near time.

The importance of Uber's brand and image might have been underestimated in the early days of the company's corporate development, characterized by multiple top-management issues. This changed lately. Uber's board of directors was restructured to adress critisism by capital markets, regulators and municipalities, Uber logo was softly redesigned and Uber's B2C services integrated in one single Uber app. All those initiatives might highlight today's brand and culture management awareness.

Last but not the least, Uber's operational excellence of its market and operations teams with their market specific knowledge in launching and scaling platform services in cities around the world is mission-critical. These teams are Uber's human interface to support consumers, drivers, couriers, restaurants, shippers, and carriers. And, they play also an important role for managing relationships with cities and regulators.

3.2.8 Core-Ecosystem Partners (CE)

One important and distinct ecosystem partner are regulatory authorities. Ride-hailing companies, being perceived as core representatives in shaping gig-economy working conditions, faced increasing regulatory scrutiny lately. Where regulatory tensions questioning the ride-hailing business model are prevalent, the value at stake, especially on Business Design sustainability and brand image, is high. The fast growth of ride-hailing companies and battles with local taxi firms, as the latter felt exposed to ride-hailing threats of substitution, forced local authorities and municipalities to strengthen regulatory oversight. Some US states as well as European cities have adjusted their local regulatory framework to ride-hailing services. A multitude of legally enforced initiatives ranging from claiming ride-hailing services as illegal like in Copenhagen, limiting the number of ride-hailing cars, to requesting specific passenger transport license as for taxi drivers or minimum wages to appease embattled local taxi firms and Uber's drivers have been initiated by multiple municipalities. Lately, Uber lost an important legal ruling in its epic battle with the city of London (Financial Times, 2021g). The UK court's decision that Uber's drivers are workers and, therefore, entitled to rights such as minimum wage is seen as one of the most significant employment cases for decades.[2] As a

[2] In the UK, workers do not have the same privileges as employees, but they are better off than self-employed as being entitled to the national minimum wage and holiday pay.

consequence of the latter, Uber has to set up a workplace pension scheme. Nevertheless, a contradicting public vote in California still allows Uber to classify its drivers as independent contractors. But, being exposed to such regulatory tailwinds questioning the ride-hailing business model demands a smooth management of regulatory affairs and collaboration with municipal and legal authorities for finding suitable compromises for all involved parties.

As drivers are customers on all three Uber platforms, insurance companies are additional important ride-hailing ecosystem partners. They may provide car insurance services at competitive prices for Uber drivers. Additional insurance coverages like for illness, maternity leave, or accidents have been negotiated by Uber in most cities. For Uber Eats, insurances are also contracted for e-scooters and e-bikes. For Uber Freight, insurance premiums play an even more prominent role as the carrier's business model is typically managed from a total cost of ownership perspective.

A third pillar of partners are technology companies. On the one side, technology partnerships are important for the platform and app development; on the other side, access to latest technologies in passenger cars and trucks has a lasting impact on Uber's services. As Uber divested its autonomous in-house development activities, these partnerships have become even more crucial lately. Therefore, Uber partnered with car OEMs like Volvo, Daimler, and Toyota.

3.2.9 Corporate Organization (CO)

Despite being part of the sharing economy, Uber has a couple of clear-cut organizational and management principles. Besides Mr. Dara Khosrowshahi as CEO and Nelson Chai as CFO, the top management of the company is supplemented by nine additional managers. As the digital platform management is mission-critical for Uber's three business lines, technology capabilities and development are deeply anchored within the top management.

Besides, the three service lines Uber Mobility for its ride-hailing activities, Uber Eats as its on-demand food-delivery platform, and Uber Freight as its B2B carrier and logistics platform represent the firm's three strategic business unit organizations.

3.2.10 Cash Flow Model (CF)

Uber' net loss for 2020 was at hefty $6.8 billion as the pandemic was a significant drag on ride-hailing revenues. Nevertheless, Uber, as well as its key US competitor Lyft, reiterated their target to become at least EBITDA positive along 2021, if the number of vaccinations will let business return to normal. 2021 might become a gamechanger for the ride-hailing Business Design if such forecast would be fulfilled. And indeed, market conditions seem to recover from pandemic lows as Uber recorded in the first quarter of 2021 with $19.5 billion of gross bookings an

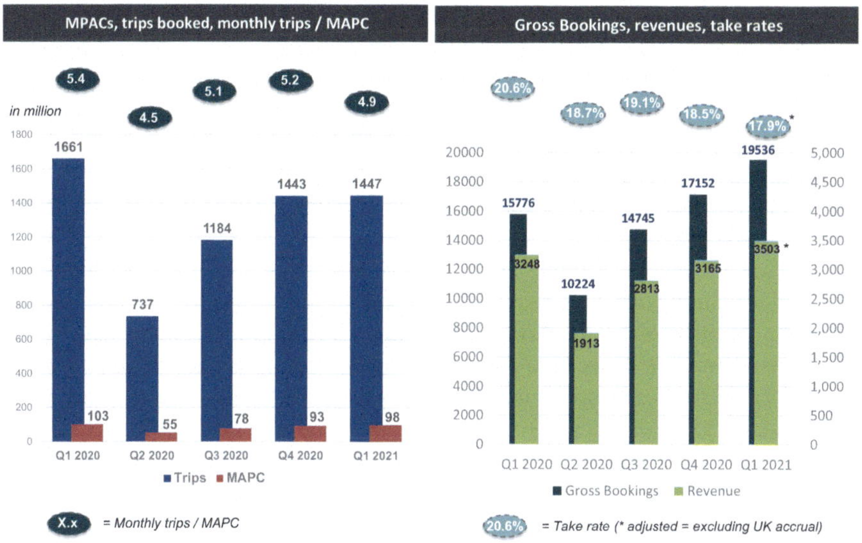

Fig. 3.4 Uber's operational and financial metrics: MAPCs, trips, trips/MAPC, gross booking, take rate, revenue

all-time high (Financial Times, 2021d). Nevertheless, adjusted[3] EBITDA was with −$359 and a −12% margin on Uber's revenues still negative in Q1 2021, despite having improved by $95 million quarter by quarter or $253 million year on year (Uber, 2021b).

The diagnostics of Uber's value drivers is a prerequisite for a sound judgement of the robustness of the Reverse DCF valuation and the likelihood of a long-term value creating ride-hailing, food-delivery, and freight logistics platform Business Design.

All three Uber platforms generate revenues through the booking of mobility services, pocketing a predefined percentage of the fee paid by their platform customers ordering such services. The overall core financials of Uber Technology, summarizing all three platforms, are provided by Fig. 3.4.

The total payment of a customer for a service is defined as gross booking, whereas the ratio gross booking per trip or order indicates the average price paid by a monthly active platform customer (MAPC) for an average ride, meal, or freight order (Uber, 2019b). Operational metrics like MAPCs, average trips per MAPC, and gross bookings as well as the take rate of Uber for its platform services are crucial drivers for defining Uber's revenue line.

[3] Adjustments in the first quarter represent foremost the $600 million accrual made for the resolution of historical claims in the UK relating to Uber's classification of drivers, which reduced on an unadjusted basis Uber's consolidated revenue to $2.9 billion and its mobility revenue to $853 million. As this reclassification is a one-time item, the further assessment references to the adjusted values.

Overall, MAPCs as well as trips on Uber's platforms collapsed during the second quarter 2020 due to the COVID-19 pandemic impacts by roughly 50% and bounced nearly back to the pre-pandemic levels at year-end 2020. Gross bookings and revenues followed a similar but less pronounced path by decreasing, respectively, by 35% and 41% between Q1 and Q2 2020. Gross bookings achieved a new quarterly high in Q1 2021 as adjusted[4] revenues with $3.5 billion, whereas the take rate on an adjusted basis decreased slightly from the pre-pandemic 20.6 to 17.9% in Q1 2021.

Uber's ride-hailing algorithms enable a dynamic pricing policy by charging riders a higher fee during demand peak times, thereby increasing gross as well as net revenues. The gross booking in ride-hailing could be decomposed in the flat or base rate and the time rate. Uber Pool charges less per person and mile in comparison to Uber X or Black as the driver may pick up or drop off other riders on the way. Nevertheless, due to the social distancing measures implemented to combat COVID-19, especially Uber Pool services faced significant headwinds and had been shut down in certain municipalities for a limited time frame. In micro-mobility, summarizing Uber's e-scooter and e-bikes business, the Company applies a usage-fee revenue model.

Uber Eats' revenue model for its food-delivery business is more complex. As it is a 3P platform, three sources of revenue exist: Uber charges a fee for each food order. Additionally, a defined percentage of the driver's fee to deliver the meal is pocketed, where the driver's price is set upon distance and duration of the food delivery. But, the third and most significant revenue source is the direct fee charged on each restaurant order, which is obviously to the detriment of restaurant owners. Whereas ride-hailing services and revenues saw a headwind, food-delivery orders and revenues profited from tailwinds during the pandemic, but did not fully compensate Uber Mobility's losses.

Uber Freight's revenue model charges a predefined brokerage service fee for each booking on its B2B platform. It is assumed that Uber undercuts peers by charging 1–3% of the total shipment price. Uber might lift brokerage fees once a substantial carrier market share is achieved (Wall Street Journal, 2019). Other revenue sources of Uber are not material.

Uber's Adjusted EBITDA was in all quarters still negative, but the EBITDA margin recovered from the early pandemic lows within the last quarters, as described by Fig. 3.5. The walk from gross bookings to Uber's revenues is very specific and tailored to its platform Business Design: For example, in its ride-hailing business Uber historically receives round about 30% of the price paid per ride, whereas the remaining 70% are pocketed directly by the drivers. Additionally, close to 10% are paid by the platform to drivers and customers as incentive, which are separate

[4] Q1 2021 revenues stood at $2.9bn including a $600 million accrual for costs Uber forecasts to bear in the years to come to settle historical wage claims in the UK related to a landmark court defeat over worker classification that will provide drivers in the UK with extra benefits. Adjusted revenues add back the accrual and came in therefore at $3.5 billion (Uber, 2021b).

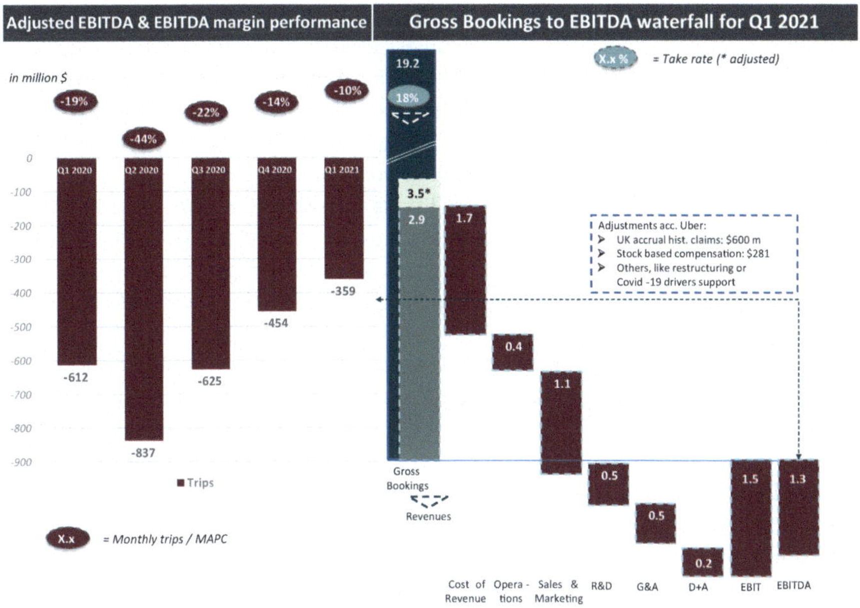

Fig. 3.5 Uber's ride-hailing revenue to EBITDA transition

and in addition to the driver's portion of the fare. Historically, these costs have been subsumed within Uber's profit and loss statement as costs of revenues as well as sales and marketing costs. In the end, these costs are an outcome of the hypercompetitive ride-hailing ecosystem where the ride-hailing firms pay referrals for the onboarding of new and bonuses for existing drivers for completing a consecutive or cumulative number of trips on the platform. Besides, significant incentives to onboard riders and diners on Uber's app are paid. Uber's gross revenue share of 30% on an average trip is reduced to a net or adjusted revenue share, described as take rate, [5] of roughly 20% of gross bookings or, for example, precisely 21.5% in Q1 2021 for its mobility platform (Uber, 2021b). Starting with the FY 2021, Uber now reports the net revenues, meaning after all driver and customer discounts, directly as its revenue line. [6]

[5] The take rates is defined as a platform's average revenue on each order, as in ride-hailing per ride or in food delivery per meal order.

[6] In its Q4 2020 financial report, Uber changed its accounting policy with respect to the recognition of excess cumulative driver payments. As formerly those have been presented within the cost of revenues, they are now directly deducted from revenues. These changes in accounting policies will lower the revenue level retrospectively, but will not impact Uber's historical loss or loss-per-share statements. Nevertheless, the diagnostics of side-payments will be less transparent in the future as directly deducted before representing net revenues.

Uber's cost levers are as well platform specific, but drivers have on all three platforms a material impact on Uber's Business Design. Although its drivers are self-employed and are not on Uber's payroll, significant incentives are paid to drivers to onboard them on the platform, to lure them away from competing platforms, or to cover claimed disadvantages of their self-employment by bonus payments. The before-mentioned costs of revenue as well as costs of sales and marketing included foremost such bonuses for referring new drivers to Uber's platform, for achieving a defined number of rides peer week or a number of consecutive trips (Uber, 2019b). Besides driver acquisition and retention, sales and marketing expenses cover also customer retention costs like customer vouchers and promotions as well as expenses for marketing campaigns.

A further crucial cost and investment lever are Uber's research and development (R&D) activities to further enhance the platform performance. Additionally, headquarters costs as finance and HR are covered under the header general and administrative costs. As stock-based compensations have a material impact, Uber historically deducts them for the calculation of its adjusted EBITDA.

Especially excessive driver incentive payments and rider referral bonuses, high R&D and platform cost, and stock-based compensations led consistently to negative EBITDA's and net profits of Uber Inc. As Uber's business still burns also cash flow, for the long-term sustainability of Uber's platform the further improvement of its cost drivers is mandatory. Recent discussions and legal disputes, especially triggered in London, of reclassifying drivers to Uber employees are further threats for Uber's cost structure. Better compensation for its drivers will either push Uber further away from profitability, or, if customers are charged higher prices, the latter may switch to other mobility services. The city of London, one of Uber's top five served megacities, may be ground zero for Uber's problems right now, but the issue is an international and even existential one for its business model. Additionally, the divestment of Uber's autonomous drive division to rival Aurora in December 2020 highlighted that robo-taxis are not going to come to rescue its platform's financial sustainability anytime soon.

Nevertheless, Uber and Lyft confirmed their target to become EBITDA positive in 2021. Additionally, Didi's performance in China provided lately empirical evidence that ride-hailing may become a profitable winner-takes-all platform by processing four-fifths of all domestic orders despite fierce competition in Chinese megacities and urban areas (Economist, 2021). All in all, the most prominent to be addressed challenge for Uber is to achieve post-pandemic breakeven and become long-term a cash flow generating platform.

3.2.11 10C Business Design Canvas for Uber

Having those strategic diagnostics of the ten modules of Uber's Business Design on hand, Fig. 3.6 provides a holistic canvas of the ride-hailing platform innovator's Business Design.

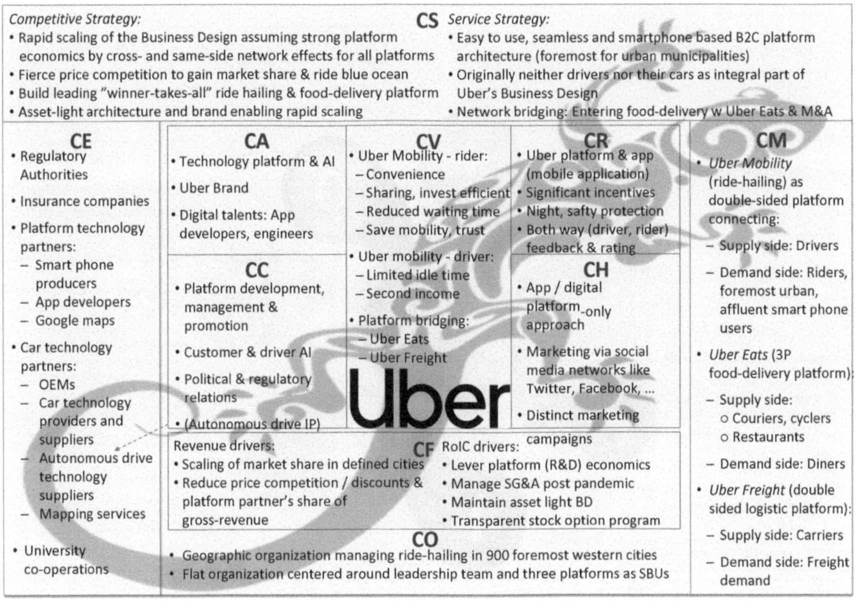

Fig. 3.6 10C Business Design canvas: Uber

3.3 Decoding Platform Value: Double-Sided Ride-Hailing Platforms

The strength of a platform Business Design, as defined in Chap. 1, is dependent on the health, defensibility, and dominance of its network. The question, if ride-hailing overall and Uber specifically enjoys the advantages of a sustainable and scalable platform, may be answered by evaluating the eight criteria of powerful platform patterns, as summarized by Fig. 3.7: The platform's architecture, its scalability, its competitiveness, the strength of same-side and cross-side network effects, the pattern of platform clusters (fragmentated versus integrated), the risk of disintermediation, the risk of multihoming, and the potential of building connected, reinforcing platforms which offer distinct synergies.

- *Platform architecture*: Ride-hailing platforms are B2C service platforms. As they match riders' interest to travel from A to B with drivers' availability, they have a double-sided platform architecture. Ride-hailing platforms compete foremost on price, service availability, and quality.
- *Platform scalability*: Ride-hailing platforms do not own the driver's car, being advantaged by balance sheet light Business Designs. Besides, the drivers themselves do not huck on the platform's income statement, as they are, at least in their traditional form, self-employed. From a platform view, the platform owner just facilitates between the rider and the driver the journey from the pickup location to

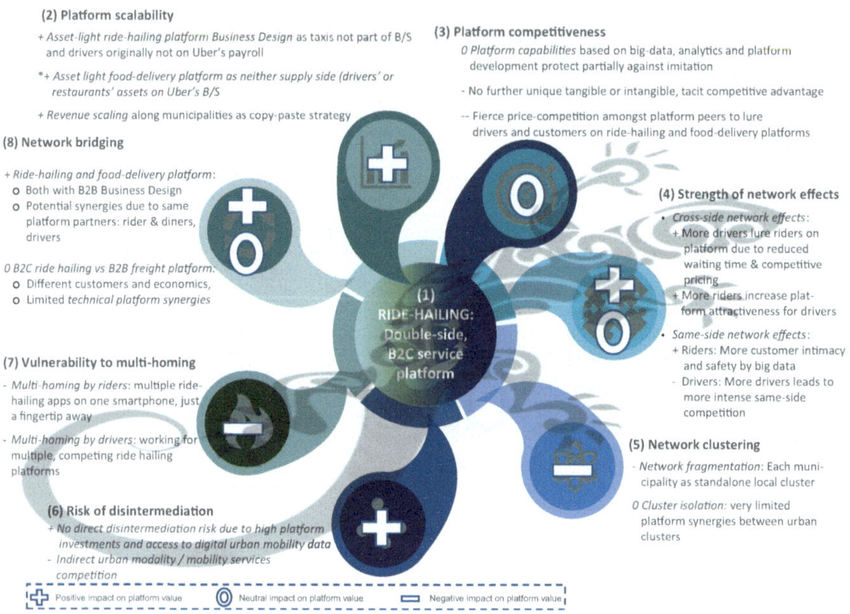

Fig. 3.7 Ride-hailing platform value and its eight strategic platform levers

the drop-off location in a seamless and efficient way. The asset-light platform architecture enables Uber and the likes to realize low costs per ride and requires limited Invested Capital to extend the platform. This fosters the scalability of ride-hailing platforms.

A strong revenue scaling architecture is also realized, as empirical evidence proved that ride-hailing platforms could easily be extended from one municipality to the next, what might be described as ride-hailing's "municipality hopping" design.

- *Platform competitiveness*: Uber's competitive advantage rests on a set of distinct technological platform capabilities like digital platform development and management, analytics paired with high-volume real-time traffic and demand data aggregation, as well as digital rider and driver intimacy technologies. This skill set is engrained in Uber's DNA and protects, at least partially, competitive imitation.

  Nevertheless, a caveat especially of ride-hailing and on-demand food-delivery Business Designs is the fierce price competition. Such value destructive competition is initiated by ride-hailing peers to lure drivers as well as customers on their platform. In the end, this might lead to a zero-value gain game, as platform competitors will most probable immediately retaliate.

  Additionally, ride-hailing platforms miss out on further differentiating competitive advantages like the distinct mRNA know-how of COVID-19 biotech platforms or creativity and fast investments in original content of streaming platforms.

- *Strength of network effects:* Ride-hailing platforms are a showcase that cross- and same-side network effects have to be separately evaluated.
- *Cross-side network effects* mimic Uber's vicious circle: By hiring more drivers on the platform, the average waiting time of riders as well as fares should drop, what may lure more riders on the platform. More riders will positively backfire on drivers, as more customers mean less idle time for taxi drivers and increased income potentials, therefore increasing the platform's attractiveness for drivers amplifying the platform's positive cross-side network effects.
- *Same-side network effects* are more complex: On the customers side, a higher number of customers offers more insights in demand patterns, rider preferences, as well as traffic and route data, which might make platform, big data, and analytics investments more attractive for the platform owner. The technology investments might reinforce ride-hailing quality and perception, ultimately increasing the platform's attractiveness for riders.
- On the driver's side, an increasing number of drivers will increase competition and might reduce income perspectives. Nevertheless, an increasing number of drivers, as on the customer side, make investments of the platform owner more reasonable. The exploitation of latest technologies might offer drivers advantages. For example, the combination of analytics with GPS data enables platforms to send drivers new requests for pickups close to their current trip or passenger drop-off location, reducing idle time and the risk that a driver will join another platform for executing the next ride.

- *Pattern of platform clusters*: Ride-hailing platforms have the caveat to share a fragmented network pattern. Each municipality is more or less its own regional network cluster with own regulatory necessities. Uber's original assessment that ride-hailing is a globally highly integrated platform was empirically proven, at least partially, as wrong, otherwise Uber would not have reduced or even quit its presence in multiple, especially Asian countries like China or India.
  Also the synergies between the local ride-hailing clusters of megacities seem to be limited as riders and drivers interact with network members outside their home municipality only very occasionally.
- *Disintermediation* might be of limited risk for ride-hailing platforms as the investment in platforms and apps as well as in underlying technologies and capabilities is significant, but at the same time mandatory. The high investments serve as a formidable barrier of entry for latecomers or competing modes of transportation. For example, the ride-sharing JV of BMW and Daimler Share Now had to leave the US market just a year after its market entrance due to a significant cash drain. Also, a significant number of drivers have to be connected with a multitude of riders, making a circumventing of ride-hailing platforms not very likely.
- *Multi-homing* is a threat on both angles of double-sided ride-hailing platforms. This holds especially true for global megacities, where digital-affluent riders use multiple ride-hailing apps on their smartphone at the same time and deciding on a single ride simply based on waiting time, costs, and driver recommendation. But,

also the drivers sometimes work for competing ride-hailing platforms to reduce their own idle time and optimize their income.

Not surprisingly, ride-hailing apps like Uber and Lyft in the USA or Didi and its local competitors in China try to escape multi-homing by providing significant bonuses for riders if they complete a certain number of trips on their platform, trying to encourage indirectly some sort of exclusivity. At the same time, drivers are as well offered significant bonuses for being hired and to work exclusively for a platform. These strategic initiatives might limit partially multi-homing but cut further into the underlying profitability and cash flows. For most ride-hailing firms, the difference between gross- and net-revenues is an astonishing 10%-point or even more.

- *Platform bridging* of ride-hailing platforms shows a mixed performance. Micromobility services might offer a close-knit platform-bridging potential. Empowered by e-scooter and bikes, they might supplement ride-hailing services and enable an end-to-end approach by solving the last-mile problem. Food-delivery platforms, sharing B2C characteristics with ride-hailing, overlap partially by their joint pool of platform partners like drivers and may create potential customer synergies between riders and diners. Therefore, ride-hailing and on-demand food delivery might offer platform-bridging potentials, what will be discussed in more detail in the next subchapter. Nevertheless, ride-hailing platforms are a double-sided network, whereas on-demand food-delivery is a three-party (3P) network. As the latter has to integrate restaurants as additional important platform partners, they have a more complex platform structure, limiting architectural platform synergies.

A final word of caution is driven by incumbent and offline backfiring. The competitive pressure of ride-hailing platforms is amplified as they compete not only with ride-hauling platform peers, but additionally with alternative modes of transportation like local taxis, public transport, and car ownership. This hyper-competition of urban transport modalities might make it demanding for ride-hailing platforms to generate reasonable RoICs above their costs of capital and lasting cash flows within their core business.

3.4 Will Network Bridging to Three-Party Food-Delivery Platforms and M&As Save Ride-Hailing?

Most on-demand food-delivery websites and mobile applications are nowadays triple-sided platforms as they connect drivers, restaurants, and diners via their app. Nevertheless, in the last couple of years, two types of on-demand food-delivery services and, accordingly, two basic platform architectures were shaped by fast growing start-ups (Poluliakh, 2021):

- Double-sided restaurant-to-consumer food-delivery (aggregator) platforms, where the restaurant is additionally to its cooking service also responsible for the delivery process, whereas the platform owner takes over the digital ordering process and acts as an aggregator and facilitator. Aggregator platforms create customer value by offering access to and comparability of various cuisines through a single app or webpage. For the diner, they offer convenience as consumers may compare on the platform's app menus and prices across a wide variety of restaurants, review restaurant ratings, and place orders. As soon as the order is confirmed, the delivery process is transferred to the restaurant and executed by the restaurant's own couriers.

- 3P platform-to-consumer food-delivery (new delivery) platforms, where the platform owner takes over not only the aggregator role, but in addition the logistics-focused food-delivery service by orchestrating the courier services. In such new delivery platform architectures, the platform provides the logistics for its restaurant platform partners. Third-party couriers become in this model, besides the restaurants and diners, the third platform partner.

Most food-delivery platform champions started as food-delivery aggregators. But, digital-affluent diners expected more and more a seamless end-to-end process, from order placement to the food's delivery on the door step, without any redirection. Not surprisingly, most food-delivery platforms transitioned their Business Design to a 3P platform-to-consumer model.

Such 3P platform-to-consumer food-delivery Business Designs grew double-digit already before the pandemic backed by significant venture capital (VC) investments, but the pandemic served as an ultimate tailwind. US online food ordering grew with a 67% CAGR between 2015 and 2018 to a $56 billion market according Euromonitor and Goldman Sachs data. The global pre-pandemic food-delivery market was estimated at around $200 billion at four times as much (Goldman Sachs, 2019). Whereas ride-hailing apps saw massive headwinds due to the COVID-19 pandemic since spring 2020, food-delivery platforms have profited from the induced lockdown and social distancing measures. The latter gave on-demand food-delivery services an ultimate boost.

Nevertheless, on a stand-alone basis, on-demand food delivery is, as ride-hailing, exposed to a hyper-competitive environment. As it represents a three-party platform, the overall platform gross bookings have to be shared with three platform partners leading to challenging business financials: High platform discounts for first-time diners, new assigned restaurants, and incentives to couriers targeting to build a tight-knit delivery network with low waiting times became standard practice of food-delivery platforms. Especially the added cost of the courier, being typically not fully compensated by an according price-per-meal uptick, is a strain on the already meagre operating margins of food-delivery platforms. So, a crucial question might be: Will on-demand food-delivery lead to improved cash flows and offer architectural synergies if integrated into ride-hailing B2C platforms?

Uber established a first footprint in the food-delivery market by establishing Uber Eats as a stand-alone business unit. As the ride-hailing business struggled in the pandemic, the company bet on the growth of its Uber Eats division. Uber Technologies Inc. reported lately on its Q1 2021 performance call that the company

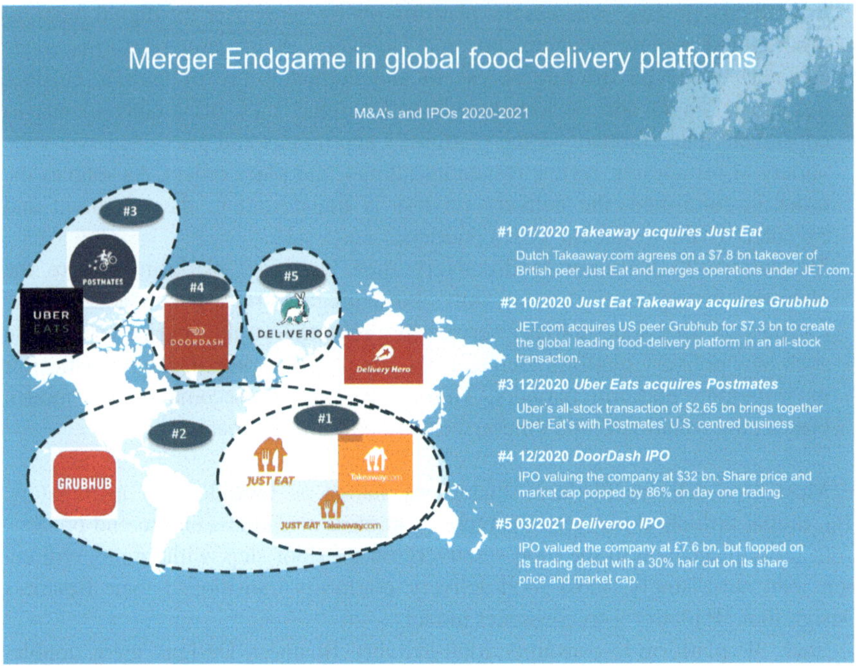

Fig. 3.8 Merger endgame and IPO frenzy within the on-demand food-delivery ecosystem. *Source*: tfX-advisory research 2021

generated revenues of adjusted $3.5 billion, with adjusted revenues in Mobility of $1.45 billion and Uber Eats of $1.75 billion. But more interesting than the absolute number was the significant portfolio shift in Uber's business. Whereas the revenues in its ride-hailing business drooped even on an adjusted basis by 41% year over year, revenues from its food-delivery platform skyrocketed by 230% year over year (Uber, 2021b, p. 16). All in all, Uber's food-delivery growth year over year compensate the steep fall in rides in Q1 2021.[7]

3.4.1 Merger Endgame and IPO's of Food-Delivery Platforms

Despite, by deploying with the transition to an integrated platform-to-consumer approach a relative new Business Design, the online food-delivery ecosystem is heavily contested and already in some sort of merger endgame, as evidenced by Fig. 3.8.

Takeaway, the originally Dutch food-delivery platform, kicked off the consolidation play in the highly competitive European on-demand food-delivery market amid

[7] Also Lyft, Uber's key competitor in its US ride-hailing business, was exposed to Q4 2020 revenue declines by 44% if compared with prior year's performance.

pressure from newcomers to the mainland European market like Uber Eats or UK's Deliveroo. In a first step, the company acquired from Delivery Hero its Germany operations—interesting wise, the latter's home market—for €930 million. The transaction included German-centered brands and platforms like Lieferheld, Pizza.de, and foodora, merged with Takeaway.com's own German platform and brand Lieferando.de. In a second step, Takeaway.com demonstrated its' European market leadership ambitions by the follow-on acquisition of the UK food-delivery platform Just Eat and by merging its own business with the transaction partner under the umbrella Just Eat Takeaway (JET).

Lately, Just Eat Takeaway acquired Grubhub, one of the leading US food-delivery platforms, for $7.3 billion [8] to create a globally leading food-delivery as-a-service market position. Also Uber Eats was rumored to have approached Grubhub with respect to a potential acquisition, but to have walked away from a deal due to likely antitrust concerns. JET's Grubhub transaction levers the strategic rationale of Takeaway's former merger with Just Eat plc, just on a global level: The merged Just Eat Takeaway.com and Grubhub business became the world's largest online food-delivery company outside of China, with strong brands, a sizeable market position in 25 countries (Financial Times, 2020b), close to 600 million orders for the joint platforms in 2019 and 70 million combined MAPCs (Techcrunch.com, 2020).

Grubhub's business model is more closely aligned with Just Eat Takeaway, which is balanced between a platform- and a restaurant-to-customer approach. In contrast, Uber Eats is a pure platform-to-consumer model by using its own couriers and delivery network to ship meals from restaurants that would traditionally not offer take-out meals for the diner. The restaurant-to-consumer platform model traditionally offered higher margins, although Grubhub's battle with Uber Eats sent it into the red in 2020.

JET competes nowadays fiercely in the European food-delivery market with UK's Deliveroo, Delivery Hero headquartered in Germany, and the Spanish player Glovo. Deliveroo, deploying on a pandemic-driven 112% growth in total transactions on its platform in 2020, went on March 2021 public. The book-building process and early trading highlighted the challenge of investors and capital markets to find a fair value for those early-stage platform Businesses Designs.

Deliveroo targeted London's biggest initial public offering (IPO) in the last decade by both measures, capital raised and market capitalization. Originally, Deliveroo headed for a market capitalization between £7.6 billion and £8.8 billion intending to sell 384 million shares [9] to investors between £3.90 and £4.60, giving

[8] In Just Eat Takeaway.com's (JET) all-share deal, Grubhub shareholders were offered 0.6710 Just Eat Takeaway.com ordinary shares in exchange for each Grubhub share. This represents an implied share value of $75.15 for each Grubhub share, a premium of around 60% compared with Grubhub's share price before rumors of the transaction emerged on capital markets. This pricing gave Grubhub a transactional equity value of $7.3 billion.

[9] Before the overallotment option, which gave Deliveroo's underwriter consortium the option to sell stocks in the secondary market

the intended capital raised a net worth of £1.6 billion at the midpoint of the price range (Financial Times, 2021b).

But, Deliveroo faced pre-IPO headwinds triggered by Uber's right-hailing decision to give its drivers' limited employee, more precisely, worker rights after the UK Supreme Court ruling that Uber's drivers couldn't be treated as self-employed. As this ruling will raise driver's costs and benefits for the respective platform owner, not surprisingly also food-delivery platforms have been hit. Due to additional volatile trading conditions and corporate governance concerns around its dual-class share structure, Deliveroo and its book-runners had to set the share price at the bottom of the initial target range at £3.9 giving the food-delivery app an IPO and opening valuation of £7.6 billion, raising £1.5 billion of equity capital (Financial Times, 2021a).

Deliveroo's much hyped IPO got even more bumpy as its shares plunged by 30% as low as 271 Pence within the first 20 minutes of its listing debut on March 31, 2021, before the share price slightly recovered and closed finally day 1 trading 26% lower than the £3.9 asking price, at 287 Pence for a market capitalization of £5.2 billion. Deliveroo's IPO flop became the worst opening-day performance in at least a decade for the London stock exchange and the comapany's shares lost further ground till May 2021 where its share price hoovered at 230–240 Pence.

This stands in stark contrast to DoorDash's IPO, Deliveroo's US peer, whose share price popped by more than 86% along its trading debut on the New York Stock Exchange on December 10, 2021 (New York Times, 2020a). Investor's enthusiasm due to the company's growth in revenues fueled by the demand for online food-delivery during the pandemic gave it an astonishing equity value of more than $60 billion at day one trading (Financial Times, 2020a). Nevertheless, DoorDash's share price lost one-third of its value between mid-February and Deliveroo's IPO timing end of March, suggesting that the European peer might have approached equity capital markets too late to profit from 2020's end-of-year tech stock IPO bonanza. The flip-sided early capital market performance of DoorDash and Deliveroo is summarized by Fig. 3.9.

In the USA, the three market players besides Uber Eats were Grubhub, which was sold, as described above, to Just Eat Takeaway lately, Postmates, and the mentioned US food-delivery market leader DoorDash, where the two latter are foremost US-focused players.

In the midst of the pandemic, Uber extended its food-delivery footprint by following a string-of-pearls M&A strategy [10]: Mid 2020, Uber Eats acquired Postmates in an all-stock transaction for $2.65 billion (Uber, 2021a). Postmates is a bolt-on transaction for Uber to strengthen and consolidate its platform position in the US on-demand food-delivery market. It will bring roughly ten million customers,

[10] Nevertheless, as for its micro-mobility business, Uber also strengthened its profit focus in food delivery by targeted divestments. The company sold its cash-draining Uber Eats Indian operation to Zomato Media Private Limited due to the hypercompetitive nature and in tradition engrained local Indian food-delivery market.

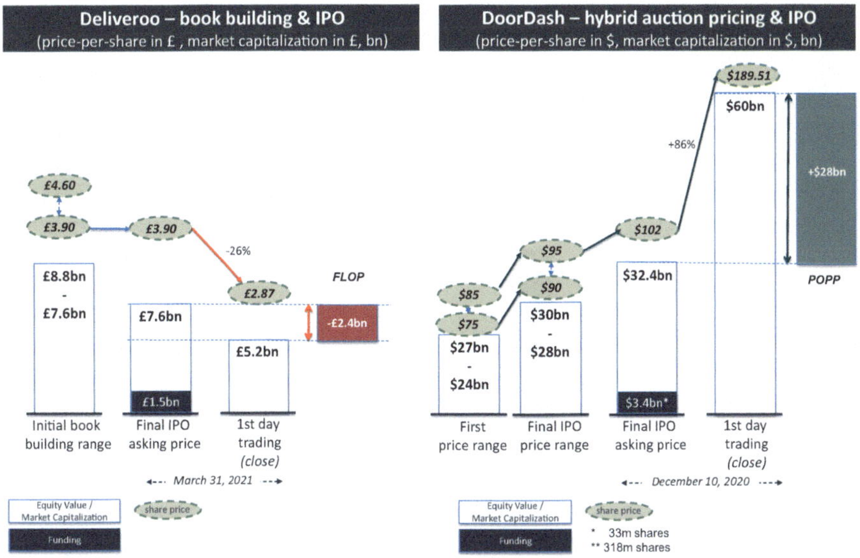

Fig. 3.9 On-demand food-delivery platform IPOs: DoorDash versus Deliveroo

Fig. 3.10 US on-demand food-delivery platform market shares and platform players

more than 100.000 merchants, and roughly $500 million revenues to the joint food-delivery platform (New York Times, 2020b).

Figure 3.10 does focus on the US food-delivery platforms' market shares. Post-acquisition Uber Eats including Postmates will be with a market share of 37% neck on neck to the market leader DoorDash with 45%. Grubhub/JET follow with 17%. Early 2021, Uber Eats acquired additionally the alcohol delivery service Drizly for $1.1 billion (Financial Times, 2020d). The latter transaction will provide Uber Eats post-closing with licenses to distribute alcohol in more than 1400 cities across the USA. Last but not the least, the company acquired the Latin American grocery app Cornershop (Uber, 2021c) extending its reach to Latin America.

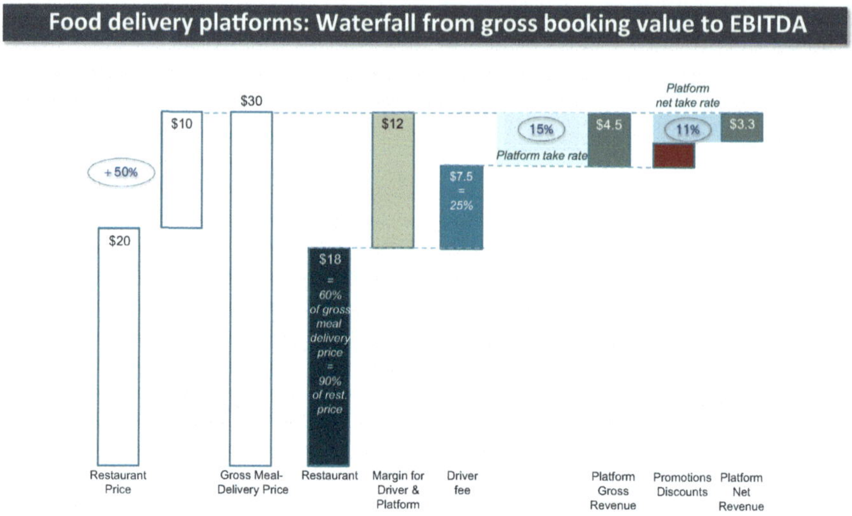

Fig. 3.11 DoorDash's 3P food-delivery platform revenue and EBIT model—indicative value waterfall

From a portfolio perspective, the merged Uber Eats and Postmates business seems to offer a strong strategic rational as food-delivery played out during the pandemic as a hedge against Uber's struggling ride-hailing core business. Additionally, the acquisition and integration of Postmates into Uber Eats gave the parent tailwinds in the hefty contested US food-delivery market.

Despite the revenue boost by more than 200% of its food-delivery business, as still in start-up mode and heavily contested, Uber Eats was still loss-making, as EBITDA in Q1 2021 stood at −$200 million or −11.5% (Uber, 2021b). But, with an impressive annual bookings run-rate in Q1 of $12 billion, the food-delivery business provided an uplift in gross booking value of Uber's overall platform to more than $19 billion.

The assessment of the stand-alone platform strength as well as value creation potential of online-food delivery platforms paired with the diagnostics of probable synergies between food-delivery and ride-hailing platforms enables an evaluation of the network bridging potentials between those two on-demand delivery-as-a-service platform Business Designs.

DoorDash released within its IPO prospectus in December 2020 some insights on the revenue and Cash Flow Model of 3P food-delivery platforms. A typical meal order costs a diner a 50% upside due to charges related to taxes, tips, and fees in comparison to an in-restaurant order. Assuming a restaurant price of $20, this would transfer to a diner's payment of $30 for at home delivery of the same meal. The restaurant nets of the meal listing price $18 equal to 90% of the in-house restaurant price or 60% of the diner's on-delivery payment. The remaining $12 will be shared between the rider, netting $7.50, and the platform, receiving $4.50 in the end from both, the customer and the restaurant. The value waterfall is described by Fig. 3.11.

But, and comparable with the ride-hailing revenue model, the consolidated take rate of DoorDash's platform was on a net basis "only" 12%, equal to $970 million of revenue on more than $8 billion of gross order volume. Reported revenues realized a plus of 226% year over year (Financial Times, 2021c). The further deductions from gross revenues reflect hefty promotional expenses and discounts to capture and to incentivize diners and restaurant platform partners. Online food delivery seems to be a tough ecosystem: It realized tremendous growth throughout the pandemic, but is as well a highly competitive business, as platforms are forced to spend significant amounts to capture and keep diners. Also, all network partners seemed in the past not really satisfied: Drivers complain about the low level of benefits, whereas restaurants dislike the typical commissions of 10%, what is from their perspective just the compensation for lead generation. Last but not the least, investors criticized the negative cash flow profile of most food-delivery platforms.

But, due to the pandemic-induced boost of food-delivery orders as well as a slightly positive normalized EBITDA of $94 million for the final quarter in 2020 (Financial Times, 2021c) and the successful listing of DoorDash, the sentiment of investors might have turned more positive. Also, the IPO proceeds of $3.4 billion may support DoorDash to scale its business and to capture network economies of scale.

For the overarching question, if the platform bridging from ride-hailing to food-delivery is a valuable portfolio move, a brief assessment of the food-delivery platform pattern is mandatory. For this evaluation, the stand-alone platform strengths of on-demand platform-to-consumer food-delivery networks along the eight platform criteria and the communalities as well as differences with the ride-hailing platform patterns will be diagnosed briefly:

- Food delivery is in case of a platform-to-consumer Business Design a three-party platform architecture and, therefore, more complex than double-side ride-hailing platforms. Besides couriers and diners, also, restaurants have to be onboarded and captured on the platform.
- In terms of *platform scalability*, this additional complexity might be a hindrance. Restaurants as additional and foremost local platform partners bring in further business and platform complexities and might limit partially scaling potentials. Also return potentials might be more challenging, as three-platform partners and the owner have to be compensated.

  Nevertheless, also food-delivery apps are asset-light Business Designs. They profit from decreasing unit costs by an increasing number of diners and platform economies of scale. Also, the revenue scaling approach is similar to ride-hailing.
- The *competitive advantage* of food-delivery platforms rests on the same technological core capabilities as ride-hailing. The joint core technologies might be one of the most fundamental arguments for platform bridging between ride-hailing and food delivery, leveraging the technology-grounded synergies between the two platform designs.

  But, competition between different food-delivery peers might be even more intense as in ride-hailing. In addition to the price competition between the different food-delivery apps, restaurants might develop their own proprietary local food delivery service to pocket platform charges by themselves. This might be especially a threat if restaurants may offer a differentiated taste or style with a distinct local fan community. An alternative strategic move by restaurants would be to switch from a platform-to-consumer to a restaurant-to-consumer model, if the take rate of platforms might become to outsized.

Also latest financials eclipsed empirical evidence how contested the food-delivery market is: Just Eat Takeaway.com faced a significant increase in pre-tax losses to €147 million, even as its revenues soared due to corona-implied social distancing measures by more than 50% to 2.4 billion in 2020. The same holds true for Deliveroo with increased losses of £224 million on 54% increased sales of £1.2 billion. As the food-delivery market is still not fully consolidated, peers invest heavily in marketing and bonus payments to diners and restaurants on their platform. This price- and market share-based competition is a significant burden for the value creation potential of online food-delivery platforms.

- For the *network effect* comparison between food-delivery and ride-hailing platforms, it must be diagnosed that both platforms share two platform partners, on the one side the riders and diners and on the other side the drivers and couriers. This offers a second source of potential synergies between the platforms.
  Both share as well some network effect patterns. *Cross-side network effects* between diners, couriers, and restaurants are strongly reinforcing each other: More diners on the platform will increase its attractiveness for restaurants and couriers. Vice versa, more restaurants on a distinct platform mean a higher diversity of tastes, attracting further diners. Besides, more food orders channeled through the platform lure more drivers on the platform increasing regional availability and reducing the waiting time for an average food order. *Same-side network effects* of restaurants might be exposed, as on the courier's side, to higher competitive pressure with an increasing number of same-side platform participants, counterbalancing partially cross-side network advantages.
- Restaurants are regional platform clients, at least, as long as they are not part of a franchise or an international restaurant chain. Food orders will always depend on the distinct local restaurant footprint of a municipality, exposing food delivery to an even more severe *risk of network fragmentation* as ride-hailing.
- The *risk of intermediation* might be not as limited as in the case of ride-hailing apps. As soon as taste preferences are known from a diner's order and the latter know about the restaurant's cooking quality, they may contact each other directly and may use the restaurant's proprietary food-delivery system for the next order, thereby side-passing the platform.
- As ride-hailing, food-delivery is exposed to the risk of *multi-homing* at all platform partners. Restaurants might use multiple food-delivery platforms, to assure customer access and delivery, couriers might join different platforms to reduce idle time, and customers might have different food-delivery apps on their mobile phone to multiply diversity and compare order costs. Multi-homing might be a prime reason for the hyper-competitive nature of on-demand food-delivery platforms.

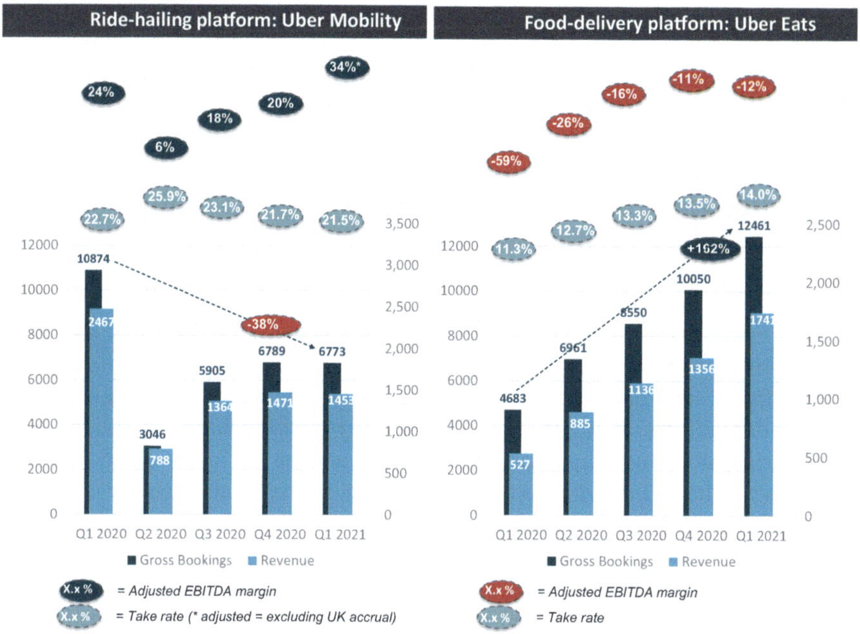

Fig. 3.12 Benchmark between food-delivery (Uber Eats) and ride-hailing (Uber Mobility) platforms

Summarized, the shared technological platform architecture and logistics demands as well as partial platform partner overlaps might provide some rational for ride-hailing and food-delivery platform synergies. Nevertheless, platform bridging from ride-hailing to food-delivery comes with the stand-alone value risk of food-delivery ecosystems due to their hyper-competitive nature. This might also be exemplified by the comparison of Uber Mobility with Uber Eats, as described by Fig. 3.12:

Uber Mobility's gross bookings and revenues fall off the cliff in Q2 2020 due to the COVID-19 pandemic, where the latter decreased by 68% in comparison to pre-pandemic Q1 2020. Not surprisingly, its ride-hailing adjusted EBITDA margin followed on close step and dropped from 24% to 6%. Nevertheless, it stayed positive and improved since then to adjusted 34% in Q1 2021 (Uber, 2021b).

Uber Eats nearly tripled its gross bookings year on year based on latest Q1 2021 financials. But take rates are still significantly lower than in ride-hailing and the EBITDA margin, despite improving significantly, achieved with −12% in Q1 2021 still not EBITDA breakeven.

All in all, on-demand food-delivery seems to be so far an even more contested platform business than ride-hailing. Also, the aftermath of the pandemic has to prove if the price premia of food-deliveries on the doorstep and stellar growth rates are sustainable post-pandemic. That will largely depend if diners, who previously loved eating at restaurants, will continue to embrace on-demand food delivery. But, equally likely, food-delivery demand will be dampened post-pandemic, the hyper-competitive nature might persist, and social and regulatory backlashes might grow. Such a scenario would hinder also long-term food-delivery platforms to become investor's darlings.

3.5 Decoding Uber's Financial Value: Reverse DCF and the Hottest Question on Wall Street

Platforms have been described in Chap. 1 as asset-light Business Designs as they typically embrace only a limited amount of tangible assets on their balance sheet and are in a prime position for scaling their business rapidly. Uber argues that its strategy is grounded on such an asset-light business architecture by pairing on its ride-hailing platform drivers with riders and on its food-delivery platform diners, restaurants, and couriers. Investors seem to share Uber's argumentation so far as equity markets value Uber higher than most automotive incumbents. This seems to be astonishing at first sight as the latter proved within the last decades their strong cash flow generating Business Designs, whereas Uber generated historically the highest losses ever before an IPO and also had encountered a significant net loss of $6.8 billion in 2020 due to the pandemic. Based on this observation, it might be interesting to question if Uber's market capitalization and implicit cash flow forecasts seem to justify its market value. In so far, Uber's stock market valuation might be indeed one of the most interesting questions on Wall Street.

For the assessment of this valuation question, the Reverse DCF approach is applied. The integrated modules are described by Fig. 3.13. The Reverse DCF concept starts with the diagnostics of the historical VC funding and capital market valuations and adds the assessment of the financial statement, explicitly the income statement, the balance sheet, and the profit to free cash flow conversion.

Based on an in-depth past and as-is performance of Uber, alternative picture-of-the-future scenarios (PoFs) are developed, whereby in this book just one of them will be discussed in detail due to size limitations. Embedded in this PoF perspective is the revenue model as a mission-critical ingredient. It serves as the backbone for the terminal value assessment as platform Business Designs' value generation is foremost driven by their growth momentum, as discussed within Chap. 1. The revenue model builds also the bridge between today and the future steady state, enabling a consistent modelling of the scaling period. Those assessments are sidelined by a detailed capital market assessment for cost of capital, financing, and valuation diagnostics. Ultimately, a valuation canvas can be described.

3.5.1 Financial Diagnostics: Past VC Funding, IPO, and Post-listing Capital Market Performance

The following financial assessment will kick off with Uber's first indicative pricing within its multiple private seed-financing rounds, Uber's book-building process and

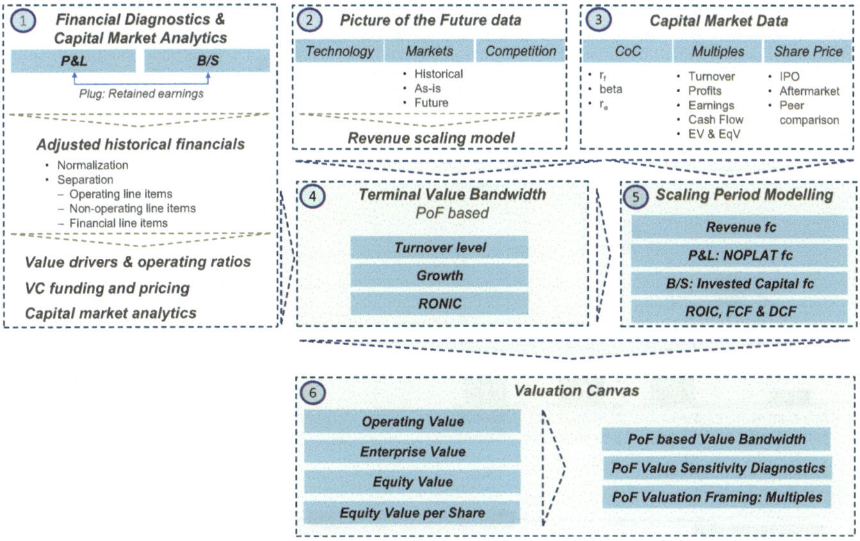

Fig. 3.13 Reverse DCF model and valuation walk concept. *Source*: tfX-advisory—Reverse DCF valuation model for platform Business Designs 2021

its IPO pricing, as well as the ride-hailing platform's post-listing stock price performance. Besides, the discussion on a suitable and tailored peer group will frame the stock-market valuation. Thereafter, the financial performance and value drivers of Uber will be assessed.

Based on this capital market perspective, a Reverse DCF valuation model will be developed based on a distinct picture-of-the-future scenario and aligned Business Design. Finally, a sensitivity assessment of the mission-critical value drivers of Uber's 10C Business Design will stress-test the intrinsic equity valuation's robustness.

Uber used a typical start-up funding model to develop its ride-hailing app and platform. The company thereby realized a stellar pricing growth throughout its multiple private funding rounds between 2010 and 2019, as highlighted by Fig. 3.14.

Uber raised in its first seed financing round back then in October 2010 round about $1.5 million, valuing Uber at the beginning of its making in a range of $4.5–5.5 million. Just 4 months later, the private backers of the series A funding round valued the company already 12 times higher than in the seed funding round at $60 million and provided additional funds of $11 million. As series B investors provided further funds between $37 and 49 million valuing Uber at around $337–347 million, series C investors valued their investment at a tenfold price of approximately $3.8 billion (Olsen, 2017). Along the following years and funding rounds from series C to G, financial sponsors provided the ride-hailing firm additional equity of $11.6–11.8 billion. All in all, Uber's raised from its inauguration till its last private funding round before its IPO in May 2019 approximately $24 billion

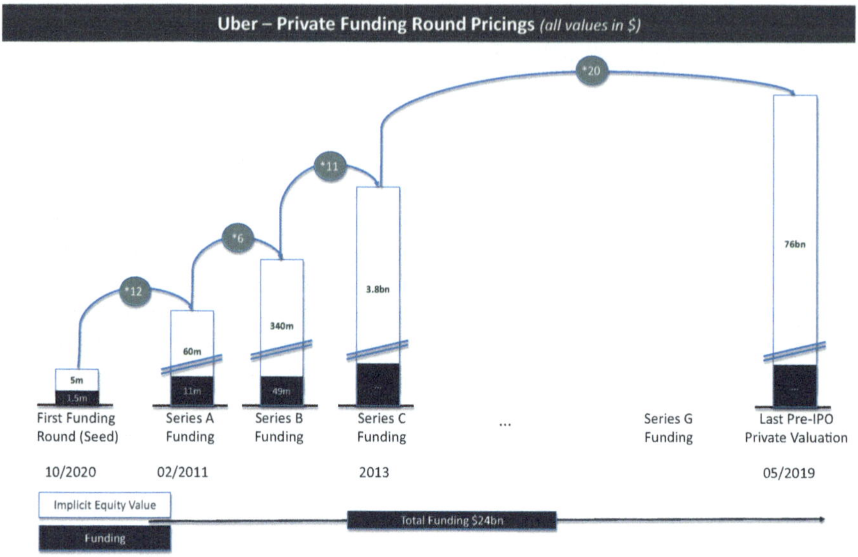

Fig. 3.14 Pricing of Uber along its seed and private funding rounds history

of seed and venture capital funding. The last private series G funding round priced Uber's market value of equity at around $76 billion (CNBC, 2019).

Despite this stellar pricing and funding development, Uber's IPO price was set by its investment banking advisors at the lower end of the book-building range of $44–$50 at $45 per share, as global investors were at the time of the IPO more cautious and valued the ride-hailing company along the book-building process at $76 billion roughly in line with the latest private funding round then. Also, some equity analysts of investment banks questioned if the raid-hailing business model might achieve breakeven ever. Nevertheless, Uber pocketed further total proceeds of $8 billion through its IPO for building its international on-demand raid-hailing and food-delivery platforms.

Figure 3.15 shows how Uber's share price fell on its trading debut below its IPO price, closing at $41.57 per share and valuing the company's market capitalization at $70 billion. The day one share price drop by 7.6% ranked Uber's IPO as the eighth worst first-day share price performance for a US-listed IPO raising more than $1 billion (Financial Times, 2019). The faltering debut of Uber followed the initial poor post-IPO performance of Uber's rival Lyft and left investors further questioning the sustainability of the still unprofitable ride-hailing business. Since then, Uber's share price was trading volatile within a wide range. Since the outset of the COVID-19 pandemic, Uber's share price volatility was additionally exposed to the uncertainties surrounding the impact of social distancing measures overall, but especially on Uber's ride-hailing business. Uber's share price reached a low at $14.82 per share on March 18, 2020, at the peak of the COVID-19 pandemic-induced global capital market tsunami. But, Uber's share price and valuation recovered consistently from

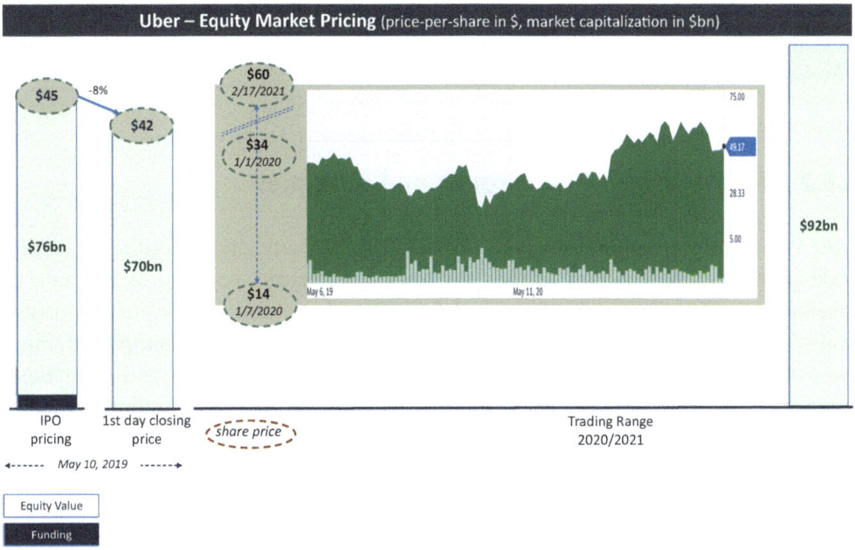

Fig. 3.15 Market capitalization, book-building range, and IPO pricing of Uber. *Source*: finance.yahoo.com, ft.com, 2021

this low, hitting an all-time high at $60 per share and trading at the writing of the book at close to $50 per share valuing Uber at $92 billion.

A more in-depth capital market assessment might compare Uber's stock price performance with its closest US peer Lyft and the overall development of the NASDAQ stock exchange: From Uber's IPO to spring 2021, the company's stock market performance pattern mimicked that one of the NASDAQ, with a significant hit during the early days of the pandemic in March 2020, but since then with a strong recovery. Nevertheless, the company's share price underperformed since its inauguration, but outperformed the broad NASDAQ index since the first vaccination breakthroughs became transparent in November 2020. Uber and Lyft shares moved as well in lockstep, but in comparison with its direct US peer, Uber shares outperformed.

Uber's actual negative profitability stands in stark contrast to its capital market valuation, implicitly assuming a stellar future performance. The net loss for 2020 hit $6.8 billion as the pandemic was a significant drag on revenues and profitability. Nevertheless, Uber reiterated its target to become EBITDA positive along 2021 (Financial Times, 2020d). Also Lyft communicated that it may achieve a positive EBITDA in Q3 2021, under the assumption that the rollout of vaccinations will let business return to normal, an assumption which might materialize according to latest market news (Financial Times, 2021f).

By comparing the recent further surge in Uber's share price and market capitalization with its still significantly loss making and cash draining past performance might raise the questions if its capital market pricing might be too elevated or mirrors simply a reasonable investment in a future dominant ride-hailing and on-demand food-delivery platform. Therefore, Uber is a perfectly demanding case for the Reverse DCF application.

3.5.2 Framing with Peer Groups and Multiples

Uber is typically perceived as a pure ride-hailing company, and according to its SIC code classification, it is part of the "taxi service industry" segment as the bulk of revenues steamed pre-pandemic indeed from its ride-hailing services as a substitution of traditional taxi services. But, this classification might be oversimplified. First, the pandemic was a booster for on-demand food-delivery services and Uber Eats' business. The latter became in 2020 not surprisingly a substantial pillar of Uber's portfolio. A more tailored peer-group and multiples assessment for Uber will incorporate not just peers from the mobility, but also from the on-demand food-delivery as well as from the freight and logistics business. Second, Uber, as discussed in the 10C Business Design and the platform value subchapters, competes on different, digital grounds than industry incumbents in the traditional food or mobility sector. As a consequence, a more holistic view on the peer group requires also the integration of established platform companies to mirror truly Uber's Business Design pattern and competitive advantage. The diversity of Uber's peer group is addressed by Fig. 3.16.

As comparable listed platform competitors for the ride-hailing business, only Lyft seems to be a reasonable peer, as other mobility platforms have their home ground in Asian markets with different demand and competitive characteristics or are still private firms. For example, Didi is a viable competitor, but a pure Chinese platform;

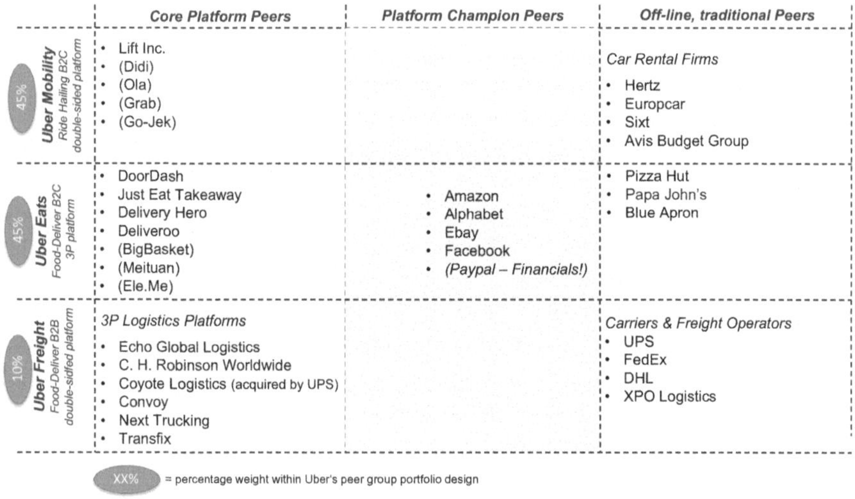

Fig. 3.16 Uber's peer-group chessboard

Grab offers its on-demand ride-hailing services exclusively in Southeast Asia, Go-Jek in Indonesia, and Ola in India.

A further, more traditional subgroup of ride-hailing peers are car rental firms like Sixt, Europcar, Hertz, or the Avis Budget Group. These companies are originally not competing on the platform level, but offer in the end as well personal transportation services. Nevertheless, one limitation of comparability might be that these services are also used for mid- to long-distance travels, whereas ride-hailing services are a more or less exclusive urban business.

Micro-mobility providers, offering foremost scooter and bike-sharing platforms, were excluded from the peer portfolio as the leading sector companies like Bird or Lime are still privately owned. Also, traditional car OEMs, often seen as Uber peers, were not considered as reasonable comparables due to their significantly differing Business Design architecture and asset-heavy pattern.

But, following the Business Design argumentation line, more mature platform companies like Amazon in e-commerce, eBay as digital trading platform, Netflix and Spotify in streaming, Alphabet in search and digital advertising, or Facebook in social media were viewed as peers, even if competing in different ecosystems.

Applying this ride-hailing assessment on the on-demand food-delivery ecosystem, the US market leader DoorDash and the merged Just Eat Takeaway/Grubhub business are seen, beside the European players Delivery Hero and Deliveroo, as suitable peers of Uber Eats including its recent acquisition Postmates. In contrast, Chinese food-delivery apps like Meituan, Ele.me, or MissFresh and Indian uprising platforms like BigBasket or Swiggy have been evaluated as not comparable, not neglecting their competitive positioning. Additionally, more traditional recipe or pizza delivery services like Blue Apron, Papa John's, and Domino's Pizza might be chosen as peers.

Last but not the least, for Uber's freight business logistics, companies like UPS, FedEx, DHL, and XPO Logistics as well as freight platforms like Echo Global Logistics, Robinson Worldwide, and others have been viewed as reasonable benchmarks (Uber, 2019b). Each of the five segments has been given a distinct weighting, thereby addressing the higher revenue contribution of the ride-hailing and food-delivery platform within Uber's business portfolio.

As discussed in Chap. 1, multiple-based valuations should be as close as possible linked to the value drivers of a Business Design. EBITDA or EBITA multiples are typically preferred (Koller et al., 2020):

$$\frac{\text{Enterprise Value}}{\text{EBIDA}} = \frac{(1-t)\left(1-\frac{g}{\text{RONIC}}\right)}{\text{WACC}-g}$$

But, as Uber and its ride-hailing as well as its food-delivery peers are still EBITDA negative, the only applicable, but not perfect multiple is the enterprise value-to-revenue ratio, which will be applied at the end of the chapter for comparing the Reverse DCF valuation with capital market derived multiples of Uber's peers:

$$\frac{\text{Enterprise Value}}{\text{Revenue}}$$

3.5.3 Pictures-of-the-Future Scenarios for Ride-Hailing, Food-Delivery, and Freight Platforms

A set of distinct picture-of-the-future scenarios frame a Reverse DCF valuation, whereby each scenario is based on a different set of assumptions. The latter take into consideration potential technological developments, for example, autonomous drive technology breakthroughs and penetration rates, alternative regulatory environments, different trends in use cases and customer preferences, and tailored competitive environments. In the Uber case study, a special attention was given to potential urban city developments and trends as those will have a substantial impact on urban mobility.

The wide set of potential future development and trend scenarios have been consolidated in three distinct pictures-of-the-future specifically for ride-hailing, food-delivery, and freight platforms:

- Picture-of-the-future A: "The digital cities that never sleep"
- Picture-of-the-future B: "Smart urban"
- Picture-of-the-future C: "Long combustion"

For exemplary purpose, the "smart urban" picture-of-the-future will be first pinpointed and then applied as the reference scenario for the later Reverse DCF valuation. Within the "smart urban" picture-of-the-future, the 2031 scenario is based on the following briefly summarized key trends:

- Urban areas will develop in the "smart urban" scenario to viable and eco-centric environments. Public places, working spaces, and private accommodations will find a new balanced urban mix, including inner-urban green spaces for CO_2 neutrality and for offering places to refresh the mind in digital times. Short distances between work, home, and leisure activities as well as digital technologies and advanced materials will shape new urban architecture. Additionally, a multi-modal mix integrating public transport, new Business Designs like ride-hailing and sharing, local taxi, and micro-mobility solutions, besides a limited traditional car-ownership model, will become the dominant mode of urban mobility.
- Such an efficient as well as environment-friendly mobility concept will become top priority of city planners and governors in the 2020s. The scenario assumes a partial shift to new mobility solutions for restructuring cities to more natural urban centers. A reduced number of parking slots will be just one policy tool to make urban car ownership less attractive. The regulatory environment will be

thought to be more ride-hailing minded. Most municipalities are assumed to have found in the steady state a new balance between local taxi interests, regulatory and city infrastructure needs, and new Business Design acceptance.
- Autonomous drive technologies are assumed to take their time due to complex urban infrastructure and real-time traffic demands. Fleets of autonomous vehicles offering "mobility as a service" will not immediately be available, but first applications of autonomous drive technologies are assumed to be at least in testing mode till 2031. Ride-sharing and food delivery might be first ideally suited ecosystems for test applications of such technology revolutions and might be pushed by digital natives.
- New technologies which pay in to improve urban living are welcomed by generations X, Y, and Z. With respect to the new automotive alphabet, the picture-of-the-future "smart urban" assumes a fast and substantial breakthrough of electric-drive technologies substituting the traditional combustion engine step by step, supported by regulatory initiatives to enable CO_2 neutrality within most communities.
- New use cases like ride-hailing or food delivery are positively perceived by citizens. Sharing will become partially the new owning by questioning the significant need of individual mobility investments especially by citizens, having access to a multitude of urban transport modes.
- On-demand food delivery will become post-pandemic not the only but an essential part of urban food consumption. Different modes like dining with friends or the family at restaurants, or at home cooking events, or simply ordering seamless a meal will characterize sprawling urban living paired with smart diversity (Financial Times, 2021c).

Based on this pinpointed "smart urban" picture-of-the-future, the financial valuation of Uber will be derived in two steps: first, by assessing the continuing value of the steady state embedded in this scenario and, second, by detailing the scaling period performance of Uber.

3.5.4 The Picture-of-the-Future Tailored Steady-State and Continuing Value Perspective

As the Reverse DCF concept starts flip-sided to the traditional valuation approach with the steady-state scenario and Business Design, the first question is when a steady state will become a steady state, characterized by a petering out of revenue growth rates and a stabilization of ROIC and RONIC [11] bandwidths of the underlying Business Design? The benchmark of decay rates of platform firms which already

[11] Whereas ROIC addresses the returns of already during the scaling period Invested Capital, RONIC describes the return and value contribution of newly, meaning during the continuing value period injected Invested Capital.

entered a more mature stage of their life cycle might provide some empirical evidence and guidance. Most platforms enter a more mature stage after 10–15 years. The picture-of-the-future scenarios assume that such a steady state to be achieved needs still a decade for ride-hailing and food-delivery. For simplicity it is assumed for the financial valuation that the continuing value phase will be entered into in 2031.

The Reverse DCF rests on the steady-state evaluation of the tight-knit platform Business Design aligned with and embedded in the chosen picture-of-the-future scenario "smart urban." The Business Design serves as the strategic framework for the financial modelling of the critical steady-state value drivers like the long-term sustainable ROIC and RONIC performance, revenue growth, profitability, and Invested Capital levels. A benchmark with established digital platforms might provide some further guidance and comfort. This might serve as a starting point, but has to be adjusted and recalibrated by the evaluation of ride-hailing double-sided and food-delivery 3P platform strengths. The 10C Business Design and platform value concept, as discussed in the previous subchapters, will provide a strategic anchor and a more detailed understanding of a reasonable valuation bandwidth.

Especially for the valuation of Uber, as the continuing value will be the true value contributor within any valuation scenario of the ride-hailing and food-delivery platform, the assumptions of the steady-state core value drivers have to be stress-tested through different lenses. The following steady-state evaluation starts with the *revenue* und *sustainable steady state growth* estimates.

Within the "smart urban" picture-of-the-future, ride-hailing is seen as an integral part of the urban modal split. Uber will become a $70 billion company, the bulk of $63–65 billion coming from its two B2C platforms ride-hailing and food delivery, the reminder from its freight B2B platform. This would imply a normalized revenue CAGR from 2019 pre-pandemic levels to the steady state of around 16%. Such a growth rate might be plausible, if compared with other, already more mature platform companies and assuming a ride-hailing favorable "smart urban" picture-of-the-future scenario. Another stress test is the comparison of Uber's ride-hailing platform revenue forecast of roughly $35–37 billion with different analyst estimates of the ride-hailing market volume in 2031, what would give Uber a steady-state market share of 15–20%.

As the substitution between urban modalities should be more or less completed till the steady state and urbanization processes are assumed to have petered out most, the underlying growth in urban transport will be more modest in the steady state. Key drivers of the long-term growth within the steady state will be more macro-economic factors as urban economic activity measured by its GDP growth or inflation rate-driven nominal price increases. The real long-term GDP growth in Western markets like the USA and Europe is assumed by most global institutions at 1.8–2% p.a., whereas the vibrant megacities might even outperform, and inflation at the same magnitude. A reasonable nominal steady-state growth rate might be in a range of 3.5–3.7% p.a.

The ROIC model has to address that the ride-hailing and food-delivery platforms have different competitive environments and economics, as discussed within the platform strength subchapter. Their ROIC and RONIC performance might still differ in the steady state, whereas their capital needs, due to platform architecture, might be quite similar. For simplicity reasons, the tailored sub-peer groups of the multiple assessment from Fig. 3.16 have been used as a proxy for the steady-state NOPLAT margin and ROIC forecasts.

The steady-state performance of the ride-hailing and food-delivery platforms was approximated by the average EBITDA margin from the sub-peer group of more mature platform companies which stood at round about 28% for the last 2 years, whereas the target EBITDA margin for the freight platform was derived by the 3P logistics platforms and carriers, which averaged 12% showing a much more competitive ecosystem due to its B2B pattern. From these segment EBITDAs, additionally corporate G&A and platform costs have to be deducted to get to Uber's definition of normalized EBITDA (EBITDA I). For G&A and platform costs, a reduction from today's 13% to 7% in the steady state, driven by economies of scale of the platform, has been assumed. This would provide a normalized EBITDA of $13.8 billion or 19% of revenues. By deducting legal expenses and stock-based compensations an unadjusted EBITDA close to $9 billion equal to a margin of 15% and by deducting depreciation and normalized taxes, finally a NOPLAT of 6.7 billion with a 9% margin would be achieved. [12]

For the Invested Capital slight economies of scale in platform investments, decreasing them from the last 3 years average of 22% to 15% of global revenues was assumed, whereas working capital needs were forecasted more or less constant at 15%. [13] This would lead to a steady-state ROIC performance of 31% within this ride-hailing favorable picture-of-the- future. [14]

All in all, those value drivers would give Uber a continuing value in 2031 of $159 billion:

$$\mathrm{CV}_{2031}^{\mathrm{Uber}} = \frac{\mathrm{NOPLAT}_{2031}^{\mathrm{Uber}} \times \left(1 - \frac{g^{\mathrm{Uber}}}{\mathrm{RONIC}^{\mathrm{Uber}}}\right)}{\mathrm{CoC}^{\mathrm{Uber}} - g^{\mathrm{Uber}}} = \frac{6.7\ \mathrm{bn} \times \left(1 - \frac{3.5\%}{31\%}\right)}{7.2\% - 3.5\%} = 159\ \mathrm{bn}$$

or an equivalent present value of the continuing value of $80 billion:

$$\mathrm{DCV}_{2021}^{\mathrm{Uber}} = \frac{\mathrm{CV}_i}{(1 + \mathrm{CoC}_i)^T} = \frac{159\ \mathrm{bn}}{(1+7.2\%)^{10}} = 80\ \mathrm{bn}$$

---

[12] By deducting legal expenses (1% of revenue), stock-based compensations (3% of revenue), and depreciation (3% of revenue) as well as taking a 25% normalized tax rate into account for the steady state

[13] Intangible assets and goodwill have been assessed to be driven by Uber's acquisition lately and not by its core operating business. Therefore, such balance sheet positions have been considered not to impact the future growth in Uber's Invested Capital.

[14] In contradiction to the planning period, where due to significant losses carried forward Uber would be not obliged to pay taxes, for the steady state, a global tax rate of 25% was assumed.

Steady-state scenarios might be framed and validated by sensitivity diagnostics of the most crucial value drivers. This might provide a better understanding of the uncertainty surrounding pictures-of-the-future scenarios and provide more reasonable valuation bandwidths. Value driver sensitivities will be addressed at the end of this chapter.

3.5.5 A Revenue Scaling and Growth Model for the B2C Ride-Hailing and Food-Delivery Platforms

The revenue model for Uber Technologies Inc. has to mirror all three platforms, ride-hailing (Uber Mobility), on-demand food-delivery (Uber Eats), and freight logistics services (Uber Freight). As mobility and food delivery share two platform partners, riders and customer—as diners or riders—and the latter are measured by Uber as MAPCs for both platforms, the same structural revenue modules may be applied. As the scaling period is structured along a decay period of 10 years, the steady-state growth and RONIC performance reference to 2031 and beyond.

A robust revenue forecast model is a crucial ingredient for the Reverse DCF and might rest on a top-down or bottom-up approach. Those revenue forecasts have to rebuild financially the platform-specific sources of revenue (Koller et al., 2020, p. 713). In the following, the applied revenue model for the ride-hailing business will be exemplary described.

The market model starts on a macro level with the assessment of the targeted regions and cities of the ride-hailing platform and an assessment on how urban mobility may develop in the next decade. In a next step, the ride-hailing share of the overall modes of transportation and its likely substitution of taxi and public transportation services might be derived. Based on this assessment, ride-hailing revenues per municipality and, paired with market share assumptions, the platform-specific revenue per distinct platform and municipality could be derived. The alternative way to estimate steady-state platform revenues is a bottom-up approach. The later will reference to the number of trips of monthly active platform consumers (MAPCs) and their average rides (for ride-hailing) or orders (for food-delivery). The second ingredient is the average fare or diners' price paid. The average fare might be further decomposed in the average miles driven multiplied with the typical fare per mile. The flow of the revenue model is shown in Fig. 3.17.

To build a top-down revenue model, the starting point is the definition of the addressable market. For the evaluation of Uber's addressable market in a first step, the targeted municipalities by Uber's platform services have to be defined. According to Uber's IPO report, the company is active in 63 countries internationally, which covers according to Uber 4.1 billion inhabitants [15] (Uber, 2019b). A

[15] World regions included for the estimate of Uber's addressable market are North America, Latin America, Europe, India, Middle East and Africa, Australia and New Zealand, Japan, South Korea, and other Asian countries excl. China. For the recalibration of the valuation, the following markets

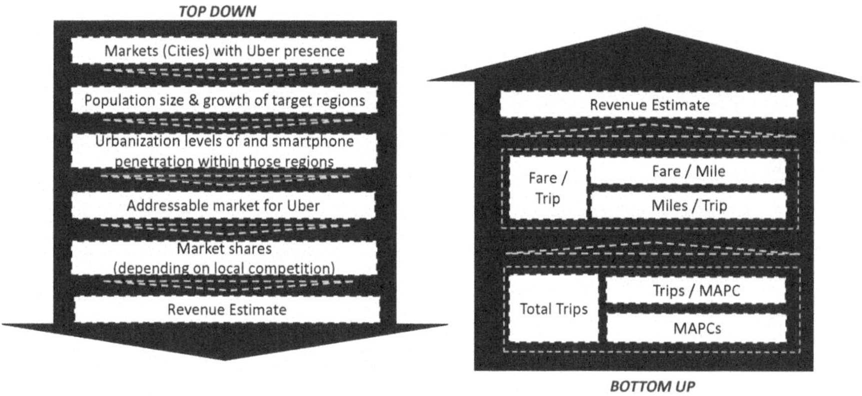

Fig. 3.17 Top-down versus bottom-up platform revenue model

more granular view, based on World Bank data for Uber's targeted markets, provides an estimate of 3.5 billion inhabitants. From the latter, the urban population is a more suitable addressable market, as Uber services are offered foremost in metropolitan areas. Urbanization levels depend on the specific region and have a significant spread from 35% in India to 82% in the USA. Urbanization levels have been calculated on an individual region level, and urban growth was estimated to peter out in the years to come. Furthermore, as Uber's services are only offered through the Uber app, smartphone ownership and availability are mandatory. As smartphone penetration rates fluctuate as well significantly from 35% in India to over 91% in the USA, these numbers have been estimated on a regional level. This reduces the all in all addressable market of citizens with smartphone ownership in metropolitan areas of Uber's target markets today to 1.4 billion and in the steady state to 1.6 billion citizens, whereby detailed numbers will also depend on Uber's successful market entrance strategy or failure in Japan and South Korea.

The second possibility to derive revenue estimates is a bottom-up approach referencing to Uber's distinct platform revenue drivers, as pinpointed by Fig. 3.18.

1. The revenue forecast for the ride-hailing platform, as highlighted in Fig. 3.18, as well as for the food-delivery platform, is foremost driven by the number of monthly active platform consumers (MAPC) using Uber's ride-hailing or food-delivery app. The calculation of total monthly active platform users MAPCs is a combination of the number of existing platform users and the number of net new riders joining the platform [16]:

have been taken as Uber's addressed core markets: USA, Canada, Latin America, Europe, Middle East, and North Africa, plus selective Asian countries including India and South Korea, besides Australia and New Zealand. China was excluded due to probable no competition as part of Uber's market exit and investment in the local champion Didi. The same holds true for Southeast Asia and Uber's equity holding in Grab. Compare as well page 3 in Uber's 2019 annual report (Uber, 2020a).

[16] The number of new riders might also turn negative in case of MAPCs joining competing platforms or in case of unforeseeable black swan effects like the COVID-19 pandemic.

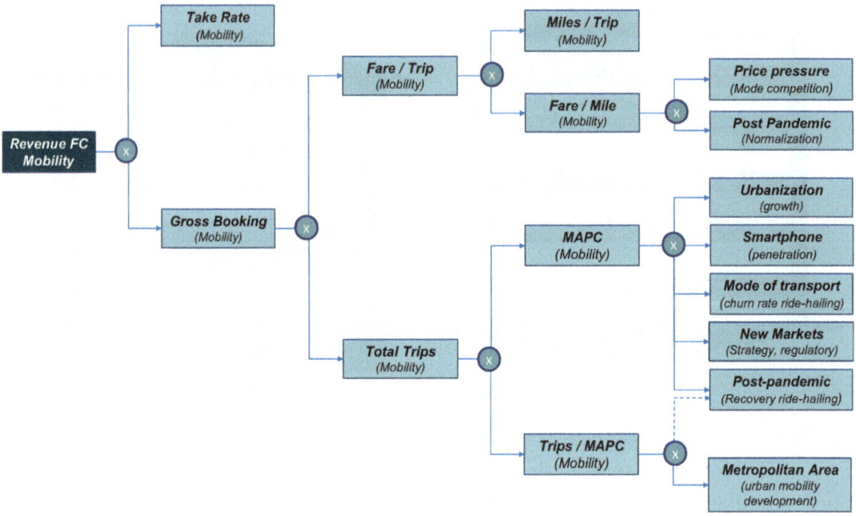

Fig. 3.18 Revenue driver tree for Uber's ride-hailing platform (Uber Mobility). *Source*: Research project tfX-advisory 2021

$$\mathrm{MAPC}_{t+1} = \mathrm{MAPC}_t + \text{new } \mathrm{MAPC}_{t+1}$$

The number of new riders depends on multiple important ingredients. As ride-hailing services are offered only in metropolitan areas and are available exclusively via smartphone apps, the growth in urbanization levels and smartphone penetration rates as well as technology affinity of target groups (generation X, Y, Z) has to be taken into account. As the picture-of-the-future "smart urban" assumes a mode of transport rotation profiting ride-hailing also the churn in the urban mode of transportation has to be forecasted. [17] This churn in urban transportation in favor of ride-hailing would superimpose the growth due to likely further urbanization trends and an increasing smartphone penetration. A forth lever of MAPC growth is the markets addressed by Uber Mobility's and Eats' strategies, which are triangled by regional regulatory frameworks. This is addressed in the simulations, for example, by modelling cases with and without Uber's market entrance and penetration in Japan or South Korea.

Last but not the least, the post-pandemic recovery will have a significant impact on MAPCs. Due to introduced social distancing initiatives to combat the pandemic, Uber's MAPC plummeted between the first and second quarter 2020 by

[17] The modelling of the forecasts with respect to the churn rate data from a recent Goldman Sachs study and alternative studies has been taken into account (GoldmanSachs, 2019). Therefore, in a separate valuation simulation, an additional 2% CAGR of the ride-hailing share of urban mobility was assumed at the beginning of the scaling period and to peter out at a growth contribution of 1% in the prior to the steady-state year 2031.

47% (Uber, 2020b). Consensus estimates are that it will take till 2022–2023 for US and European economies to return to pre-pandemic levels. The same is assumed for Uber's ride-hailing MAPC numbers recovering to pre-pandemic volumes in 2022, whereas Eats MAPCs are assumed to stabilize at the elevated levels of the pandemic and grow slightly thereafter. A robust reference is the most recent numbers of MAPC of Uber, which grew by 19% within Q4 2020 to 93 million MAPCs and increased further in Q1 2021 to 98 million MAPCs (Uber, 2021b). In the last quarter of 2020, the number of trips surpassed the milestone of 1 billion for the first time since the pandemic kicked off. The overall MAPC post-pandemic growth as estimated in the scenario "smart urban" is roughly in line with latest studies (Business Wire, 2020).

All in all, those five drivers translate into the growth rate of MAPCs g^{MAPC}:

$$\mathrm{MAPC}_{t+1} = \mathrm{MAPC}_t \times \left(1 + g_{t+1}^{\mathrm{MAPC}}\right)$$

2. To get to the number of total trips or orders n_t the number of monthly active platform users MAPC_t has to be multiplied with the average number of rides per platform user in case of ride-hailing platforms or average on-demand food orders in case of food-delivery platforms $n_t^{\varnothing}$:$n_t = \mathrm{MAPC}_t \times n_t^{\varnothing}$

With more vaccines available and social distancing measures slowly phased out, also, the average rides per platform user are assumed to recover to pre-pandemic levels till 2022. Additionally, average rides will depend long term foremost on the development of metropolitan areas, where for the "smart urban" scenario, a stepwise development to more green cities with more renewable power usage and CO_2 neutrality would give comfort for further ride-hailing growth. Besides, the regulatory framework might limit or support ride-hailing Business Models and firms.

For the evaluation of the robustness of Uber's forecasted MAPC growth, the platform user development of digital firms having already entered some sort of steady state like Facebook, Netflix, or PayPal, has been used as further benchmark. In light of this empirical evidence, growth rates starting with 25% and decelerating to 11% for the next decade after introducing their new Business Design, the growth pattern assumed in the picture-of-the-future scenario "smart urban" seems plausible.

3. To get to gross bookings of ride-hailing and food-delivery services, as channeled through Uber's platform, the number of total trips or orders n_t has to be multiplied by the average fare per trip or order price $f_t^{\varnothing}$. For ride-hailing Business Designs, the latter might be further decomposed in the two sub-drivers:

- Average miles per ride: $m_t^{\varnothing}$
- Average fare per mile: $\frac{f_t^{\varnothing}}{\text{mile}}$
  The historical price development provides some interesting insights. In the last years prior to the pandemic, a fierce competition on market share of the ride-hailing peers put downward pressure on fares (Statista, 2021). But, during the pandemic, and despite a massive downturn in the number of rides, average fares increased double digit. For the revenue-scaling model, it is assumed that post-pandemic price pressure will resume with a price drop of 8–9% in 2021 and 2022 returning to pre-pandemic set price levels in 2023. A further 1% p.a. price decrease is assumed for the outer years. The argumentation line is here: that on the one side, ride-hailing and mode of transport competition will be still post-pandemic a drag on prices for ride-hailing and the hyper-competitive nature of the food-delivery market and the re-opening of restaurant will lower at home diner's prices. On the other side, the need to achieve breakeven will be the number one priority of listed ride-hailing and food-delivery corporations and might limit the amount of price competition between the peers mid- to long term.

4. Given those market levers, the gross-bookings gb_t on the Uber Mobility and Eats platform might be derived as:

$$\text{gb}_t = n_t^{\varnothing} \times f_t^{\varnothing}$$

By applying the take rate of Uber Mobility tr^M (%) and Uber Eats tr^E on the respective gross bookings, the revenues of the Uber Mobility and Uber Eats are derived. The take rates included in former times as well the incentive payment-induced bridge between gross and net sales, which is engrained in the ride-hailing and food-delivery Business Design. The calculation here refers to Uber's nowadays application of net revenues r by netting out additional customer and driver incentives, bonus payments, and referrals. Uber's Mobility take rate stood in Q1 2021 at 22%, whereas Eats realized a take rate of 14% (Uber, 2021b), mirroring the even more competitive nature and triple-sided pattern of the on-demand food-delivery ecosystem.

The revenue methodology is exemplified for Q1 2021 revenues of Uber:

- For Uber Mobility's (ride-hailing) revenue forecast:

$$r_t^M = \text{gb}_t^M \times \text{tr}^M = 6.8 \text{ bn} \times 21.5\% = 1.45 \text{ bn}$$

- For Uber Eats (food-delivery) revenue forecast:

$$r_t^E = \text{gb}_t^E \times \text{tr}^E == 12.5 \text{ bn} \times 14\% = 1.75 \text{ bn}$$

3.5.6 A Revenue Scaling and Growth Model for the B2B Freight Platform

For the freight platform, a similar, but less complex revenue model was developed. As Uber Freight is only present in the USA and Europe, studies focusing on those two regional markets have been assessed. In general, the truck and logistics market growth follows the GDP development, but at a superimposed level.

The US and European truck markets are expected to recover quite robustly from their pandemic-induced drop in tonnage levels according to recent reports. For 2022, a GDP growth recovery of 5% is assumed,[18] which will transfer in a significant freight uptick, as evidenced by Uber Freights Q1 2021 year-over-year freight growth of 51% (Uber, 2021a). Long-term freight growth is modelled in line with GDP growth of 2.5% $\pm$ 0.5%. This would be also in line with the latest APA report that freight volumes might increase by a quarter or so within the next decade. This growth would be significantly lower than during the high times of globalization in the 1990s and early 2010s.

Due to the forecasted post-pandemic sluggish long-term growth in the underlying freight logistics market, the only true escape route for Uber Freight to scale its business might be to build a viable digital freight platform powerhouse which is capable to compete with freight market benchmarks like C.H. Robinson Worldwide or Echo Global Logistics. Both peers have roughly a 2.1–2.2% share of the US logistics market, whereas Uber Freight stands at roughly 0.1%. The picture of the future "smart urban" assumes that Uber successfully manages to slightly catch up with the benchmark duo with a share of 0.5% of the logistics volume in the steady state. This assumes that CH. Robinson Worldwide and Echo Global Logistics as truck freight logistics pure plays have also long-term a competitive advantage compared with their challenger Uber Freight.

Combining the truck freight volume growth with the intended market share gains provides the baseline for the Uber Freight revenue forecasts.

3.5.7 The Revenue to EBITDA Conversion

Revenues for 2021 are forecasted at $15.4–15.6 billion, a roughly 40% increase year on year foremost driven by a ride-hailing platform growth rebound due to the sequenced phase-out of social distancing measures in cities around the globe. Eats' revenues would stay with $6.5–6.7 billion close to the elevated levels during the pandemic, and as confirmed by Uber's Q1 performance. Uber Mobility is forecasted to see an uptick from its Q1 2021 revenues of $1.5 billion to $2.1–2.3 billion in Q4 2021 and for the full year at $7.3–7.5 billion. Uber Freights revenues are forecasted in a bandwidth of $1.3–1.5 billion, where renewed business activity

[18] The assumed 5% GDP growth in Uber Freight markets in 2021 mirrors a 6% GDP growth for the USA and a 4% GDP growth for the EU.

will boost logistics demand. After a second strong recovery year 2022, revenue growth is modelled in line with more mature platform companies and the discussed trends in urbanization.

For a top-down estimate of the steady-state revenue to EBITDA conversion peers in Uber's three lines of businesses ride-hailing, food-delivery, and logistics have been benchmarked with respect to their profit-margins. The long-term target ratios of those three platform service lines have been described in the continuing value subchapter. For example, the peer group of the mobility segment may be designed by a portfolio of listed rental companies and a second portfolio of listed platform firms. The argumentation would be here that car rental firms are partially comparable with ride-hailing companies with respect to their offered services, whereas platform companies may have a more comparable Business Design, making both reasonable peers. Nevertheless, platform firms might be more applicable benchmarks as they also share the asset-light financial architecture of ride-hailing and food-delivery platforms. Their average peer group EBITDA margin of 28% was taken as target ration for Uber Eats and Uber Mobility, which is forecasted to be achieved in the steady-state year 2031.

For the Uber Freight business, the same procedure has been deployed, whereas the peer group was tailored around listed freight operators and logistics companies like UPS, DHL, FedEx, Echo Global Logistics, XPO Logistics, or C.H. Robinson Worldwide. As this is a pure B2B play with a lens on efficiency, cost of ownership, and cost of transport, the average EBITDA margin is not surprisingly for such a high-competitive ecosystem lower as for the B2C platforms. The logistics champions subsegment achieved an average EBITDA margin of 12% what was assumed as Uber's continuing value target margin for its freight business. Uber Freight is still in start-up mode and loss-making with an EBITDA margin of −13% in Q4 2020. It is assumed that breakeven is achieved in 2026 and the peer groups' target ratio in 2031 as steady-state performance.

3.5.8 Moving from Segment EBITDA to Corporate EBITDA and Free Cash Flows

To calculate the segment EBITDA (EBITDA I) from Uber's segment platform EBITDA's for its three lines of business, Mobility, Eats, and Freight, the corporate and platform costs have to be deducted. A platform Business Design should offer substantial economies of scale. This was assumed by the gradual decrease of platform costs from 14% to 7% of revenues long term, but in absolute terms such costs would nevertheless increase from $2 billion to $5 billion, allowing Uber to scale and adjust its platform continuously. [19]

[19] Platform costs are a significant cost driver of any platform company and are therefore in the center of interest of Uber's cost management approach. For a robust midterm estimate of such costs, mature platform peers R&D costs have been benchmark to design a probable target rate.

For the transition from the segment EBITDA of Uber to its corporate EBITDA performance (EBITDA II), further cost and expense items have to be deducted like legal advisory costs, stock-based compensations, and depreciation. Legal advisory costs are assumed to level out from today's inflated 3% at 1% of revenues once the legal disputes with major metropolitan areas around ride-hailing Business Designs and gig-workers are solved. Nevertheless, legal disputes are assumed to remain partially as a long-term Uber playing field due to the fierce competition between the modes of transportation.

Stock-based compensations are as well assumed to scale down from the post-IPO elevated 5% of revenues to a normalized level of 3%, whereas for depreciation and amortization only minor economies of scale are assumed as continuous platform investments will be necessary driving them down from 4% to long-term 3% of revenues. For other, minor cost items, historical levels have been applied. [20] Finally, interest expenses have been modelled based on Uber's financing structure and tax rates calculated as a weighted average global tax rate at 25%. Tax payments will be in the underlying valuation model only relevant for the outer planning years due to Uber's significant amount of losses carried forward. By subtracting these cost items the NOPLAT performance within the scaling phase could be modelled as baseline input for the free cash flows.

3.5.9 Invested Capital and Cost of Capital

For Invested Capital the working capital performance in the scaling phase was assumed in line with the continuing value to improve only marginally to 15% of revenues, whereas for property, plant, and equipment as well as operating leases, economies of scale in platform costs have been assumed. The latter are forecasted to decrease within the scaling period from 21% to 15%, but in absolute terms increase to $10 billion or by 150% till 2031, giving the company again the probably necessary headroom to scale its platform architecture. With these ingredients of the income and balance sheet line items of Uber's three platforms, the free cash flows for the picture-of-the-future "smart urban" could be modelled as summarized by Fig. 3.19:

The cost of capital approach references to the traditional weighted average cost of capital (WACC) framework as an enterprise valuation approach is applied. The WACC are defined as the blended costs of equity and after-tax cost of debt weighted by their respective market value-based contribution to the financing mix of the company. For Uber's cost of equity diagnostics, the traditional Capital Asset Pricing Model (CAPM) is applied. The risk-free rate of the 10-year US government bond yield stood at the point of valuation at 1.6% and the implied equity market risk

[20] The P&L position other income (net), which is in Uber's case foremost driven by its income and expenses from its investment in its Chinese ride-hailing Didi and its other equity investments, was not explicitly modelled, as details for those peers' Business Designs and outlooks were not available.

	2021	2022	2023	2024	2025	2026	2027	2028	2029	2030
Revenues	15.607	19.458	24.334	29.810	35.811	42.195	48.807	55.119	61.176	66.352
yoy growth	*40%*	*25%*	*25%*	*23%*	*20%*	*18%*	*16%*	*13%*	*11%*	*8%*
Adjusted EBITDA - I (Segments)	-1.340	-1.153	-680	109	1.207	2.694	4.586	6.880	9.508	12.384
EBITDA margin (%)	*-9%*	*-6%*	*-3%*	*0%*	*3%*	*6%*	*9%*	*12%*	*16%*	*19%*
Adjusted EBITDA - II	-2.546	-2.321	-1.991	-1.323	-481	742	2.381	4.433	6.854	9.545
EBITDA margin (%)	*-16%*	*-12%*	*-8%*	*-4%*	*-1%*	*2%*	*5%*	*8%*	*11%*	*14%*
EBIT	-3.196	-3.169	-2.830	-2.367	-1.578	-532	917	2.808	5.068	7.653
EBIT margin (%)	*-20%*	*-16%*	*-12%*	*-8%*	*-4%*	*-1%*	*2%*	*5%*	*8%*	*12%*
NOPLAT	-3.196	-3.169	-2.830	-2.367	-1.578	-532	917	2.808	5.068	7.653
NOPLAT margin (%)	*-20%*	*-16%*	*-12%*	*-8%*	*-4%*	*-1%*	*2%*	*5%*	*8%*	*12%*
Depreciation & Amortization	670	810	982	1.164	1.352	1.539	1.717	1.868	1.994	2.076
Operating CF	-2.526	-2.359	-1.848	-1.203	-226	1.007	2.634	4.675	7.061	9.730
Investment in Invested Capital	1304	2041	2494	2782	3035	3224	3344	3273	3811	3629
Free Cash Flow	-3.829	-4.400	-4.342	-3.985	-3.260	-2.217	-711	1.402	3.251	6.101
Discounted Cash Flows	-3573	-3830	-3526	-3019	-2305	-1462	-437	805	1741	3049
WACC: 7,2%										

Fig. 3.19 Reverse DCF model (excerpt) for Uber's valuation embedded in PoF "smart urban"

premium at 4.5% (Damodaran, 2020). Uber's beta, as measure of its stock sensitivity benchmarked to a diversified peer portfolio, was estimated by different capital market studies in a range 1.18–1.22, higher than the average market risk.[21] The estimate of Uber's average cost of debt, based on its 2020 financial statements and annual report, was calculated at 7.2% pre-tax, or 5.4% post tax. Using market weights of debt and equity, Uber's WACC stands at 7.2%.

3.5.10 The Walk from Operating to Enterprise and Equity Value

By discounting Uber's picture-of-the-future "smart urban"-based continuing value and the free cash flows of the scaling period with the WACC of 7.2% provides an operating value of $67 billion:

$$\text{Operating Value (OV)} = \sum\nolimits_{t=1}^{\infty}(\text{DCF}_t) + \text{DCV} = -13\ \text{bn} + 80\ \text{bn} = 67\ \text{bn}$$

Despite the supportive assumptions of the picture-of-the-future "smart urban," the scaling period would be contributing a negative value, thereby pinpointing the dependency of Uber's equity market value on the long-term outlook and continuing value assumptions.

The valuation flow from Operating to Equity Value is summarized by Fig. 3.20.

Adding excess cash of $5.7 billion, as well as Uber's equity stakes at carrying value at $12.9 billion,[22] the enterprise value EV would total $86 billion:

[21] To get a more robust beta estimate for the still limited capital market history of Uber, the levered beta of the company was benchmarked with the unlevered beta of a tailored, more-broadly defined peer group and re-levered by applying Uber's debt-to-equity ratio. This beta assessment will be detailed in the second edition, having more historical capital market data available for a more granular cost of capital assessment.

[22] According to Uber's Q1 2021 report, the company holds the following ownership positions: 14% in Didi (China's ride-hailing champion), 16% in Grab (acquired as part of Uber's Southeast Asian

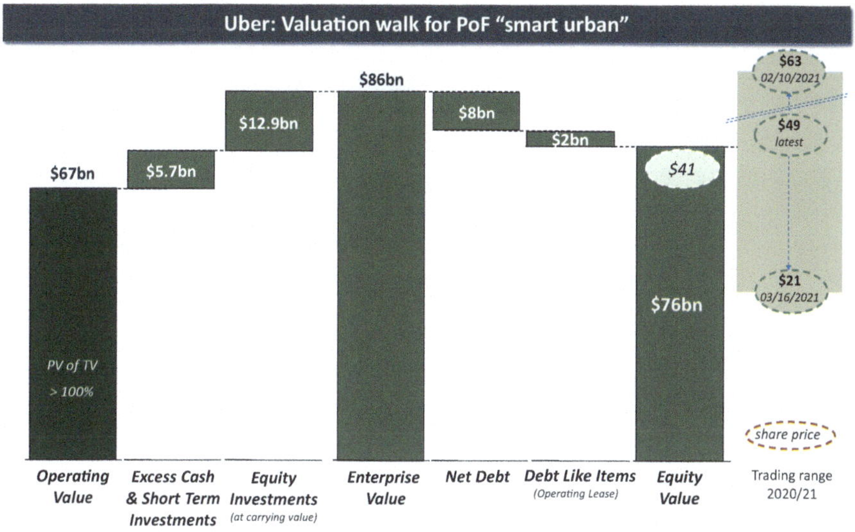

Fig. 3.20 Uber's valuation walk from operating to equity value for the PoF "smart urban"

$$\mathrm{EV} = \mathrm{OP} + (\text{excess cash} + \text{equity holdings}) = 67\ \mathrm{bn} + 19\ \mathrm{bn} = 86\ \mathrm{bn}$$

Finally, by deducting long-term debt of \$7.6bn and debt like items of \$1.7bn, the equity value (EqV) of \$76 billion, equivalent with an intrinsic valuation-based share price estimate of \$41 per share, is derived. This valuation walk from operating to equity value is summarized within Fig. 3.20:

$$\text{Equity Value EqV} = \mathrm{EV} - \mathrm{Debt} = 86\ \mathrm{bn} - 10\ \mathrm{bn} = 76\ \mathrm{bn}$$

3.5.11 Value Driver Sensitivity and Valuation Canvas

For a holistic valuation of Uber, the above picture of the future "smart urban"-based valuation has to be stress-tested with sensitivity assessments for its most crucial value drivers like the cost of capital or the MAPC development. Additionally, the Reverse DCF has to be compared with other picture-of-the-future scenarios and with the ride-hailing and food-delivery peers, as summarized by Fig. 3.21.

The sensitivity of Uber's valuation with respect to the cost capital is significant, as the true value contribution by the platform's free cash flows is realized in the outer years of the scaling period and, foremost, within its terminal value, as highlighted

---

operations and market divestment to Grab in 2018), 26% in Aurora (acquired as part of its autonomous drive divestment to Aurora), 33% in Yandex Taxi, 8% in Zomato, 6% in Joby, and 31% in the electric scooter company Lime (Uber, 2021b).

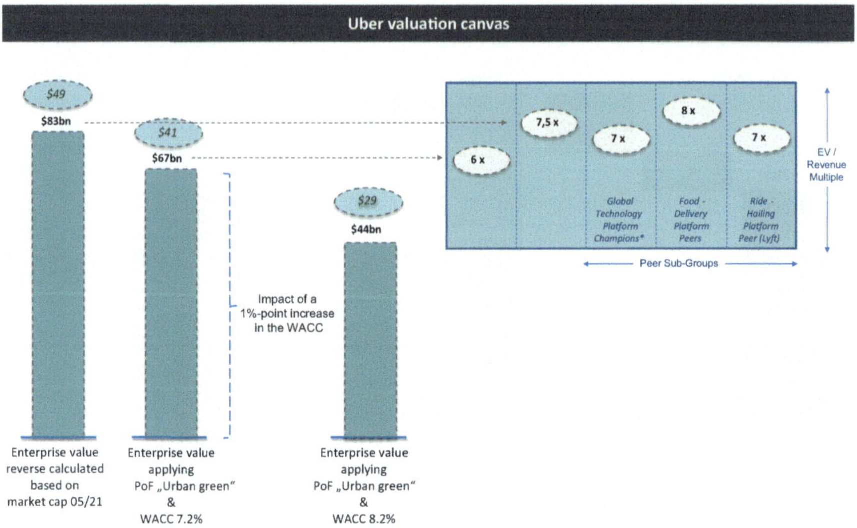

Fig. 3.21 Uber valuation canvas (exemplary)

within Fig. 3.21. A hike in the inflation rates and in government bond yields, as discussed at the time of writing this book, would be to the detriment to Uber's valuation.

The comparison with capital market peers is only possible by applying a revenue multiple, as Uber as well as its ride-hailing and food-delivery contenders still operate with negative profitability. The revenue multiple proves that the indicated valuation range would be in line with today's capital market perspective.

The valuation of Uber revealed not just the value levers, as described by Fig. 3.22, but also the most crucial risks of its platform Business Designs:

- All three platforms are exposed to a hyper-competition nature. Near-term especially its food-delivery platform Eats, due to the actual endgame in this still young ecosystem and its triple sided-platform architecture, will demand customer capture and retention payments. But, also ride-hailing competition has to overcome not only competition with peers but also with other modalities of urban transportation.
- A second, more short-term threat to be addressed by Uber are regulatory risks questioning the viability of ride-hailing and food-delivery platforms: Uber and Lyft lost a combined market value of more than $20 billion in the week since US labor secretary Marty Walsh first signaled the Biden administration's intent to look more closely at the platform economies' classification of its workers (Financial Times, 2021e).
- A mission-critical question for improving long-term profit margins and achieving cash flow breakeven of all its platforms is the reduction of excessive side

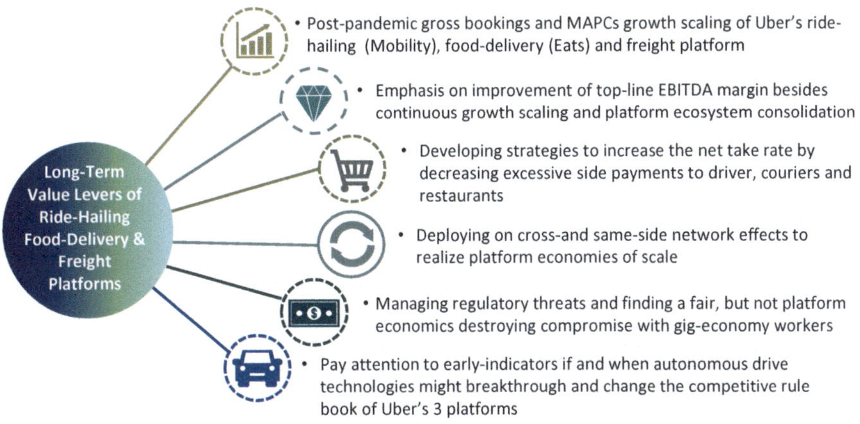

Fig. 3.22 Long-term value levers of ride-hailing, food-delivery, and freight platforms

payments and incentives for its multiple platform partners. This holds true for riders and diners but also for its drivers, couriers, and restaurants. But, it will become a delicate act to find the balance between increasing Uber's net take rate and profits versus retaliating competitive pressure.

- Very-long-term technology developments, especially of autonomous drive approaches, might change fundamentally the rules of the game of all three platforms and may open the market entrance of even more powerful technology champions with proprietary technologies, as Google and the likes.

But Uber provided lately clear indicators of its emphasis to strengthen the profitability and cash flow performance of its platform Business Design as exemplified by multiple recent portfolio restructurings:

- Exchanging its JUMP investments and micro-mobility ambitions for an equity stake in the electric scooter and e-bike specialist Lime
- Selling its autonomous drive assets and capabilities as part of its subsidiary Apparate USA LLC to Aurora Innovation, Inc., thereby closing in essence its "other bets segment"[23]
- By streamlining its core business lines with targeted divestures like Uber Eats India or its European Freight Business (Uber, 2021c) lately
- And, finally, by tailored acquisitions to strengthen its market position in the merger endgame of the food-delivery platforms, especially by acquiring Postmates

[23] As part of the divestment of Apparate USA LLC to Aurora Innovation Inc., Uber made also a $400 million cash investment in Aurora and entered into a collaborative agreement with Aurora pursuant to which the two partners will cooperate with respect to the launch and commercialization of autonomous drive technologies for Uber's ride-hailing network.

References

AD Little. (2020). *Rethinking on-demand mobility—Turning roadblocks into opportunities.* https://www.adlittle.com/en/insights/report/rethinking-demand-mobility

Business Wire. (2020). *Ride hailing—Global market to decline from $60.5 billion in 2019 to $52.1 billion in 2020, recovering to $85.5 billion by 2023.* https://www.businesswire.com/news/home/20200611005704/en/Ride-Hailing%2D%2D-Global-Market-to-Decline-from-60.5-Billion-in-2019-to-52.1-Billion-in-2020-Recovering-to-85.5-Billion-by-2023%2D%2D-ResearchAndMarkets.com

CNBC. (2019). *Uber ends its first day of trading down more than 7%.*https://www.cnbc.com/2019/05/10/uber-ipo-stock-starts-trading-on-the-new-york-stock-exchange.html

Damodaran, A. (2020). *Implied ERP by month for previous months.*http://pages.stern.nyu.edu/~adamodar/.http://pages.stern.nyu.edu/~adamodar/

Economist. (2021, February 15). *Why China's Didi can succeed where Uber has struggled.*https://www.economist.com/business/2021/02/15/why-chinas-didi-can-succeed-where-uber-has-struggled?

Feix, T. (2020). *End-to-end M&A process design—Resilient business model innovation.* Springer Gabler.

Financial Times. (2019). *Uber shares close nearly 8% below IPO price.* Financial Times. https://www.ft.com/content/01579114-72b8-11e9-bf5c-6eeb837566c5

Financial Times. (2020a, December 9). *DoorDash shares jump 86% amid IPO franzy.* https://www.ft.com/content/c9f8f03f-6b82-4828-84e2-7ac25966b7d1

Financial Times. (2020b, June 10). *JET to combine with Grubhub.* https://markets.ft.com/data/announce/detail?dockey=1323-14573213-0M7T4H9GPM6PPD87QSELE3M3NF

Financial Times. (2020c, December 7). *Uber abandons effort to develop own self-driving vehicle.* Financial Times. https://www.ft.com/content/e55ce767-0ede-4096-aa3b-1d26671f3772

Financial Times. (2020d, February 11). *Uber's food-delivery growth fails to offset ridesharing decline.* Financial Times. https://www.ft.com/content/1950a6c0-06b3-4d0b-9f7b-d5ef29f36cce

Financial Times. (2021a, March 31). *Deliveroo shares tumble as trading begins in London.* https://www.ft.com/content/ef1a6585-1560-4cfd-a90f-2a6145fe3257

Financial Times. (2021b, March 22). *Deliveroo targets IPO valuation of up to £8.8bn.* https://www.ft.com/content/22314a4b-5647-48b2-991c-d70639f7ccda

Financial Times. (2021c, February 26). *Delivery group DoorDash sees new habits enduring beyond Covid.* https://www.ft.com/content/3844b5a4-20f2-4ba9-befd-8ca52b1d092d

Financial Times. (2021d, May 5). *Uber leans on delivery business as rideshare demand remains flat.* https://www.ft.com/content/f720516f-6bee-4033-b496-62fc31722662

Financial Times. (2021e, May 6). *Uber seeks to assure investors over rising US regulatory threat.* https://www.ft.com/content/54ee1a47-c274-416f-ae0b-d894bdacafe9:https://www.ft.com/content/54ee1a47-c274-416f-ae0b-d894bdacafe9

Financial Times. (2021f, June 7). *Uber's UK rides business roars back to pre-pandemic levels.* https://www.ft.com/content/d577e2b5-b7e0-449d-a3ac-78f16a808546

Financial Times. (2021g, February 20). *Uber loses landmark UK battle as Supreme Court rules drivers are workers.* Financial Times. https://www.ft.com/content/9ef3a1c5-328c-460d-9261-33ea991cae62

Goldman Sachs. (2019, June 4). *The future of mobility.* https://www.goldmansachs.com/insights/pages/gs-research/future-of-mobility/report.pdf; https://www.goldmansachs.com/insights/pages/gs-research/future-of-mobility/report.pdf

Jahromi, M., & Zhang, T. (2020). *Sharing economy and the impact of collaborative consumption.* Edited by I. R. de Luna et al. Hershey: IGI Global (Advances in Finance, Accounting, and Economics). http://services.igi-global.com/resolvedoi/resolve.aspx?doi=10.4018/978-1-5225-9928-9

Koller, T., Goedhart, M., & Wessels, D. (2020). *Valuation—Measuring and managing the value of companies.* John Wiley & Sons.

New York Times. (2020a, December 10). *DoorDash soars in its first day of trading*. https://www.nytimes.com/2020/12/09/technology/doordash-ipo-stock.html

New York Times. (2020b, July 5). *Uber buys postmates for $2.65 billion.* https://www.nytimes.com/2020/07/05/technology/uber-postmates-deal.html

Olsen, D. (2017). *Uber by the numbers: A timeline of the company's funding and valuation history.* https://pitchbook.com/news/articles/uber-by-the-numbers-a-timeline- of-the-companys-funding-and-valuation-history

Poluliakh, Y. (2021). *Two types of on-demand food delivery platforms – Pros and cons.*https://yalantis.com/blog/three-types-of-on-demand-delivery-platforms-pros-and-cons/

Reihart, R. (2018). *Snapshot: Who uses ride-sharing services in the U.S.?*https://news.gallup.com/poll/237965/snapshot-uses-ride-sharing-services.aspx

Shaheen, S. (2018). Shared mobility: The potential of ride hailing and pooling, UC Berkeley: Transportation Sustainability Research Center. In Sperling D. (Ed.), *Three revolutions.* Island Press.

Statista. (2021). *Average quarterly cost per ride of ridesharing services in the United States from 2017 to 2019.*https://www.statista.com/statistics/890167/average-cost-per-ride-ridesharing-united-states/

Techcrunch.com. (2020, June 10). *Just eat takeaway confirm's it's gobbling up Grubhub.* https://techcrunch.com/2020/06/10/just-eat-takeaway-confirms-its-gobbling-up-grubhub-in-a-7-3b-deal

Uber. (2019a). *An operating system for everyday life.*https://www.uber.com/newsroom/everyday-life-os

Uber. (2019b). *Form S-1 registration statement—Uber Technologies Inc.*https://www.sec.gov/Archives/edgar/data/1543151/000119312519103850/d647752ds1.htm

Uber. (2020a). *2019 annual report.*https://d18rn0p25nwr6d.cloudfront.net/CIK-0001543151/f272e038-1c89-456c-acf8-cea0cffe544d.pdf

Uber. (2020b). *Form 10-Q. For the quarterly period ended June 30, 2020.* https://d18rn0p25nwr6d.cloudfront.net/CIK-0001543151/6be7ca8c-d5b0-44b5-96ea-7322b601fa82.pdf

Uber. (2021a, May 5). *Uber announces results for first quarter 2021.*https://investor.uber.com/news-events/news/press-release-details/2021/Uber-Announces-Results-for-First-Quarter-2021/

Uber. (2021b, May 5). *Q1 2021 earnings—Supplemental data.*https://s23.q4cdn.com/407969754/files/doc_financials/2021/q1/Q1-2021-Supplemental-Slides.pdf

Uber. (2021c, February 10). *Uber announces results for fourth quarter and full year 2020.*https://investor.uber.com/news-events/news/press-release-details/2021/Uber-Announces-Results-for-Fourth-Quarter-and-Full-Year-2020/default.aspx

Wall Street Journal. (2019). *Uber turns over nearly all freight revenue to truckers, analyst says.* https://www.wsj.com/articles/uber-turns-over-nearly-all-freight-revenue-to-truckers-analyst-says-11559691301

The Streaming Revolution in Global Media and the Down of an Epic Battle

4

Abstract

One of the most fascinating empirical cases on digital disruptions reshaping the strategic rules of competition within an established industry is global entertainment. The streaming revolution exposed even media behemoths like Disney to a "digital tsunami" which triggered a spectacular investment boom, comparable with the railways in the 1860s or the car industry in the 1940s. Netflix is nowadays the global market leader in film streaming, having lured more than 200 million subscribers on its platform. Netflix's 10C Business Design will be benchmarked with Disney's lately strategy revitalization by its multi-billion 21st Century Fox (TFCF) acquisition and the introduction of its own streaming platform Disney+. After the discussion of the different Business Designs of the streaming endgame contenders, the strength of subscription-based video-on-demand (SVoD) platforms is assessed by applying again the eight platform value drivers, as defined within Chap. 1. Besides the mandatory investments to scale technologically entertainment platforms, also significant content investments (originals) are part of most streaming platforms' DNA. Such investments are in contradiction to the typical asset-light characteristic of platforms, but are a crucial ingredient of their competitive advantage. The Reverse DCF valuation of Netflix, embedded in "the streaming gambit" picture of the future, supplements the discussion of entertainment streaming platforms.

One of the most fascinating empirical cases on digital disruptions reshaping the strategic rules of competition within an established industry is global entertainment. The streaming revolution exposed even the media behemoths to a "digital tsunami" which triggered a spectacular investment boom, comparable with the railways in the 1860s or the car industry in the 1940s. A modern yardstick of the significance of the streaming revolution is, besides the significant volume of investments, the number of monthly active users or subscribers (MAPCs) of a platform. Netflix realized an

T. Feix, *Valuing Digital Business Designs and Platforms*, Future of Business and Finance, https://doi.org/10.1007/978-3-030-83632-0_4

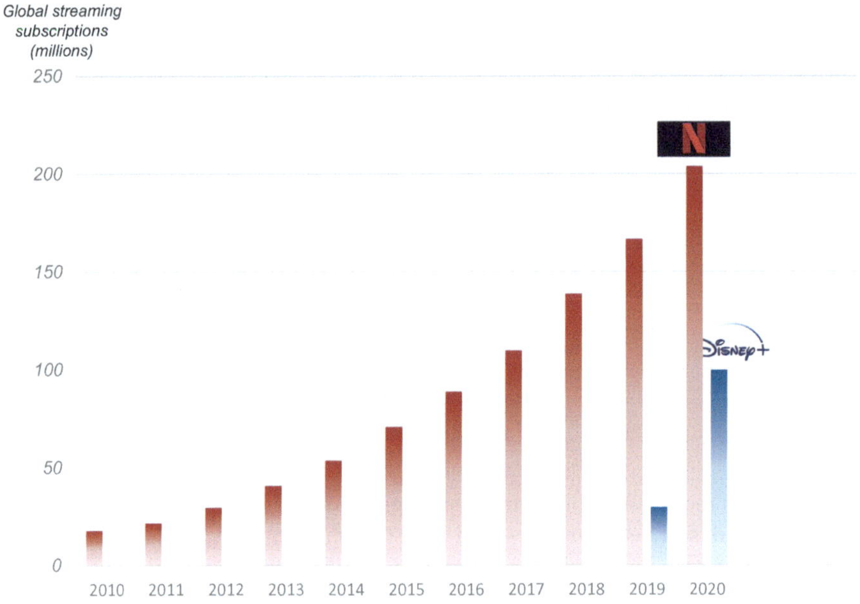

Fig. 4.1 Global streaming subscribers: Netflix head start versus Disney+ catch-up strategy

exponential subscriber growth within the last decade. Having gained 210 million subscribers till the end of the first quarter 2021, Netflix is nowadays the global market leader in film streaming. The former linear entertainment distribution disrupter became in just a decade the streaming incumbent.

The entertainment giant Disney, coming late to the streaming market, realized a jumpstart after introducing Disney+, besides its minor streaming endeavors Hulu and ESPN+. In 18 months, meaning in roughly a tenth of the time it took the challenger Netflix, Disney lured 116 million viewers on its streaming platform and plans to have 325 million subscribers by 2024 (Economist, 2021a). The subscription performance of the two streaming contenders is summarized by Fig. 4.1.

Entertainment streaming platforms provide creative content on their platform from artists, thereby connecting the latter with entertainment consumers, meaning viewers, listeners, or gamers. This double-sided approach is enlarged to a three-party concept, if streaming platforms offer advertisers to place commercials on the platform, targeting the platform's entertainment community. The Business Designs of entertainment double-sided or multi-sided platforms are significantly different: Double-sided streaming platforms use typically monthly subscription-based revenue models, whereas 3P networks are ad-financed platforms. Both approaches might be combined within freemium concepts, where the "free" platform partners uses a basic, often by advertisements interrupted and ad-funded service, whereas subscribers get for their fee a premium membership with uninterrupted streaming experience. For platforms applying a freemium approach, the churn rate from free users to subscribers is an important value driver.

Examples are YouTube using an ad-funded model; Netflix, Amazon Prime, or Apple's streaming services Apple Music and Apple TV+ applying a pure subscription model; and Spotify in deploying a freemium approach. The content of a streaming platform defines the perceived entertainment quality of viewers or listeners. Therefore, especially film streaming platforms started lately to create also their own, high-quality content, branded as originals.

Innovators like Netflix in film streaming or Spotify in music streaming created for traditional media business strategies uncontestable blue oceans by addressing multiple viewer USPs like convenience, as well as permanent and seamless availability on any digital device combined with near unlimited variety of genres and languages based on a long-tail strategy. Side by side to their streaming technology platform, the innovators built also the above-described new revenue models based on monthly recurring video-on-demand (VoD) subscriptions. More than 700 million viewers (Economist, 2019e) have flocked on such platforms already before the pandemic, but the latter gave VoD streaming Business Designs an ultimate boost. Netflix crossed in 2020 the 200 million streaming membership milestone and achieved 37 million paid net subscription additions during this pandemic dominated year (Netflix, 2021b).

The caveat, at least for originals producers, is that streaming became a costly, meaning investment heavy business. Entertainment companies have to lavish continuously significant funds and cash flows on creating new original content or for licensing attractive films, series, and documentaries as a prerequisite to lure additional paying members on their platform. Netflix, for example, spends yearly between $12 and $14 billion on new content creation. Also Disney intends to multiply its annual content investment from today's $2 billion to $8–9 billion for Disney+ and $14–16 billion across all its streaming channels, which include as well Hulu and ESPN+, where the latter is a sports-focused streaming platform. This strategy will set it on par with Netflix's investments by 2024 and will fund the release of around 10 new "Star Wars" series, 10 Marvel comic book-based series, 15 further original series, and the same amount of feature films, all going straight to Disney+ (Economist, 2020). In so far, streaming is an investment-heavy Business Design and counterintuitive if compared with the typically asset-light pattern of platform companies, as described in Chap. 1. Due to these content investment needs, American streaming companies built up a significant debt pile of more than $500 billion (Economist, 2019e).

The streaming-induced disruptive innovation and the massive shift of viewers' preferences from traditional entertainment channels to the new streaming platforms challenged entertainment incumbents to re-vitalize their Business Design or risking to become meaningless. Even global media giants like Disney had to recalibrate their strategy. Figure 4.2 on value diagnostics highlights how Netflix became a game changer and neck-on-neck competitor of established global incumbents like Disney within the last decade. The streaming inventor multiplied its revenues 20-fold between 2010 and 2020, and with a CAGR of 38%, its market capitalization growth outpaced even its revenue growth. Netflix is at the point of writing this book with a $255 billion market valuation of its equity priced in line with Disney Inc.

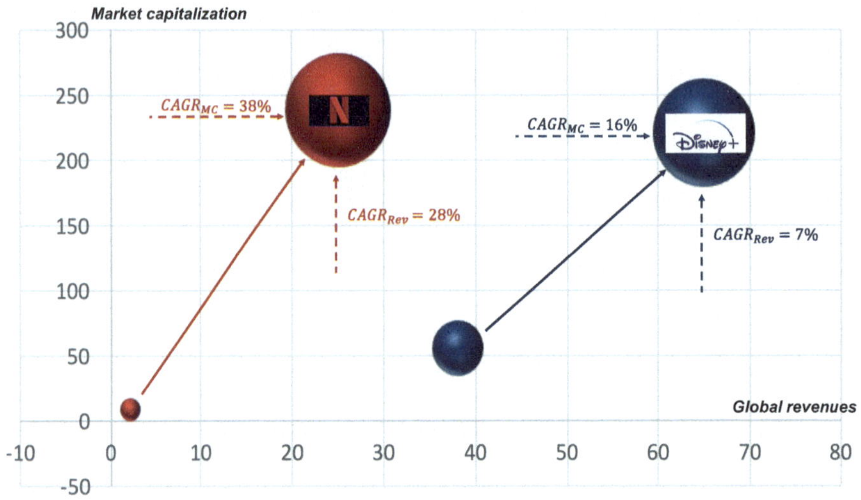

Fig. 4.2 An epic streaming and valuation battle on the horizon: Netflix versus Disney valuation diagnostics

But, the entertainment behemoth became lately a poster boy of a successful tech-driven turnaround and for a successful off- to online platform retaliation strategy. [1] Having applied for decades a dominant, vertically integrated Business Design centered on its DNA of "content is king," Disney realized the seismic, technology-enabled shift in its core entertainment market in the last years. By acquiring most of the assets of the 21st Century Fox franchise and merging two powerful content libraries, as well as by introducing its own on-demand streaming services Disney+, ESPN+ with focus on sport content, and HULU, which is a jointly owned streaming service of entertainment companies, the company re-innovated its strategy successfully.

This sea change in the competitive and technological environment of the global media ecosystem led to an investment bonanza of more than $650 billion on content build-up and acquisitions within the 5 years before the pandemic (Economist, 2019c). This multibillion investment spree reshaped the global media ecosystem and the way entertainment is created, produced, and distributed, as well as how viewers consume it.

On the M&A markets, especially 2019 was exposed to frantic deal-making activities where alone three mega-deals counted for more than a $215 billion transaction volume. Besides the before-mentioned acquisition of the 21st Century Fox assets by Disney for $74 billion, AT&T acquired Time Warner for $104 billion, while Comcast strengthened its European network by the acquisition of the local broadcaster Sky for $40 billion.

[1] The conceptual framework of off- to online platform retaliation strategies has been introduced and described within Chap. 1 on platform strategies.

Lately, AT&T reversed its former acquisition by spinning off WarnerMedia and merging it with Discovery. This $43 billion transaction [2] showed two things. First, the continued reshaping of the global media landscape. Second, the need for global scale as even WarnerMedia with its streaming service HBO embedded within the AT&T empire seemed to be unable to compete on global scale with Netflix, Disney +, and the likes. The new entity will become globally the second largest media empire by revenues after Disney (Economist, 2021b).

Just a week after AT&T unraveled its entertainment endeavor, Amazon acquired the Metro-Goldwyn-Mayer (MGM) studio, the legendary film studio behind the "James Bond" franchise as its arguable crown jewel, for close to $9 billion. As the transaction includes MGM's overall expansive content library with more than 4000 movies, including global hits like "The Terminator" or "Rocky," as well as compelling TV shows such as "Fargo," the deal will enlarge Amazon's own entertainment content library significantly. The strategic rational of all of those transactions was foremost to create enough content for enticing viewers for exclusive streaming services and to create the necessary scale to fund further content investments. As the latest wave of transactions within the media sector sums up to $240 billion, six times higher compared year on year, the renewal of global entertainment of the early 2020s has found no halt so far (Financial Times, 2021a).

The significant growth rates in digital-affluent monthly active streaming platform users went not unnoticed by digital natives. Whereas Netflix as streaming innovator and Disney as traditional entertainment power house are media pure plays, technology giants entered the streaming ecosystem by competing on different grounds. Apple and Amazon may see streaming more as a strategic supplement to strengthen their online service portfolio than entertainment as an attractive stand-alone business by itself. Apple is rumored to have invested more than $2 billion into originals and for luring high-profile directors as well as actors from Hollywood as entrance ticket for its new streaming service Apple TV+. Amazon, by leveraging its Prime members' access, invested with $5 billion per year even more (Economist, 2019b). And, those technology companies have deep pockets of cash, which may be deployed in the years to come on building an even more powerful streaming empire. It is highly probable that the streaming market will be exposed to a streaming endgame in the 2020s.

[2] As part of the transactions, AT&T will receive a $43 billion upfront payment as a mix of cash, stocks, and sold-off debt. Besides, AT&T shareholders will own 71% of the new, merged entity with Discovery. The transaction therefore values WarnerMedia at about $100 billion (Economist, 2021b). The Discovery/WarnerMedia combination's indicative enterprise value will approach $150 billion (Financial Times, 2021b).

4.1 Streaming Endgame

All those investments led to a hyper-contested streaming market fueled by Schumpeterian competition between giant streaming contenders like Netflix, Disney, Discovery/Time Warner, Comcast, ViacomCBS, Amazon, and Apple, following diverse corporate strategy approaches to scale their proprietary streaming platform. The core streaming platforms and their main strategies are summarized in Fig. 4.3.

Disney, AT&T or now Discovery/TimeWarner, ViacomCBS, and Comcast might face thereby a challenging trade-off. On the one side, being exposed to streaming pure plays like Netflix and technology giants' integrated online service bundles they are forced to boost the transition of their traditional media Business Design into a twenty-first-century streaming model. As such, AT&T released its HBO Max service in 2019 moving its then owned WarnerMedia franchise even more to streaming, while Comcast extended the reach of its ad-supported Peacock streaming business (Economist, 2019d). On the other side, all those streaming investments undermine the incumbent's existing lucrative, still cash flow-generating traditional media business, a traditional strategy deadlock, which might be only overcome by deploying an ambidexterity approach.

As more than 500 scripted series are nowadays released per year, it is to be asked when the spending binge will come to a halt. Creative destruction will consolidate

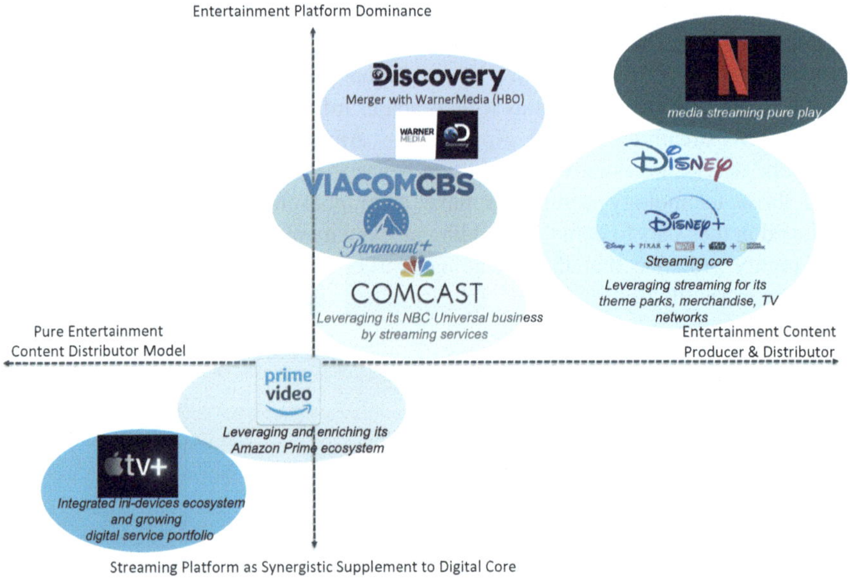

Fig. 4.3 The seismic shift of streaming strategies creating a hyper-competitive entertainment ecosystem

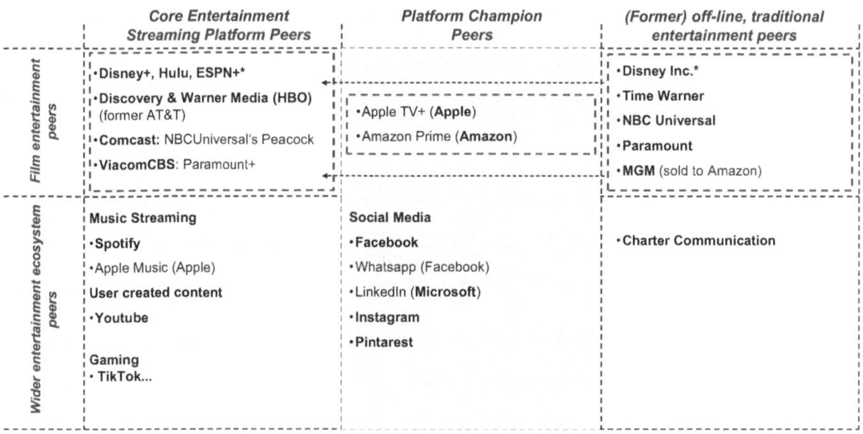

Fig. 4.4 Netflix's entertainment and streaming ecosystem and its peers

sooner or later also the global streaming market and might lead to "the biggest hangover Hollywood has ever seen" (Economist, 2019b). It will get interesting which streaming strategies and platforms will succeed, and only some endings will be happy ones for equity as well as debt holders.

Driven by the tailwinds of the pandemic for locked-down viewers, the transition of traditional entertainment to streaming saw another boost. At the beginning of 2021, Netflix was still leading the streaming revolution with its more than 200 million subscribers, but Amazon Prime says to have in the meantime a reach to 150 million Prime members, whereas Disney+ seems to be the fastest-growing streaming service with more than 100 million subscribers. WarnerMedia's HBO and NBC Universal's Peacock+ follow with round about 40 million subscribers leaving big screens and joining flat screens.

To evaluate streaming platforms from a broader perspective of consumer entertainment, the peer group assessment may include, besides the streaming contenders, any, foremost digital company competing for consumers' leisure time and attention. Such a wider scope with respect to the peer group design might include music streaming or social media platforms like Facebook, WhatsApp, and LinkedIn, as described by Fig. 4.4.

4.2 Game Changer M&A Within the Media Ecosystem: Disney Acquires 21st Century Fox

Transactions have been for decades part of media companies' and, especially, Disney's DNA. In the 2010s, entertainment champions used acquisitions foremost to build vertically integrated media Business Designs incorporating both ends of the media value chain, entertainment content creation, and traditional media content distribution: Comcast acquired NBC Universal in 2013. AT&T took over satellite

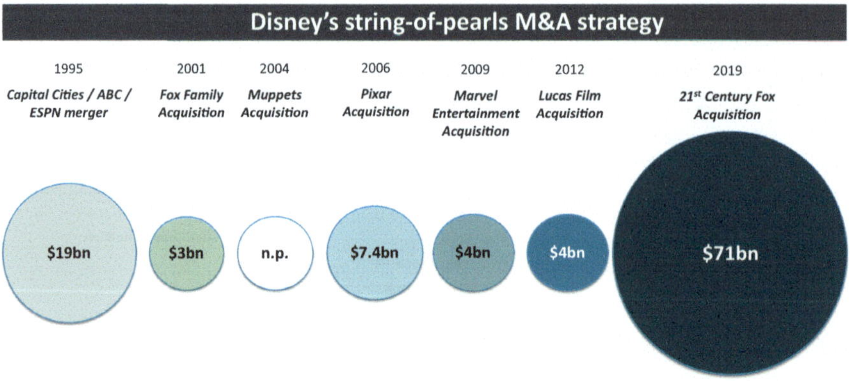

Fig. 4.5 Disney's string of pearls M&A strategy and entertainment portfolio revitalization

television specialist Direct TV in 2015 for $67 billion before acquiring in 2018 the Time Warner franchise including HBO for $104 billion just to spin it off and merge it with Discovery in 2021, as described above (Economist, 2019d).

Disney, in stark contrast to its peers, expanded horizontally by a string-of-pearls transaction strategy: After its acquisition of Pixar's animation studios, the "Star Wars" franchise, Lucasfilm, and Marvel Entertainment, its megadeal to acquire 21st Century Fox from Rupert Murdoch was an ultimate milestone in building a powerful content library with a portfolio of global characters.

Disney's corporate development, littered by these original content and film-portfolio acquisitions, followed a clear strategic rational: one the one side, to enlarge its global entertainment portfolio and, on the other side, to extend its technology capabilities with respect to animation, streaming, and further technology enablers shaping probably the future entertainment ecosystem. Thereby, Disney developed a lasting influence on what content we view and how we view movies, shows, and news, as highlighted by Fig. 4.5.

- On the content side, multiple tailored acquisitions enlarged Disney's abundant catalogue of own-created classics. The $19 billion transaction of *Capital Cities ABC/ESPN* in 1995 was an entrance ticket to the world of sports, besides its extension into supplementary cable TV networks. The 2001 acquisition of the *Fox Family Channel* for $3 billion added content foremost for teens and young adults like "Pretty Little Liars" to the then kids-centered Disney portfolio. It was also the starting point for the close relationships between Disney and Fox owner Rupert Murdoch. The next transactional milestone was the acquisition of *the rights of The Muppets Show* in 2004, one of the longest-running franchises. But two transactions might stand out within Disney's content-driven acquisitions: A further line of classics was added in 2009 by the $4 billion acquisition of *Marvel Entertainment*, the home of superheroes with blockbusters like "The Avengers," "X-Men," or "The Fantastic Four." The Marvel acquisition positioned Disney hardly contestable due to its global box office power. The 2012 $4 billion acquisition of *Lucasfilm* with its Star Wars saga, as one of the most valuable entertainment properties of all time, gave Disney's franchise portfolio an ultimate boost.

- On the technology end, the early acquisition of ABC supplemented Disney's distribution approach by *ABC's* cable channel network and 225 affiliated stations (Kemet, 2019; Kim & Mauborgne, 1999; Uber, 2019). The *Pixar studios* acquisition in 2006 for more than $7 billion is another prime technology example and strengthened especially Disney's animation capabilities for its movie development and production. Jointly, the companies developed a sequence of highly successful films like "Finding Nemo," "The Incredibles," or lately "Soul." The 2017 acquisition of *BAMTech*, a New York-based streaming media start-up company, intended to strengthen its direct-to-consumer capabilities to build up Disney+ as a capable streaming platform.

But, a true game changer in the entertainment ecosystem was Disney's acquisition of 21st Century Fox (TFCF[3]). This transaction offered multiple strategic advantages for Disney, an extension of its international reach, a further shift from vertical to horizontal entertainment dominance, and a springboard, by its content extension, for introducing a highly valuable streaming video-on-demand (SVoD) service, in Disney's terminology its direct-to-consumer (DTC) business. As a further outcome of the TFCF acquisition, Disney became the market leader of the studio film industry with a consolidated market share of 31%. Disney's Chairman and CEO Robert Iger underlined the strategic rational of the deal within his transaction announcement "combining Disney's and 21st Century Fox's wealth of creative content and proven talent creates the preeminent global entertainment company, well-positioned to lead in an incredibly dynamic and transformative era (Twenty-First Century Fox, 2019)."

A transaction between Disney and Fox was rumored in spring 2017. The TFCF franchise became since its inauguration in 1935 one of the most attractive entertainment assets spanning across six continents. It was the home of shows like "The Simpsons," broadcasting cable networks like FX, the Fox Sports Network, the Fox News channel, National Geographic, the rights to 28 US Fox TV stations, more than 350 international channels, as well as a portfolio of movie favorites like the "Fantastic Four" or "X-Men."

The transaction also targeted to combine two financially powerful media giants with EBITDA-margins in the 20–30% range, as pinpointed in Fig. 4.6. The two companies entered on December 14, 2017, into a preliminary purchase agreement that valued the targeted assets of TFCF originally at $52.4 billion, targeting one of the biggest transactions the entertainment industry had ever seen. At the time,

[3] After the acquisition of the outstanding capital stock of 21st Century Fox, Inc. the acquired business was subsequently renamed TFCF Corporation (TFCF) (Walt Disney, 2019). Therefore, in the following, TFCF will be used as abbreviation to describe the acquired company, its assets, or the transaction between Disney TFCF.

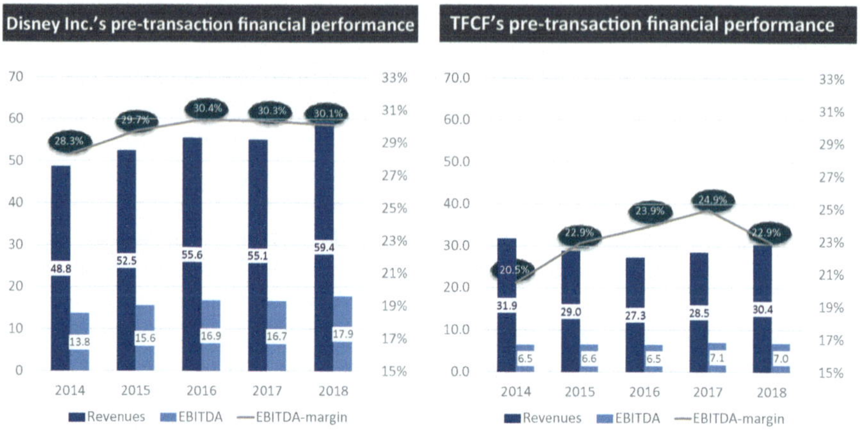

Fig. 4.6 Pre-transaction value diagnostics Disney (acquirer) and TFCF (target). All financial data based on SEC 10-K reports and Financial Statements of Disney and TFCF for the financial years 2014 through 2018

including TWCF's net debt of $13.7 billion, the total transaction value stood at $66.1 billion.

The two transaction partners also detailed the deal structure: Disney intended to acquire the TFCF's iconic collection of films, series, and cable networks, the Fox's film and TV studios, the networks National Geographic and FX, the Indian and Southeast Asian pay-TV broadcaster Star TV, and stakes in Sky, Endemol Shine Group, and Hulu, as well as regional sports networks. The transaction structure proposed to not include the Fox Network and Fox News which were intended to be carved out and set up as a stand-alone entity Fox New before closing the transaction with Disney.[4]

Disney's own originals and entertainment content with favorite titles including its animated features, "Marvel" and "Star Wars" films, paired with the potentially added Fox's repertoire of content, including the "X-Men," "Alien," the "Predator" franchises, the license rights for "Star Wars IV," and shows like "The Simpsons," "Family Guy," and "The X-Files," seemed like a perfect match to offer viewers globally one of the most attractive entertainment portfolios. The acquisition intended also to bolster Disney's plans to become a dominant streaming service platform, making it a capable contender to Netflix.

But, due to the attractiveness of TFCF's assets and the perception of a merger endgame at the time in the entertainment ecosystem with a multitude of high-profile transactions underway, a bidding war kicked in between Disney and Comcast. Both contenders saw the TFCF acquisition as a potentially transformative transaction to

[4] This is an important detail, as sometimes the transactions is wrongly perceived as if Disney acquired the listed TFCF with all its assets. Transaction multiples applied on "Fox old" comprising all assets are therefore misleading.

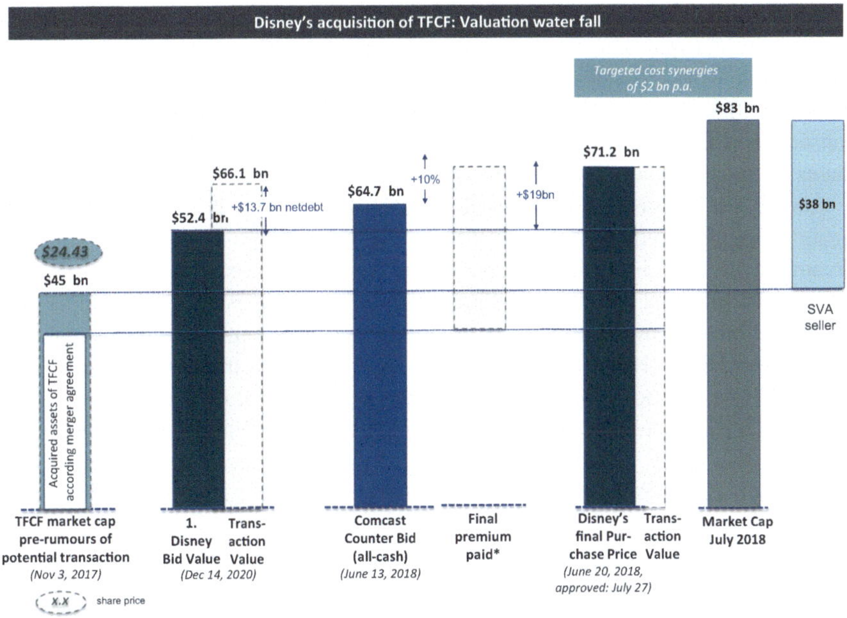

Fig. 4.7 Valuation diagnostics of the bidding war between Disney and Comcast for TFCF assets

build an impressive catalogue of movies, shows, and channels. The ultimate intent was also for Comcast to use an enlarged entertainment content as a Trojan horse to enter the competition with streaming innovators like Netflix or HBO.

After 2 years, Disney finally won a fierce bidding contest, and the two transaction partners announced jointly the deal on March 19, 2019, becoming effective a day later and by Disney paying $51.57 per share[5] or $71.2 billion as a total equity value for TFCF (Twenty-First Century Fox, 2019). As Disney acquired with the transaction also $19.2 billion of TFCF debt and $19.8bn of cash, the total transaction value stood also at close to $71 billion. Disney's offer topped Comcast's final offer of $65 billion by 10% while also providing shareholders of TFCF the option of receiving cash instead of stock. The means of payment was a 50-50 split, by paying $35.7 billion in cash and offering 343 millions of shares of the new joint company (Walt Disney, 2019). Disney targeted with the transaction $2 billion of pre-tax synergies per year to be captured till 2021 (Twenty-First Century Fox, 2019, p. 7; Walt Disney, 2019). The valuation flow of Disney's transformative acquisition is summarized by Fig. 4.7.

[5] More precisely and as set forth in the Merger Agreement, at the effective time of the Acquisition, each shareholder of TFCF had the choice to exchange shares of TFCF common stock in par for $51.572626 in cash (the "cash consideration") or alternatively in 0.4517 shares of common stock of the new holding company "New Disney," defined as TWDC Holdco (the "stock consideration"), incorporating both transaction partners' assets (Twenty-First Century Fox, 2019).

Before executing the transaction, TFCF completed its spinoff of a portfolio of distinct TFCF assets like the Fox News Channel, the Fox Sports, and Business broadcast networks, besides certain other assets and liabilities, integrating them into the spun off entity "New Fox." TFCF distributed prior to the execution of the transaction with Disney according rights to its existing shareholders for all issued shares of this new entity (Walt Disney, 2019).

Already the merger document indicated that the ultimate target was not only to create an unparalleled entertainment library but to extend post-transaction the joint streaming offering, including ESPN+ for sports enthusiasts, the Disney+ SVoD service anticipated at the time to be launched late in 2019, as well as Disney's and TFCF's combined ownership stake in the general entertainment DTC streaming service Hulu, LCC (Hulu [6]). For the latter, Disney received through the transaction with TFCF an additional 30% stake in stepping up its total ownership position to 60%, which was post-acquisition increased further to 67% (Walt Disney, 2020, p. 3). In so far, the TFCF transaction opened up a probable epic battle for the global streaming market dominance between Disney and Netflix.

4.3 Decoding Strategic Value: Netflix Versus Disney+ 10C Business Designs

For the two entertainment contenders, their dedicated Business Designs will be assessed in the following, before analyzing the platform strength of entertainment streaming services.

4.3.1 Netflix

Reed Hastings and Marc Randolph co-founded Netflix by offering online movie rental services in the USA. The early revitalization of its Business Design in the mid-2010s through the introduction of on-demand, subscription-based services gave Netflix a head start in streaming. By strategically deploying these tailwinds, the company positioned itself as one of the most influential entertainment empires nowadays.

[6] In 2006, Hulu partnered with a portfolio of high-caliber media and social network firms like AOL, NBC Universal, Comcast, Facebook, MSN, Myspace, and Yahoo! to distribute their content and to build a viable competitor by its reach to Netflix. Disney joined in as stakeholder in 2009, giving HULU rights to content from both ABC and Disney Channel for an equity stake of 30%.

4.3.2 Competitive Strategy and Purpose (CS)

Netflix invented a new dominant design in the entertainment ecosystem by introducing and rapidly scaling its subscription-based on-demand streaming (SVoD) platform. Today, it is the most successful entertainment platform and a globally perceived brand with more than 200 million subscribers. As the company is a SVoD pure play, it has the strategic advantage in comparison to media behemoths not to be caught by a legacy of traditional TV or cable assets. The company has not the necessity to follow an ambidexterity approach, where the growth in new streaming services goes in the end to the detriment of a still cash flow generating traditional media business.

The growth of its streaming platform is based upon a long-tail strategy offering a wide variety of genres as well as languages and combining blockbusters like "Narcos" or "House of Cards" with niche or localized content. Besides, its platform offers, by combining big data with analytics technologies, individual viewer preferences-tailored film recommendations and services. This segment-of-one approach creates an ultimate customer experience, luring viewers on the platform and creating platform economics.

The content strategy follows a high-quality approach by investing yearly up to $15 billion in new original content creation and by acquiring media talents and first-class entertainment capabilities in an addition to licensed content. These massive investments serve, besides its global brand and entertainment capabilities, as a substantial barrier of entry. Nevertheless, the funding of such significant entertainment investments is a financial burden for streaming players.

Netflix also reinvented the media revenue model by introducing subscription-based video-on-demand (SVoD) services. Different subscription-pricing models are tailored around distinct viewer priorities.

4.3.3 Core Value Proposition (CV)

The streaming disruption has created an enormous windfall for consumers. From a viewer's perspective, the traditional entertainment service model was simple. First, viewers flocked to cinemas for watching new releases, which were after two to three months offered as video rentals. Additionally, advertisers have been from the very beginning part of the traditional media viewer's journey, where the former paid cable or TV networks for their access to viewers.

The success of HBO, the then-owned cable channel of Time Warner, with weekly series like "Sex and the City" brought in the 1990s empirical evidence that viewers are willing to pay premia if they experience attractive entertainment content. Nevertheless, the content was still distributed through pay-TV channels. The ultimate turning of the media tide was brought to customers by Netflix's innovative streaming service offering.

Netflix recreated entertainment USPs for its viewers on multiple ends: It offers through its streaming platform seamless and convenient high-quality entertainment.

Its services are 24/7 available on a fingertip on any mobile device, laptop, or TV at any location, even offline. Convenience is addressed by its digital, on-demand pattern, which also enables a direct platform-viewer interface and makes any intermediary obsolete.

As for viewers variety is the species of life, Netflix offers on its platform a wide portfolio of TV shows, documentaries, and movies, as well as a significant number of genres and languages. Due to the subscription model, Netflix viewers can access the platform's film catalogue unlimited.

Netflix leverages also customer intimacy, which logs in viewers on their platform, as it runs an effective data algorithm for its proprietary recommendation system. By adding more translated subtitles of various languages as well as local films, the needs of international viewers are taken into account and strengthen platform patterns. In comparison to traditional cable and pay-TV networks, the viewer experience will not be interrupted by marketing adds, increasing customer experience significantly.

4.3.4 Customer and Markets (CM)

Globally viewers substituted pay-TV at home and theater visits by streaming quite rapidly. Proved by empirical evidence in the US entertainment market, especially the younger-than-34-year-old viewer segment is cutting off the cord as their time spent watching pay-TV dropped between 60% and 80% within the last decade (Economist, 2019b). But, also for the elder viewers the transition to streaming seems irreversible.

Netflix viewers have more to choose from attractive subscription prices: Viewers can pick from different streaming packages that cost typically less than $10 compared with $80 or so for a typical cable bundle offer. For its on-demand entertainment services, Netflix designed three subscription plans, a basic, a standard, and a premium offering. The subscription plans are tailored around the number of devices and viewers and provide unlimited access to Netflix's exhaustive film content.

The viewer reach seems unlimited, as diversity is addressed by a vast offering of genres and entertainment content like movies, series, TV shows, or lately documentaries and animated features. Moreover, Netflix has been expanding to over 190 countries (Netflix, 2021a). The internationalization was backed by offering locally produced and according regional preferences-adjusted content which became partially not only local hits but global blockbusters like in the case of "La Casa de Papel." This strategy to grow the local original content slate was extended lately and proved successful. "Lupin," a charming Parisian burglar story transferred into a nowadays more action-thrilling environment, was not just in France, but as well as in dozens of other countries a number 1 bestseller, ranked #2 in the US top ten list of Netflix, and probably had more than 70 million viewers within the first 28 days after its release (Netflix, 2021b, p. 3).

The significance of the international markets for Netflix's overall growth momentum became transparent in the last years. Whereas for subscribers 2017 turned out as a tipping point where international viewers overtook North American ones, the same

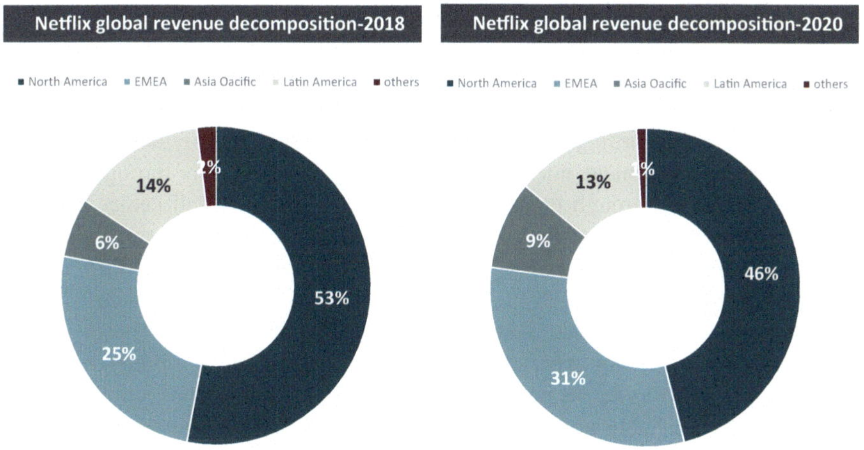

Fig. 4.8 Netflix's regional growth engines

development was perceived for revenues 2 years later. The significant growth in new paying memberships of 36 million in 2020 was with 83% driven by international markets outside North America (Netflix, 2021a).

Nowadays, besides North America with 46% of global revenues, especially Europe became a growth engine for the company and contributes 31% of global revenues. Besides, Latin America with 13% and Asia Pacific with 9% are important markets for the company and offer significant growth potentials. Nevertheless, also US viewers are still joining the streaming platform and grew from 65 million to 74 million paying subscribers between 2018 and 2020 (Netflix, 2021a).

International subscribers might offer the bulk of growth options for Netflix, but the caveat is that abroad growth might come potentially with higher costs to win viewers due to the need of tailor content for each regional entertainment market with its unique viewer preferences and tastes. The regional decomposition of Netflix's revenues is summarized by Fig. 4.8.

Also the quality of the produced originals by Netflix was proven lately, as evidenced by the crop of Oscar and Emmy nominations for its streamed content. Especially the Emmy nomination became a neck-to-neck contest between HBO and Netflix. At the 71st annual Emmy Awards, the last prior to the pandemic, the two streaming contenders accounted for 50% of the nominees for outstanding drama series and three of the seven for outstanding comedies (Economist, 2019a).

Netflix's market strategy intends to become an engrained part of the cultural zeitgeist by big viewership titles like "The Crown" with more than 100 million viewers since its launch, or "Bridgerton" and "The Queen's Gambit" with more than 60 million viewers within the first 28 days.

4.3.5 Customer Relationship (CR)

The capturing of new viewers as well as the interaction with and retention of existing subscribers is obviously, as being a platform company, a foremost digital approach. To simplify the onboarding process on the platform, Netflix provides an easy-to-understand and convenient interface. Nevertheless, Netflix offers through its web portal by live chat, through email inquiries, or simply by its call center multiple support options for its subscribers. Specifically, the online live chat service should provide a human touch and feel of the otherwise anonymous interface of the streaming platform.

Throughout the digital entertainment journey on the platform, viewers may set up and manage their viewing experience according to their individual preferences and priorities. The self-service set preferences are managed through the Netflix app and website and are available any time. Additionally, the Netflix recommendation hitlist intends to personalize its entertainment experience.

Also the payment process is fully digitalized. The monthly subscription fee is automatically transferred from the customer's bank account to Netflix until cancellation of the subscription. Netflix's marketing strategy integrated also offerings like gift cards and grants various discounts as promotional plan to strengthen viewer relationships.

4.3.6 Channels (CH)

Essentially, Netflix's platform and app itself is the core channel through which its vast variety of entertainment content is distributed. In contrast to its key competitor Disney, which uses three streaming channels, Disney+, ESPN+, and Hulu, Netflix centers all its content on one streaming platform. With its streaming channel, Netflix serves as an intermediary for the distribution of entertainment content from producers to viewer, but is taking over the producer role as well in case of its original content.

Despites its platform dominance, Netflix deploys further channels. Through the co-operation with Apple's app store, the Netflix app is widely applied on Apple devices leveraging Netflix's entertainment distribution throughout the Apple ecosystem.

Additionally for marketing, social media networks such as Facebook or Instagram, especially to reach out to younger viewers, are used by Netflix. Through these social media channels, Netflix places trailers or updates to inform about new movies or series and to interact with viewers. It is also an integral part of its strategy to shape a zeitgeist philosophy. For its localization efforts, Netflix uses selectively traditional media channels as newspapers, magazines, or sponsored programs as in the case of movie festivals.

4.3.7 Core Assets (CA)

A few, distinct core assets play a central role for the streaming platform Business Design of Netflix and define its competitive advantage.

The company's streaming platform infrastructure is at its heart as it enables Netflix to deliver its entertainment content to ever more viewers. Netflix will be hard to dislodge as it onboarded more than 200 million global subscribers on its streaming platform, giving it a head start for the streaming endgame.

To create a seamless customer journey, Netflix invested heavily in advanced digital technologies. The development of big data approaches, analytics, and content-focused algorithms should further improve viewer convenience and individualize the viewer's entertainment experience. For example, Netflix introduced lately digital parental controls so that families have more control over the content viewed and parents may set filters at the title level or by maturity rating. New digital options enable to create profile-specific lock PINs or customized autoplay settings and create transparency into themes and content viewed. Another new service approach based on digital analytics should enable viewers to find more easily the right film, series, and shows to watch. Subscribers might be reminded about highlighting titles as far as a year away or may watch instantly a title chosen by Netflix's recommendation engine tailored for a distinct viewer avoiding time-consuming browsing (Netflix, 2021b). All in all, with those digital core assets, the company intends to offer best-in-class viewer quality and more effective streaming services.

A further mission-critical asset is the extensive library of original and licensed content of Netflix. It has 47,000 TV episodes and 4000 films in its American catalogue alone. That is significantly more than its core peer Disney+ with roughly 7500 episodes and 500 films at the starting point of Disney's streaming service. Netflix spends, as described earlier, around $15 billion or so a year on new originals development and licensed material (Economist, 2019d) extending its content library further. In 2021 entertainment content spend is expected at $12 billion by Netflix. But also its contenders invest heavily to compete: Disney is forecasted to invest $15 billion, WarnerMedia/Discovery $19 billion, NBC Universal $6.5 billion, and ViacomCBS another $11 billion (Economist, 2021b).

Last but not the least, Netflix created a global brand name that seems to be appealing to all ages, preferences, and localities. Netflix is a legally registered and protected trademark. Its content library and its brand are from financial perspective intangible assets. The entertainment content on the Netflix platform is protected by its copyrights and trademarks. In addition, the company owns an extensive patent portfolio.

4.3.8 Core Capabilities (CC)

The development, improvement, and scaling of its streaming platform, the design of algorithms for its recommendation engine, or the shaping of intuitive viewer interfaces request strong capabilities in latest technologies like AI, cloud computing, analytics, or data mining. Netflix cooperates with top universities to acquire talents with respect to such technology capabilities and co-operates with leading technology firms.

Another core capability is, especially for its original content development, the management of entertainment talents, actors, celebrities, and scriptwriters. The latter play a vital role to lure viewers on its platform and to avoid a customer drain to the uprising competing streaming services. As these talents come from around the globe and are typically highly creative, this is a challenging task and is addressed up to Netflix's top management.

As Netflix viewer growth comes more and more from non-saturated international markets, the global brand management will become in the next years also a predominant task. The brand management plays also a vital role for positioning Netflix as a leading entertainment creator and as being part of the actual "zeitgeist."

4.3.9 Core-Ecosystem Partners (CE)

Netflix paid in the first years after the launch of its SVoD platform significant amounts for the rights to stream beloved licensed content like "Friends" or "The Office." This enabled the company to lure viewers on the platform. In time, Netflix began producing its originals. The success of this strategy kicked in notably in 2013 with the release of the first season of the political drama "House of Cards." But, this significant and cash flow burning strategic move brought the new challenge for the company to acquire and to co-operate with scriptwriters, actors, and a hemisphere of creative talents within the global entertainment industry far beyond the Hollywood studies. Netflix built therefore sensitive informal networks and ties with writers and actors.

With the success of its originals and by winning multiple, highly respected entertainment awards, Netflix's transition from a licensed content distributer to a creative, serious, and high-quality entertainment producer was step by step well accepted within the entertainment community. This may pay in on Netflix's competitive advantage as the proprietary original content differentiates the company's platform and sharpens its brand's uniqueness by setting it apart from its streaming peers.

A second important ecosystem partner group are technology companies in fields like big data, cloud systems, or analytics. As entertainment content provider, additionally, co-operations with hardware producers offering TVs, laptops, tablets, smartphones, or other devices are essential for Netflix to optimize viewer experience and quality.

Beyond those actual partners, in the midterm, the gaming industry may become an interesting ecosystem to co-operate with. Both, streaming and gaming, compete in the end for the limited entertainment time of their consumers. Additionally, gaming is known to apply successfully latest technologies, being a formidable benchmarking partner for the continuous improvement of streaming content and integrating more dynamic viewer-content interactions.

4.3.10 Corporate Organization (CO)

Netflix organization mimics a tailored structure-follows-strategy approach, applying a regional organizational layer separating between national and international markets, a content-driven layer separating original content production from licensed content management, and a coordinating headquarters functional layer:

- On the regional level, Netflix addresses the different needs between its domestic, more mature streaming business (US subscribers) from its international, often still in start-up mode streaming markets (non-US subscribers). This geographic scope within its organizational structure plays an important role for Netflix's international growth ambitions as it enables the company to implement regionally tailored content and marketing approaches addressing different market trends or viewer preferences.
- As Netflix manages with its originals and licensed films two distinct entertainment contents with significantly different entertainment business and management success factors, also, the organizational structure along those lines has strategic importance. The value chains of film licensing and originals production, management or distribution, requests significantly differ management capabilities and styles.
- Additionally, some headquarters' function within Netflix's entertainment content-driven organizational structure are quite unique if compared with other industries or peers: For example, its talent group is responsible for improving Netflix viewer's experience continuously; its product group designs, builds, and optimizes Netflix productions; or its content group is responsible for all content provided to subscribers including original series from around the world.

4.3.11 Cash Flow Model (CF)

Netflix is today not just measured by subscribers the SVoD champion. With revenues of $25 billion, an operating profit of $4.6 billion, and for the first time positive free cash flows, the company became also a financial powerhouse lately. This went also not unnoticed by capital markets, as evidenced by Fig. 4.9. The market capitalization of Netflix stood at more than $246 billion with an implicit share price of $555 per share at the point of writing this book. In the last decade, the price per share increased thereby from $25 to $542 at year-end 2020 more than 20-fold, with a CAGR of 39%.

Therefore, equity capital markets seem to appreciate Netflix's strategic shift from a DVD rental to a global streaming platform player. Compared with its core streaming contender Disney as well as the broader diversified NASDAQ index, Netflix outperformed on equity capital markets its peers within the last years. The pandemic was an additional booster for the company's share price, which nearly doubled year over year as viewers flocked on its platform due to stay-at-home and social distancing measures. But, also Disney's shares performed well since the

Fig. 4.9 Development market capitalization and share price Netflix versus Disney versus NASDAQ. *Source*: finance.yahoo.com 2021

company introduced successfully its own streaming platform Disney+ and intends to catch up with its contender.

As Netflix's share price and market capitalization even outperformed the revenue and profit growth, according multiples like enterprise value-to-revenue or enterprise value-to-EBITDA more than doubled since 2014 onward. Whereas the former indicates with 10 times revenues an upside outlier pricing, the latter is with 15 times EBITDA in a more long-term entertainment and platform peer benchmark upper range.

To assess in more detail the value drivers of subscription-based streaming video on-demand (SVoD) platform Business Designs, the *financial diagnostics* and the *capital market analytics modules* of the *Reverse DCF model* will be applied on Netflix's financial performance from 2010 to 2020.[7]

Netflix built an enticing, diversified entertainment catalogue by aggressive investments in its originals development, as well as by content acquisition to become the dominant viewer platform and the #1 choice when it comes to leisure time spending. The actual target is a yearly investment of $15–16 billion to develop new originals and acquire licensed content. This is summarized by Fig. 4.10.

In so far, Netflix deploys not the advantages of an asset-light Business Design. Nevertheless, the pairing of its streaming platform with tailored, significant investments in mission-critical entertainment content, originals as well as licensed, might play out as the true competitive advantage of its platform and a formidable barrier of entry protecting high margin zones.

[7] The financial diagnostics model is applied in the Netflix case study by an in-depth assessment of Netflix's audited financial statements and SEC reporting, especially the 10-K reports for the last 10 years 2010–2020. A more detailed discussion and breakdown of the financial assessment will be provided within the Reverse DCF valuation subchapter.

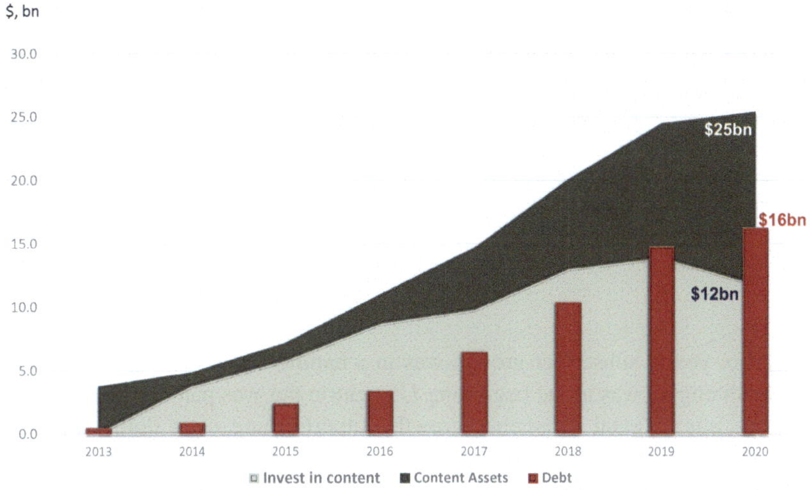

Fig. 4.10 Netflix's content investments, content assets, and indebtedness. Includes the balance sheet positions net current content assets and net non-current content assets as carved out from Netflix's 10-K SEC reports for the financial years 2013 till 2020. Debt includes the balance sheet positions short-term debt and long-term debt as carved out from Netflix's 10-K SEC reports for the financial years 2013 till 2020

This investment spree was funded by burning yearly $3 billion of cash and by accumulating a debt pile of more than $16 billion, foremost long-term interest-bearing liabilities. Not surprisingly, scepticism if Netflix is able to grow its streaming platform quickly enough to outpace interest and debt repayments have been worrying debt as well as equity investors and heightened before the pandemic kicked in.

But, it seems that the company's investment thesis played out as it achieved in 2020 a major financial milestone. By luring more than 210 million subscribers on its platform, the streaming platform champion achieved its cash flow breakeven, after years of cash drain due to its high investments in entertainment content. Still in the 2 prior years, free cash flow was with −$4.8 billion in 2018 and −$3.9 billion in 2019 significantly negative. The management confirmed on its Q1 2021 earnings call not only to achieve positive cash flows in 2021 but to sustainably grow cash flows beyond 2021. The projected free cash flow performance from subscription payments paired with a $8.2 billion cash balance and an $750 million undrawn credit facility will probably enable the company to fund in the future further content growth without onboarding additional debt. Much more, the company made the announcement to be able to buy back shares on the equity market due to its strong cash flow performance and to repay its 5.375% bond maturing out of free cash flow funds.

The core value drivers mirror exactly Netflix's strategy to enter the streaming market as a blue ocean around 2013 and its scaling of the streaming business since then to become the dominant player in the global SVoD entertainment ecosystem. Platform subscribers grew from 19 million in 2010 to close to 204 million paying viewers at year-end 2020 with a CAGR of 27% significantly outperforming media

Netflix Financial Diagnostics - Condensed IS

		2010	2011	2012	2013	2014	2015	2016	2017	2018	2019	2020	
		0	1	2	3	4	5	6	7	8	9	10	
Subscribers (#, m)		18	22	30	41	54	70,8	89	111	139,259	167,090	203,663	27,46%
growth y-o-y			22%	36%	37%	32%	31%	26%	24%	26%	20%	22%	
										100,0%	100,0%	100,0%	
REVENUES	1.670.249	2.162.625	3.204.577	3.609.282	4.374.562	5.504.656	6.779.511	8.830.669	11.692.713	15.794.341	20.156.447	24.996.056	27,73%
growth y-o-y		29%	48%	13%	21%	26%	23%	30%	32%	35%	28%	24%	
EBIT		283.641	376.068	49.992	228.347	402.648	305.826	379.793	838.679	1.605.226	2.604.254	4.585.289	32,09%
EBIT margin		13,1%	11,7%	1,4%	5,2%	7,3%	4,5%	4,3%	7,2%	10,2%	12,9%	18,3%	
Depreciation & Amortization		340.068	839.619	1.702.083	2.241.680	2.781.798	3.547.045	4.924.978	6.330.385	7.656.457	9.319.826	10.922.622	
Depreciation		38.099	43.747	45.469	48.374	54.028	62.283	57.528	71.911	83.157	103.579	115.710	
Amortization		301.969	795.872	1.656.614	2.193.306	2.727.770	3.484.762	4.867.450	6.258.474	7.573.300	9.216.247	10.806.912	
EBITDA		623.709	1.215.687	1.752.075	2.470.027	3.184.446	3.852.871	5.304.771	7.169.064	9.261.683	11.924.080	15.507.911	37,90%
EBITDA margin		28,8%	37,9%	48,5%	56,5%	57,9%	56,8%	60,1%	61,3%	58,6%	59,2%	62,0%	
Net Income (Loss)		160.853	226.126	17.152	112.403	266.799	122.641	186.678	558.929	1.211.242	1.866.916	2.761.395	
Earnings (net income or loss) per share													
Basic		0,44	0,61	0,04	0,28	0,63	0,29	0,44	1,29	2,78	4,26	6,26	

Fig. 4.11 Reverse DCF model for Netflix: Excerpt of financial diagnostics and capital market module

peers. Also, yearly subscriber growth was in a bandwidth between 20% and 37%. The growth engine was at the beginning US centric but was paired especially since 2015 with international subscriber growth outperforming even domestic growth rates.

The revenue model of the streaming innovator is based on the discussed subscription model, which comprises three types of SVoD service packages with tailored monthly subscription fees, where most viewers pay $10 or less per month. Nevertheless, the company was able, despite the hypercompetitive nature of the streaming market, to rise the subscription price per month by $1 to $14 for its most popular plan lately, providing empirical evidence for Netflix market impact and customer's willingness to pay for quality entertainment. Overall, Netflix was successful to increase its average revenue per member between 2018 and 2020 from $9.88 to $11.02 (Netflix, 2021b, p. 2). Besides its subscription-based revenues, Netflix also generates some further revenue streams from movie studios with Netflix originals for popular series like "House of Cards" or "Fuller House."

Netflix revenues grew in line with its subscriber growth with a CAGR of 27.7% in the last decade. Implicitly, this means that subscriber fees are quite robust and that growth was not bought with viewer discounts, offering thereby significantly better and more sustainable financial performance perspectives. Netflix global revenues of $25 billion in 2020 are regionally balanced, with North America contributing 46%, Europe and Africa 31%, Latin America 13%, and Asia Pacific 9%.

Netflix's profitability improved with some delay, but in line with its significant revenue growth since 2016/2017. As EBIT margins have been sluggish hovering around 4–5% in the mid-2010s, since 2017, they took off and achieved 18% in 2020. Also EBITDA margins followed the same path. But, even more remarkable is the comparison and stark difference between EBIT and EBITDA margins, which highlights the pattern of global streaming entertainment platforms. For example, in the last financial year 2020, Netflix amortized $10.8 billion of its media content, whereas depreciation of tangible assets coming in at $0.1 billion were more or less negligible. This also means that Netflix's EBIT of $4.6 billion and a margin of 18% transform to an EBITDA of $15.5 billion with an impressive margin of 62%. Netflix's financial diagnostics is framed by Fig. 4.11.

On a granular cost diagnostics level, the most crucial cost drivers embedded in Netflix's Business Design are foremost its licensed content acquisition and the costs for producing new originals. Besides, technology-driven costs like customer payment processing, platform maintenance and development costs, and marketing and sales expenses are additional cost drivers.

The increasing profitability improved also Netflix's net income and equity position. The marginal net income till 2016 increased consistently since then and achieved \$3.2 billion in 2020. This allowed Netflix, by plowing back profits, to increase its retained earnings to \$7.5 billion and its total book value of equity to \$11 billion. In line with the increase in Netflix's total stockholder equity and the petering out of its debt onboarding, the debt-to-book- as well as market-equity ratio and, therefore, Netflix's financial resilience improved significantly lately. Due to the funding needs of entertainment content creation and licensing, the debt-to-book equity ratio increased from 2013 to 2018 from 0.5 to 2, but bottomed out 2018/2019 and dropped in 2020 to a more long-term sustainable ratio of 1.5. This might become even more important if, in case of a robust post-pandemic recovery, interest rates might increase as indicated by the upswing of US yields since February 2021. Ultimately, 2020 became the before-described tipping point for Netflix's financial and cash flow performance.

4.3.12 10C Business Design Canvas: Netflix

A brief summary of Netflix's Business Design is provided by the canvas of Fig. 4.12. It indicates how the new, digital technology enabled subscription-based video-on-demand (SVoD) platform Business Design, and Netflix's consistently implemented

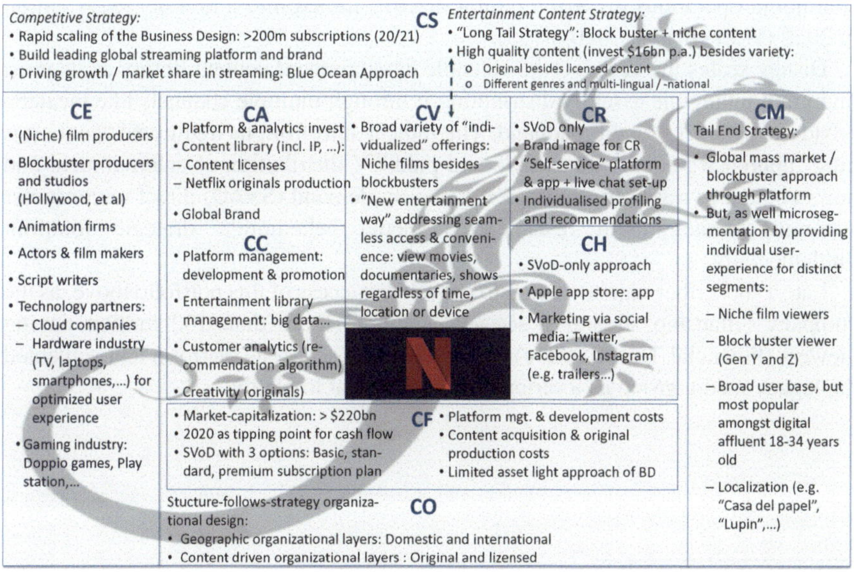

Fig. 4.12 10C Business Design: Netflix' SVoD streaming platform

entertainment strategy challenges the traditional, multi-billion global entertainment industry.

By propelling the streaming service to more than 200 m subscribers, the old entertainment guards had been forced to respond strategically. A successful off- to online platform retaliation strategy will be exemplified in the following by assessing how Disney revitalized its Business Design by introducing its proprietary on-demand streaming service Disney+.

4.3.13 Disney and Disney+

Disney's strategic corporate development is a different story than the Netflix case, making this neck-on-neck competition insightful. Disney, established in 1923, built for nearly 100 years since its existence an impressive catalogue of blockbusters and unlimited number of TV shows. Disney is today a globally diversified entertainment group combining a multitude of pay- and broadband TV channels, news networks, entertainment content production, and, ultimately, experience parks. Lately, the direct-to-consumer, meaning its proprietary streaming platforms Disney+, Hulu, and ESPN+, were added.

For its financial year 2018, the year prior to its TFCF acquisition and the COVID-19 pandemic impacts on its business,[8] Disney reported $60 billion of global revenues. Revenues of the financial year 2019 were lifted by the acquisition of TFCF Inc. to $69.6 billion, but declined significantly due to the pandemic in 2020 to $65.4 billion, whereas profits were more dramatically hit. Net income from continuing operations off $10.9 billion in 2019 turned into a loss of –$2.4 billion in 2020 (Walt Disney, 2020, p. 33).

Disney scales the access to its valuable entertainment content library as its most important intangible asset by distributing it through multiple channels like theaters, broadcast networks, and broadband. The radical shift from its traditional "content is king" approach paired with a cable and paid-TV distribution of entertainment and news content to a subscription-based video-on-demand (SVoD) direct-to-consumer streaming strategy will reshape the media behemoth's strategic footprint fundamentally.

Latest subscriber numbers seem to prove the success of this portfolio move, as the company's flagship streaming services captured more than 100 million paying viewers (Financial Times, 2021c) in less than 2 years on its platform and cemented the legacy media group as a serious streaming rival to Netflix.

[8] Therefore, and especially for benchmarking, normalization, and valuation purpose, the FY2018 might be an important reference point.

4.3.14 Competitive Strategy and Purpose (CS)

Disney's Business Design was grounded for decades on a vertically integrated customer entertainment value stream from the production to the distribution of entertainment content and to steer viewers ultimately to its theme parks as well as to buy its merchandises centering around its globally known and admired characters. The distribution strategy of the vertically integrated Business Design delivered traditionally media content through channels like theaters, broadcasting TV like the company's ABC television network, and cable networks like its Disney channel, ESPN for sports entertainment, or FX.

The media giant targets to lever synergies and creative capabilities in between its different strategic business units by building a consistent entertainment flow along the customer journey. This dominant entertainment Business Design, especially its significant investment in intangible assets like entertainment content and brand building, served as a substantial barrier of entry against potential contenders in the past.

The "content-is-king" DNA of Disney was put into practice by its buy-and-build strategy of an enviable film collection, including acquired franchises like the "Star Wars" imperium from Lucasfilm, the Marvel Studios, or Pixar Animation, besides by its own characters and blockbusters. But, Disney's former dominant entertainment Business Design built around blockbusters and box offices will be forward looking less valuable as fewer viewers frequent cinemas, seeing the SVoD model as a viable, convenient, and more-and-more preferred alternative. Disney+ as its main, proprietary in-house streaming service seems an obvious solution as the company releases films through its streaming platforms directly online to its consumers.

4.3.14.1 Joint Business Design: Impact of TFCF Acquisition and Disney+ Streaming Platform

With the described multibillion, heavily contested takeover of the TFCF assets, the traditionally family- and kids-centered content was significantly enlarged, on the one side content wise with a broad catalogue of blockbusters like "Avatar," series like "The Simpsons," and additional channels. On the others side, the TFCF acquisition also enlarged Disney's global reach, as the international footprint of the target supplemented the still more US-centric footprint of the acquirer.

This broadened entertainment portfolio was intended to serve as an ideal spring board for Disney's own streaming platforms. Additionally, Disney strategically stopped licensing its films to Netflix, even by forgoing $2 billion per year in licensing profits (Economist, 2019b). This will provide the company the strategic advantage once the former film licenses finally expire in 2021 that it will have full control of the access to its valuable film library content.

Besides, Disney gains a new source of digital competitive advantage, direct relationships with its viewers, and deep, data-based insights with respect to their entertainment preferences. This will enlarge its potential to develop target-group tailored original recommendations. In November 2019, the company launched its long-awaited SVoD service platform Disney+ with Disney, Pixar, Marvel, Star

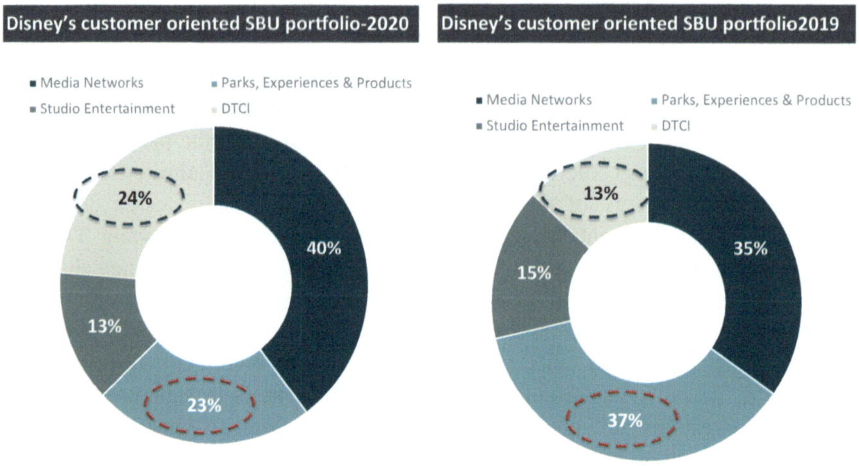

Fig. 4.13 Disney's portfolio revitalization and SBU shift

Wars, and National Geographic branded content in the USA, followed by an international rollout.

4.3.15 Core Value Proposition (CV)

Disney's mission along the last decades was and still is to be perceived as one of the world's leading entertainment and news companies, from production to distribution, of a broad and differentiated portfolio of media and entertainment content, services, and merchandise products paired with strong brands, as pinpointed by Fig. 4.13. The company targets to balance creativity and innovation to achieve a unique entertainment journey and to add enticing visitor experience within its theme parks.

The market strategy of Disney is centered on the approach to reach out to its global entertainment community and their aligned value propositions by a multi-channel offering. Disney's tectonic entertainment distribution portfolio shift by scaling its new streaming services was further pushed by the severe impact of the COVID-19 pandemic. As Disney's parks and shops have been shuttered due to social curbs, its direct-to-consumer streaming endeavor DTCI skyrocketed, whereas its parks and merchandise business collapsed, as shown in Fig. 4.13.

4.3.15.1 Joint Business Design: Impact of TFCF Acquisition and Disney+ Streaming Platform

The transaction of TFCF broadened Disney's value proposition, by adding valuable entertainment content, for example, in sport event broadcasting or in news distribution, besides widening its film catalog with a wide variety of movies and series. This wider setting extended Disney's value proposition beyond its traditionally family- and kids-centered approach and characters.

The introduction of its own streaming services came with the overall SVoD advantages for its viewers, addressing USPs like convenience, 24/7 availability, tailored entertainment content which is instantly available, and a wide variety of film genres and series.

4.3.16 Customer and Markets (CM)

Disney traditionally targets with its foremost family-oriented films and series as well as by its international brand positioning the entire global entertainment mass market. Despite having been focused in content production and marketing on children, teens, and families, the company ultimately created an entertainment experience for viewers across all ages. In the last years, Disney paired this global mass market approach with a more diversified approach with respect to ethnicity, exemplified by its Indian market approach, fields of interest with distinct channels like ESPN for sports entertainment, or age as by its latest movies and video game releases targeting especially generation Y viewers. Besides, through its news channels and TV networks, Disney addressed the US and global news-interested community and supplemented its entertainment audience. The company's regional revenue decomposition is provided by Fig. 4.14.

Additional important business partners and customers of the traditional Disney Business Design are:

- Theaters, as enabler of the distribution of its new film content to its global audience
- Independent merchandise shops supplementing its own merchandising outlets, where the latter have an especially strong stance within the Disney theme parks
- Advertisers and marketing partners

Fig. 4.14 Disney's revenue decomposition 2019

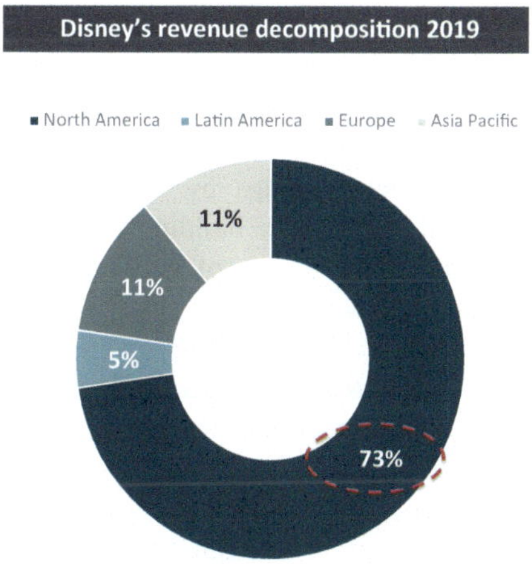

Advertisers are a sometimes overlooked customer segment within the entertainment ecosystem. For Disney, the sale of advertising time and space on its networks and related platforms as well as through its TV stations is an important revenue stream.

A final and since the early 2010s in importance growing customer group has been the raising SVoD platforms as Disney leveraged the cash flow potential of its large film library by licensing it out to its then streaming business partners like Netflix and others. This market strategy was substantially altered by building its proprietary streaming service Disney+.

4.3.16.1 Joint Business Design: Impact of TFCF Acquisition and Disney+ Streaming Platform

The TFCF acquisition broadened the customer access of Disney as the targeted audience of the acquired company's entertainment content are more adults, and with its channels TFCF foremost addresses news and sport event-interested viewers. But, the transaction also internationalized further Disney's market approach.

The market introduction of Disney+ was from the very beginning an international approach for Disney targeting a global audience. After the release of the Disney+ services within its home market, the company introduced the new platform in Europe and Asia Pacific just a couple of months later.

4.3.17 Customer Relationship (CR)

Disney follows a double-pronged strategy to develop intimate, long-lasting customer relationships. On the one side, especially the theme parks as well as the merchandises sold in its own shops excel a direct customer interface which enables the company to learn more about customer behaviors and interests. This allows also to build customer awareness and emotional ties with its entertainment community via its global characters.

On the other side, and from a revenue and cash flow perspective even more important, are the indirect customer interfaces by distribution and selling its entertainment and news content to a global audience through theaters and its own broadcasting networks and TV channels an integral part of its Business Design. But, also here the company circumvents the potential customer distance of indirect customer relationships by a multitude of pillars: Disney creates an emotional customers lock-in by building a global brand loyalty and character awareness. In addition, the exposure of celebrities in its film franchise may pay further in on customer attraction.

4.3.17.1 Joint Business Design: Impact of TFCF Acquisition and Disney+ Streaming Platform

The acquisition of TFCF offered from a customer relationship point of view a perfect fit, as the company intends as Disney to catch viewer attention and to create an emotional buy-in through its celebrities and characters like "X-Men," "Fantastic

Four," or "The Simpsons." Character and brand awareness will probably also play post transaction an important role for the joint company's Business Design and strategic advantage within the global entertainment market.

A much more disruptive approach for its entertainment and news community relationships was Disney's introduction of its SVoD services Disney+, Hulu, and ESPN+. As described within Netflix's Business Design assessment, leading entertainment streaming platforms overcome the anonymity of a digital-only approach by building a viewer-tailored, segment-of-one customer experience with user recommendations along analytics of the subscriber's viewing history and patterns, by introducing local content and by further marketing strategies.

4.3.18 Channels (CH)

As in its customer relationships, also in its channel strategy Disney implemented a double-sided, multi-channel approach. Its TV-oriented entertainment and news content is distributed foremost through its owned TV channels, media networks, as well as parks and resorts in addition to paying third-party TV and cable networks. Especially its movie content was traditionally distributed by independent theaters around the world before it was licensed with a time lag of two to 3 months to international TV and cable companies or distributed through its proprietary channels.

Also, Disney's consumer products are sold through its own shops, as well as by independent retailers. In a pre-streaming world, for example, Disney's DVD sales have been channeled through independent retailers and made them a viable cash flow contributor. For its marketing and brand strategy, Disney deploys on a large online presence through social media networks like Facebook, Instagram, or Twitter.

Before implementing its proprietary streaming service, especially Netflix was used as a further SVoD channel to distribute Disney's entertainment content through licensing contracts. In so far, the streaming inventor served, as described earlier, at the beginning of the SVoD development as customer and distribution partner.

4.3.18.1 Joint Business Design: Impact of TFCF Acquisition and Disney+ Streaming Platform

This was altered, as Disney introduced its own streaming platforms Disney+, Hulu, and ESPN+. As the company stopped the licensing of its entertainment content to streaming competitors, it will deploy this content in the future exclusively on its proprietary streaming platforms intending to provide an exclusive USP for its subscribers.

As on the customer side, also on the channel side the TFCF acquisition brought a significantly enlarged footprint as it adding numerous pay-TV channels as well as news, sports, and broadcasting channels.

4.3.19 Core Assets (CA)

Disney's empire rests on distinct, for the entertainment industry highly valuable tangible and intangible assets, but as well includes some legacy assets, as shown in Fig. 4.15.

Comparing the ratio of total assets to revenue between Netflix and Disney, the stark difference between traditional and platform Business Design patterns becomes obvious. Whereas Disney's total assets, measured on book values, are 2.8 times of its revenue, Netflix's ratio stands at 1.2 times. Nevertheless, as the entertainment industry's competitive advantage rests on significant investments in attractive originals and licensed content, both companies' asset value for its entertainment content stands pretty close at $25 billion. In so far, also Netflix's streaming-only model is not a pure asset-light platform architecture.

For Disney's entertainment business, the international development and production network of original content like its Disney, Lucasfilm, National Geographic, and Marvel Studios paired with animation studios like Pixar, are mission-critical assets. The same holds true for its ABC-branded broadcast television network, its owned US TV stations, or its specialized media networks and cable channels like ESPN, Disney, and FX. These tangible assets are supplemented by its theme park investments around the world and sum up to $27 billion of tangible assets. Additionally, Disney's acquisition history to acquire attractive entertainment targets, even

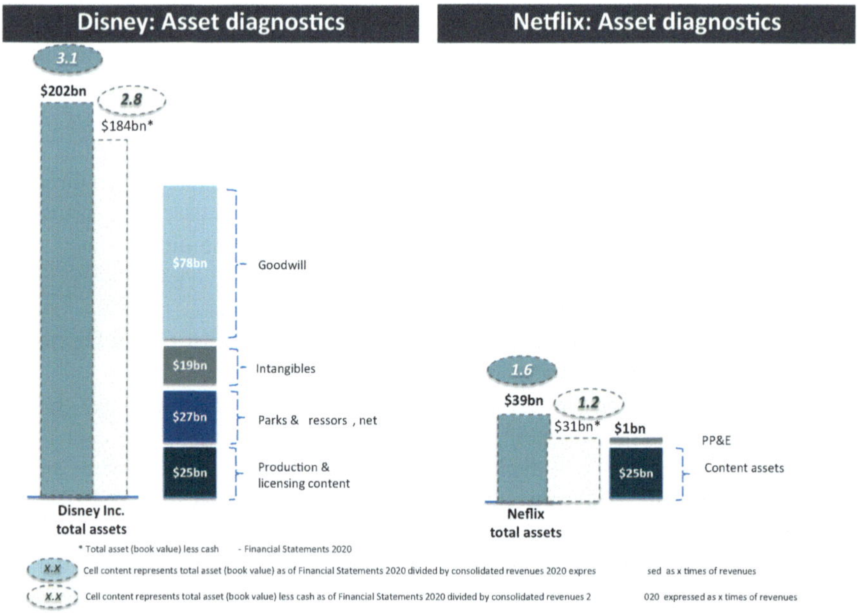

Fig. 4.15 10C Core asset diagnostics: Netflix versus Disney

at elevated prices, comes with the burden of a sizable goodwill of $78 billion. Those two balance sheet positions alone make up more than 50% of the sum of assets.

Strategically at least the same importance have Disney's brand and characters portfolio and its extensive film, series, and shows library as highly valuable intangible assets. The latter include all movies from Disney franchises, including Star Wars, Marvel, and Pixar, as well as all movies and animation films from Disney itself. The Disney brand and the value of its characters supplement the list of intangible core assets. Especially those intangible assets request also in a streaming world significant, continuous investments but are mandatory for a differentiation strategy in the highly contested entertainment ecosystem.

4.3.19.1 Joint Business Design: Impact of TFCF Acquisition and Disney+ Streaming Platform

The negative side of the acquisition of highly attractive targets is the before-mentioned goodwill, onboarded on Disney's balance sheet. But, as highlighted by the TFCF acquisition, transactional advantages like the enlarged asset value of Disney's content library and the extended character and brand portfolio, as well as TFCF's tangible TV and cable network might overcompensate the deal's disadvantages.

Streaming is a costly business, as entertainment companies lavish funding for fresh shows and films to lure subscribers. Disney plans to double its annual content investment to about $15 billion by 2024, at which point its streaming business would turn a profit, the company predicted (Financial Times, 2021c, 2021e). This will change the relative magnitude of the balance sheet's core assets, but will still request lasting investments.

4.3.20 Core Capabilities (CC)

What makes Disney outstanding and shapes its competitive advantage is the company's capability to create and produce emotional entertainment experience for its viewers. This is exemplified by the long list of global blockbusters and media awards for its original contents. Storytelling and creating emotional ties is part of Disney's DNA. Closely aligned is its core capability to manage its fast original content library and to scale successful blockbusters, spin-offs, or series like in the case of "Star Wars" and the "Marvel Heroes."

Disney's highly capable brand management is the backbone for creating and continuously developing its consistent brand and characters' perception around the world and along all entertainment channels. Disney's marketing and creativity place its talent acquisition and capture as a top priority for its management team. Also, Disney's core HR management target is to attract, retain, and develop such highest quality talent. Its global management program is designed to develop creative talent and to prepare them for future leadership roles. This human capital development strategy is paired with a high-performance culture which facilitates internal talent mobility and inclusiveness.

As described in the introductory part of this chapter, Disney is a serial acquirer and integrated sequentially multi-high-level transactions. The successful pairing of internal entertainment content development and external growth strategies is a further core capability of the company. This is exemplified, as even though Disney realized multiple acquisitions over the last years, the company has been able to preserve its creative and unique culture inspired by its founder Walt Disney.

4.3.20.1 Joint Business Design: Impact of TFCF Acquisition and Disney+ Streaming Platform

Disney's success in acquiring the TFCF franchise and to win the contested bidding war highlighted the company's M&A capabilities. The merged company will also bring together highly capable, creative, and technology-minded talents to further strengthen the joint company's creative pool and ever-more important entertainment and platform technology skills. TFCF will also add international entertainment experience as well as news and sports market knowledge and capabilities.

4.3.21 Core-Ecosystem Partners (CE)

To build its holistic Disney entertainment world, the company co-operates with a multitude of different players within the entertainment and technology ecosystem to supplement its own capabilities. Such co-operation partners involve:

- Theaters and theater chains, as Disney built since its origin close to 100 years ago an intimate relationship with such partners for orchestrating the launch, the marketing, and the broadcasting of its newly released films
- Celebrities, artists, actors, as well as novel and scriptwriters hired for Disney's originals production
- Not just Hollywood studies for the development of mainstream, blockbuster movies development, but also Indie and niche film studios for specialized or regional content creation
- Specialized animation studios to supplement its own Pixar capabilities
- Co-operations with gaming players, extending Disney's entertainment journey into this adjacent, but fast-growing entertainment ecosystem
- Additional, co-operations with technology players, e.g., to optimize home-viewing quality, sound experience, analytics for recommendation engines, and many more

Disney intends to create a distinguished and unique entertainment experience with its ecosystem partners for its customers. Therefore, the orchestration of and long-term successful partnering with this bandwagon of diverse companies is critical for the company to fulfill its value proposition, despite being perceived as a global entertainment powerhouse.

4.3.21.1 Joint Business Design: Impact of TFCF Acquisition and Disney+ Streaming Platform

The TFCF transaction enlarged the global reach to important entertainment and technology ecosystem partners. By scaling the size of the company, the joint entity will also become an even more important entertainment business partner.

The introduction of its SVoD platforms made new technology capabilities mandatory. Therefore, in the years to come, the creative ecosystem partners will be supplemented by ever-more technology partners and start-ups to further develop the viewer experience and entertainment journey.

4.3.22 Corporate Organization (CO)

Disney has a multidivisional organizational structure. The globally diversified entertainment giant's highest-level organizational layer separates Disney's activities in the following four strategic business units (Walt Disney, 2020):

- "Media Networks"
- "Parks, Experiences, and Products"
- "Studio Entertainment"
- "Direct-To-Consumer and International (DTCI)", comprising its streaming and international business

Despite this SBU structure, Disney promotes through its corporate departments an interdivisional cooperation to create synergies in between the various strategic business units.

4.3.22.1 Joint Business Design: Impact of TFCF Acquisition and Disney+ Streaming Platform

Pre-transaction TFCF structured its operations in two strategic business units:

- "Cable Network Programming" comprised the production of original content and licensing of news and sports programming content, distributed primarily through cable TV networks, satellite and telecommunication operators, or US online video distributors.
- "Television," which focused on broadcasting and distributing programs under the FOX brand

Post-transaction, the acquired assets from TFCF have been integrated in the global Disney organization.

In autumn 2020, Disney announced a strategic reorganization of its media and entertainment activities to scale its streaming DTC business globally. The three primary strategic business units "Media Networks," "Studio Entertainment," and "DTCI" will be reorganized into four strategic groups: three content groups, comprising "Studios," "General Entertainment," and "Sports" focusing on originals development and production. The developed and produced entertainment content of those three groups will be distributed through all traditional channels and streaming DTC platforms. The fourth group "Distribution" will be in charge for this distribution and commercialization of the entertainment content across all channels and platforms. The "Distribution" group will also be accountable for media and entertainment operating results globally and according reporting (Walt Disney, 2020).

4.3.23 Cash Flow Model (CF)

Disney's market capitalization achieved with $344 billion an all-time high at the point of writing this book. But, in the last 18 months, the capital market performance of the entertainment giant was quite volatile. Between 2015 and 2019, the company's shares traded foremost in a narrow range between $100 and $115, before increasing in 2019/2020 pre-pandemic to $150 per share. Disney's business was severely impacted by the pandemic as its once-mighty theme parks were shuttered and movies closed. Not surprisingly, Disney's share price dropped by a third during the early days of the pandemic and the introduction of coronavirus social curbs. Nevertheless, as Disney's powerful kickstart of its streaming strategy became transparent on capital markets, its market capitalization rebounded fast and reached new highs lately, as evidenced by Fig. 4.16.

In line with its capital market development, Disney's revenues of its traditional business lines and their operating profits deteriorated significantly in 2020 due to social distancing measures requiring the closures of theaters and theme parks. Global revenues plummeted from $69.6 billion in 2019 to $65.4 billion in 2020, whereas net income from continued operations deteriorated from $13.9 billion to −$1.7 billion, whereas the latter was also depressed by $5.7 billion of restructuring charges and should be a one-time effect.

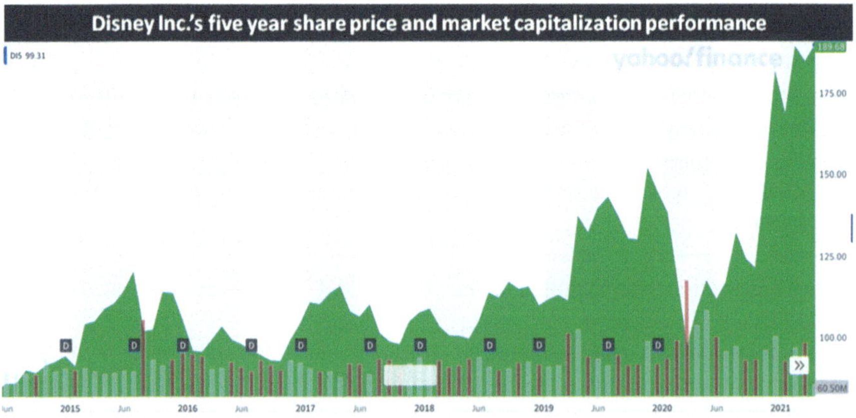

Fig. 4.16 Disney's share price and market capitalization performance. *Source*: finance.yahoo.com 2021

Disney's most crucial cost drivers are its marketing costs, besides film acquisition and licensing, as well as original production costs. A more detailed breakdown for Disney makes only sense on SBU level as the Business Design and also the cost structure of the different lines of business are quite diverse.

Global revenues steam from its cable networks and broadcasting, advertising fees, TV distribution licenses and fees, theater distribution rights payments, publishing, and gaming. Volume-wise, the bulk of those traditional revenue streams is based on pay-TV and on advertisement payments. With viewers on traditional channels rapidly declining and switching to streaming, such advertisement payments dry up. But, Disney had a head start into its streaming endeavor, as described. Multiplying the 100 million subscribers the company gained till the end of 2020 with an average subscription price of around 6$ per month, the subscriber numbers would translate in a revenue estimate of $7 billion just 18 months after having started Disney+.

4.3.23.1 Joint Business Design: Impact of TFCF Acquisition and Disney+ Streaming Platform

Aggressive estimates forecast that Disney's streaming revenue, comprising all its streaming activities like Disney+, Hulu, and ESPN, might achieve up to $30 billion till 2025 or so (Forbes, 2020). Bullish analysts even believe that Disney+ might break even already by 2022 and eventually attracting 45 million subscribers in North America and 115 million abroad giving its streaming service an additional boost.

Disney's streaming revenue model is essential for its streaming approach. As in Netflix's case, it is subscription-based: Disney+'s standard subscription comes in on the cheaper side of the market at $6.99 per month, whereas a bundle of its streaming services Disney+, ESPN+, and the ad-supported version of Hulu are marketed at $12.99 per month in the US market.

With an average streaming subscription price range of $7–8 per month, that would equate to more than $10 billion in recurring revenues from the new services midterm translating into roughly a fifth of the company's global revenues. Disney plans to double its annual content investment to about $15 billion by 2024, at which point its streaming business would according management estimates break even.

4.3.24 10C Business Design Canvas Pre- Versus Post-TFCF Transaction and Disney+ Streaming Platform

The comparison of the "pre and post" canvases of the 10C Business Design should highlight how Disney's Business Design underwent a portfolio revitalization by acquiring the TFCF franchise and by introducing and scaling its proprietary SVoD streaming platform Disney+.

This pre-TFCF transaction and prior to its streaming services introduction Business Design, as pinpointed in Fig. 4.17, was significantly altered in the last 2 years by the transformative transaction of TFTC's most attractive assets and the corporate portfolio revitalization by the scaling of the Disney+ streaming business, as highlighted in Fig. 4.18.

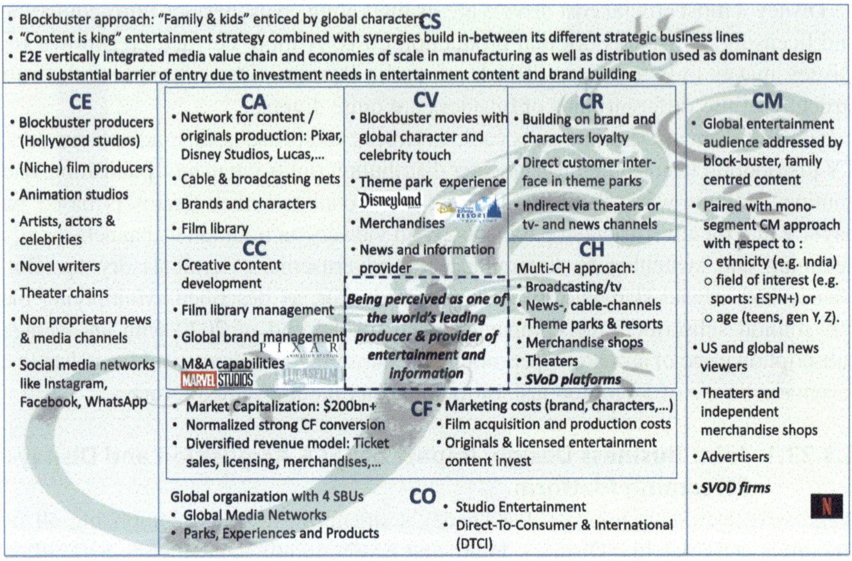

Fig. 4.17 10C Business Design: Disney *pre*-TFCF acquisition and Disney+ streaming platform launch

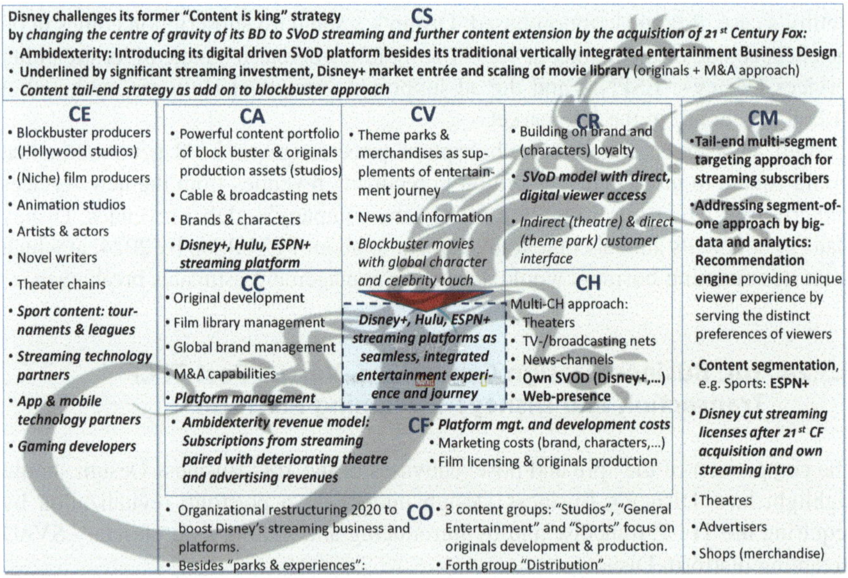

Fig. 4.18 10C Business Design: Disney *post*-TFCF acquisition and Disney+ streaming platform launch

4.4 Decoding Platform Value: SVoD Entertainment Streaming Platforms

The latest significant growth in streaming viewers and subscribers of SVoD entertainment streaming platforms like Netflix, Disney+, HBO, and others might indicate a strength of such Business Designs. But, due to their young history, empirical evidence is missing on their long-term sustainability, their lasting competitive advantages, and their value creation potential.

As defined in Chap. 1, the health, defensibility, dominance, and sustainability of a platform Business Design depend on a set of distinct platform value drivers. This holds also true for SVoD streaming platform Business Designs in the entertainment industry, which will be assessed in a next step.

Streaming platforms have been defined as a dedicated subgroup of service platforms. They match entertainment content developers with subscribers as viewers, as in the case of film-streaming services, or listeners, as in the case of music-streaming services. As not just the revenue model but also the content strategy of music and movie platforms are diverse, the explicit focus in the following assessment will be on film-streaming platforms. The latter's eight value drivers are summarized by Fig. 4.19.

- *Platform architecture and core:* SVoD entertainment streaming platforms match as double-sided B2C network creative content providers with entertainment consumers, meaning viewers. A distinct characteristic of leading SVoD platforms

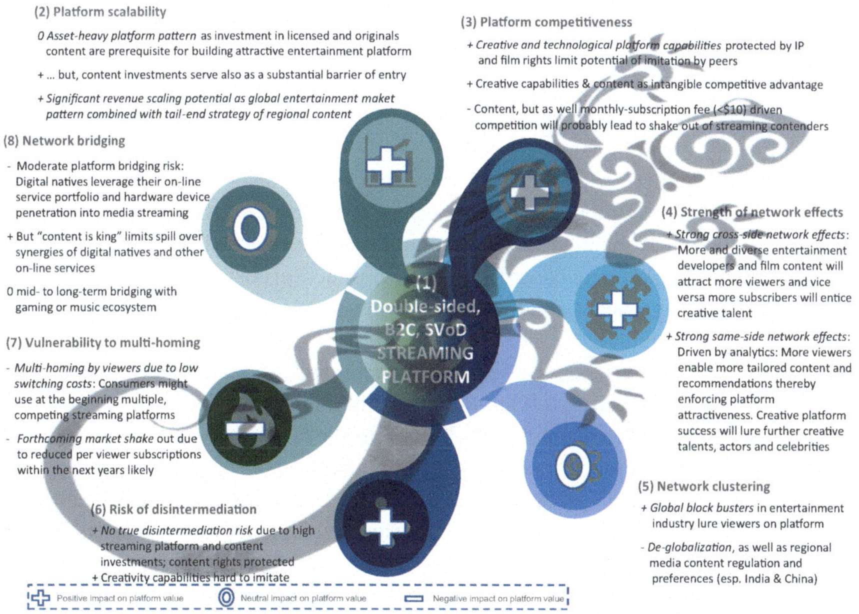

Fig. 4.19 SVoD entertainment streaming platform value and its eight levers

is that they produce and offer own content branded as originals, besides licensing in entertainment content from third-party providers like studios. In so far, such SVoD platforms pair the typical platform matching pattern with their own content creation.

Within the film entertainment ecosystem, the platform architecture is seldom extended to a three-party concept, where advertisers place commercials on the platform, or a freemium model. VoD streaming platforms deploy typically a subscription-based revenue model (SVoD) like in the case of Netflix or Disney +. This stands in stark contrast to music platforms, which pair such subscription models foremost with freemium approaches or for-free add-based revenue models, often described as basic subscription.

- *Platform scalability*: SVoD streaming platforms are disrupting the global entertainment industry. They shift the transaction model from the ownership of a film CD, the payment for a standardized network program, or the purchase of a theater ticket to a monthly subscription-based payment model, which offers 24/7 nearly unlimited variety of entertainment content in a convenient way. Such services individualize the viewers' entertainment experience through individual preferences-based recommendations.

  Nevertheless, as also for SVoD platforms content is king, they are *investment- and asset-heavy Business Designs*. This stands in stark contrast to the typical platform pattern, or if compared with ride-hailing, online food-delivery, global accommodation, and e-commerce platforms. Besides the technology development costs, especially the significant investments in licensed and original content are a prerequisite to build an attractive content library that lures the viewer on SVoD streaming platforms. These heavy investment needs may hinder an even faster scalability but serve as a perfect barrier of entry.

  Especially Netflix's and Disney's performance proved the significant revenue scaling potential of global entertainment streaming platforms by their exponential subscriber growth in the last years. Whereas Disney builds foremost on its global characters, Netflix added to its blockbuster content local entertainment approaches for its international subscriber growth. This tail-end strategy of regional content is enabled as new content may be released at negligible costs on its streaming platform. Nevertheless, the production costs of such international content is still significant and might offer long-term regional specialists or niche players a market entrée.
- *Platform competitiveness*: Beside their technological architecture, *streaming platform capabilities are* built around their entertainment content. As the proprietary film, series, and documentaries library, as the core of any SVoD platform, is protected by IP or film rights for original content or by licensing contracts for third-party content, SVoD streaming Business Designs offer a significant and lasting protection against imitation. The originals content production sets SVoD streaming services also apart from their music counterparts, as music-streaming services like Spotify typically serve as an intermediary pure play between artists and listeners without any own creative content development or production,

whereas film-streaming leaders produce their own originals, which supplement licensed content.

Technological streaming platform and creative capabilities might be tacit, and competition might long-term catch up. But such capabilities are also deeply engrained in the streaming Business Designs and short- to mid-term hard to copy by new entrants. Also, those technological capabilities are permanently renewed and new functionalities integrated by Netflix and Disney, and also pay in as a valuable barrier of entry of SVoD entertainment ecosystems. Additionally, creative capabilities by acquiring and managing high-quality writers and actors is a complex endeavor. Netflix and Disney mastered this challenge by multi-year experience, which additionally limits the potential of new contenders.

In contradiction to these competitive strengths of streaming platforms, the significant competition between the dominant streaming players like Netflix, Disney+, Comcast, ViacomCBS, Discovery/WarnerMedia, Apple TV+, or Amazon Prime, with aggressive price settings for monthly subscription fees, often below $10 per month, creates a hypercompetitive ecosystem. Also, in the years to come the entertainment industry might be exposed to a shakeout, once viewers will consolidate their subscription to one or two leading SVoD services. Nevertheless, the leading SVoD players have been able to increase their subscription fees due to their attractive content, which sets them apart from ride-hailing or food-delivery platforms.

- *Strength of network effects:* SVoD streaming platforms offer significant cross- as well as same-side network effects.

  Cross-side network effects: As content counts in entertainment, an attractive and diversified portfolio of high-quality streaming content will lure viewers on the platform. And, the more subscribers are on the platform and the higher the potential audience, the higher the likelihood that highly regarded scriptwriters and actors will join the platform owner, partially signing even exclusive contracts for new originals content production. The same holds true for important ecosystem partners like film studios or technology partners, including hardware manufacturers or game developers. This will attract further viewers creating strong cross-side network effects.

  Same-side network effects: Driven by analytics and big date technologies, streaming platforms develop recommendation engines which enable intimate, individual preference-driven viewer experiences. The more viewers subscribe on a distinct platform, the more tailored and accurate might be such recommendations, and the more entertainment content might be offered on the platform, reinforcing its value for viewers. Additionally, word of mouth on streaming hits or favorite actors creates strong same-side viewer network effects, as the ushering in the age of "binge-watching" proved. Additionally, the more successful such a streaming platform is in winning admired awards and being perceived as a creative powerhouse, the more attractive it will be for further actors, writers, and celebrities to join, creating same-side network effects as well on the entertainment producer side.

- *Pattern of platform clusters*: The ultimate question of platform cluster characteristics is, if global platforms offer a significant strategic advantage for their customers in comparison to local network approaches. The attractiveness of global blockbusters or series may be a strong argument for global streaming platform dominance. Additionally, all SVoD contenders try to position their entertainment services on international markets by developing a global brand recognition.
  Open borders have set the scene in global entertainment for decades, since global charters and talents are admired around the world. This is also evidenced, as a majority of streaming subscribers now live outside America, the home turf of streaming champions. But, across the world, these elements are in the last years at risk as the political establishment in a multitude of countries as well as voters veered away from open trade and free global markets. This tendency to a more de-globalized world has a direct influence on the entertainment industry and might work to the detriment of global entertainment producers and distributers. Additionally, regional viewer preferences may hinder an unlimited extension of global streaming platforms as the latest Indian streaming market developments proved.
- *Disintermediation*: Disintermediation risks seem to be very limited as streaming platforms request significant investments in content acquisition and production paired with intimate competitive advantages in technology and creative capabilities. Additionally, content rights are typically protected by enforceable IP rights limiting further disintermediation risks.
- *Multi-homing:* Multi-homing might be the most severe danger zone for streaming platforms. Due to the significant competition in the entertainment ecosystem, viewers have to pay typically less than $10 per month or so for a single subscription offering unlimited platform access. Those low monthly subscriptions lead implicitly to low switching costs. Besides, also technologically, streaming platforms could be switched at a fingertip on the smartphone.
  At this still early stage of the new entertainment world, many subscribers use multiple, competing streaming platforms to test and try different technologies and compare their distinct entertainment content. The risk might be an ultimate shakeout in the streaming market once standards are set and viewers made their preferred choice. Viewers might then limit their subscriptions to one or two preferred platforms. Such a streaming platform endgame seems highly likely in the post-pandemic 2020s.
- *Platform-bridging:* Platform bridging is for streaming platforms a double-sided sword. On the risk side, digital natives like Apple or Amazon leverage their own ecosystems, which incorporate ever more online services to counter the potential maturity of their core business, to enter the streaming space. Apple builds even in parallel a music streaming and, with Apple TV+, a movie-, series-, and show-streaming platform which might be merged one day to one ultimate entertainment platform for its i-device ecosystem.

But, it will become interesting in the 2020s, if the technology giants are able to extend their footprint in the highly creative entertainment business when it comes to original content development. Early challenges of Apple, despite having invested significant amounts for actors, prove that this may not become an easy task. But, the tech giants have such deep pockets that they may at a later consolidation stage even acquire an established streaming contender, to strengthen their own streaming platform.

An upside potential for streaming natives might be to apply platform-bridging strategies into adjacent ecosystems of the broader entertainment world by reaching out to music or gaming. But, as especially the latter became due to their focus on the young, technology-affluent generation powerful entertainment contenders, they might retaliate such moves or might even initiate first-mover strategies.

This shaping of the global entertainment industry in the 2020s might become one of the most interesting as well as brutal endeavors of business model and strategy transformations in the 2020s shifting ecosystem boundaries, creating new customer experiences, and reallocating capital market investments.

4.5 Decoding Netflix's Financial Value: Reverse DCF

The following enterprise and equity valuation is, as the former platform assessments, based upon the Reverse DCF model. The financial diagnostics of Netflix's past performance as well as its capital market performance was discussed within the CF module of the 10C Business Design. The financial valuation of the platform will refer to this financial diagnostics at multiple points.

The valuation part kicks off with a short description of the picture-of-the-future (PoF) scenario the streaming giant's valuation exemplary rests upon. Thereafter, the steady-state performance and the rolled backward discounted cash flows will be derived. The detailed planning period value will be paired with the discounted continuing value to get to an operating value estimate for Netflix. The traditional walk from the latter to enterprise value by adding excess cash and non-operational assets and, ultimately, equity value by deducting debt and debt-like items will be described and a valuation canvas derived. The latter will be finally framed by a multiple assessment of entertainment and digital platform peers. The Reverse DCF valuation model is framed by Fig. 4.20.

4.5.1 Picture-of-the-Future Scenario "The Streaming Gambit"

The PoF "the streaming gambit" is a scenario within which the Business Design of SVoD platforms will become the primary means of at-home entertainment and successfully competes with theaters also after lockdown restrictions of the COVID-19 pandemic will be phased out. The following characteristics might describe such a potential scenario briefly, before the question if under such favorable

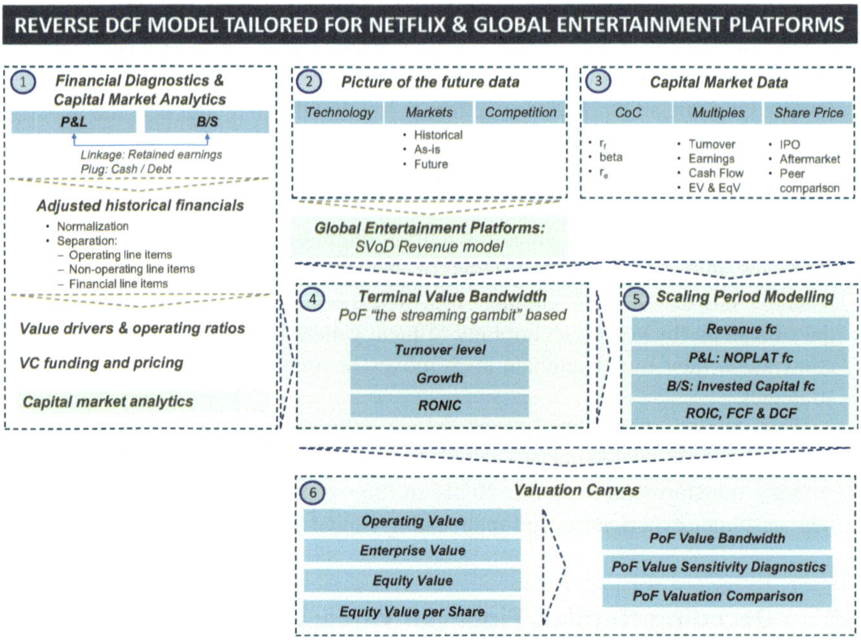

Fig. 4.20 Reverse DCF model tailored for SVoD entertainment platforms and PoF "the streaming gambit"

streaming ecosystem trends the elevated stock-price and market capitalization of digital streaming champions like Netflix might be justified.

"The streaming gambit" picture-of-the-future rests on the following assumptions:

- The world economy will swiftly recover from the corona pandemic burdens due to an efficient out-phasing of lockdown restrictions and social distancing measures. Following the latest updates on global growth forecasts of NGOs, this scenario assumptions might seem to be justified.[9] Especially the USA seems to recover fast from its pandemic lows due to its successful and fast vaccination program.
- Nevertheless, mutant strains and changes in social patterns will have a lasting impact on human interaction and safety standards, placing at-home events and streaming also long term as viable alternatives to outside entertainment events.
- The unique selling proposition advantages of streaming like convenience of a 24/7 instant accessibility and at-home viewing; the fast variety of films, documentaries, and series; as well as tailored recommendations based on analytics of former viewing preferences will provide streaming with long-term competitive advantages if compared with other modes of entertainment at home like

[9] The latest World Economic Outlook update in May 2021 was especially bullish, increasing its growth predictions for the world economy to 5.6% for 2021 and 4.5% in 2022.

cable or pay-TV or outside like theaters. This won't lead to a full substitution, but will enable further gains of the entertainment share of wallet by streaming players. Streaming might integrate even gaming components making the viewer experience even more interactive and dynamic.

- From a technological point of view, streaming advantages like platform access, convenience, and stability will be consistently further improved by newest technological developments. This might include even more tailored recommendation engines based on machine learning algorithms, availability of stable and fast 5G networks with close to perfect entertainment experience, and other forthcoming enabling technologies.
- A continuous stream of new originals and powerful series, integrating local content and tastes combined with a wide variety of genres, will offer unlimited entertainment options. By luring viewers long term on distinct platforms, streaming services-centered entertainment communities will be created and will part of the 2020s "zeitgeist."
- Fierce competition between the streaming contenders will lead to a shakeout phase. Just two to three streaming platforms per region will survive and shape the post-shakeout period. The massive investment needs for creating a continuous stream of content, originals, as well as licensed films and series, paired with the creativity needs of the entertainment industry and a global brand positioning, will build strong market entry barriers limiting imitability and fast second strategies.

Based on those core assumptions of the picture-of-the future "the streaming gambit," a likely valuation bandwidth may be determined and framed with peer multiples. The Reverse DCF starts once more with the steady state before working through the transition period of the scaling period.

4.5.2 Steady State and Continuing Value

For the steady-state evaluation of Netflix, the key value driver formula of the continuing value has to be tailored for the entertainment ecosystem specifics and the distinct B2C SVoD entertainment platform Business Design [10]:

$$\mathrm{CV}_{2031}^{\mathrm{NFLX}} = \frac{\mathrm{NOPLAT}_{2031}^{\mathrm{NFLX}} \times \left(1 - \frac{g^{\mathrm{NFLX}}}{\mathrm{RONIC}^{\mathrm{NFLX}}}\right)}{\mathrm{CoC}^{\mathrm{NFLX}} - g^{\mathrm{NFLX}}}$$

Therefore, four core financials have to be estimated for Netflix, whereas those estimates should be consistent with and close-knit to the above described picture-of-the-future "the streaming gambit": Its most likely NOPLAT level in a post-scaling phase, the sustainable steady-state growth rate of entertainment streaming

[10] Within the financial formulas, the NASDAQ capital market abbreviation for Netflix "NFLX" will be used.

platforms, the Return on New Invested Capital, or more specific, entertainment content, and the company's long-term cost of capital in line with its targeted financing structure have to be determined.

For the NOPLAT estimate, the revenue level of Netflix at the beginning of the steady state and its return on new investments in media content are crucial ingredients. "The streaming gambit" scenario assumes a shakeout within the streaming industry, where ultimately two to three dominating streaming platforms might survive. Netflix, as probably one of those global streaming survivors, is estimated to have 440–450 million subscribers on its platform and to achieve a steady-state revenue volume of $56 billion. Both indicators would imply roughly a doubling of the platform's actual number of subscribers and revenues.

These might be, based on the underlying scenario, reasonable assumptions. The growth from 210 million subscribers today to 450 million subscribers in 2031 would lead to a CAGR of 8%, what would be in line with the overall entertainment growth rate realized by Disney in the pre-pandemic year's. Decomposing the target rate of viewers on a regional level, Netflix might achieve 100–110 million viewers in its US home market, 110–120 million users in the European and African markets, 90–100 million users in Latin America, and 120–130 million platform users in Asia Pacific. For the latter, the significant market entrance investments in India, especially as the country has in average a young, technical-affluent, and entertainment-minded population, will have a significant impact on Netflix's long-term growth in the region. At first sight, the Chinese market with its huge population might seem as well as an interesting playing field for entertainment streaming contenders. But, due the local content requirements paired with the US-China political disturbances, the unwillingness of Chinese viewers to pay for streaming content, and the implicit acceptance of pirate copies may give this local market no priority for international streaming companies in contrast to many other industries.

A comparison with Disney's streaming targets is also interesting. As the company had a head start into its streaming endeavor, gaining more than 100 million subscribers in 18 months after having launched its main streaming channel Disney +, the company announced an aggressive target to achieve up to 260 million viewers for its Disney+ platform and more than 300 million paying members across all its three streaming services till 2024. Compared with these numbers, the growth estimate of Netflix to add 1.15 times of its viewer base during the 10 years of the scaling period might look even conservative, as Disney would target a threefold subscriber number to be achieved in just 3 years. [11]

The *long-term growth* rate has to be estimated at the point of time when growth peters out from the early significant growth rates and the market begins to stabilize. The growth rate has to mirror market trends, use cases, competitor dynamics, and also the targeted SVoD revenue model of the steady-state scenario. The

[11] A recent study of a leading investment bank used a subscriber bandwidth of 500–535 million subscribers as a 10-year forward estimate, which was perceived to be too bullish for the contested streaming ecosystem and potential regional market access limitations.

methodology to derive the steady-state growth rate might be based on a top-down or scaling approach, as described in Chap. 1. As a reasonable long-term entertainment growth, 3% have been derived from multiple studies, also from today's perspective with the ever-increasing entertainment content a realistic, maybe even on the low-end, estimate.

The EBIT and NOPLAT margins Netflix might sustain in the steady-state period were forecasted at 26% and 20% respectively, and its ROIC at 26%. Compared with the margins the company achieved already in 2020 and especially in Q1 2021,[12] with a normalized[13] EBIT margin of 18% and 27%, respectively, this seems reasonable within "the streaming gambit" scenario. That the ROIC outperforms the EBIT margin only slightly shows the asset-heavy platform pattern of Netflix's Business Design and the also long term as mandatory assumed significant investments in entertainment content. The increase in subscribers and revenue should enable the company to capture some economies of scale, especially on its massive content investments and its global marketing expenses. Nevertheless, it is assumed that the streaming contenders will have to invest year by year significant amounts in new originals and licensed content.

Stress-testing Netflix's NOPLAT and ROIC estimates again by benchmarking those with its key contender Disney shows reasonable and robust results. A most likely comparable year for a long-term comparison might be 2018, before Disney's financial indicators have been distorted by the acquisition of 21st Century Fox in 2019 and the corona pandemic kicking in in spring 2020. In 2018 Disney's NOPLAT margin came in at 23%, roughly in line with the long-term Netflix estimate. The cost of capital, based on a WACC approach, has been assumed consistent with the scaling period at 6%.

Taking those financial estimates into account, the continuing value at the end of the scaling period would be around $324 billion:

$$CV_{2031}^{NFLX} = \frac{11\ \text{bn} \times \left(1 - \frac{3\%}{26\%}\right)}{6\% - 3\% = 324\ \text{bn}}$$

This would translate into a present value of the continuing value of around $181 billion:

$$DCV_i = \frac{CV_i}{(1 + CoC_i)^T} = \frac{324\ \text{bn}}{(1+6\%)^{10} = 181\ \text{bn}}$$

[12] The EBIT margin of 27% in Q1 is expected to be not sustainable during the year due to higher content investments and costs targeted throughout the year but should improve significantly year over year to 23%.

[13] The normalized margin assumes a US/international standard tax rate of 25%. This assumption is higher than the actual realized tax rate of Netflix.

4.5.3 Scaling Period and Free Cash Flows

The scaling period is set at 10 years to enable a decay of the actual high growth rates and a petering-out of the transition from traditional entertainment Business Designs to streaming platforms. By backward and forward modelling of the key financial indicators between today's performance and the targeted performance of the steady state, consistent with "the streaming gambit" picture-of-the-future, a quite robust financial model might be achieved.

The starting point are Netflix's revenues of $25 billion, as realized in the last financial year 2020. The expected robust economic growth for 2021 and 2022 due to the phase-out of pandemic restrictions, especially in the USA, may have two contrasting effects on Netflix's streaming service revenues. On the one hand, higher income levels, less threats of recession-induced unemployment, and pent-up demand most probably will increase consumer's spending levels for leisure time activities like tourism and entertainment. On the other side, the step-by-step easing of social distancing measures may partially re-shift entertainment spending to live events, restaurant, or gym visits. Nevertheless, the transition from traditional cable TV to streaming will still support Netflix's growth line consistently throughout the next years.

The applied scaling model assumes with a 15% subscriber growth rate for 2021 and 10% for 2022 lower than Wall Street consensus estimates for Netflix. Netflix subscriber growth with four million new subscribers in Q1 2021 (Financial Times, 2021d) came in lower as its management-own forecast and Wall Street expectations. And, also most of Netflix's peers realized a higher growth momentum. Netflix management argued that this might be just a short-term slowdown in growth due to the massive pull forward in 2020 in terms of subscriber growth with its 36 million paid net adds. Also, due to the COVID-19-induced near global entertainment production shutdown in early 2020, some high-profile content title launches of Netflix have been pushed into the second half of 2021. By production of new entertainment content running since spring 2021 for the first time since the pandemic in most regions close to full steam again and more than 500 titles in post-production, pre-launch phase, this will allow Netflix to release at least one new original film per week in 2021 which should bolster short- to midterm revenue growth rates (Netflix, 2021b, p. 4).

Underlining the company's platform growth expectation is also the empirical evidence provided by Netflix's president and Co-CEO Reed Hastings during Netflix's Q1 earnings call, that the first re-openings in the USA showed no noticeable material negative effect on subscriber growth. Therefore, a reacceleration of growth toward the end of 2021 due to the launch of big titles is assumed as likely.

Furthermore, the robustness of top-line forecast might also be proven: If growth would come in at more conservative levels in the next one or 2 years, this may be compensated by higher growth rates in the outer years, as a quite rapid decay from the double-digit growth rates to the steady-state target growth of 3% is assumed. Last but not the least, a widely used market study estimates the SVoD growth in the forthcoming years till 2025 to grow with a CAGR of more than 11% and offering

	2021	2022	2023	2024	2025	2026	2027	2028	2029	2030
Revenues	28.745.464	32.482.375	35.730.612	38.589.061	41.676.186	44.593.519	47.715.065	50.577.969	53.106.868	54.700.074
yoy growth	*15%*	*10%*	*10%*	*9%*	*8%*	*7%*	*7%*	*6%*	*5%*	*3%*
EBIT	6.535.695	7.503.122	8.383.000	9.193.571	10.080.182	10.947.499	11.886.847	12.783.463	13.615.211	14.222.019
EBIT margin (%)	*23%*	*23%*	*23%*	*24%*	*24%*	*25%*	*25%*	*25%*	*26%*	*26%*
NOPLAT	4.901.771	5.627.342	6.287.250	6.895.178	7.560.137	8.210.624	8.915.135	9.587.597	10.211.408	10.666.514
NOPLAT margin (%)	17%	17%	18%	18%	18%	18%	19%	19%	19%	20%
Depreciation & Amortization	12.561.015	14.193.947	15.613.342	16.862.409	18.211.402	19.486.200	20.850.234	22.101.248	23.206.311	23.902.500
Invested Capital	21.559.098	24.361.781	26.797.959	28.941.796	31.257.140	33.445.139	35.786.299	37.933.477	39.830.151	41.025.055
Free Cash Flow	3.011.257	2.824.659	3.851.072	4.751.342	5.244.793	6.022.624	6.573.976	7.440.419	8.314.734	9.471.610
Discounted Cash Flows	2.840.809	2.513.936	3.233.434	3.763.508	3.919.214	4.245.713	4.372.069	4.668.211	4.921.478	5.288.897

Fig. 4.21 Reverse DCF model: Scaling period core financials forecasts for Netflix's valuation

with a penetration rate of 14% some headroom for the Reverse DCF forecasts (Statista, 2021).

Margin improvements on EBITDA, EBIT, and NOPLAT level are modeled at 4–5% points, as shown in Fig. 4.21 which summarizes the cash flows and their ingredients for the valuation. Profit margins and cash flows are derived from a more granular cost driver level assuming partial economies of scale foremost in platform as well as content investments and expenditures. A stepwise improvement is assumed, which might be a fair assumption for scale-driven cost and profit improvements. The EBIT margin would improve from 18% in 2020 (or compared with elevated levels of Q1 2021 of 27%) to 26% in 2030, normalized NOPLAT to 20%, and ROIC to 26% within the 10-year scaling period. Netflix's management forecasts are more aggressive, by targeting a yearly margin increase of 3% points for the years to come (Netflix, 2021b). Therefore, a valuation based on those bullish assumptions would come up with a higher valuation and is integrated in the later valuation canvas.

Investment needs in new content, as major driver of Netflix's Invested Capital, might be a continuous drag on cash flows, but due to the fact that amortization as non-cash expense has to be added back in cash flow calculations and due to the scaling of its platform, free cash flows would still significantly improve from $3 billion to $9.5 billion ultimately. Summing up the discounted cash flows, modelled consistently for the transition path from the actual performance to the steady-state performance of the picture-of-the-future "the streaming gambit," would result in a net present value of $40 billion:

$$PV_{t=2021}^{2030} = \sum_{2021}^{2030} \frac{FCF_t}{(1 + CoC)^t} = 40 \text{ bn}$$

The present value of the scaling period would contribute roughly 20% of the operating value.

4.5.4 Operating, Enterprise, and Equity Value of Netflix Embedded in "The Streaming Gambit" PoF

Consistent with the Enterprise-DCF concept, Netflix's value of operations (OP) is calculated as the sum of the streaming champion's DCFs within the scaling period and the present value of the continuing value (DCV):

$$\text{Operating Value} = \sum\nolimits_{t=1}^{10} (\text{DCF}_t) + \text{DCV} = 40\text{ bn} + 181\text{ bn} = 221\text{ bn}$$

For the valuation walk from operating value (OP) to enterprise value, the excess cash and cash-like items as well as non-operating assets have to be added, resulting in an operating value of $229 billion:

$$\text{EV} = \text{Value of Operations OP} + \text{excess cash} = 221\text{ bn} + 8\text{ bn} = 229\text{ bn}$$

For the final walk from enterprise value to equity value, debt and debt-like items have to be subtracted. In Netflix's case, short- and long-term debt of $15.6 billion, onboarded in former years to fund its substantial investment in entertainment content production and licensing, results in an ultimate market value of equity of $219 billion or a corresponding, intrinsic share price estimate of $482 per share:

$$\text{Equity Value EqV} = \text{Enterprise Value} - \text{Debt} = 229\text{ bn} - 15\text{ bn} = 214\text{ bn}$$

The management of the streaming company also announced lately that it intends to maintain a gross debt bandwidth of $10–15 billion in the next years (Netflix, 2021, p. 5). The full valuation walk is summarized by Fig. 4.22.

To achieve a more robust valuation bandwidth than a single-shot value matrix, simulating different assumptions in the cost of capital and growth rates might be applied and create a valuation canvas.

4.5.5 Valuation Canvas and Framing

A simplified comparison of the "the streaming gambit" picture-of-the-future backed equity valuation with a valuation roughly in line with Netflix's management forecasts might provide further insights. For the latter, the margin improvements forecasted by Netflix's top management have been paired with the identical subscriber growth assumptions as in the former scenario. Additionally, the robustness of the valuation will be stress-tested by a brief sensitivity analysis simulating the impact of changes in the company's cost of capital or steady-state growth forecasts on its equity value. The valuation sensitivities and scenarios are summarized by Fig. 4.23.

The valuation according to the management assumption of a margin uplift of 3% points year by year was simulated till 2024 where Netflix would ultimately achieve an EBIT margin of 30%, which was frozen for later years. This margin development was paired with the growth forecast of "the streaming gambit" PoF. The combination of the forecasted streaming growth momentum and the management's margin

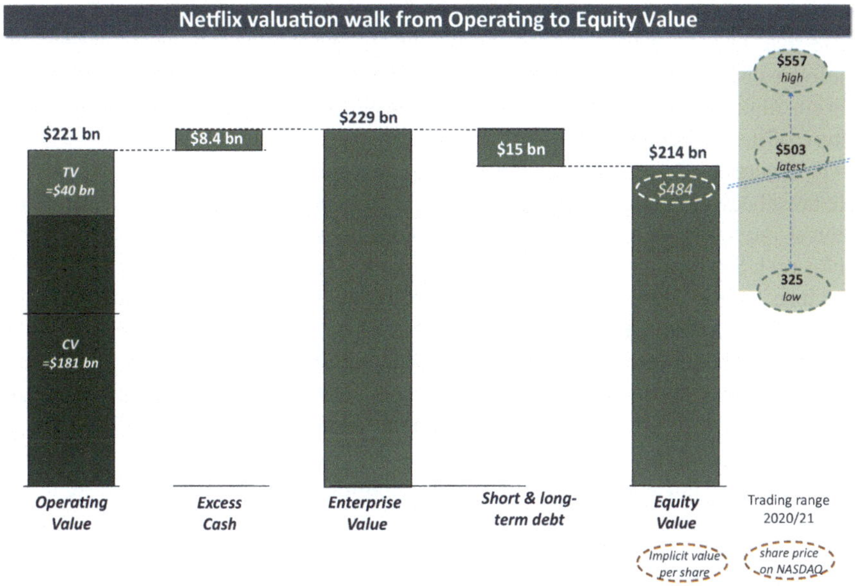

Fig. 4.22 Netflix valuation walk from operating to enterprise to equity value

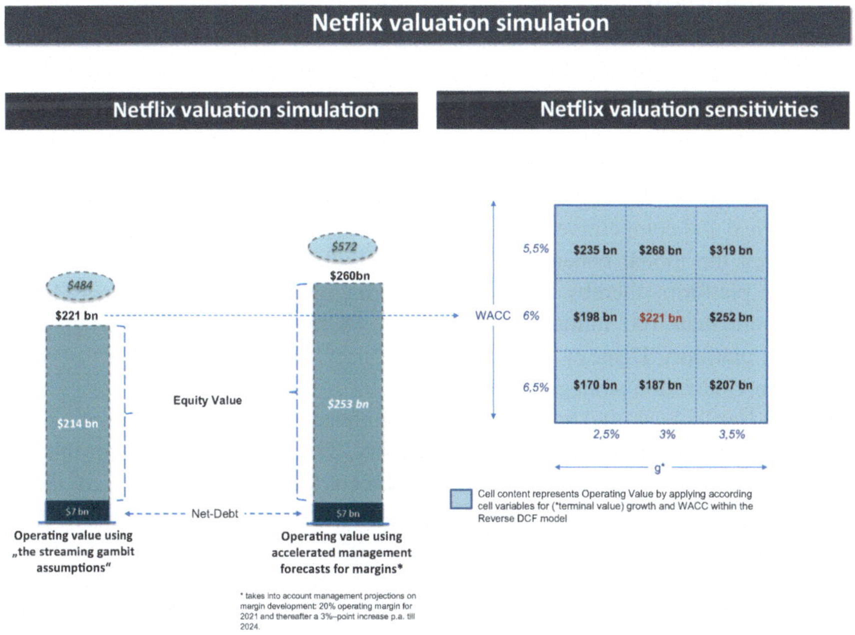

Fig. 4.23 Netflix Reverse DCF valuation scenarios and value driver sensitivities

improvement would lead to an uplifted operating value estimate of $260 billion. An EBIT margin in the range of 30% might seem extreme, but is archived by digital and platform champions. Nevertheless, the combination of a significant growth and margin improvement at the same time might be limited by the hyper-competitive nature of the global entertainment streaming market.

To determine a sensible valuation bandwidth, the cost of capital and the growth rate have been chosen to illustrate the impact of long-term value driver assumptions. Interest rate changes, as evidenced at the point of writing this book by increasing yields on US government bonds or induced by changes in Netflix's financial funding structure, have a sizable impact as Netflix realizes significant cash flows in the outer years, where present values are more impacted by cost of capital changes as close by cash flows. The long-term growth of streaming platforms is due to the scaling-driven value creation of such Business Designs a second mission-critical variable. A change in the long-term growth rate, once more by a 0.5%-point change, will shift the equity value by around $30 billion.

An alternative framing might use a trading multiple assessment of close-by listed film-streaming competitors or might broaden the valuation comparisons by also including more adjacent entertainment platforms or traditional entertainment companies and further pictures-of-the-future.

4.6 Summary

The streaming revolution within the global entertainment industry, initiated by Netflix for films, series and documentaries or by Spotify and YouTube in the music ecosystem, is an interesting learning of how long-standing, powerful old guards in an assumed shielded, highly profitable industry may ultimately be forced to adopt a new strategic game plan by being exposed to seismic shifts in their technological and competitive ecosystem. The need to revitalize its Business Design forced even the global behemoth Disney to rapidly introduce and scale its own streaming platform, thereby competing with its own traditional business lines. Luring more than 100 million subscribers in 18 months on its just established streaming platform, Disney+ provides empirical evidence on the upsides of such portfolio revitalization strategies.

Lately, Netflix backfired by underlining its global entertainment ambitions and its strategy to consistently enlarge its content library. The streaming innovator inked a multi-year deal with Sony Pictures Entertainment for streaming rights of Sony studio's movies, including the forthcoming Spider-Man films (Wall Street Journal, 2021). 2020 was also the year Netflix crossed the milestone of 200 million subscribers, with 37 million new viewers having joined the platform. The beginning of the 2020s might be remembered as the down of an epic streaming battle between those two leading global entertainment streaming contenders, as described at the beginning of this chapter. It might also lead to a brutal industry shakeout as seven streaming entertainment powerhouses compete with different strategic approaches on the viewers' limited leisure time.

Nevertheless, the attractiveness of streaming platforms, as described by the eight platform strengths, seems to make it worthwhile to fight this battle. Entertainment platforms have not only evidenced significant scalability patterns, but offer also a sustainable competitive advantage as such SVoD entertainment platform patterns request significant content investment as well as creative capabilities and talents. Due to these barriers of entry, entertainment platforms will probably be a hardly to be contested arena by outsiders and will limit the risk of dis-intermediation. Significant network effects exist cross and same side. Cross side, more variety, more creative talent, more well-known actors, and more celebrities will lure ever more subscribers on the platform to watch films, series, and documentaries. Vice versa, the increasing global reach and subscriber numbers of such platforms make them attractive for talents and high-profile actors to join in. Last but not the least, the latest strategic moves and releases of Netflix like "Bridgerton," "Lupin," or "The Queen's Gambit" seem to contribute to an international zeitgeist, creating a strong international bonding and network.

An interesting development might be on how alternative entertainment platforms like music, film, or gaming may ultimately compete on limited customer leisure time or might even lead to bridging strategies in between such ecosystems.

References

Economist. (2019a, September 28). *Despite producing quality shows, Netflix and HBO face headwinds.* https://www.economist.com/business/2019/09/28/despite-producing-quality-shows-netflix-and-hbo-face-headwinds

Economist. (2019b, March 20). *Streamlined—Disney, AT&T and Comcast v Netflix, Amazon and Apple.* https://www.economist.com/business/2019/03/30/disney-at-and-t-and-comcast-v-netflix-amazon-and-apple

Economist. (2019c, March 20). *The $650bn binge—Fear and greed in the entertainment industry.* https://www.economist.com/weeklyedition/2019-11-16

Economist. (2019d, November 14). *The future of entertainment.* https://www.economist.com/briefing/2019/11/14/the-future-of-entertainment

Economist. (2019e, November 14). *Who will win the media wars?* https://www.economist.com/leaders/2019/11/14/who-will-win-the-media-wars

Economist. (2020, December 12). *Disney plans to match Netflix in its spending on streaming.* https://www.economist.com/business/2020/12/11/disney-plans-to-match-netflix-in-its-spending-on-streaming

Economist. (2021a, February 25). *Tech competition—The rules of the tech game are changing.* https://www.economist.com/leaders/2021/02/27/the-rules-of-the-tech-game-are-changing?

Economist. (2021b, May 22). *The streaming wars—Monster of a merger.* https://www.economist.com/business/2021/05/20/the-warner-discovery-deal-and-the-future-of-streaming

Financial Times. (2021a, May 26). *Amazon agrees deal to buy MGM for $8.45bn.* https://www.ft.com/content/a796bb0e-bb92-4ac2-9bac-77f75e8b40c8

Financial Times. (2021b, May 18). *AT&T/Discovery: Getting your money back will have to do.* https://www.ft.com/content/9b3757bb-45ad-4d3a-80b5-bc386f75c07f?segmentId=1d846c0f-a9f0-a1db-a1f9-95194756b089:https://www.ft.com/content/9b3757bb-45ad-4d3a-80b5-bc386f75c07f

Financial Times. (2021c, February 11). *Disney+ added 8m subscribers over Christmas.* Financial Times. https://www.ft.com/content/49581411-5650-4448-8325-ce12f85ee86b

Financial Times. (2021d, May 14). *Netflix outpaced by old media companies it thought to dethrone.* https://www.ft.com/content/48c06611-1c17-4941-96cc-b085dfe05cdf

Financial Times. (2021e, February 3). *Spotify boosts subscriptions but warns of "uncertainty" ahead.*https://www.ft.com/content/68a0b358-7573-4255-be9b-0f048ac50928

Forbes. (2020, May 11). *Disney+ has the potential to become a $30 billion giant in only 5 years.* https://www.forbes.com/sites/genedelvecchio/2020/05/11/disney-plus-has-the-potential-to-become-a-30-billion-giant-in-only-5-years/

Kemet, H. (2019, November 12). *A timeline of Disney's media acquisitions.*https://www.complex.com/pop-culture/2019/11/disney-acquisition-timeline

Kim, C., & Mauborgne, R. (1999). Creating new market space. *Harvard Business Review, 77(1)*, 83–93.

Netflix. (2021a). *10-K report for FY 2020.* https://www.sec.gov/edgar/search/?r=el#/dateRange=custom&category=form-cat1&ciks=0001065280&entityName=NETFLIX%2520INC%2520(CIK%25200001065280)&startdt=2010-03-23&enddt=2021-03-23&filter_forms=10-K

Netflix. (2021b, Januar 19). *Shareholder letter Q1 2021.*https://s22.q4cdn.com/959853165/files/doc_financials/2021/q1/FINAL-Q1-21-Shareholder-Letter.pdf

Statista. (2021). *Video-streaming (SVoD).*https://de-statista-com.ezproxy.hs-augsburg.de/outlook/dmo/digitale-medien/video-on-demand/video-streaming-svod/weltweit#weltweiter-vergleich; https://www.statista.com/outlook/dmo/digital-media/video-on-demand/video-streaming-svod/worldwide

Twenty-First Century Fox. (2019, March 19). *SEC form 8-K.* https://sec.report/Document/0001193125-19-079716/

Uber. (2019). *An operating system for everyday life.*https://www.uber.com/newsroom/everyday-life-os

Wall Street Journal. (2021, April 8). *Netflix inks deal for rights to Sony Movies, including coming Spider Man films.* https://www.wsj.com/articles/netflix-inks-deal-for-rights-to-sony-movies-including-upcoming-spider-man-films-11617901201?page=1

Walt Disney. (2019, March 19). *Disney and 21st Century Fox announce per share value in connection with $71 billion acquisition.* https://thewaltdisneycompany.com/disney-and-21st-century-fox-announce-per-share-value-in-connection-with-71-billion-acquisition/

Walt Disney. (2020). *Financial year 2020 annual financial report.* https://thewaltdisneycompany.com/app/uploads/2021/01/2020-Annual-Report.pdf

Airbnb: From Double-Sided Accommodation to Multi-sided Experience Platform?

5

Abstract

Airbnb is today the most popular global online accommodation community. The platform matches travelers seeking authentic experiences with hosts offering unique, inspiring accommodations around the world. Therefore, Airbnb is in its origin a double-sided service platform for home-sharing. The company also became a synonym for the overall sharing economy. But, as the company's strategy intends to stretch out from an accommodation to a holistic experience platform, the company might even be in a transition stage to a multi-sided platform. Chapter 5 first describes Airbnb's revolution within the global hospitality industry by introducing its double-sided accommodation rentals platform. Additionally, its tailored 10C Business Design is compared with those of international hotel groups, highlighting the advantages of its asset-light platform architecture. Thereafter, the rentals platform feverish awaited, and spectacular initial public offering (IPO) will be described. With a pop of 114% on its opening share price in day one trading, its IPO became one of the most successful in corporate America's recent history, giving the rentals platform a market capitalization north of \$80 billion. The evaluation of Airbnb's eight platform value drivers highlights the potential shift from a double-sided accommodation to a multi-sided experience platform. The final financial valuation introduces the picture-of-the-future scenario "the age of connecting and belonging," before evaluating the accommodation platform with the Reverse DCF approach.

Airbnb is today globally the most popular online accommodation community. The platform matches hosts, who would like to list and offer their accommodation for a stay with private as well as business travelers, searching for and booking such accommodations through Airbnb's app. Therefore, Airbnb is in its origin a

T. Feix, *Valuing Digital Business Designs and Platforms*, Future of Business and Finance, https://doi.org/10.1007/978-3-030-83632-0_5

double-sided service platform for home-sharing. [1] The company also became lately a synonym for the overall sharing economy. [2, 3] But, as the company's strategy intends to stretch out from an accommodation to a full experience platform, offering visitors a variety of supplementary services at their targeted destination, the company might even be in a transition stage to a multi-sided platform.

5.1 Airbnb's Revolution as Global, Double-Sided Accommodation Rentals Platform

Airbnb was born in 2007 when the then two self-employed designers and friends Brian Chesky and Joe Gebbia began renting out an airbed in their San Francisco apartment during a local technology conference. The two intended to make an extra money with their side hustle while working on their social media start-up. After the two hosts welcomed three guests to their San Francisco home, their simplified business idea that travelers may pay discounted rates to stay in the spare bedrooms of local hosts took off, and their company became the poster boy of the so-called sharing economy turning private property into a new income stream.

Their idea was easily scalable as by renting out beds of hosts, an accommodation platform bears not the significant investment needs of traditional hotels while charging a commission for acting as a double-sided platform matchmaker between hosts and guests. First bookings were extended to a full-flagged business model for renting spare beds in cities during large conferences which typically encounter the problem of scarcity with respect to available and affordable hotel rooms. Later, the spare bed-renting idea was unfolded into an entire Business Design centering around a platform-based rental of entire accommodations or properties.

In 2009, Nathan Blecharczyk joined in, and Airbed and Breakfast was founded as Airbnb. More than 800 million stays have been booked since then on Airbnb's app in almost every country across the globe (Airbnb, 2021a). The platform offers nowadays globally seven million properties in over 100,000 cities (Economist, 2019). Airbnb became in the last years so successful that even global hotel incumbents like Marriott tried to copy Airbnb's Business Design by launching their own proprietary platforms like "Homes & Villas."

But 2020 played out to be a game-changer in Airbnb's young corporate history. The company started the year by preparing its long-awaited initial public offering, only to put nearly anything on hold as the black swan effect of the COVID-19

[1] Following the definition of platform patterns within Chap. 1

[2] Chua et al. (2019) describe Airbnb's value proposition as enhancing a simple sharing of personal properties or belongings.

[3] Botsman et al. (2010) define the term "sharing economy" broadly as an ecosystem that rests on sharing underused assets or services for free or for a fee directly from individuals. Sharing is therefore a peer-to-peer approach in which assets or services are shared between private individuals, either free or for a fee, typically enabled by the web.

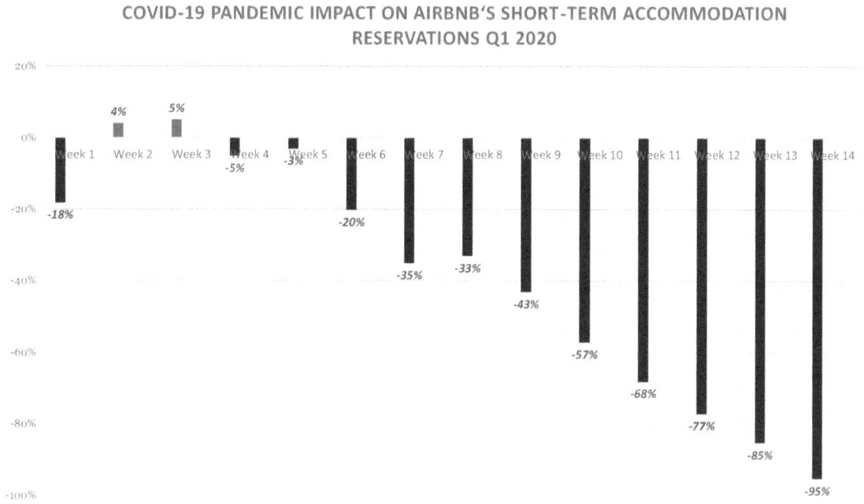

Fig. 5.1 COVID-19 pandemic impact on Airbnb's short-term accommodation bookings year over year (%). *Data-source*: Airbnb.com 2021

pandemic sent the world into lockdowns and global travel as well as tourism to a standstill in Spring 2020, as exemplified in Fig. 5.1 for Airbnb's bookings.

Airbnb's Business Design was hit hard in its core by the pandemic due to the induced social distancing measures. COVID-19 grew fast into an existential crisis: In April 2020, the worst month of the crisis, gross bookings on the rentals platform have been nearly completely wiped out, as pinpointed in Fig. 5.1 it became the moment of truth where its founders realized that travel and tourism is going to change, and probably might never go back to be the same as prior to the pandemic. Airbnb's management described the pandemic's impact on global tourism within its 2020 shareholder letter: "2020 was the year when nearly everything changed—the way we live, the way we work, and the way we travel" (Financial Times, 2020a).

The company immediately restructured its business, laying off 25% of its employees, cut marketing expenditures, and stopped any projects outside its core rental business, sharpening its focus. Airbnb was even forced in Mai 2020 to raise $2 billion in emergency funding from investors to counter the cash drain due to collapsing online bookings.

Revenues in the second quarter of 2021, the first quarter of the pandemic, collapsed by 72%, as indicated by Fig. 5.2. But, in the summer of 2020, the company saw slowly new booking patterns emerging, indicating a path to recovery as many remote workers tried to find comfortable accommodations for their new "digital only" work-life balance. Guest stayed longer, often for at least a month, at a rate higher than what would have been able to charge for traditional tenants.

Airbnb seemed to be more resilient than most of its peers while being still hit hard by the COVID-19 pandemic. Gross bookings on the platform were close to $24 billion and revenues $3.4bn for the full-year 2020, down by 37% and 30%,

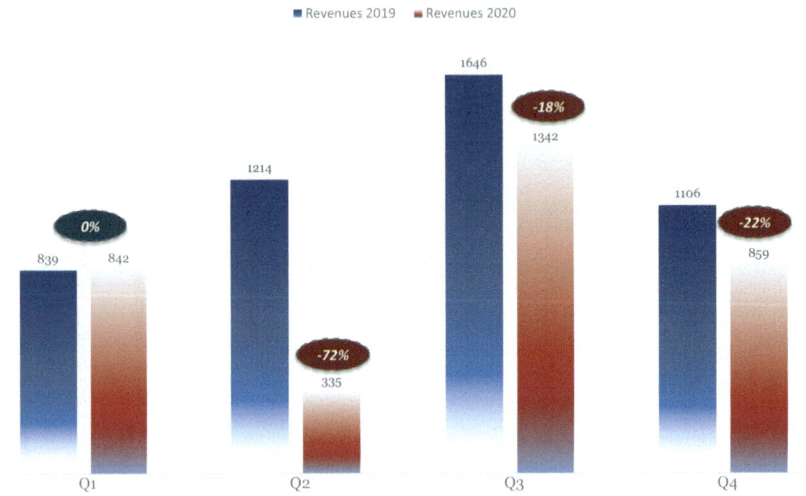

Fig. 5.2 COVID-19 pandemic impact on Airbnb's top-line revenues. *Data-source*: Airbnb's Shareholder Letter Q4 2020

respectively (Airbnb, 2021c), even if less severe than the overall market which lost 50% of its value, proving Airbnb's resilience and fast management response. But, the long-term, post-pandemic impacts on Airbnb's Business Design may not yet be fully apparent.

The San Francisco-based company's stellar stock market debut on December 10, 2020, might have come as a surprise. But, maybe, it is simply a sign of significant investor confidence in the strength and resilience of Airbnb's home-sharing platform, its potential to outgrow from a home rental to an overall travel experience platform, as well as the long-term recovery prospects of the global travel and tourism industry post-pandemic at large.

Airbnb's shares more than doubled on its first trading day to $146 per share on the NASDAQ stock exchange, giving the company a market capitalization of roughly $87 billion, more than twice of the market value of equity of the globally largest hotel giant Marriott (Financial Times, 2020d). Airbnb's IPO might, hopefully, be remembered as a sharp turnaround of how the corona pandemic hit global tourism.

The revolution by Airbnb's global accommodation platform Business Design is pinpointed in the value-growth matrix of Fig. 5.3: In the aftermath of its IPO, the market capitalization of the accommodation platform was higher than the combined value of its three global peers Marriot, Hilton, and International together.

Global hotel giants addressed lately the eternal threat of accommodation platforms by participating in the home-sharing business and increasingly try to revitalize their own Business Design by integrating platform patterns. This was evidenced by Accor's acquisition of Onefinestay, a London-based start-up that provides an Airbnb-like approach for high-end homes combined with a hotel-like service for hosts and travelers. Marriott, the largest hotel company in the world, joint

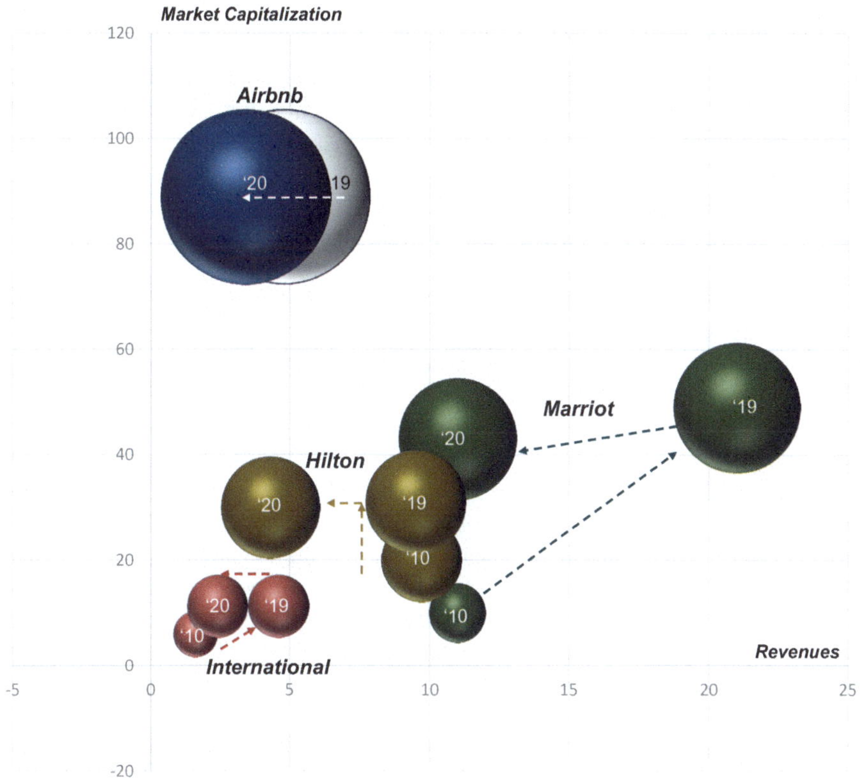

Fig. 5.3 Airbnb's value creation and growth benchmark with global hotel peers

forces with Hostmaker to break into the sharing economy creating TributePortfolioHomes.com, which enables travelers to book a stay in London homes. Vice versa are platform firms starting to list hotel rooms. HomeAway realized this through its Expedia Affiliate Network, while Airbnb retaliates by integrating bed-and-breakfast and boutique hotels. In so far, the global tourism market will be even more contested in the 2020s.

In the following, the growth potential and resilience of the home-sharing pioneer's Business Design as well as the strength of its accommodation platform will be explored in detail, before the Reverse DCF model tries to find a picture-of-the-future scenario-based fair value bandwidth for Airbnb as one of the equity capital market favorites.

5.2 Decoding Strategic Value: Airbnb's 10C Business Design

Airbnb's 10C Business Design diagnostics not only will assess the home-sharing pioneer's as-is working principles, but will also evaluate the intended strategic move from a global accommodation rentals platform to a full-service travel and hospitality platform addressing a much wider market of estimated $3.4 trillion revenues globally, according to Airbnb. This might be mission critical for the later analysis of Airbnb's growth prospects and platform strength, as this potential transition would have a lasting impact on the rental sharing platform's long-term strategic and financial valuation.

5.2.1 Competitive Strategy and Purpose (CS)

Airbnb's mission to connect travelers seeking authentic experiences with hosts offering unique, inspiring accommodations around the world highlights the platform's double-sided architecture. Accessibility of the platform is provided by Airbnb's website and mobile app.

The company's strategy follows a global approach by liaise hosts and visitors from everywhere on its accommodation platform and by building a global and reliable brand name. The latter is seen, beside its technology platform, as a competitive advantage. Trust plays for both platform partners, the hosts and the guests, a mission-critical role in arranging a stay with an, at the beginning of the booking process, anonymous counterparty. The accommodation booking platform offers their hosts a global reach of potential visitors and its travelers a nearly unlimited variety of accommodations at their targeted destination. In so far, Airbnb follows a personalized tail-end strategy in contrast to the volume strategy of most hotel giants focusing on hotel bed capacity utilization.

As Airbnb does not own any of the offered properties listed on its platform, again in stark contrast to the traditional hotel business model, the company profits from a typical asset-light platform Business Design, as discussed in Chap. 1. The revenue model is based upon a commission for each booking from both platform partners. In so far, the revenue and Cash Flow Model are closer to a one-time transactional approach as for ride-hailing and less to a streaming-based subscription model.

An important part of Airbnb's DNA is the design, the implementation, as well as the orchestration of an easy-to-use, convenient accommodation booking process. A personalized, enjoyable journey experience based on an intimate host-guest relationship is targeted by the platform's USP. This USP paired with a digitally enabled, frictionless travel processes should combine the best of both worlds, the service excellence of leading hotels and the intimacy of private homes. As technology-driven Business Designs encounter the risk to be perceived as anonymous, Airbnb invests heavily to address emotions and to build a cozy community. Ultimately, hosts should offer an "one-of-a-kind" stay and an unparalleled, unique travel experience which let guests experience the world in a more authentic, connected way (Airbnb, 2021a). Additionally, the platform's rating system should foster transparency and trust throughout the travel journey.

As Airbnb scales the integration of booking local experiences like restaurant and museum visits, guided tours, or sport events, on its platform to personalize the guest's experiences, it onboards multiple additional platform parties. Therefore, its strategy shifts its center of gravity from a pure accommodation rentals platform to an overall experience platform. This strategic move also alters the platform architecture from a double-sided to a multi-sided approach. The holistic experience strategy and according personalization of the traveler's stay also set it further apart from the standardized offers of traditional hotel peers.

Hotel giants, exposed to Airbnb's global platform approach, retaliated lately by launching their own proprietary booking platforms. But, Airbnb responded with a countermove, by letting apartment hotels list their rooms on its app and by investing in properties tailored for Airbnb rentals.

5.2.2 Core Value Proposition (CV)

As a double-sided platform, Airbnb has to create a convincing value proposition for both platform partners, hosts and guests alike.

Airbnb creates for travelers its value proposition by providing on its platform a wide variety of potential homes to rent at affordable prices, especially if compared with hotels. Instead of the traditional traveling and hotel experience to feel, at least partially, as stranger, the platform tries to create personal experiences by building ties between its guests and hosts or even the wider local community. This is evidenced by Airbnb's latest marketing campaign "made possible by hosts" and makes the company partially unique, by giving its hosts a central role in its customer value delivery. It also integrates guests to shape the company's core value proposition (Airbnb, 2021c, p. 8). The rentals company addresses thereby comfort, safety, and trust paired with unique experience for its travelers along the whole visitor journey. The ultimate target is to draw travelers to the platform by creating images and stories around a holistic and authentic journey experience.

The onboarding, selection, and booking process is empowered by a seamless navigation on the platform, especially by a simplified placement process for hosts and booking process for guests: The host places his or her accommodation together with a profile on Airbnb's platform. The placement is supplemented by reviews, ratings, and recommendations of former guests, intending to build trust between two originally strangers and fostering a buy-in of the Airbnb visitor community. Additionally, hosts might provide photos and detailed descriptions about their accommodation like number of rooms or their interior, as well as further information about the neighborhood and possible experiences close by to the accommodation. This should provide potential guest more comfort in selecting the best fitting place to stay. In case the traveler is interested to rent an offered accommodation, the guest sends the host a message through Airbnb proprietary messaging system. Hosts have then a 24-hour acceptance response time. The price of the accommodation is set by the host and depends on the timing and length of the stay. But, Airbnb also supports its hosts in their price setting through the platform's predictive pricing algorithm that will recommend tailored rental fees for its hosts.

Airbnb takes a counter-position to the foremost standardized, look-alike hotel rooms of global hotel chains by initiating an individual touch point of the guest-host relationship and by making available a diversity of private homes. Besides, by having created the globally most powerful accommodation platform, Airbnb levers its vast array of guest data, feedbacks, recommendations, and traveler-generated content to tailor the stay according to the individual interests and needs of each guest.

For example, local information and events provided by event managers as well as authentic guidebooks created by local hosts should enable visitors to organize their own unique travel experience according to their interests. Nearby shopping, restaurants, visiting, museums, and event recommendations of local hosts may be additionally valuable to experience the destination more authentically and go much beyond old-style flyers guest might find still in most hotel lobbies.

But also for its hosts, as second platform partner, Airbnb offers a multitude of value adds. Foremost, the platform creates for hosts an additional income stream for renting out a room or their entire home, for example, if they are on holidays. This might be paired with the desire of most open-minded hosts to meet interesting people, getting new ideas, and maybe becoming even friends with some guests.

For hosts, as for travelers, the convenient, seamless, and save platform architecture and booking processes play out as a significant USP: The guests' identity and payment credentials are already verified pre-visit by ID and credit card background-checks on the platform. Additional comfort with respect to the counter parties is provided by the guest review ratings. A multitude of further support services like accommodation booking management, cleaning services, and others are provided by request through Airbnb's platform. Separate, mission-critical advantages are, due to most host's typically missing technological and payment infrastructure, the platform's robust money transfer processes guaranteed by Airbnb and the offered insurance coverages for listed properties, if demanded.

Last but not the least, the platform defines "rules of the game" for the traveler's stay like recommended hospitality standards, hosting guidelines addressing safety, hazards, neighborhood information, or dispute resolutions.

5.2.3 Customer and Markets (CM)

As a double-sided platform, Airbnb serves two customer segments, hosts and travelers. In its IPO prospectus Airbnb described its total addressable market to be \$3.4 trillion, decomposed in \$1.8 trillion for short-term stays, \$0.2 trillion for long-term stays, and \$1.4 trillion for experience services.

Each night, roughly two million people around the world stay in an accommodation of Airbnb's hosts (Economist, 2019). Travellers may be separated by the purpose of their trip in business and leisure travel guests, as both segments have to be addressed by their significantly different use case. Whereas the first might be interested foremost in an optimized accommodation specific value-for-price ratio, the latter might be interested in an overall trip experience with local insights at reasonable pricing.

The lately introduced sub-brand Airbnb Plus targets the upscale leisure family market and business travelers, by offering premium services. Homes of Airbnb Plus have been verified for quality, comfort, design, maintenance, and other amenities,

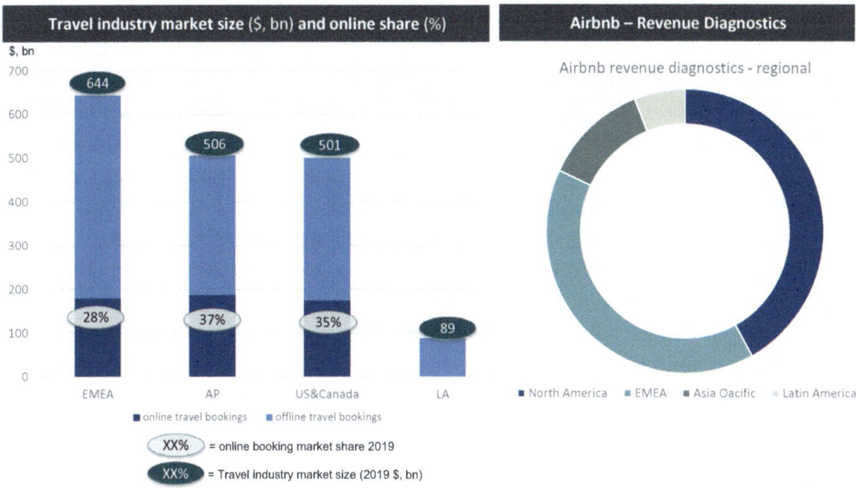

Fig. 5.4 Global travel industry market size and Airbnb's regional revenue and pricing diagnostics. Data-source: Statista, 2021

besides offering easy check-in, premium Internet access, and fully equipped kitchens (Airbnb.com, 2021a).

Another important segmentation criteria is obviously the geographical location the traveler intends to visit, as described by Fig. 5.4. Besides, the traveller's preferred area like countryside, suburban, or metropolitan, the number of travelers like single, couple, or family trips plays an important role for the market segmentation. The latter will have an influence on the preferred type of accommodation like renting a single room, a flat, or even an entire house.

These high-level segmentation approaches are supplemented by a detailed micro-segmentation based on big data and analytics approaches to tailor the accommodation and trip experience along visitors' preferences coming close to a segment-of-one treatment. As explained later in more detail, with Airbnb Experiences, the platform extends this approach of an individualization of the traveler's visit by offering supplementary hiking tours, museum visits, local events like concerts or flea markets, as well as food or wine tours. Airbnb outperforms in so far by large most hotels in the personalization of travelers' experiences not just by offering a wide array of homes and locations enabling genuine micro-segmentation and the "perfect match" between guest and host, but by a holistic traveler's experience, giving the later an unique experience every time.

Hosts, as the second partners on Airbnb's accommodation platform, come from around the world offering places to stay. The host might be differentiated along similar criteria as location, type of offered accommodation, and their role as sole host or integrated travel agent, where the latter is also responsible to coordinate visits of local events or trips.

Airbnb extended its loyalty program in recent years to lock hosts on their platform. Hosts may earn the status of "superhosts" pending on highly rated customer reviews, quick response time to guest questions, and the number of stays in their accommodation. The recognition as a "superhost" is a significant marketing incentive and differentiator for accommodation providers. Additionally, Airbnb built in recent years a community with its hosts, which became transparent in its IPO prospectus and latest capital market reports (Airbnb, 2021c).

Airbnb started lately to cooperate with property developers like Niido to transform buildings into Airbnb units, where both companies gain 25% of the generated revenues of such rebuilt accommodations (Mody & Gomez, 2018, p. 3). This approach might further pay in to build a trustful as well as collaborative ecosystem and platform community. But, it will position the rentals platform even more into direct competition to hotels and might lead to less individualized offers.

5.2.4 Customer Relationship (CR)

Airbnb has to blend the platform's relationship with its potential travelers searching for an attractive accommodation with the relationship to its four million hosts offering their room, apartment, or house on the platform.

The customer relationship with travelers is built around their whole journey, what provides the platform multiple contact points with its travelers: from the traveler's onboarding on the accommodation platform, the planning of their trip as well as of further arrangements, the booking process, the payment process, ultimately, to the customer capture as part of the Airbnb community for follow-on bookings. Thereby, Airbnb combines the scalability and quality standardization advantages of digitalized processes with intimate relationships, especially through the direct host-guest interaction during the traveler's stay.

Most transactions are fully automated through the app and web page, for example, the signing process on the web page or app. Nevertheless, customer embeddedness is targeted by a multitude of processes. Visitor issues and complaints are addressed immediately through the Airbnb app, massaging systems, e-mail, or hotline. The same holds true for any inappropriate behaviors or risks on both sides, the hosts' and the guests'. As the host's and the guest's platform experience and relationship are built upon trust and the exchange of sensitive data, the company invests significantly in the protection of privacy and any personal data.

The mid- to long-term capture of host and traveler engagement on the platform is targeted by distinct referral programs based on a reward system with credit points expressed as a discount for the traveler's next accommodation booking on Airbnb's platform.

The platform-host relationship is ultimately steered by the assessment of the accommodation provider if the platform offers an additional and continuous income stream. The host's core interest centers typically on the access to the wide pool of potential guests, at the same time demanding an adverse selection of black sheeps to protect the hosts property from wrongdoings or bad guest behavior. Additionally, the host's perception of the platform's process quality, as evidenced by its response time to accidents, damages, or complaints, the assurance of a seamless 24/7 on-boarding of travelers, or the coordination with local event managers and co-operation partners, plays an important role for the perceived host-platform relationship.

5.2.5 Channels (CH)

As a digital native, Airbnb leverages more or less all social media networks to initiate traveler awareness, platform interest, and onboarding. Sponsored digital advertisements and marketing campaigns are placed frequently on YouTube, Facebook, Twitter, Instagram, and the likes as well as hospitality tight-knit web pages like Lonely Planet or others. Especially for the capture of new and engagement of existing accommodation platform users, social media channels like Airbnb's Instagram posts and Facebook pages play an important role. Airbnb supplements these third-party digital social networks by a number of proprietary channels like its Airbnb Newsroom and Airbnb Citizen channel, through its web page, and Airbnb's Facebook landing page.

Nevertheless, word of mouth plays an additional, imminent role for Airbnb's platform placement and fits precisely with Airbnb's push for unique and inspiring user stories described by the latest Airbnb campaign "made possible by hosts" (Airbnb, 2021c). The download of the Airbnb app is possible in any mainstream app store.

5.2.6 Core Assets (CA)

Core assets have been described throughout the book as those assets which stand out for a Business Design's unique characteristics. For Airbnb, the following assets might make a true difference for its accommodation rentals platform.

First, the company developed a technological leading accommodation platform and app. This platform is continuously enlarged by onboarding additional users and guests as well as by integrating new features and co-operation partners along the whole travel experience. Important characteristics of the platform are its seamless working search engine and algorithms for finding accommodations in a defined target region. The platform is strengthened by strong and lasting network effects:

- Cross-side network effects exist as a larger number of hosts and a diverse set of accommodation types increase the attractiveness for travelers, and, vice versa, a larger pool of potential global visitors pushes further hosts' interests to list their accommodation on Airbnb's platform.
- Same-side network effects exist as more travelers will lead to more variety in accommodations offered by hosts on the platform and will make local recommendations and information more broadly available. This serves as an additional customer advantage for the next marginal traveler.

Airbnb created, side by side to its technology platform, a global brand and app, which is crucial to be perceived as a trustworthy transaction and platform partner for global accommodation bookings. The brand image is reinforced emotionally through the users themselves, meaning host and visitor-generated content and surrounding stories, including photos and images.

Additional highly valuable core assets are the company's talents and employees. Their core capabilities in technology fields like platform and app development or algorithm design are matched with an in-depth understanding of the tourism industry and hospitality specific process knowledge.

5.2.7 Core Capabilities (CC)

This detailed understanding of the company's tourism ecosystem and technology skills as the company's true DNA enables Airbnb's employees to design processes which are clear-cut for both platform partners and address the needs of hosts and visitors like trust and comfort. Prime examples might be here the recommendation and rating as well as guest and host feedback systems.

The further scaling and development of Airbnb's platform requests latest technology skills like analytics or data science and mining capabilities. These capabilities are boiled down on a granular, tourism industry-specific level, e.g., for further tailoring the platforms' recommendation algorithms, optimizing the check-in process, or integrating further safety features and cross-checks along the booking or payment processes.

All-in-all, Airbnb's capabilities intend at the same time to tame negative network effects, for example, by easing guest-host interactions or by improving and fastening the complaint management process, as well as to foster positive feedback loops for scaling the platform by enlarging the amount of hosts, accommodations, and covered cities or by integrating complementary tourism services on the app. Ultimately, guests and hosts should be enticed by the platform-enabled travel experiences.

5.2.8 Core-Ecosystem Partners (CE)

For embedding the accommodation selection and stay of its travelers into a more holistic travel experience requests the cooperation with a multitude of tourism ecosystem partners:

- Tourism and event agencies might support hosts with supplementary services like guided tours or local art, restaurant, or nightlife events.
- To create a positive perceived travel image, photo sequences, and image posts on social media networks like Instagram became an integral part of Airbnb's brand story. The company hires for distinct events, like accommodation photo shootings or street events, professional photographers, bloggers, and freelancers.

- On the technology side, global and local digital map providers, latest GPS data-enabled location positioning or online payment solution providers, cloud technology providers, or digital ID identification and fraud detection firms are important partners to supplement Airbnb's core capabilities. Airbnb additionally acquired selectively a bundle of tech start-ups which might scale future supplementary platform offerings, functionalities, or enabling technologies.
- Insurance companies are also transactional partners for the platform and its hosts as they ensure trust by their insurance payments in case of damages in the hosts' accomodations.
- Access to business travelers' alliances with travel platform providers like Concur or Flight Centre gave Airbnb host's access to corporate travel managers. The latter have some discretion which platforms, accommodation providers, or hotel chains they enlist in line with corporate travel policies providing a vast potential of business guests.
- Capital markets, especially early backers, seed financiers, and venture capitalists enabled the financial means for the fast scaling of Airbnb's platform through multiple private funding rounds before the company ultimately filled its IPO and became a listed corporation in December 2020.

A final set of important co-operation partners are local communities, regulators, and politicians. The latter serve as key partners to position Airbnb as accepted and trusted accommodation provider. The discussions centering around the social, communal, and financial responsibility of the accommodation platform highlighted the importance of those relationships.

Regulators and politicians in multiple communities complain that the typical Airbnb host has changed from the original "mom and dad renting out a spare room" to professional host renting out several accommodations or even a portfolio of properties. Only 21% of Airbnb's listings are still spare bedrooms, whereas more than half of all listings are managed by hosts with at least two properties on the platform. [4] The chief concern echoed by city officials is here the partial conversion of private into full-time tourist accommodations and the potential impact on the affordability of local housing.

According regulations put in place might threaten Airbnb's presence in some cities. For example, after tightening local rules on hosts in San Francisco in 2018, the number of available listings on Airbnb plummeted by 50%. Airbnb counter-argued that its presence increases local spending and tourism revenue. Lately, the company stated in its IPO prospectus that it came to agreements in around 70% of its top 200 cities. Additionally, as each of those top cities accounts for less than 2.5% of Airbnb's total booking revenue (Financial Times, 2020a), the company's overall business is still highly diversified. The proactive liaise with such a multitude of cities, communities, regulators, and other political groups seems to have played out

[4] According to data from Financial Times and Transparent, a research firm focusing on short-term rentals (Financial Times, 2020a)

to be more beneficial in comparison to other platforms' more aggressive and confrontative stance with local regulators.

5.2.9 Corporate Organization (CO)

At first glance, Airbnb's structure might seem highly complex, but is clearly strategy minded in addressing the demands of its dynamic and technology-driven accommodation booking platform business embedded within an even wider travel and tourism ecosystem. Airbnb's organizational structure, often described as a prime example of a holacracy [5] organization offering significant flexibility, has also matrix organizational characteristics. The latter provide some structural framing.

The governance and process flows between core management layers are clearly defined. The CEO and founder Brian Chesky is the interphase between the management and the Board of Directors. The Vice Presidents of Airbnb's core departments directly report to the CEO. [6] These core departments mimic in detail Airbnb's platform and hospitality market specifics on top level and also within the departments:

- On top level, by the design of departments and responsibilities like "VP for trips," "VP for engineering," "VP for design," "VP for product and home operation," or "business affairs and legal office."
- On the individual department level, for example, the department for "trips" includes directors and teams for the operations of trips, product leads, or quality leads for trips, whereas the department for design is decomposed in directors and teams for research, for the design of operations, for the design of trips, for the design management for guests, and product content leads.

Despite this structural framework, cross-functional co-operation between those departments is initiated especially on the project level. Product and project managers work with their virtual team, staffed by team members from different departments like engineering, research, data science, and others, vertically. These teams have full authority and decision-making power to drive their project through the organization, whereby the VPs of experience or design might have a review right for more sizable

[5] A holacracy organization might be described as an organizational archetype that replaces traditional hierarchical organizational architectures and management styles by self-management of fluid teams, as decision power is widely dispersed throughout the organization teams and individual team members are empowered (Holacracy, 2020). Nevertheless, the alignment with the company's ultimate purpose and strategic direction has to be assured. A very nuanced article on the strengths but also challenges of firms applying holacracy organizational principles to fulfill on the ultimate goals of reliability and adaptability of organizational designs might be found in the *Harvard Business Review* article from Bernstein et al. (2016).

[6] The departments by itself have further layers below the Vice Presidents like directors, product managers, and support staff.

projects. A vertical design team of a new product might include managers from engineering, design, research, and data science with significant authority building holacracy elements into Airbnb's organization. These vertical teams target three strategic directions, product initiatives, platform or infrastructure initiatives, and new growth initiatives. The latter might become mission-critical for Airbnb's intended transition from an accommodation rental to a full trip advisory and travel experience platform.

Airbnb's organizational design was stress-tested by the pandemic and showed resilience by consistent cost-cutting initiatives, by pulling back from businesses outside of its core home-sharing business and by adjusting the platform to post-pandemic new realities.

5.2.10 Cash Flow Model (CF)

Airbnb realized lately one of the most successful initial public offerings (IPOs) of America's recent capital market history: Its share price popped at the opening of its first day trading at the NASDAQ stock exchange by 114% with a corresponding price per share of $146, giving the rentals platform a market capitalization of $87.2 billion (Financial Times, 2020d). As Airbnb's extraordinary successful start as listed company surprised many capital market participants and stands in stark contrast to its pandemic-fueled operational challenges at the beginning of the year, its details will be discussed explicitly within the next subchapter.

The equity valuation might seem elevated at first glance as the San Francisco-based accommodation booking service's businesses collapsed due to the pandemic and only recovered lately. Airbnb's bookings on its platform stood at 193 million nights and experiences for 2020, a decrease of 41% year over year, whereas its gross booking value decreased only slightly less by 37% to $23 billion. As cross-revenues came in at $3.4 billion, a 30% reduction compared with the prior year, the company reported a loss in line with the prior year on adjusted EBITDA level of $251 million and a net loss of $4.6 billion inflated by charges related to the company's IPO [7] (Airbnb, 2021c).

Nevertheless, bookings and revenues seem to have at least stabilized in Q4 2020, and adjusted EBITDA was back close to brake-even. And, Airbnb is also a different story as, unlike some other Silicon Valley platform companies, it began already in 2016, 9 years after its inauguration, to generate positive cash flows and a year later reported to have crossed EBITDA breakeven with $93 million (Financial Times, 2020a).

The assessment of the long-term financial prospects of the home-sharing pioneer has to identified and assessed the platform's value drivers like ROIC, long-term growth forecasts, and mission-critical cost items. Airbnb generates its revenues from facilitating guest stays at the accommodations offered by its hosts on its platform.

[7] Especially $2.8 billion of stock-based compensation expenses (Airbnb, 2021c)

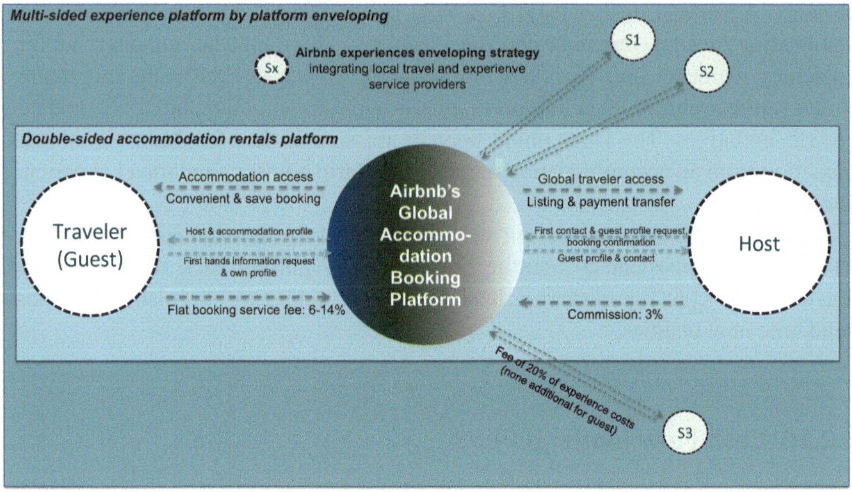

Fig. 5.5 Airbnb's double-sided, commission-based revenue model enveloping multi-sided experience

The rentals platforms *revenue model* rest upon a commission model, charging a service fee as a percentage of the booking value from both platform partners, hosts and guests. Airbnb collects the booking value from guests on behalf of the hosts as well as guest fees using the guest's pre-authorized payment method. After check-in, Airbnb disburses the booking value to the host, less the fees due from the host to the company (Airbnb, 2021b, p. 93).

Figure 5.5 describes the revenue streams between the platform and its partner's. Airbnb is said to charge its guest a service commission fee per transaction of 6–12% and its hosts a fee of 3%.[8] Some peers like HomeAway apply a different pricing strategy and charge a listing fee instead of Airbnb's transactional commission from their hosts. Event fees are flip-sided to booking commissions, as no service fees are charged from guests, whereas a 20% fee is charged from event hosts or local service providers, who typically use Airbnb as a supplementary advertising platform for their offering. Additionally, Airbnb passes some of its costs directly onto their host like in the case of Google search costs, or in case the host's booking request was initiated through Google ads, whereas the host may opt out. Airbnb offers also supplementary services. As a prime example for the latter serve professional photographers or cleaning service in selected cities for Airbnb listed properties, where the platform charges a distinct service fee.

At first sight counterintuitive has been the development of average daily rates ("ADRs"), which track the gross booking value per night and which increased year over year by 13% to $128 in Q4 2020. This price increase was driven by a regional

[8] Hosts pay a 3% transaction fee if they select a flexible cancellation policy, 4% for a moderate, and 5% for a strict cancellation policy.

shift to North American bookings, where ADRs tend to be higher than in other parts of the world. Also, more guests booked entire homes, relative to private or shared rooms, and prices are higher for the former.

Moving from Airbnb's top-line revenue development to its earnings performance, besides its US-GAPP reporting also a normalized perspective will be provided. This seems to be mandatory due to the company's more than $2.8 billion in non-cash stock-based compensations paid in 2020 along its IPO. Airbnb was required along its IPO to recognize a significant portion of stock-based compensations provided to its employees in the last several years (Airbnb, 2021c, p. 3), a typical procedure of Silicon Valley listings.[9]

Airbnb's adjusted EBITDA performance, excluding stock-based compensations, proved to be quite resilient throughout the pandemic due to the company's cost discipline by managing down operating expenses[10] and its focus on its core accommodation rental business. In its IPO quarter, Airbnb' reported an improved adjusted EBITDA of $21 million, compared with a prior year Q4 EBITDA loss of $276 million. For the full year, Airbnb's 2020 adjusted EBITDA stood at −$276 million, more or less in line with 2019's performance of −$253 million, despite the platform lost in 2020 a third of its revenues, equal to −$1.4 billion.

To manage Airbnb through this demanding year 2020, the attention of the Airbnb's management was on the most crucial *cost drivers*, which will be more in-depth assessed within the Reverse DCF valuation. The following costs play a center role for Airbnb's performance (Airbnb, 2021c) and are detailed in Fig. 5.6[11]:

- *Cost of revenue*: covering Airbnb's payment processing costs, data center hosting costs for the platform, amortization of internally developed software, and acquired technology (Airbnb, 2021b, p. 62), are roughly 25% of Airbnb's revenues. The ratio was fairly stable during the pandemic as cost of revenue declined in 2020 in line with the decreasing revenues of the platform. The reasons have been lower payment fees associated with lower booking volumes and cost-containment initiatives of Airbnb's management.
- *Cost of operations and support* primarily consist of personnel-related expenses and third-party services costs, customer relations costs including refunds, and allocated costs for information technology (Airbnb, 2021b, p. 62). In the last years, such costs floated around 17% of revenues but increased to 26% or, on an adjusted basis, to 22% in 2020. The gross margin was in the last years trading in a range of 58–59% and decreased only slightly during the pandemic, based on a normalized level.

[9] Additionally, Q4 2020 net income was impacted by a mar-to-market adjustment of $872 m referencing to the recognition of an increased value of its warrants issued in line with its long-term loan agreement entered into in April 2020 and triggered due to Airbnb's share price increase (Airbnb, 2021c).

[10] Excluding stock-based compensation and stock-settlement obligations

[11] Airbnb's condensed consolidated statements of operations from its latest financial statement 2020 have been used. The adjusted statements have been reverse engineered based on Airbnb's provided information on stock-based compensation expenses.

	Condensed IS		Adjusted IS	
	2019	2020	2019 adj.	2020 adj.
Revenues	4.805.239	3.378.199	4.805.239	3.378.199
Cost of revenue	1.196.313	876.042	1.196.313	876.042
% of revenues	*25%*	*26%*	*25%*	*26%*
Operations & support	815.074	877.042	814.257	733.045
% of revenues	*17%*	*26%*	*17%*	*22%*
Product development	976.695	2.752.872	920.063	874.079
% of revenues	*20%*	*81%*	*19%*	*26%*
Sales & marketing	1.621.519	1.175.325	1.597.600	740.053
% of revenues	*34%*	*35%*	*33%*	*22%*
G&A	697.181	1.134.851	681.002	590.765
% of revenues	*15%*	*34%*	*14%*	*17%*
Restructuring charges		151.355		151.555
% of revenues	*0%*	*4%*	*0%*	*4%*
Total costs & expenses	5.306.782	6.967.487	5.209.235	3.965.539
	110%	*206%*	*108%*	*117%*
EBIT	-501.543	-3.589.288	-403.996	-587.340
	-10%	*-106%*	*-8%*	*-17%*
			Cross-check stock-based comp	
			97.547	3.001.948

Fig. 5.6 Airbnb's condensed income statement incl. stock-based compensation adjustments

- *Product development costs* include platform and app infrastructure costs as well as the development costs for new features, for the ongoing fine-tuning of algorithms, and for other platform-enabling technologies. These costs jumped, due to stock-based compensations along Airbnb's IPO, from 20% of revenues in 2019 to 81% in 2020, but are on an adjusted basis with 26% of revenues more in line with prior years. Platform development might realize some economies of scale once the platform matures but might be in the next years more a variable cost item as further platform developments might be necessary to scale the booking to an experience platform.
- *Sales and marketing costs* include, besides the traditional marketing mix like band, performance, and field operations costs, as well market expansion costs for exploring hosts and accommodations in new cities or for adding new supplementary service lines. Sales and marketing-related costs have been traditionally a third of Airbnb's revenues but have been reduced in 2020 by a consequent cost management to 22% of revenues on an adjusted basis. Especially lower performance marketing and brand campaign expenses contributed to such cost initiatives.

- General and administration, meaning foremost headquarters services and personnel-related expenses for management and administrative functions, are typically 15–17% of revenues on an adjusted basis.

Airbnb was already pre-pandemic focusing to become more efficient and profitable as a preparation for its targeted initial public offering, but the COVID-19 pandemic and downward spiraling bookings accelerated the company's focus on cost management meaningful.

Fast forward to the short-term outlook 2021, Airbnb's management communicated that its core priority will be to prepare the accommodation platform for the expected rebound in travel activity. As COVID-19 vaccines are rolled out and social distancing restrictions are probably lifted step by step in the second half of 2021, the company's midterm priorities will be the management of the expected travel rebound and the further transition to an entire end-to-end experience platform for hosts and guests alike (Airbnb, 2021c).

5.2.11 10C Business Design Canvas: Airbnb

Figure 5.7 summarizes Airbnb's 10C Business Design canvas, highlighting the architecture and inner working mechanisms of the accommodation rentals platform.

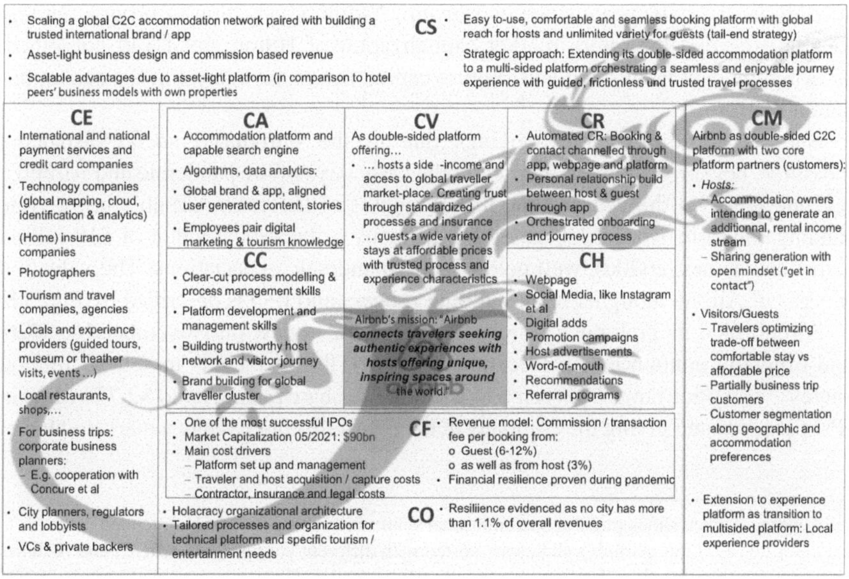

Fig. 5.7 10C Business Design canvas of Airbnb

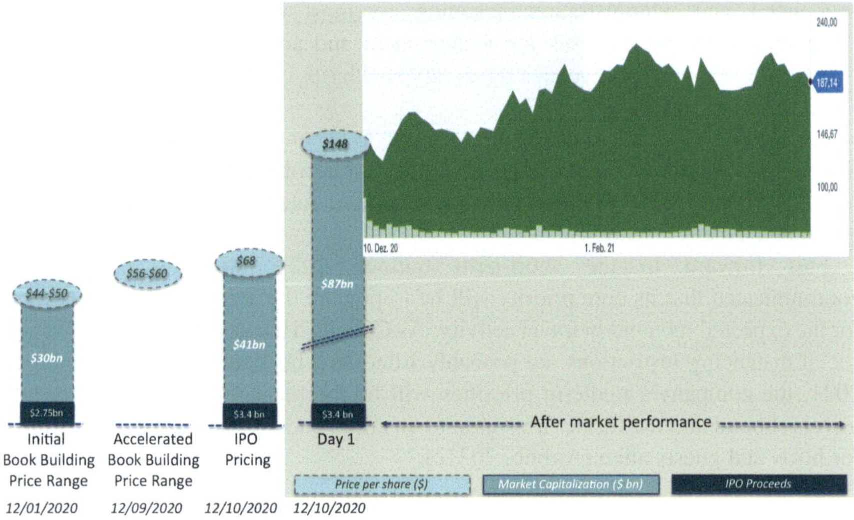

Fig. 5.8 Airbnb's accelerated book-building price range, final IPO pricing, and market capitalization. *Data-Source*: finance.yahoo.com 2021

5.3 Airbnb's IPO: Sailing on Capital Market Tailwinds

Already in 2017, 10 years since its start-up, Airbnb's valuation in private funding rounds exceeded the entire market capitalization of Hilton and Hyatt combined, showing the significant seed and venture capital investors' interest in the accommodation platform.

But, as accommodation bookings due to the introduced social distancing measures, not surprisingly, collapsed in the early days of the pandemic and Airbnb's revenue fell by a third during the first 9 months of the year, Airbnb's last private funding round in April 2020 gave the company a theoretical value of $18 billion (Financial Times, 2020d), well below its pre-pandemic expectations. The valuation process of Airbnb along its book building process and IPO is described by Fig. 5.8.

Airbnb filed its preliminary prospectus for SEC review on November 16, 2020, and officially announced on December 1, 2020, that it intends to sell 55 million shares [12] in a price range between $44 and $50 per share raising up to $2.75 billion in IPO proceeds and giving the company at the top of this price range a market value of

[12] Including a green shoe option of 5 m additional shares increasing the $2.5bn intended proceeds to the described $2.75bn. Airbnb's shares are vested with different voting rights, where class A shares own one voting right, class B shares 20, and class C as well as H no voting rights (Airbnb, 2021b, pp. Exhibit 4.1: 1–2). As it is the case for most Silicon Valley unicorns, especially founders and early bakers will hold foremost B shares, having control over the company even in case of owning less than 50% of outstanding shares.

its equity of $29.8 billion (Financial Times, 2020b).[13] This valuation at 8.8 times 2020 revenues of $3.4 billion would have been slightly higher than Booking.com's as well as significantly higher than Expedia's trading multiple at this point of time. The three founders, Brian Chesky, Airbnb's chief executive, Joe Gebbia, and Nathan Blecharczyk, announced to still hold 42.2% of the voting rights in their listed company post its initial public offering.

Nevertheless, as US technology stocks saw a significant uptick since the pandemic-driven equity capital market lows in April 2020 and traded on record highs at year end 2020, investors, encouraged by the news on breakthroughs of Sars-CoV-2 vaccines, were looking forward to significantly improved post-pandemic travel prospects. Airbnb's go-to-market announcement was therefore perfectly timed and well received. Along its accelerated book-building process, the company and its lead underwriters of its IPO lifted the original price range to the book building range of $56–$60 per share.

As the macro drivers seemed to provide an ideal timing for Airbnb's feverish awaited initial public offering (IPO), the rentals platform's initial public offering was finally priced at $68 per share, significantly above its updated target range (Financial Times, 2020c). This pricing of the company's shares implicitly allowed Airbnb to raise proceeds of $3.4 billion from its initial public offering. Ultimately, the rentals platform was listed on the NASDAQ stock-exchange under the ticker-symbol ABNB.

At its IPO pricing, Airbnb's implied market capitalization of $41 billion was greater than its travel booking peer Expedia with a market capitalization of $18.2 billion, but still below Booking.com's market capitalization of $86 billion.

In a sign of significant investor confidence in Airbnb's home-sharing platform strength's as well as the long-term recovery prospects of the travel and tourism industry post-pandemic at large, Airbnb's shares received a further boost at the opening of the trade at the NASDAQ stock exchange, trading at $148 per share on day one, an 114% uplift from its offer price. At the first day trading price, the home-sharing company's market capitalization stood at $87 billion, roughly three times the initial book-building price range and more than twice the market capitalization of Marriott or Hilton, the largest global hotel groups. Airbnb's spectacular stock market debut on NASDAQ was one of the most successful in corporate America's recent history. At the time of finalizing the book, the rentals platform's shares traded on a comparable level.

[13] On a fully diluted basis incorporating also employee stock options and restricted shares, the market capitalization would have been equal to $33bn.

5.4 Decoding Platform Value: From Double-Sided Accommodation to Multi-sided Experience Platform

To assess Airbnb's transition from a double-sided accommodation to a multi-sided experience platform, the platform's strength will be evaluated along the eight platform value drivers, as described by Fig. 5.9.

- *Platform architecture and core*: Airbnb's origin as pure accommodation rentals platform had a consumer-to-consumer C2C (private host to private traveler), double-sided architecture, matching the traveler's interest to find an attractive accommodation at reasonable prices with the host's interest to earn an extra dollar. By the transition from an accommodation to a holistic experience platform and the integration of experience partner's on its platform, Airbnb became a multi-sided Business Design.
- *Platform scalability*: Airbnb is one of the true pioneers of the typical *asset-light platform designs.* Neither assets from the accommodation provider nor from the seeker are part of Airbnb's balance sheet. Airbnb's app simply connects a wide variety of affordable to high-end accommodations with a global community of private and business travelers. This offers Airbnb a unique competitive advantage in comparison to its traditional asset-heavy peers like hotel-chains.
  Obviously, the most significant advantage of Airbnb's asset-light architecture is the *global scalability potential* of its platform at neglectable cost for onboarding

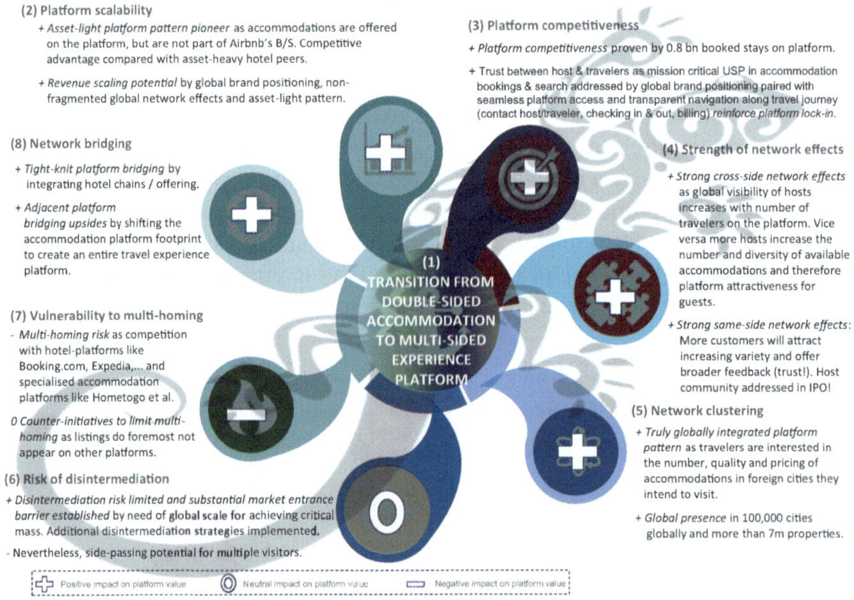

Fig. 5.9 Airbnb's global accommodation and experience platform value and its eight levers

new hosts or travelers. This is further enabled by the non-fragmented global network effects of its platform and a global brand positioning ensuring trustworthy processes and host-traveler relationships.

The asset-light Business Design of Airbnb plays not only out to be a competitive advantage for its growth ambitions. It also provided evidence of its resilience during the pandemic-induced standstill in bookings. The platform's management was able to manage down all major cost categories, streamlining its organization, and adopting rapidly to new use cases like bookings closer to home or for remote working (Airbnb, 2021c). The bookings on its platform seem also to rebound faster than expected, proving further the adaptability of Airbnb's platform Business Design.

- *Platform competitiveness*: Airbnb's *platform gravity* is mirrored by more than 800 million bookings through its app. Trust between host and travelers is a mission-critical USP for both double-sided accommodation platform partners. This is fully addressed not only by seamless accommodation search and booking processes. Also the navigation process through the limitless varieties of accommodations fulfills ease-of-use needs.
  Additionally, the entire travel journey is processed with full transparency, starting with the first contact and exchange between the two pre-transaction strangers, the host and the traveler, building a two-party intimacy. This pattern is supported by a secure and controlled checking in and out process as well as save billing procedures through the platform. All those trustworthy process standards reinforce Airbnb's platform lock-in.
- *Strength of network effects:* The accommodation platform is built upon strong cross-side as well as same-side network effects:
  C*ross-side network effects* are enabled as the app connects accommodation providers with seekers around the world: The platform offers on the one side global visibility for hosts and their accommodations and on the other side an enormous variety for private and business travelers. A rising number of hosts and variety in accommodations increases the platform's attractiveness for guests, and, vice versa, the more travelers use Airbnb's app, the more interesting the platform gets for potential hosts. The strength of this self-enforcing feedback loop increases with the number of hosts and guests using the platform for their bookings, creating a "winner-takes-all" pattern. Additionally, Airbnb hosts often are renters at a different or even same time of the year, switching their role as platform partner and becoming an even more engrained part of Airbnb's community.
  On a more granular level, cross-side effects are evidenced as Airbnb creates together with its local platform partners a growing list of guidebooks for major destinations similar to traditional travel guides, but with a much more local and unique note. This might emotionally entice guests for a distinct destination by providing an individualized trip perception. This initiates positive cross-side network effects which might be compared with Netflix's approach to address individual viewer preferences. Such tail-end approaches are enabled by technology-empowered platforms with wide, in a best case, global reach.

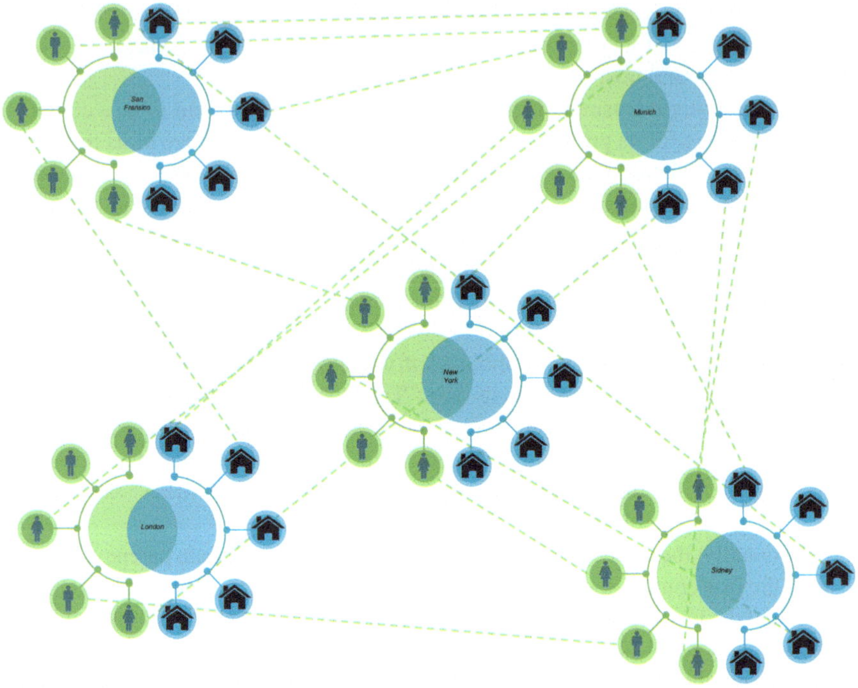

Fig. 5.10 Airbnb's global accommodation platform cluster

Strong same-side network effects exist on the accommodation seeker's side as more travelers will attract more hosts increasing further the variety of accommodation offerings and the platform attractiveness for guests. Additionally, the more visitors comment on their experiences and provide ratings on the platform, the more accurate and trustworthy might this feedback mechanism by building further trust. On the host side, Airbnb built a strong community, which also reinforces itself with the number of platform hosts.

- *Pattern of platform clusters*: As described by Fig. 5.10, Airbnb's listings are a global play. Any property anywhere may potentially appeal to any global traveler.

Global accommodation might be one of the strongest global network clusters as private and business travelers are interested in the number, quality, and pricing of accommodations in foreign cities or countries they plan to travel to and not in their hometown. On Airbnb's app, travelers connect with hosts around the world. As its accommodation platform is truly a globally integrated network cluster, it is also less vulnerable to potential peers as the latter would have to build a platform with global scale on their own to compete against Airbnb. The need to gain global scale for achieving critical mass is a substantial market entrance barrier.

- *Disintermediation*: This need of global scale to achieving a critical mass of attractive accommodation offers of hosts on the platform limits as well the potential *risk of disintermediation.* Nevertheless, in principle, once the connection between the traveler and the host is established, they could potentially side-pass the platform for the next visit.
  Airbnb implemented as counter action additional disintermediation strategies. For limiting first contact disintermediation risk, the app withholds the host's detailed address and mobile number until the booking on the platform and payments are finally set. Additionally, the host faces the risk to being cut off Airbnb's global visitors access in case of diagnosed side-passing efforts or other wrongdoings, not an attractive trade-off for accommodation owners.
- *Multi-homing:* The market dominance of Airbnb's platform and its outperformance in network effects was in former times evidenced as listings on its platform did not appear on any other platform. But, as ultimately accommodation platforms might compete not only with peers like Booking.com or Expedia, but as well with booking platforms of hotels, hotel chain proprietary booking systems, or travel agencies for the traveler's trip arrangement and accommodation booking, multi-homing might be the biggest platform threat for Airbnb.
  Accordingly, competition is creeping up, and hosts started to multi-home partially using other channels as well as Airbnb. Thirty-four percent of the homes listed on Airbnb's platform can also be booked elsewhere in the meantime. Additionally, hosts with multiple listings may use Airbnb's global reach and brand as a channel to capture new guests, but may switch to alternative, cheaper platforms for their repeat business (Financial Times, 2020a). Airbnb addresses such threats by initiating counter initiatives to limit such multi-homing trends.
- *Platform-bridging:* The extension to tight-knit or even more adjacent ecosystems may offer Airbnb substantial growth options, enlarging the reach of the platform and strengthening its barriers of entry further. But, such platform bridging might come also with slower growth due to the increasing complexity of platform partnerships. The question if and in how far Airbnb is able to successfully introduce new, additional services beyond its core home-sharing business is a widely discussed question on capital markets, as the company targeted in its IPO prospectus this close to $3.4 trillion total addressable global hospitality market.
  To supplement its accommodation offerings by integrating hotels might be a potential *tight-knit platform-bridging* approach, but might place the platform even more in direct competition with hotel booking platforms like Booking.com and direct hotel bookings. An additional risk might be that the intimacy of private homes get lost. This tight-knit bridging strategy seems nevertheless to be already targeted by Airbnb as evidenced by its acquisition of HotelTonight in 2019.

  A more *significant, adjacent platform bridging* would be the shift of the center of Airbnb from an accommodation platform provider to an entire travel experience platform. And indeed, Airbnb seems to have further idea on a launch pad for such a beyond accommodation approach which might open up many new avenues to local experience and revenue extensions.

One element of this strategy is to provide an integrated, entire trip arrangement, defining or at least navigating "where to go, what to do and how to get there, not just where to stay." This might be enabled by co-operations with a multitude of partners of the wider travel ecosystem from rental car firms, airlines, museums, to local restaurants and events. Such an integrated trip advisory service bundle is already partially offered by Airbnb Luxe, where a trip designer orchestrates and arranges anything from trip logistics to restaurant and museum visits or local sightseeing tours.

Airbnb Experiences goes even beyond by linking on its platform guests with locals offering guided city tours, biking trips, joint cooking events, or sightseeing paired with local events. Airbnb addresses with its experience products, according own data, an $1.4 trillion subsegment of the above described overall addressable market. Since launching Experiences in 2016, however, Airbnb has until now not shared performance indicators of this subsegment (Financial Times, 2020a).

All in all, how Airbnb addresses and captures this platform-bridging potential from accommodation rental to travel experience will play a central role for the company's likely longer-term growth ambitions.

By assembling the eight platform strength drivers for the global accommodation network, Airbnb seems to have the potential to create a powerful, global digital Business Design. Beyond building on these network strengths, Airbnb addressed weaknesses typically encountered by platforms early on.

Airbnb side-passed the controversial discussion and disputes with national regulators about "gig economy" worker exploitation, unlike ride-hailing companies which had to accept the city of London decision that Uber drivers are their workers. As the platform partner of travelers is partly a property and partly a service, these vexed discussions might be circumvented. Additionally, Airbnb applied a cautious and co-operative approach with respect to regulators. The accommodation platform could agree with more than 500 global cities about the status of its accommodations until now.

5.5 Decoding Airbnb's Financial Value: Reverse DCF

5.5.1 Short Term: Preparing for the Travel Rebound

A year after the world was hammered by the global pandemic with its lockdowns and social distancing measures, Airbnb prepares for a forecasted significant travel rebound. The company believes that people are yearning for travel and human interaction as soon as restrictions are gradually lifted.

But, the company also expects that when travel does return, it will look different than pre-pandemic. The rentals company described this expected shift in its latest shareholder letter as "in 2021, travel will be less about where you go and when you go, and more about who you are with and what you can do together. We will see a shift from mass travel to meaningful travel" (Airbnb, 2021c).

Additionally, the increase in remote working will provide more flexibility around where and when visitors will travel. Airbnb's analytics identified also a shift in how potential travelers search on its platform as almost 40% of them seem to be flexible with respect to timing or location of their stay. A recently conducted survey by Airbnb of American traveler habits confirmed its forecasted trends: When travel returns, it will center around connections. The travel type US citizens have missed most was spending time with their family and friends. After their own health and the safety of others, the top reason with 37% of respondents for getting vaccinated is the ability to connect with their friends and their family, followed by 32% for the ability to feel safe to travel. And, with 56%, a majority prefers a domestic or local destination versus just 21% who want to visit some place international and further away (Airbnb, 2021c).

Airbnb believes to be uniquely positioned to take advantage of those trends and developed a plan for 2021 and beyond that may help the company to capitalize on the probably coming travel rebound.

5.5.2 Picture-of-the-Future Scenario: "The Age of Connecting and Belonging"

The Reverse DCF valuation for Airbnb will be framed exemplary by a picture-of-the-future scenario which might be phrased as "the age of connecting and belonging." Such a scenario is obviously not the only plausible one. As described within Chap. 1, the PoF idea is to create a set of distinct scenarios to build up a robust valuation range.

But, the "age of connecting and belonging" PoF might be a likely scenario as it blends a couple of first post-pandemic trends into one consistent mosaic: Driven by the hope to escape out of the pandemic at the beginning of the 2020s and by having learned about the burden of social distancing, the value architecture of societies might be, at least partially, recalibrated in the years to come. The "age of connecting and belonging" picture-of-the-future deploys this idea. Social intimacy and ties, family values, and societal embeddedness might become the new imperatives of such a future value architecture of "connecting and belonging." Ownership and materiality will lose influence, and sharing and self-awareness, including ecological values, will gain ground. This scenario, with a dedicated view on its impact on the tourism ecosystem and hospitality industry, will be briefly described, as it will serve as a reference point for the Reverse DCF valuation:

- The post-pandemic world within the picture-of-the-future "the age of connecting and belonging" might change the central role of "ownership" in Western economies and societies: In a digitalized, post-consumerist society, the emphasis might shift much more to an "access-based consumption," highlighting aspects of wellness and well-being, beyond materialism (Mody & Gomez, 2018). Such a development would obviously provide comfort for Airbnb's positioning within the global tourism industry, as having emphasizing sharing and a sense of community within the hospitality ecosystem from its origins.

- Pine and Gilmore (1988) described the notion of the uprise of the experience economy already at the turn of the millennium by four distinct elements, escapism, education, entertainment, and esthetic. Mody and Gomez (2018) broadened that view in the context of travel-based experiences by adding characteristics like personalization, communitas, localness, hospitableness, serendipity, and ethical consumerism. Airbnb elevates such a sense of community and localness as travelers sharing space with others and with hosts will drive more authentic experiences embedded in the host's neighborhood.
- Such a world which places an emphasis on personal relationships, friendships, family values, and partnerships would mean for the global hospitality ecosystem that the preference where to stay during the holidays might change significantly. Preferences might shift from hip hotspots or mega-cities to the greater outdoors, meaning national parks, hiking spots, or non-crowded seaside resorts. And indeed, Airbnb identified in early 2021 a shift in travelers' behaviors for trips closer to home in more remote, rural destinations and preferring longer stays in bigger homes offering more space (CNN, 2021). This stands in stark contrast to the pre-pandemic favorite bookings of vacations abroad and in hip urban centers.
- This might be paired with, and not in contradiction to, an increasing attitude toward individualization and personalization in a digital, anonymous world of generations X, Y, and Z.[14] Individualization might involve a shift to a "new luxury"—seeking out unique, authentic experiences that serve as a launch pad for self-fulfillment.
- Coming out of a hybrid at home working, teaching, and family zoom fatigue reality during the pandemic having supercharged a "co-everything" world, integrating work and life much beyond the traditional but not deeply grounded work-life balance discussions may sustain also post-pandemic. Future travelers might look for accommodations as a bread of a residence, hotel, experience, and WeWork space embedded in a local community.
- Technology might play in this scenario an important role as enabler as digital tools and connectivity have changed and will change the way we live and how we work in an ever-more connected world. The availability of high-speed Internet in a 5G world, unlimited cloud-based digital storage, and deep-routed analytics might become gamechangers in the 2020s and may allow ever more distance working. The hospitality industry must factor in how to embed the trend of distance working, where longer-term rentals of accommodations providing comfort and intimacy, as well as high-quality and digital infrastructure, might stand on top of the priority list of travelers and digital distance workers.

[14] Generation Z that follows Millennials will also be the major force in the tourism market by 2040.

	Core Platform Peers	Platform Champion Peers	Off-line, traditional Peers
Global players (listed)	• **Booking.com** • **Expedia** o Homeway Inc. (affil. of Expedia) o VRBO (affil. of Expedia)	• Amazon • Alphabet • Netflix • Paypal • Ebay • Facebook	Hotel Chains • **Marriott International, Inc.** • **Marriott Vacations Worldwide Inc.** • **Hilton Worldwide Holdings Inc.** • **Hilton Grand Vaccation Inc.** • **InterContinental Hotels Group PLC** • Accor SA • Hyatt Hotels Corporation • Shangri-La Asia • Mandarin Oriental International Ltd. • Resorttrust, Inc • NH Hotel Group, S.A. • Melia Hotels International, S.A. • Kyoritsu Maintainance Co. Ltd • Fattal Holdings Ltd.
Local players & hospitality specialists (listed)	• Tripadvisor (US) • *Trip.com (China)* • *MakeMyTrip (India)* • *Webjet (Australia)* • *Triviago (Germany)* • *Despegar.com (Argentina)* • *OnTheBeach (UK)* • *Edreams Odigeo (Lux)* • *Lastminute.com (Netherlands)* • *Holidaycheck (Germany)* • *HostelWorld (Ireland)* • *Travelzoo (US)* • *Couchsurfing*		

Fig. 5.11 Airbnb's ecosystem peer-group

Summarized, the picture-of-the-future scenario "the age of connecting and belonging" might challenge the hospitality industry to re-think their story and how to address the above-portrayed trends by revitalizing their strategic approach:

5.5.3 Steady State and Continuing Value

For the steady-state evaluation of Airbnb, the platform has to be embedded in the underlying picture-of-the-future scenario "the age of connecting and belonging" and the forecasted steady-state performance benchmarked with a tailored peer group.

The long-term growth rate for the hospitality industry and the global accommodation market was assumed with 4%, slightly outperforming the expected global GDP growth, but lower than pre-pandemic growth of 5% (OECD, 2020, p. 20). For the long-term RONIC performance estimate, the tailored peer-group of Airbnb might be calibrated by a mix of traditional hotel chains and accommodation providers, the global online competitors Booking.com and Expedia, a set of regional online-hotel and accommodation contenders, as well as true platform peers. Such a wide-scope peer group is provided by Fig. 5.11.

- The closest benchmarks for Airbnb might be online travel agencies and hotel booking platforms with global reach like Booking.com or Expedia. Nevertheless, already, those platforms peers might not be fully comparable with Airbnb, as the formers' partners are hotels and not private hosts. Booking.com was with a pre-pandemic revenue of $15 billion in 2019 the global booking platform market leader with an online travel agency market share of roughly 43% (Statista, 2021), whereas Expedia is second with $12 billion revenues.
- Regional, tier 2 midsized online travel agencies have significantly less revenues and according market shares. Only Ctrip with $5.1 billion and the travel advisory

platform Tripadvisor with $1.5bn crossed the $1 billion revenue milestone in 2019. Due to their local footprint, they might be only partially comparable with Airbnb's global platform approach.
- Global platform champions like Amazon, Alphabet, Netflix, PayPal, eBay, Facebook, and others might not fit from the perspective of addressed markets. Nevertheless, for selective financials like long-term revenue decay periods or platform investment needs, they might provide useful insights.
- Global hotel chains like Marriot International, Hilton Worldwide Holdings, InterContinental Hotels Group, Accor SA, Hyatt Hotels Corporation, Shangri-La Asia, or Mandarin Oriental International might be perceived at first glance as perfect benchmarks. Nevertheless, they have with respect to a peer group assessment with Airbnb the mirrored problematic of tech giants. They fit perfectly well from an industry perspective, but do not share platform characteristics. But, as Airbnb competes with them directly for the share of wallet of global tourists and travelers, they will be referenced as benchmark and included in the peer group discussion.

For the forecast of the long-term, steady-state platform profit and ROIC as well as RONIC performance embedded in the picture-of-the-future scenario "the age of connecting and belonging," an EBIT margin of 18–19% and a NOPLAT margin of 14–15% were forecasted. These margins are in line with the pre-pandemic margins of top-performing hotel peers like Hilton, [15] but below Booking.com's operating profit margins which hoovered in the mid-30% range pre-pandemic. Airbnb's steady-state ROIC performance would be in line with Facebook's, but with a different decomposition, as the accommodation rentals firm NOPLAT margin would be significantly lower, but its capital-turnover much faster. [16] Further, no changes in the tax rate or cost of capital have been assumed, if compared with the scaling period.

The continuing value at the end of the scaling period, by applying above assumptions, would be round about $134 billion:

$$CV_{2031}^{Airbnb} = \frac{2.1\text{bn} \times \left(1 - \frac{4\%}{71\%}\right)}{5.5\% - 4\%} = 134 \text{ bn}$$

This would translate into a present value of the continuing value of around $79 billion:

[15] Hilton Worldwide Holdings Inc. realized pre-pandemic an operating profit margin of 18%, calculated on the financials provided in its 2019 10-K SEC report. The company outperformed its contenders InterContinental Hotels Group PLC with 14% or Marriott International Inc. with 9%, where the computations are once more based on the respective 10-K SEC reports for 2019.

[16] Facebook's Invested Capital is inflated by its goodwill of $19 billion for its acquisitions and a quite significant investment in PP&E, with a $46 billion total, according to the social media giant's latest 10-K SEC report.

$$\mathrm{DCV}_{2031}^{\mathrm{Airbnb}} = \frac{\mathrm{CV}_{2031}^{\mathrm{Airbnb}}}{(1+\mathrm{CoC})^{T}} = \frac{134\ \mathrm{bn}}{(1+5.5\%)^{10}} = 79\ \mathrm{bn}$$

5.5.4 Scaling Period and Free Cash Flows

In its short-term outlook for its revenues, Airbnb forecasted a year-over-year decline in Q1 2021 which is expected to be less than that of Q4 2020, as a gradual improvement in guests' willingness to book accommodations was perceived lately. However, Airbnb's management argues to have still limited visibility for a robust growth outlook for 2021 given the difficulty in determining the pace of vaccine rollouts and the related impact on willingness to travel. Therefore, the management didn't provide an outlook for the rest of 2021 so far (Airbnb, 2021c).

Nevertheless, short-term, especially 2021 and into 2022, pent-up demand among leisure travelers will support the revival of the tourism industry overall as national social distancing measures have been phased out or, most likely, will be reduced step by step. Additionally, as latest data on US travelers show sharp price increases for domestic short-term rentals in the greater outdoor, rentals platforms like Airbnb might become the preferred accommodation booking choice for those looking to social distance. Accommodation booking platforms might, as in the downturn, outperform hotels in the post-pandemic recovery over the next years. This unbalanced growth might even intensify as during the pandemic sharply declined business travel and international holidays might not bounce back sharply short-term and might continue to weigh especially on the hotel segment of the travel ecosystem (Financial Times, 2021).[17]

For the scaling phase of the picture-of-the-future scenario "the age of connecting and belonging," a partial recovery of the bookings from their pandemic lows is forecasted in 2021, whereas a full recovery is assumed to take two years. This seems to be plausible, as a regional staged phase out of social distancing measures and recovery of the hospitality industry, depending on the vaccination progress, seems to be likely. The midterm growth was assumed to decay from Airbnb's early days highs and is forecasted in line with the online travel industry development. Nevertheless, a slight uptick simulating small market share gains by Airbnb is assumed as the platform seems to be well placed in "the age of connecting and belonging" scenario to profit from its brand positioning. Airbnb's take rate from gross bookings was forecasted to improve marginally from today's 14% to 15% of gross booking revenues, and is in line with the platform's charged fees from guests and hosts. Therefore, revenues increase as well more than industry average within the scaling

[17] Airbnb's average daily rates (ADRs) for rentals are up by 35% in Q1 2021 compared with the prior year, and numbers of nights booked in rural areas increased by 50%, whereas urban bookings are down by 65% (Financial Times, 2021).

	2021	2022	2023	2024	2025	2026	2027	2028	2029	2030
Revenues	4.560.569	5.994.962	7.391.426	8.753.755	9.911.792	10.874.951	11.772.489	12.626.378	13.542.202	14.389.031
yoy growth	*35%*	*31%*	*23%*	*18%*	*13%*	*10%*	*8%*	*7%*	*7%*	*6%*
Adjusted EBITDA	-109.454	11.990	206.960	472.703	792.943	1.152.745	1.553.969	1.994.968	2.491.765	3.021.697
EBITDA margin (%)	*-2%*	*0%*	*3%*	*5%*	*8%*	*11%*	*13%*	*16%*	*18%*	*21%*
EBIT	-200.665	-107.909	59.131	297.628	594.707	935.246	1.318.519	1.742.440	2.220.921	2.733.916
EBIT margin (%)	*-4%*	*-2%*	*1%*	*3%*	*6%*	*9%*	*11%*	*14%*	*16%*	*19,0%*
Taxes (*25% on global profits after usage/expiratio*	*0*	*0*	*0*	*0*	*0*	*0*	*0*	*0*	*0*	*25%*
NOPLAT	-200.665	-107.909	59.131	297.628	594.707	935.246	1.318.519	1.742.440	2.220.921	2.050.437
NOPLAT margin (%)	-4%	-2%	1%	3%	6%	9%	11%	14%	16%	14%
Invested Capital	912.114	1.198.992	1.478.285	1.750.751	1.982.358	2.174.990	2.354.498	2.525.276	2.708.440	2.877.806
Net Investment in Invested Capital	304.038	286.879	279.293	272.466	231.607	192.632	179.508	170.778	183.165	169.366
(IC as % of revenues)	*20%*	*20%*	*20%*	*20%*	*20%*	*20%*	*20%*	*20%*	*20%*	*20%*
Free Cash Flow	-504.703	-394.788	-220.162	25.162	363.100	742.614	1.139.011	1.571.662	2.037.756	1.881.071
Discounted Cash Flows	-478.391	-354.698	-187.493	20.311	277.820	538.578	782.998	1.024.093	1.258.578	1.101.237
WACC: 5.5%										

Fig. 5.12 Airbnb's valuation embedded in the PoF "the age of connecting and belonging": scaling period

phase. All in all, revenues will grow threefold from 2021 to 2030, achieving $14.4 billion at the end point of the scaling phase. Airbnb would be a $15 billion company by entering the steady state, consistent with the continuing value assumptions and described by the valuation overview of Fig. 5.12.

Memorizing a strong pent-up demand from the pandemic's lows, a further shift to online travel bookings, as well as Airbnb's platform and brand strength embedded in picture-of-the future scenario "the age of connecting and belonging," the forecasted revenue growth might seem plausible.

On the cost side, the financial diagnostics of Airbnb's proved a fairly stable COGs ratio between 40% and 42%, providing implicitly a gross margin of 58–60%. The gross margin is assumed to improve from the reduced pandemic levels of 52% in Q1 2021 to ultimately 62% in 2030, slightly above pre-pandemic levels. The driver of this improvement is, besides the recovery of the business industry, the assumption of slight economies of scale, especially in the costs of operations and support. For the three further important cost drivers, additional explicit assumptions have been chosen:

- Product/platform costs: Pure product and platform development costs, coming from normalized, pre-pandemic levels of 15–19%, are assumed to decrease by economies of scale, typically for a platform company, to a steady-state rate of 10% of revenues. But, this would mean in absolute terms that product and platform costs would still double to $1.5 billion p.a. in the scaling phase as continuous accommodation platform reinvestments and further product enhancements to extend the experience ecosystem will be mandatory to realize the anticipated growth rates.
- Sales and marketing costs: The same argumentation might hold true for marketing and sales expenses. These costs hoovered at a third of revenues pre-pandemic and pre-IPO. The further platform growth should provide Airbnb headroom to reduce market-related costs to a quarter of revenues, in line with the cost improvements during the pandemic, but still increasing significantly in absolute terms to $3.6

billion. The long-term level of market-related costs would be quite close to the significant improved marketing costs of 22% within Q1 2021.

- General and administration costs: G&A, as typical fixed costs, my decrease by a third from pre-pandemic levels in relative terms to 9–10% of revenue, but would also double in absolute terms, as Airbnb might have to invest in a more global organizational structure.

This financial skeleton of the picture-of-the-future scenario "the age of connecting and belonging" would lead to a significant EBIT improvement from close to break even in 2021 to 18–19% of revenues, but would be in line with leading hotel peers in pre-pandemic times and might be also achievable for an accommodation rentals platform firm. [18]

The Invested Capital side of Airbnb's asset-light balance sheet mirrors perfectly the pattern of a platform Business Design. The most significant working capital positions "funds receivable and amounts held on behalf of customers" on the operating asset side match with the "funds payable and amounts payable to customers" on the operating liability side. As also the further working capital positions would roughly nil out, [19] free cash flows would not be dragged down during the growth scaling phase by significant working capital needs like it is the case for traditional Business Designs. For the non-current assets of Invested Capital (excluding goodwill) and capital expenditure calculation, Airbnb's PP&E, operating leases, and intangibles, which summed up to 18–21% of revenues in the last years, have been identified as Airbnb's crucial long-term assets. As further platform and intangible investments will be necessary and might compensate some economies of scale, a constant invested capital target rate of 20% of revenues has been assumed.

The tipping point of cash flow break might be achieved in this scenario in 2024. As the cash flow surplus has to compensate the prior years' negative cash flows, the discounted cash flow contribution of the scaling period would be limited to $4 billion.

5.5.5 Airbnb's Enterprise and Equity Value of "The Age of Connecting and Belonging" Scenario

The summed up discounted cash flows of the scaling period paired with the discounted continuing value would give the accommodation platform an operating value of around $83 billion under the described assumptions of the picture-of-the future "the age of connecting and belonging":

---

[18] Airbnb's significant losses carried forward have been modelled by postponing tax-related payments till tax provisions have been fully depleted. A global/US tax rate of 25% was ultimately assumed.

[19] For the detailed working capital calculation, from Airbnb's 10-K report operating cash, pre-payments, and other current assets, accounts payables, and taxes payables as part of the balance sheet position accrued expenses and other liabilities were classified as working capital items.

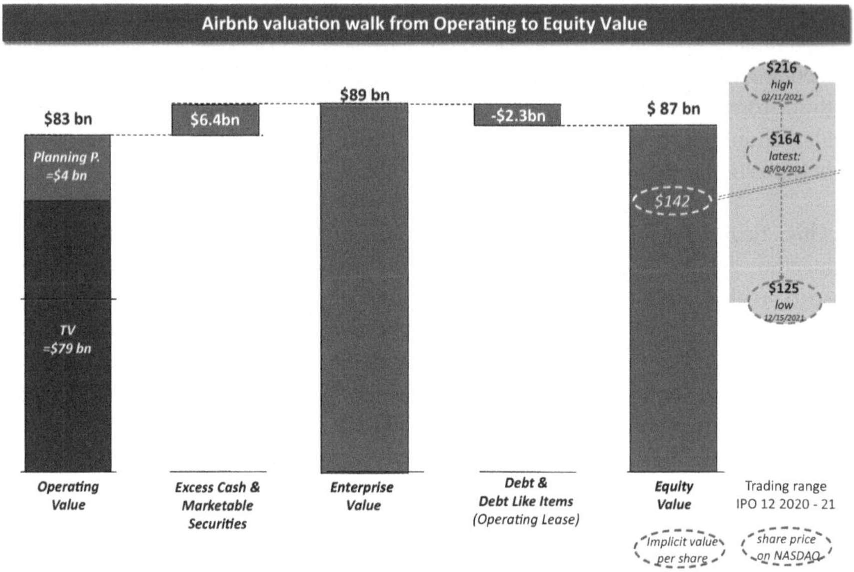

Fig. 5.13 Airbnb's valuation walk within the POF "the age of connecting and belonging"

$$\text{Operating Value} = \sum\nolimits_{t=1}^{\infty} (\text{DCF}_t) + \text{DCV} = \$4 \text{ bn} + \$79 \text{ bn} = \$83 \text{ bn}$$

The decomposition in the scaling period and the terminal value highlights the sensitivity of this scenario with respect to the continuing value performance assumptions. As described by Fig. 5.13, for the valuation walk from operating value (OP) to enterprise value Airbnb's excess cash, which increased significantly due to its IPO proceeds, and the marketable securities have to be added, resulting in an operating value of $89 billion:

$$\text{EV} = \text{OP} + (\text{excess cash} + \text{marketable securities}) = \$83 \text{ bn} + \$6.4 \text{ bn} = \$89 \text{ bn}$$

From the enterprise value of $89 billion, debt of $1.8 billion, and debt-like items, in Airbnb's case operating lease liabilities of $0.5 billion, have to be deducted to get a final equity value estimate of $87 billion:

$$\text{EqV} = \text{EV} - (\text{Debt} + \text{Operating Leases}) = \$89 \text{ bn} - \$2.3 \text{ bn} = \$87 \text{ bn}$$

By dividing the equity value by the platform firm's undiluted shares outstanding, an indicative price per share of $142 would be achieved.

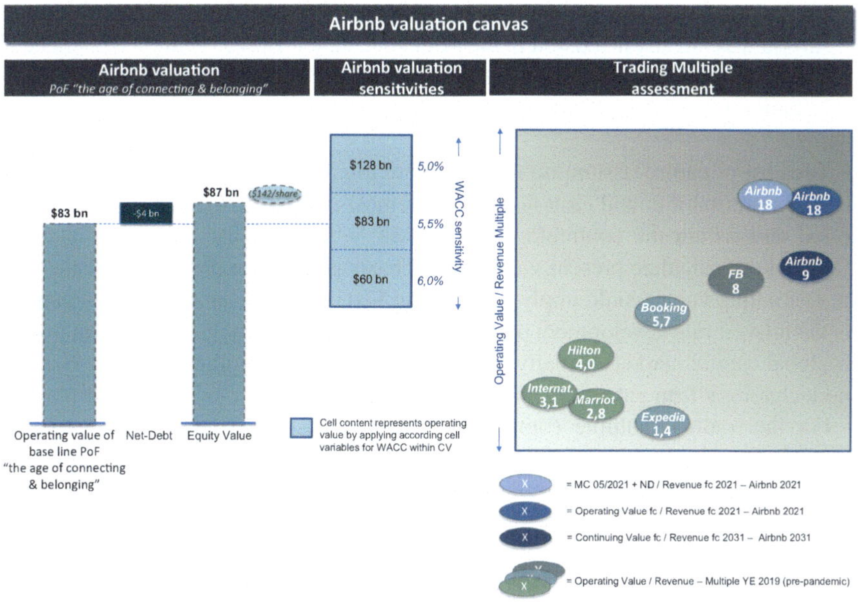

Fig. 5.14 Airbnb's valuation canvas

5.5.6 Valuation Canvas, Framing, and Summary

To put this scenario into a broader perspective, the sensitivity assessments and peer comparisons of Fig. 5.14 will finally frame this value estimate of Airbnb.

In a full flagged valuation of Airbnb, the following stress tests would be added:

- *Additional scenarios*: Besides the picture-of-the-future "the age of connecting and belonging," additional scenarios broaden the perspective of valuation outcomes and sharpen the understanding which trajectories are most important for the management team to track.[20]
- *Sensitivity assessment*: For platform Business Design, the sensitivities with respect to the growth momentum and growth decay period, the long-term return perspectives depending on the sustainability of a platform's distinct competitive advantage, and the cost of capital are especially worthwhile to analyze. The simplified working mechanisms of valuation sensitivities for the Airbnb case are exemplified here by the cost of capital simulations.

[20] In this book, the focus was to present briefly the picture-of-the-future "the age of connecting and belonging." Alternative scenarios developed for stress testing the Airbnb valuation have been "slowbalization," mirroring the impact of a more regionalized world on the global hospitality industry, and "roaring 2020s," mimicking a significant rebound of the tourism markets beyond the base-line scenario in the next 3 years due to potential significant pent-up demand and available cash resources saved and accumulated during the pandemic by households.

- *Peer group-based trading multiple comparison*: The tailoring of a peer group for Airbnb was already discussed in the prior subchapter. Based on this assessment, a trading multiple comparison was added in Fig. 5.14, which shows that Airbnb's valuation is on the high side from a multiple perspective.

The cost of capital assumption has a severe impact on the valuation outcome, as Airbnb's profitability and cash flows are foremost realized at the end of the scaling period and within the continuing value phase, where the discount factor plays a major role to calculate present values. A 50 basis-point increase of interest rates in the continuing value would imply a more than $20 billion hit for Airbnb's valuation. As the interest rate development post-pandemic is one of the major discussion points on global capital markets actually, this risk might be an overall concern for Nasdaq and technology firm valuations in the near future.

For the trading multiple comparison, the two hospitality platform contenders Booking.com and Expedia, hotel giants like Marriott, Hilton, or InterContinantal, as well as a global platform champions like Facebook provide insights for Airbnb's valuation. The three hotel contenders traded at a 3–4 times revenue multiple prior to the pandemic, whereas the booking platform peers had a wider spread with Expedia of less than two times and Booking.com with close to six times. Airbnb's trades with a market capitalization of $87 billion somewhere at 18 times expected revenues in 2021 far beyond such multiples. Even compared with an established digital champion like Facebook, trading at eight times pre-pandemic and nine times on trailing-12-month revenues actually, Airbnb's valuation seems on the high side.

But, by referencing to Airbnb's continuing value, once having achieved steady-state performance, the revenue multiple of nine times would be in line with Facebook's relative capital market pricing, what might seem plausible within a picture-of-the-future "the age of connecting and belonging" scenario. Also, Airbnb's significant platform strength, measured by the eight platform value drivers, as pinpointed by Fig. 5.9, and its relatively strong competitive positioning within the global experience ecosystem might justify such a continuing value bandwidth of Airbnb.

References

Airbnb.com. (2021). https://www.airbnb.com/plus

Airbnb. (2021a, February 21). *Airbnb announces fourth quarter and full year 2020 results.* https://investors.airbnb.com/press-releases/news-details/2021/Airbnb-Announces-Fourth-Quarter-and-Full-Year-2020-Results

Airbnb. (2021b, February 26). *Form 10-K report—Annual report.* https://d18rn0p25nwr6d.cloudfront.net/CIK-0001559720/84dcc076-235d-4520-805c-0e64b6fe8c40.pdf

Airbnb. (2021c, February 25). *Shareholder letter Q4 2020.* https://s26.q4cdn.com/656283129/files/doc_financials/2020/q4/Airbnb_Q4-2020-Shareholder-Letter_Final.pdf;https://s26.q4cdn.com/656283129/files/doc_financials/2020/q4/Airbnb_Q4-2020-Shareholder-Letter_Final.pdf

Bernstein, E., Bunch, J., Canner, N., & Lee, M. (2016, July–August). Beyond the Holacracy Hype. *Harvard Business Review*, 1–13.

Botsman, R., Rogers, R., Foley, K., & Tantor, M. (2010, September). *What's mine is yours: The rise of collaborative consumtion*. Tantor Media Inc.

Chua, E., Chiu, J., & Bool, N. (2019). Sharing economy: An analysis of Airbnb Business Model and the factors that influence consumer adoption. *Review of Integrative Business & Economics Research, 8*, 19–35.

CNN. (2021, May 5). *Airbnb CEO identifies 5 trends that are unlikely to reverse*. https://edition.cnn.com/2021/05/25/tech/airbnb-pandemic-business-travel/index.html

Economist. (2019, October 10). *Airbnb and Uber are chalk and cheese*. https://www.economist.com/business/2019/10/10/airbnb-and-uber-are-chalk-and-cheese

Financial Times. (2020a, December 7). *Airbnb IPO: A barometer for travel after the pamdemic*. https://www.ft.com/content/d47d875d-bf7f-4527-a879-a3f33761c78f

Financial Times. (2020b, December 20). *Airbnb looks to raise up to $2.5bn in IPO*. https://www.ft.com/content/c5450812-c45d-4833-a99f-22a390e5d3e4

Financial Times. (2020c, December 9). *Airbnb price shares well above range as IPO frenzy continues*. https://www.ft.com/content/d5aa43db-1aee-472f-abff-9ee315aa2e0c

Financial Times. (2020d, December 10). *Airbnb soars on debut in last IPO bounce*. https://www.ft.com/content/a1c5cc26-b224-470a-84fe-8a6575fd33dc

Financial Times. (2021, April 26). *Prices for US rentals in the greater outdoor rise*. https://www.ft.com/content/9ff30cae-9105-46a5-90c9-8fe0fa006dfc

Holacracy. (2020). *Why practice holacracy?* https://www.holacracy.org/explore/why-practice-holacracy

Mody, M., & Gomez, M. (2018). Airbnb and the hotel industry: The past, the present, and future of sales, marketing, branding and revenue management. *Boston Hospitality Report. Boston University*.

OECD. (2020). *OECD tourism trends and policies 2020*. OECD Publishing.

Pine, J., & Gilmore, J. (1988). *The experience economy*. Harvard Business School Press.

Statista. (2021). *Online travel market worldwide*. https://www.statista.com/topics/2704/online-travel-market/

The manufacturer's authorised representative in the EU is Springer Nature Customer Service Centre GmbH, Europaplatz 3, 69115 Heidelberg, Germany. If you have any concerns regarding our products, please contact ProductSafety@springernature.com

Printed and bound by CPI Group (UK) Ltd, Croydon, CR0 4YY
30/09/2026
02225691-0003